The History of
SCOTTISH LITERATURE

Volume 2

THE HISTORY OF SCOTTISH LITERATURE
general editor Cairns Craig

Volume 1   Medieval and Renaissance *editor R D S Jack*
Volume 2   1660 to 1800 *editor Andrew Hook*
Volume 3   Nineteenth Century *editor Douglas Gifford*
Volume 4   Twentieth Century *editor Cairns Craig*

DICTIONARIES from AUP

THE SCOTTISH NATIONAL DICTIONARY
(18th century to the present day)
in ten volumes

THE COMPACT SCOTTISH NATIONAL DICTIONARY
in two volumes

A DICTIONARY OF THE OLDER SCOTTISH TONGUE
From the twelfth century to the end of the seventeenth
Volumes 1 to 6 (and continuing)

THE CONCISE SCOTS DICTIONARY
editor-in-chief Mairi Robinson

GAELIC DICTIONARY
Malcolm MacLennan

The History of
SCOTTISH LITERATURE

Volume 2

1660–1800

edited by Andrew Hook

general editor Cairns Craig

ABERDEEN UNIVERSITY PRESS

First published 1987
This edition 1989
Aberdeen University Press
A member of the Pergamon Group

© The Contributors 1987

The publisher acknowledges subsidy from the Scottish Arts Council towards the publication of this volume.

British Library Cataloguing in Publication Data

The History of Scottish literature.
  Vol. 2: 1660–1800
  1. English literature—Scottish authors
  —History and criticism 2. Scottish
  literature—History and criticism
  I. Hook, Andrew
  820.9'9411   PR8511

  ISBN 0-08-035055-0
  ISBN 0-08-037726-2

Printed in Great Britain
The University Press
Aberdeen

Contents

List of Contributors

IAIN GORDON BROWN, a graduate of Edinburgh and Cambridge, and a Fellow of the Society of Antiquaries of London, is Assistant Keeper of Manuscripts in the National Library of Scotland. He is the author of *The Hobby-Horsical Antiquary; Poet and Painter: Allan Ramsay, father and son; Allan Ramsay's Rise and Reputation; The Clerks of Penicuik*, and is editor of *Scott's Interleaved Waverley Novels* (1987).

ALASDAIR CAMERON is a lecturer in Theatre Studies in the University of Glasgow. He is assistant editor of the Journal, *Theatre Research International* and is a member of the Board of Tay Theatre Company. He is at present at work on a history of the theatre in Scotland, planned in conjunction with the Scottish Theatre Archive for which he has academic responsibility.

GEOFFREY CARNALL is a Reader in English Literature at the University of Edinburgh. He is co-author (with John Butt) of vol 8 of the *Oxford History of English Literature*, dealing with the mid eighteenth century.

JOHN R R CHRISTIE is a historian of science in the Department of Philosophy in the University of Leeds. He has published many articles on Scottish Science in the eighteenth century.

THOMAS CRAWFORD was until his recent retirement a Reader in English at the University of Aberdeen. His best-known books are *Burns: a study of the poems and songs* and *Society and the Lyric*, and he is joint editor of *Longer Scottish Poems Volume Two 1650–1830*. He is currently President of the Association for Scottish Literary Studies.

DOUGLAS DUNCAN holds a doctorate from Aberdeen University and is at present Professor of English at McMaster University, Hamilton, Ontario. His publications include *Thomas Ruddiman* and *Ben Jonson and the Lucianic Tradition*.

F W FREEMAN, a graduate of Aberdeen and Edinburgh and Postdoctoral Fellow at the Institute for Advanced Studies in the Humanities, Edinburgh University, is Senior Associate Member of St Antony's College, Oxford University. His publications include *Robert Fergusson and the Scot's Humanist Compromise* and his articles on Allan Ramsay, Robert Fergusson and the Vernacular Movement have appeared in several journals including *The Bibliotheck, Studies in Scottish Literature* and *Scottish Literary Journal*.

ANDREW HOOK is Bradley Professor of English Literature at Glasgow University. His interest in both Scottish and American literature is reflected in his book *Scotland and America 1750–1835*. He has edited *Waverley* for the Penguin English Library, and his publications include articles on James MacPherson, Scott, Hogg, Carlyle and Macaulay.

ALEXANDER KINGHORN has recently retired after 34 years in university teaching in USA, Canada, West Indies, Denmark and the Middle East. He has served on the editorial board of *Studies in Scottish Literature* since it started in 1963, and was co-editor with Dr Law on Vols III to VI of the Scottish Text Society edition of Allan Ramsay. His publications include *Middle Scots Poets*, *Barbour's Bruce* and *Mediaeval Drama*.

ALEXANDER LAW was until his retirement one of H.M. Inspectors of Schools. He is responsible for *Education in Edinburgh in the 18th Century*, and worked with Professor Kinghorn on Vols III to VI of the Scottish Text Society edition of Allan Ramsay, and also on *Poems by Allan Ramsay and Robert Fergusson*.

CAROL MCGUIRK is the author of *Robert Burns and the Sentimental Era*. An Associate Professor of English and Comparative Literature at Florida Atlantic University, she is currently compiling a comprehensive bibliography of Burns criticism (tentatively entitled 'Robert Burns: A Research Guide').

JOHN MULLAN is a Research Fellow at Jesus College, Cambridge. His current study of sentimentalism, *Sentiment and Sociability*, is about to be published.

HUGH OUSTON is Principal Teacher of History, Beeslack High School, Penicuik. He graduated from Christ Church, Oxford and did research in Oxford and Edinburgh before training as a teacher in Aberdeen. He was a contributor to *New Perspectives on the Politics and Culture of Early Modern Scotland*.

IAN ROSS is Professor of English at the University of British Columbia, Vancouver, Canada. His publications on eighteenth-century Scotland include *Lord Kames and the Scotland of his Day*, and he is now at work on a major biography of Adam Smith.

MARY JANE (WITTSTOCK) SCOTT is the author of *James Thomson, Anglo Scot*. Her articles on Scottish topics ranging from the Renaissance to the twentieth century have appeared in *Studies in Scottish Literature*, *Scottish Literary Journal*, *Neophilologische Mitteilungen*, *The Bibliotheck*, and the *Journal of the Architectural Heritage Society of Scotland*.

RICHARD B SHER is Associate Professor of History and Associate Dean of the College of Science and Liberal Arts at New Jersey Institute of Technology in Newark, New Jersey. The author of numerous publications on the Scottish Enlightenment, he is currently engaged in editing a collection of essays on connections between Scotland and America in the eighteenth century.

KENNETH SIMPSON is a graduate of the Universities of Glasgow and Strathclyde. He teaches English and Scottish Literature at Strathclyde and has particular interest in the eighteenth century and the development of the novel. His publications include essays on Burns, Smollett, Galt, Stevenson, and Sterne; a collection of critical essays on Fielding; and forthcoming, a study of eighteenth-century Scottish Literature, *The Protean Scot.*

DERICK S THOMSON has been Professor of Celtic at Glasgow University since 1963. He has written widely on Celtic and Scottish Gaelic topics, edits the Gaelic quarterly *Gairm*, and has published several collections of his Gaelic verse, including the Collected Poems, *Creachadh na Clarsaich.* He is author of *An Introduction to Gaelic Poetry* and *The Companion to Gaelic Scotland.*

GORDON TURNBULL is a member of the Department of English at Yale University. He is currently pursuing research on Boswell at Yale.

Introduction

ANDREW HOOK

How far do the years between 1660 and 1800 which this, the second volume in a history of Scottish literature, purports to cover, compose any kind of coherent period? History is an ongoing process making any form of periodization inevitably problematical. Allan Ramsay in *The Gentle Shepherd* (1725) suggests that the restoration of Charles II in 1660 brought back the good times for the common people of Scotland, but that was not a view shared by large numbers of Scots at the time. For them, the good times dawned with the Glorious Revolution of 1688 when the Catholic King James II was driven from the British throne and a Protestant succession ensured. Perhaps then 1688–1800 represents a truer, more coherent period? But a mere nineteen years brings us to one of the most decisive moments in Scotland's history. Does not the Act of Union of 1707, depriving Scotland of its independent Parliament, mark a change of such magnitude that its consequences are with us even today? Perhaps therefore 1707–1800? Yes; except that in 1715 and again in 1745 some at least of the Scottish people were prepared to take up arms to try to overthrow the social and political order of which the Union of 1707 was a key constituent. And 1800? Clearly no more than a year which marks the passing of one century into another.

The kind of difficulty involved in establishing period boundaries is clear. But a particular problem for literary and cultural history is the relevance for these areas of study of boundaries initially established in terms of political or social history. It is the broad argument of this entire history of Scottish literature that the individual literary work is best understood within the widest possible cultural context—including, that is, all those social, political, economic, religious, and intellectual forces which together determine the nature of society at any given time. But this approach does not mean that literature and culture are simply seen as disappearing into the wider context, changing and developing at the same time and at the same speed as its other constituents. In fact, a period that makes a great deal of political sense may make little cultural sense. And the converse is also true. 1660, as I began by suggesting, could be regarded in religious and political terms, as a less significant starting-point than 1688, but, as this volume indicates, 1660 does make excellent cultural sense.

For that sense to become evident, however, the avoidance of another potential pitfall is necessary. Cultural history is not to be seen as a single line of development, an inevitable progress from a lower to a higher level of cultural achievement: Scottish culture moving from, say, the barbarism of the seventeenth century to the enlightenment of the eighteenth. Of course

1

it is possible to look back from the vantage point of an enlightened 1800 and imagine that one sees just such a forward movement—from the 1697 when Thomas Aikenhead, an Edinburgh student, was hanged for repeatedly declaring that 'theology was a rhapsody of ill-invented non-sense,' or from the 1722 when the last Scottish execution for witchcraft occurred in Sutherland. None the less, even if one accepts that Scotland in 1800 was a very different country from what it had been in 1660, and that in some areas progress had indeed been made, its cultural history is still not to be understood as simply a question of reading the past in terms of the future. The so-called Whig interpretation of history, which saw the past in terms of a struggle between progressives and reactionaries with the progressives (the Whigs) always finally winning, has long been out of favour with most historians. The Whig interpretation of cultural history, however, tends to remain much in evidence.

What 1660 meant for Scotland's cultural history was the renewal of continuity with the past. As the early essays in this volume indicate—and Hugh Ouston's opening essay in particular—Scottish culture in the period between the Restoration and the Union of 1707 was in inspiration strongly royalist, aristocratic, and Episcopal, with roots stretching back to the Scottish Renaissance Court. The social, political, and religious traditions with which that culture was bound up, that is, were destined to suffer, in 1688, historical defeat. Political power would be transferred irrevocably to different traditions. But for a time at least the older culture remained in place; that as the eighteenth century went on it became less and less the mainstream of Scottish cultural life does not diminish its importance for the period after 1660, nor make it irrelevant to subsequent developments in the eighteenth century. Indeed F W Freeman's essay on Fegusson shows precisely how a major poet can turn cultural loss and political defeat into imaginative triumph.

After 1688 it was inevitable that in the long run the Jacobite, Episcopal strain in Scottish culture would be overtaken by developments linked to the Hanoverian, Whig, Presbyterian ascendancy in Scotland's social and political life. But Tory Jacobitism did not disappear. It moved out of the world of political reality into the language of sentiment and feeling where its power of survival becomes one of the many paradoxes which characterize eighteenth-century Scottish culture. Nor, in this context, should the full significance of the world of feeling be underestimated. As John Mullan's essay indicates, the increasingly commercial and materialist culture of Scotland in the later eighteenth century was uneasily aware that some of its most cherished values were identified with feelings denied any form of legitimate social existence. Feelings might embody truths suppressed elsewhere.

In any event, a nostalgic Jacobitism is understandable enough in writers such as Allan Ramsay and Robert Fergusson whose political sympathies were clearly Tory in nature. What indicates its pervasiveness, however, is the fact that an identical political nostalgia appears in the work of writers who were upholders of the Hanoverian status quo, including even those—like James Thomson, Tobias Smollett, and James Boswell—who saw in the existence of the United Kingdom an opportunity to seek literary fame in London. But a paradox of this kind is no more than an index of the divided self which is Scotland's eighteenth-century culture.

The essays in this volume do nothing to dispel the idea that particular historical circumstances ensured that Scottish literature and culture in the eighteenth century would be characterized by tension and uncertainty, even though these on occasion may be disguised beneath nationalist over-assertion or a polite complacency. What the Union of 1707 achieved in this connection was critically important: renewed focus on the meaning of Scotland. The closer political union with England inevitably involved a questioning of what remained of Scotland's separate identity. What was post-Union Scotland? A nation, a country, a region, a province, a colony, or what? Was Scotland a co-partner in the United Kingdom, North Britain, or a remote province, marginally separate, totally unequal? The eighteenth century found no way of resolving such questions. Nor, as Iain Brown's essay indicates, is there any simple equation between political and cultural sympathies: even those who were directly responsible for the Union could remain emphatic and powerful defenders of Scotland's independent cultural identity. And once raised, the identity problem refuses to go away. Anyone who dips into *The Scots Magazine*—the one conspicuously successful Scottish literary magazine of the eighteenth century, published without interruption from 1739 to 1826—will be struck by how often issues are aired which remain issues in 1800 and even today: about cultural assimilation and cultural independence; about the survival or disappearance of the Scottish language and Scottish speech; about the consequences of the spread of standard education and improved Anglo-Scottish communications. (It is salutary to remember that, until well after the middle of the eighteenth century, there was only a single monthly stage-coach between Edinburgh and London, the journey taking between ten and sixteen days, and passengers often making their wills before setting out.) The question of cultural identity ceases to be a question and becomes an unbroken thread in the pattern of Scottish culture itself.

Language is inevitably a closely related issue. Was standard English to be the language of Scotland outside the Gaelic-speaking areas of the north and west? Yes and no was the characteristic eighteenth-century answer. The Scottish vernacular gained new life through a Union-inspired revival of interest in the older Renaissance poets such as Henryson, Dunbar, and Gavin Douglas, through a growing taste for the popular tradition of Scots ballad and song, and ultimately through the contemporary vernacular poetry of Ramsay, Fergusson and Burns. At the same time the enlightened Scots literati aimed to write an English prose as pure and correct as anything written in London and the South. Scottish self-consciousness in this area was clearly extraordinarily acute. Language often appears to be the point at which a more generalized cultural uneasiness becomes specific; language focuses, for example, both the central issue of 'politeness' and what David Daiches and others have seen as the tension between the inner- and other-directed, nationalist and internationalist, dimensions of eighteenth-century Scottish culture.

'Politeness' is a complex concept which is central to highly important areas of Scottish culture from the later seventeenth century on. As a socio-intellectual term it seems to define inter-related modes of social conduct and discourse, the classic expression of which the Scots identified with the essays of Addison and Steele. More generally, the cultural implications of politeness appear to be related to the widespread desire to avoid any return by Scottish society to the factional bitterness and divison which had made the Scottish experience in the seventeenth century so often a matter of violence and bloodshed. (Consider here, for example, what Gordon Turnbull has to say about Boswell's account of the dramatic confrontation between his father and Dr Johnson.) The importance of the term in relation to the practicalities of life is suggested by Thomas Somerville's autobiographical recollection that William Robertson suggested it was the lack of polish of the Scottish Members of Parliament in London immediately after the Union that was the main cause of their weakness. (Yet Somerville could regard the need to be dressed à la mode in order to attend Court in London in 1769 as an occasion of 'fun and merriment' for him and his friends.) Hence Douglas Duncan's essay on Scholarship and Politeness and is rightly not the only contribution in which the centrality of this concept is indicated.

As I have suggested, the language question in eighteenth-century Scotland has long been seen as related to considerations of the attachment of Scottish culture either to the nationalist and antiquarian rediscovery and revitalization of Scotland's own history and traditions, or to the wider world of Enlightenment and learning in Europe as a whole. Poetry in vernacular Scots was capable of survival into the eighteenth century; prose was not. Hence for the Scottish historians and philosophers, moralists and essayists, critics and scientists, there was no alternative to English. (Latin ceases to be viable early in the century.) It is out of this situation that the temptation arises to identify authentic Scottish literature in the eighteenth century with the use of the vernacular. That temptation is one that for different reasons this volume firmly resists. (And this resistance, in turn, helps to explain aspects of the structure and contents of the volume itself.)

In the first place, the eighteenth century itself never defined literature in such a way as to exclude history, philosophy, biography, essays, sermons, and the rest; and while Geoffrey Carnall's essay indicates that the gap between the practice of major historians such as Hume and Robertson, and that of a novelist such as Scott, was not in fact especially wide, Ian Ross shows us that for a historian like Hume, poetry and culture generally were very much part of his proper concern. Hence it would be wrong for a history of the literature of the period to exclude from consideration a majority of the works which contemporaries at home and abroad saw as the strongest evidence of Scotland's literary achievement: even if English were indeed the language through which that achievement was expressed.

Much more important, however, is the distortion of Scottish literary historiography which an undue privileging of the use of the vernacular inevitably produces. To assume that Burns is part of Scottish literature because he uses (some of the time) a Scottish vernacular diction, whereas James Thomson belongs to English literature because he chose to write in English, is to produce a very partial picture of Scotland's literary culture in the eighteenth century. Yet to a substantial degree this is precisely what has happened. Use of the vernacular has often been accepted almost as a test of Scottish virility; cultural nationalism has always been happier with the Scottish vernacular than with Scots-English. The result has been a grossly over-simplified account of the development of Scottish literature from the early Makars on. The vernacular definition of Scottish literature, for example, consigns all writing in Scots Gaelic to a form of Celtic ghetto. What Derick Thomson's essay in this volume demonstrates is not only the imaginative achievement of Gaelic poetry in its own right, but also the degree to which that poetry was not isolated from the rest of Scotland's literary culture. That it is the Anglo-Scot James Thomson who should emerge as a major influence on Gaelic writing is particularly telling.

However, it is not only Mary Jane Scott's essay which challenges the received view of the 'Englishness' of Thomson and his fellow Anglo-Scots poets, and the consequent literary historiographical preoccupation with the exponents of the vernacular. Kenneth Simpson's essay on Smollett shows equally well how an author's consistent use of English is in no way incompatible with an entirely natural and spontaneous recourse to established Scottish literary conventions and Scottish habits of thought and feeling. Indeed Alexander Kinghorn and Alexander Law on Ramsay, Thomas Crawford on Scots songs, and Carol McGuirk on Burns himself, all refuse to take any kind of over-simplified view of the linguistic situation of the Scots writer in the eighteenth century. Professor McGuirk in fact turns conventional literary history on its head by locating a major source of Burns's artistic and imaginative strength precisely in the Anglo-Scottish dimension of his work.

The divisions in Scottish culture in the seventeenth century were at bottom religious in nature. The eighteenth century had no wish to return to the violence and war that such divisions had produced in the past; but inevitably religious tension remained, even if it now took different forms. After 1690 there was no longer any threat to the hegemony of the Church of Scotland in the country's religious life. On the other hand, the emergence of the philosophical Enlightenment in Europe did ultimately represent a threat to traditional religious values. In Scotland what matters is the significance of the challenge to conventional religion which the scepticism of David Hume, Lord Kames, and their Edinburgh circle, actually involved. For the great mass of the Scottish people, whose staple reading-matter remained the King James Bible and religious works such as Thomas Boston's *Human Nature in Its Fourfold States*, Bunyan's *Pilgrim's Progress*, and Ralph Erskine's *Gospel Sonnets*, one suspects that

Hume's ideas remained uninfluential and largely unknown. None the less, the immediate popularity of those Counter-Enlightenment Aberdeen philosophers who attempted to refute Hume—George Campbell, James Beattie, and Thomas Reid—and the speed with which their Common Sense philosophy was welcomed throughout Europe and America, do suggest that established authority everywhere did see the potential threat to the existing moral ordering of society that scepticism represented.

However, within Scotland, religious tension is most in evidence in the internal conflicts which soon appeared within the structure of the Church of Scotland itself. These produced either the secession from the established Church of small groups not prepared to accept the authority of the parent body, or, more significantly, a continuing struggle throughout the eighteenth century between a Popular or traditional Calvinist grouping within the Church, and a Moderate party, inclined towards a more liberal, less austere, and more 'polite' approach to the Church and its role in society. It was probably this clash between the Moderates and their opponents that made questions of religion, morality, philosophy, ideology and conduct, of significant concern not only to intellectual elites but to large numbers of ordinary Scottish people. Inevitably, then, this central division in the country's religious life made an impact on the period's literary culture. One strain in Calvinist culture had always been uneasy over the status of 'carnal learning'. In consequence, Presbyterian clergymen in the early eighteenth century remained troubled and uncertain over their response to secular literature: the open and long-running hostility to the threatre, and in particular the outcry occasioned by John Home's writing of *Douglas*—Home was himself a clergyman—alluded to both by Richard Sher and Alisdair Cameron, are but the most open manifestations of such Presbyterian disquiet. In cultural terms, however, it was the association between Moderation and politeness that proved decisive. Douglas Duncan's account of the stylistic problems facing Robert Wodrow, the historian and proponent of the Popular party in the Church, suggests very well how it was Wodrow's opponents—the Moderates—who had become identified with polite discourse and English norms of good taste. Hence after mid-century, Moderate clergymen were to become, as Professor Sher shows, probably the largest single professional group contributing to the literature and learning of the Scottish Enlightenment.

A final area of tension in Scotland's eighteenth-century literary culture worthy of note is that referred to in my own essay in this volume. The conditions of authorship in eighteenth-century Scotland were clearly somewhat problematical. An independent professional career as a writer was scarcely possible—at least if one wanted to remain at home in Scotland. Printing, publishing, book-selling, patronage—the scale of all of these remained modest. Inevitably, then, Scotland's literary output, year by year, was never great. Yet, astonishingly, a handful of Scottish texts achieved amazing popularity throughout the western world: Scott's fantastic popular triumph with the Waverley Novels in the early nineteenth century should not be allowed wholly to overshadow the enduring fame achieved by such eighteenth-century works as Ramsay's *The Gentle Shepherd*, John Home's tragedy *Douglas*, James Macpherson's *Ossian*, various collections of popular Scots songs and ballads, and the poetry of Burns. These works retained an enthusiastic audience for almost a century, and created an enduring image of Scotland that was much more romantic than rational. Yet, by 1800, the successes of the Scots literati—the histories of Hume and Robertson, the Common Sense philosophy of Reid and Stewart, the criticism and aesthetics of Kames and Blair, the social enquiries of Adam Smith, Adam Ferguson and John Millar—and, in particular, the widespread adoption of their works as college and university texts, ensured that Scotland was everywhere recognized as a centre of Englightenment learning. This conjunction of Romanticism and Enlightenment around 1800 is another Scottish paradox meriting further exploration.

What has just been said about the popularity of eighteenth-century Scottish literature, and its relatively narrow base, helps to explain some of the features of this volume. No individual author or text has been seen as the exclusive concern of just one contributor. As the volume aims to provide a sense of the cultural context within which individual writers worked, themes and topics have been given as much attention as particular authors or literary genres; politics, for example, has been seen as relevant to pastoral, and Presbyterianism to poetry and plays. One result is that important texts are looked at in more than one essay; hence readers who are interested in what is said about a specific work are advised to use the Index.

The volume does not pretent to provide an exhaustive history of Scottish literature in the eighteenth century. There are writers who get only a passing mention, others who get no mention at all. And in the case of writers who are given more extended treatment, there is frequently no attempt to 'cover' all of their work. Contributors were encouraged to pursue their topics in the context of the period as a whole, so the chronological development of the volume—from the Restoration to Romanticism—is unobtrusive. The range of the volume, as has been said, is intended to be wide. None the less, readers may be disappointed to find some areas or topics or approaches apparently neglected: not much, for example, on the contributions to Scottish literature of the different Scottish regions; not much on the significance of English hostility towards the Scots after the Jacobite rising of 1745 and the accession to power somewhat later of the Scottish Earl of Bute; not much on women's writing.

Women's writing is a political issue of today, and as such demanded careful consideration. Eighteenth-century Scotland had its women writers—Lady Wardlaw, Lady Grizel Baillie, Jane Elliott, Mrs Alison Cockburn, Lady Anne Barnard, Lady Anne Lindsay, Lady Nairne, and others—all of them remembered for occasional poems or songs in Scots; but it is difficult to see them as representing very much more than further evidence in favour of Thomas Crawford's argument that the popular culture of eighteenth-century Scotland was able to appeal across traditional class barriers. Only in the early nineteenth century does writing become for Scottish women a possible source of supplementary income. Yet Mr Crawford's essay also makes it clear that, particularly within Scotland's popular culture, a woman's voice was often powerfully present.

A final word of explanation. The decision not to modernize spellings in quotations is deliberate: particularly in the early contributions, retention of the original forms provides a valuable insight into the use of English in Scotland at a particular historical moment.

The Editor of such a volume as this is bound to incur debts. I should like to thank all my contributors for their cooperation and amiability. But to Kenneth Simpson and Thomas Crawford—and to Nicholas Phillipson most of all—I owe special thanks for invaluable help, advice, and encouragement. Finally I wish to record my gratitude to Ingrid Swanson; her work as secretary has made the whole project possible.

Glasgow, 1987

FURTHER READING

GENERAL AND POLITICAL HISTORY

Cowan, I B, *The Scottish Covenanters* (London, 1976)
Ferguson, W, *Scotland: 1689 to the Present* (Edinburgh, 1968)
—— *Scotland's Relations with England* (Edinburgh, 1977)
Lenman, B, *The Jacobite Risings in Britain 1689–1746* (London, 1980)
Meikle, H W, *Scotland and the French Revolution* (Glasgow, 1912)
—— *Some Aspects of Later Seventeenth-Century Scotland* (Glasgow, 1947)
Mitchison, R, *Lordship to Patronage: Scotland 1603–1745* (London, 1983)
Riley, P W J, *The Union of England and Scotland* (Manchester, 1978)
Scott, P H, *The Union of Scotland and England* (Edinburgh, 1979)
Smout, T C, *A History of the Scottish People 1560–1830* (London, 1969)

CULTURAL HISTORY

Camic, C, *Experience and Enlightenment: Socialization for Cultural Change in Eighteenth-Century Scotland* (Edinburgh, 1983)
Campbell, R H and A S Skinner (eds), *The Origins and Nature of the Scottish Enlightenment* (Edinburgh, 1982)
Chapman, M, *The Gaelic Vision in Scottish Culture* (London and Montreal, 1979)
Chitnis, A C, *The Scottish Enlightenment: A Social History* (London, 1976)
Daiches, D, *The Paradox of Scottish Culture* (London, 1964)
—— *Literature and Gentility* (Edinburgh, 1982)
Davie, G E, *The Democratic Intellect* (Edinburgh, 1961)
Graham, H G, *The Social Life of Scotland in the Eighteenth Century* (London, 1899)
Hont, I and M Ignatieff (eds), *Wealth and Virtue: the Shaping of Political Economy in the Scottish Enlightenment* (Cambridge, 1983)
Hook, A D, *Scotland and America, 1750–1835* (Glasgow, 1975)
Houston, R A, *Scottish Literacy and the Scottish Identity* (Cambridge, 1985)
McElroy, D D, *Scotland's Age of Improvement: A Survey of Eighteenth-Century Literary Clubs and Societies* (Pullman, 1969)
Mitchison, R and N T Phillipson (eds), *Scotland in the Age of Improvement* (Edinburgh, 1970)
Sher, R B *Church and University in the Scottish Enlightenment: the Moderate Literati of Edinburgh* (Princeton and Edinburgh, 1985)
Strang, J, *Glasgow and Its Clubs* (London and Glasgow, 1857)

LITERARY HISTORY

Craig, D, *Scottish Literature and the Scottish People, 1680–1830* (London, 1961)

Crawford, T, *Society and the Lyric: A Study of the Song Culture of Eighteenth-Century Scotland* (Edinburgh, 1979)

Daiches, D, *Robert Burns* (New York, 1950)

Graham, H G, *Scottish Men of Letters in the Eighteenth Century* (London, 1901)

MacQueen, J, *Progress and Poetry: The Enlightenment and Scottish Literature* (Edinburgh, 1982)

Watson, R, *The Literature of Scotland* (London, 1984)

Chapter 1

Cultural Life from the Restoration to the Union

HUGH OUSTON

From William Robertson in 1759 until as late as the 1960s, most historians regarded the seventeenth century in Scotland as a period of cultural stagnation, either because of the removal of the Court to London in 1603 or because of the century's intense preoccupation with religious issues. A more sophisticated but related analysis has argued that there was a disjunction between the experience of Scotland, the language that embodied it, and the beginnings of the anglicisation of Scottish polite culture. Only recently have historians begun, first, to look for the origins of the Scottish Enlightenment of the eighteenth century in the totality of Scottish culture, that is, not just in literature and philosophy; and secondly, to examine the actual concerns of the seventeenth century, including religion, on their own terms. These two trends are in fact coming to be complementary. Scottish culture from the Restoration to the Union can now be described in terms not primarily literary or philosophical, and it can be seen to include a number of themes whose interaction did much to stimulate the subsequent social enquiries of the eighteenth century. I will try in this essay to describe briefly these varied and contrasting themes and to highlight the most prominent common quality they developed before the Act of Union of 1707: their appeal to the professional classes. It is my contention that the most important contribution of the late seventeenth century to a distinctive Scottish cultural tradition was the confirmation of the professions' role within its development.

There was an element of paradox in this role. The energies which gave social strength to the country's central professional institutions in the Restoration period were originally anglophile, aristocratic and courtly. These energies also led to the Union of Parliaments of 1707, which denuded Scotland of its traditional social and political leadership, thus leaving the professions to play a dominant part in the survival of a distinctive Scottish intellectual life. In the 1680s the professions claimed an important cultural role in a tradition dating self-consciously from the Renaissance, the Jacobean Court, and the Reformation. Soon after the Union, however, the intellectual interests which they derived from this tradition were providing fertile ground for the innovative ideas of the eighteenth century. So the period 1660–1707, far from being an intellectual parenthesis in Scotland's history, had written through it a line of continuity in the form and content of Scottish culture from the Renaissance to the Enlightenment.

In 1660 Scotland lacked, and by 1707 had developed, an intelligentsia—made up largely of lawyers, doctors, academics and ministers. The emergence of such a group of thinkers, and the institutional and intellectual developments associated with them, was the most significant development of late seventeenth-century Scottish culture. This development can be traced through the social, economic and political history of the period, against a background of comparative domestic peace, the possibility of wealth, and the security of a property-based social structure. Through successive political quarrels over ecclesiastical organisation, parliamentary identity, royal succession and economic problems, the Scottish professions built up a leading role in their country's cultural history.

The ambitions of the professions were originally patronised in the post-Restoration period by King James II and VII, who, while still Duke of York, resided in Scotland as High Commissioner between 1679 and 1682. His aim to secure a loyal political power base in Scotland coincided with the desire of several professional groups for royal patronage. The language in which that patronage was expressed was still that of the Renaissance tradition of the 'Virtuoso', a model which combined royalist and aristocratic social status with a broad intellectual curiosity. Virtuoso enquiry embraced scientific and antiquarian learning, and Latin and vernacular literature and philosophy, all conceived of as parts of a unity of knowledge.

The accident of the Glorious Revolution of 1688 took away Royalist political protection and opened the professions to the influence of restored Presbyterianism and, later, to the ideas thrown up by the vigorous political debate over the nation's identity. The Union of 1707, finally, took away both Parliament and aristocracy, leaving the professions to try to confirm for themselves a role in circumstances very different to those of the 1680s. That they were able to do so with such success in the course of the following century was largely due to the institutional and intellectual identity which they had developed since the Restoration. At the dawn of the Enlightenment, that is, the learned achievements of the nation had largely come to be vested in professional institutions originating in an aristocratic tradition looking back to the Renaissance.

The members and subsequent imitators of these institutions maintained significant aspects of the Virtuoso ideal. First, they still felt an obligation to their country, to their professions, and to the concept of the 'advancement of learning', and thought all three obligations interdependent. Secondly, they defined learning in the broadest sense: it included not only the social disciplines of law, medicine and theology, but also touched on such diverse objects of enquiry as antiquarianism, book-collecting, geography and history, oral poetry and popular belief, classicism, natural history, educational policy and economic improvement. Such Virtuoso pansophism may have been growing dated even in Scotland by 1707, in the sense that the unrigorous method it pursued seemed inadequate to the followers of

Newton, but the range of interests it bequeathed was already that of the French philosophes and their Scottish counterparts. The integration of such diverse areas of enquiry remained a distinctively Scottish cultural tradition. Throughout the period from 1660 to 1707, great respect was held, as it always had been, for English and continental models, but a central and overriding concern can be discerned as early as the Union within the diversity of Scottish culture: reflection on man in his social and natural environment.

What were the concerns of the new Scottish professional class as it consolidated its role in Scottish culture during the post-Restoration period? First was a concern for social status. In his notes for a description of Scotland in 1695, Sir Robert Sibbald, a leading physician and Virtuoso throughout this period, commented on the growing link between the legal profession and the landed classes:

> a great part of the Nobility . . . have made and increased their Estates, by being Members of the College of Justice, or session, and obtaining the Erection of Church Benefices.

Sibbald's own success in the foundation of the Royal College of Physi cians of Edinburgh in 1681 was due crucially to his convincing the future James VII that personal royal patronage should be accorded to the doc tors' high social status. This status involved intellectual obligations: when in 1707 a surgeon claimed 'Are we not Gentlemen, have not we had a liberal Education?', a rival physician replied:

> I always thought, that by a liberal Education is meant . . . a competent knowledge in the Latine and Greek Tongues, Philosophy and the other liberal Sciences . . . as makes a Man that applys himself to the Studie of Divinity, Law, Medicine &c. capable to understand . . . Standart Authors . . .

The true specialist professional, that is, had to have the general cultural education of a gentleman, and in fact the social aspirations of the profes sions were bound up with the wider question of the status of the gentry, based on property, which was manifesting itself in the 1680s and 1690s through entail and enclosure legislation, and through an interest in heral dry, precedency, freemasonry and formal societies such as the Royal Company of Archers and the Order of the Thistle.

These related social and professional aspirations were encouraged in the 1680s by James VII as he developed his political influence in Scotland, but they outlived the Revolution of 1688 in which that influence was des troyed. They can still be seen in the Scotland described by John Slezer in his *Theatrum Scotiae* of 1695, dedicated to the nobility and gentry, and in the vigour of these classes in the intellectual debates of the last years of the Scottish Parliament. The typical Renaissance Virtuoso had been a gentle man—though a few nobles such as the Earl of Perth and his sister the

Countess of Errol aspired to the role. After 1660, however, the ideal spread increasingly to professionals of a lower social origin such as Archibald Pitcairne the physician, Professors James and David Gregory the mathematicians, James Sutherland the horticulturalist, and clergymen such as George Sinclair the demonologist and James Gordon the topographer. For professionals such as these, the association of learning with improved social standing was an important incentive in encouraging them to pursue intellectual achievement.

The second defining concern of such figures was virtue, conceived as an intellectual as well as a moral mode of self-fulfilment. In the early seventeenth century Sir James Balfour had written that 'the fontaine and Spring of Nobility is ather wertew or Authority of ye Prince.' Virtue as defined by Balfour was a feudal social ideal. However, to the royalist professionals of the post-Restoration period, such as the Lord Advocate, Sir George Mackenzie, it included moral and intellectual qualities. For Mackenzie, these derived from the Stoic belief that virtue was based on knowledge and reason, and a similar recognition is implied by the historian Gilbert Burnet's description of Sibbald as 'the most learned antiquary in Scotland, who had lived in a course of philosophical vertue.' In other words, Sibbald was a Virtuoso.

A third distinctive feature of the new professional class was their commitment to the 'advancement of learning' as a patriotic programme. Such learning might include the full range of Virtuoso enquiry, which aimed to define and explore a Scottish cultural identity. For example, Sibbald himself looked back to Sir James Balfour and his Jacobean circle as sharing

> a common love of letters . . . and a mutual desire of benefitting and adorning their country by the preservation of its historical and literary treasures

—and worked towards this ideal until his own death in 1722. Many of his contemporaries shared such a nostalgia both for the pre-civil war political order and for the cultural achievement of Renaissance Scotland.

Such nostalgia among the Virtuosi working before 1688 helped to define the social context of their intellectual aspirations, but it was also part of a shared political, philosophical and methodological outlook. Many held to a royalist political conservatism of a kind most fully worked out in the defence of the political establishment by Sir George Mackenzie as Lord Advocate between 1677 and 1689. Mackenzie was motivated above all by fear of a repetition of the 'great rebellion', as the Civil War was defined, the best protection against which was the continuation of the established order of James VI's reign into those of his grandsons. Mackenzie repeated Jacobean arguments against the dangerous belief of the sixteenth-century scholar and historian George Buchanan in an 'ancient constitution' as a rival to theories of absolute monarchy. In Mackenzie's writings, 'present positive law', or law in action, reflected and defended God's intention for human society, which was demonstrated in the philosophical premise that man's soul had been imprinted with 'some common principle whereby he is led to love order.' In the assertion of such a principle, political and philosophical conservatism came together. A similar conjunction appeared in Sibbald's *Scotia Illustrata* of 1684 which used a medieval, Aristotelian taxonomy to provide a framework for an account of Scotland's natural history. Sibbald wrote this book in his newly-appointed role as Geographer Royal, investigating anew a recently stabilized country, and as such it is a political statement; but it is also a recognition of the unity of knowledge, and its inclusive approach reflects the empirical, even credulous methodology of the Virtuoso.

Sibbald was a key figure in Scottish cultural life from the 1670s, when he gathered round him a group of young professionals who were returning from completing their studies in Europe, including Andrew Balfour, Sir James' younger brother, who had been tutor to Lord Rochester. Sibbald corresponded with one of these men 'anent maitter of learning, especially moral philosophie, the knowledge of the world, and of men . . .' At the same time the young James Gregory, Professor of Mathematics at St Andrews from 1670–74, hoped to found an observatory there so 'we may be enabled to keep correspondence with learned and inquisitive persons.' These hopes for intellectual coordination became an explicit programme on the arrival of the Duke of York in Scotland in 1679. From the first, James skilfully linked intellectual patronage to royalist party loyalty, partly by identifying such loyalty with social and intellectual qualities. In consequence, the royalist belief in the necessity of order was used to justify the setting up of formalised institutions:

> whatever arguments are given for the establishment of societies of men in General, the lyke may be adduced for the erection of particular Faculties and Corporationes . . .

By the 1680s the intellectual community to which Sibbald and Mackenzie belonged saw itself as a means through which royalist and aristocratic government would enable Scotland to 'begin to contend with the happiest of our neighbours', as Sibbald hoped.

Thus, during the 1680s, the coincidence of James' political ambitions with the intellectual aspirations of the Scottish professions led to the founding of several new institutions. The Royal College of Physicians was given a charter in 1681, its members having already helped to set up the first botanical garden in the 1670s. The Surgeons were also given a royal college in 1681, though it was held up for fourteen years by professional jealousy. New professorships were filled in mathematics, botany and medicine at the College of Edinburgh, which was first called a University in 1685, and three years later was also due to receive a royal charter confirming its status and importance. Sibbald, as mentioned above, was appointed Geographer Royal in 1682. The town of Edinburgh itself was given a new charter in 1688 encouraging the physical metamorphosis which did not take place for another seventy years. The legal profession, independent of direct royal patronage but led by the royalist Virtuoso Mackenzie, was developing its intellectual facilities—a new constitution in 1686, and the Faculty of Advocates' Library, set up in 1679 and inaugurated a decade later in anticipation of a role for the profession which also took half a century to fulfil. Taken together, all these developments moved the professions firmly towards leadership of Scottish polite culture.

Within this professional structure, the cultural interests and standards of individual writers varied widely. The advancement of medicine was particularly uneven, despite the new College of Physicians' concern with standards. This was partly due to the difficulties of establishing the institutions of a profession against the medieval guild structure of Edinburgh. The doctors found support from the central government and the lawyers, but they were divided both from the surgeons and among themselves. In 1684–5 a young group of Leyden graduates had attempted to oust the founders of the College; this may have accounted for a long delay in publishing the first Pharmacopeia. The appointment of Drs Sibbald, Halkett and Pitcairne as professors of medicine in 1685 was intended to provide examination of doctors by a 'duly constitute faculty of medicine as is usual in the Universities of other nationes.' In fact, such examinations were not carried out, nor did the professors of medicine teach. However the physic garden continued to flourish under James Sutherland, Professor of Botany from 1676, who was patronized by the Town Council with the encouragement of both the landed classes and the medical professions. Sutherland did write a Latin description of the garden, and Dr Thomas Burnet a medical handbook, *Hippocrates Contractus*, in 1685, and the College of Physicians began to collect a small library of works on related subjects.

The library's growth was interrupted by the revolution of 1688, and the following decade saw a major intellectual argument in the medical community. This centred on Dr Pitcairne, who spent a year as Professor of Medicine at Leyden University from 1692–3. He allied himself with the surgeons in an attempt to develop an anatomy school in Edinburgh, and also split the physicians over the issue of the treatment of fevers and his belief in rational medicine. Presbyterian patronage through Principal Gilbert Rule of Edinburgh University further clouded the issue, though the incorporation of the surgeons, the establishment of the anatomical theatre, and the publication of the *Pharmacopeia* in 1696 were real advances which were to be built on in the eighteenth century by Scottish doctors taught by Pitcairne's pupil at Leyden, Boerhaave.

Sibbald saw no distinction between the work of a doctor and that of a Virtuoso. He had established learned conferences among his friends in the late 1670s and continued these monthly after the foundation of the College, himself lecturing on a non-medical subject. His antiquarian and geographical work had the same aim, the discovery and description of past and present as part of the investigation of an ordered universe and participation in an ordered society. Already involved in contemporary cartography, Sibbald was made Geographer Royal specifically in order to produce a natural history and geography of Scotland. To this end he published an advertisement asking for information from the nobility, gentry, clergy, royal burghs, universities and colleges. Of identifiable contributors to *Scotia Illustrata*, thirty-eight were ministers and there were replies from all the other groups, although the Highlands were underrepresented. The same method of collecting information was used by cartographers such as Pont and Gordon earlier in the century, and by Adair and Slezer in the 1690s.

The nature of Virtuoso intellectual standards is shown by Sibbald's indiscriminate collection of information and its organisation into preconceived Aristotelian classifications and 'curiosities' which confirmed or departed from these. The same order was imposed on zoological, historical and social material. Thus Virtuoso scientific enquiry was the antithesis of the Baconian method. The learning to which it contributed was not a series of principles which experiment could call into question but an absolute and constant corpus of knowledge which was slowly being uncovered. The practical application of this knowledge did not require any methodological innovation. What stimulated it was rather an improvement in political circumstances:

> because the face of the country, by the peace and quiet we enjoy under his Majesties happy Government, is quite changed from what it was of old . . . therefore a new and full description was much desired by all ingenious persons.

Throughout the rest of his life Sibbald continued in the same intellectual tradition working, for example, on whales, roman antiquities and county history, but by 1706, as he wrote to Hans Sloane of the Royal Society in London, he could 'find . . . few here curious of that sort of learning'. Yet he kept up a regular if difficult exchange of information with the Royal Society, sending young Episcopalian intellectuals south and receiving books from London. There are references to the use of the 'Museum Balfourianum' as a conference room for the doctors, to a 'Club of Antiquaries' in 1702, and to the proposed establishment of a Royal Society for Scotland: none the less, the main themes of Sibbald's later career were isolation and discontinuity.

Sibbald's failure testified to the weakness of the intellectual tradition to which he belonged. By the 1690s, the Virtuoso ideal was under attack from those Scottish thinkers who had espoused a more Baconian approach to knowledge, largely under the influence of Isaac Newton. James Gregory, for example, dismissed the work of George Sinclair, sometime Professor of Philosophy at Glasgow: 'ye must not call experiments new inventions otherwise ye are making new inventions every day . . .' Pitcairne likewise censured Sibbald as 'a writer certainly diligent and industrious, but not always correct; rather superstitious and credulous.' Both the Gregories and Pitcairne were correspondents of Newton, and were the first Scots in their fields of optics, mathematics and medicine to attempt to apply Newtonian standards of experiment. David Gregory also remained interested in

Scottish intellectual life in the 1690s and 1700s, though he became Savilian Professor of Astronomy at Oxford in 1691. Pitcairne's activities in the same period included Latin versification, playwriting and the encouragement of the work of the young Jacobites Thomas Ruddiman and Robert Freebairn, who were also to set new critical standards in their fields of editing and publishing after the Union. Thus the influence of Pitcairne and the Gregories was transmitted not only through their professional work but through a truly Virtuoso range of interests.

The rising prestige of the lawyers, like that of the doctors, was partly a question of the profession's enhanced social status as arbiters of a world where, in Mackenzie's words, 'government is the King's and property the subject's birthright'. The gentry cemented their alliance with the legal profession by joining it in increasing numbers towards the end of the century. The 1688 revolution confirmed that the alliance was based on social status, as it survived the collapse of the Stuart dynasty who had indirectly encouraged the development of the legal profession only at the price of highly politicising it.

The late seventeenth century saw a crucial development in the theory, forms and process of Scots law which gave it the strength to maintain its individuality after 1707. By then, the institutions and intellectual traditions which had developed during the previous fifty years had given the legal profession a distinctive cultural role in Scotland. It is clear that one reason for the lawyers' continuing social and intellectual influence in the 1690s—just as in the case of the doctors—was the strength of the institutions established under Stuart patronage in the previous decade. The roles of the Court of Session and the Lord Advocate had become more clearly defined, the Court of Justiciary had extended royal justice, and both Mackenzie and Lord Stair had written Institutions, differing but comprehensive statements of the theory of Scottish law, and useful guides to its practice. Both men had intellectual ambitions outside their profession, and Mackenzie in particular saw a role for lawyers themselves as purveyors of learning to the nation. The library of the Faculty of Advocates was to be a vital medium for this. It was first mentioned in 1679 when it was proposed that new advocates should contribute a sum to its upkeep 'considering that the office and employment of advocats being a liberal profession.' Mackenzie oversaw its rapid development through to 1689 when he delivered its inaugural oration, reemphasising its national purpose:

> Therefore on the death of their owners, let lawyers' libraries flow, like streams to the ocean, into this library common to us all.[1]

Mackenzie naturally saw learning and literature as worthy interests of an aristocratic Virtuoso, a role to which professional men of gentle breeding could aspire. Hence up to 1707 the intellectual patronage of the Faculty of Advocates continued to reflect the Virtuoso tradition. In 1701 John

Spottiswoode, Dean of the Faculty and Keeper of the Library, proposed an 'Act for erecting the Advocates into a Society' which although not passed also supposed a wider role for the profession. Once again the ideal had been proposed by Mackenzie, in his *Idea Eloquentiae Forensis Hodiernae* of 1681:

> if they, who lived in the first Dawn of Learning, made so great a Noise in the World, what may be expected from our Advocates, who are born in a happier Age, and assisted with all the Advantages that Leisure, Riches, a liberal Education and the respectful Observance of Clients can possibly afford them?

It was George Mackenzie himself who fulfilled his own ideal most completely. The quality of his writing in its variety of styles far exceeds that of any contemporary. However after 1672 the most interesting feature of his contribution to Scottish culture was his determination to concentrate on the advancement of learning through his professional work, and in this he resembled the rest of the Scottish Virtuosi:

> When I was too young, to write in my own Profession, my love to my Countrey tempted me to write Moral Philosophy, and to adventure on a Play and a Poem, but now that I find, that our Countreymen could be happy enough in these, if their inclinations were not less than their abilities, I have abandoned those Employments . . .

As Lord Advocate, Mackenzie wrote treatises on criminal law, government policy, royalist political philosophy, including antiquarian and heraldic works, and his *Institutions of the Laws of Scotland*. In all these areas, however, his work had a strong political purpose: the defence of the Restoration establishment. The development of the institutions and ideology of the legal profession was itself a vital part of this defence, and the cultural achievement of the profession was interdependent with it. For example, his first forensic work, the collection of pleadings of 1672, explained contemporary excellence both by the improvement in eloquence since Cicero's time and by the politically favourable atmosphere of monarchy.

Mackenzie's non-legal literary achievements were likewise motivated by his professional status and his political principles. His writings were imitative in style and patriotic in sentiment, as was much of the work of his Virtuoso contemporaries. It is worth remembering that the Jacobean courtly tradition from which his work derived was both anglophile and nationalist, and that this major theme of Virtuoso culture did not involve the tensions to which it was subject after 1707. Indeed it can be argued that one of the reasons for the survival of a distinctive Scottish culture after the Union was the confidence with which English intellectual influences had been imitated and adapted in the late seventeenth century. The use of an English literary style derived from the move of the Scottish Court to London in 1603 and from Scottish writers such as Drummond of Hawthornden, but also, more profoundly, from the Calvinist Reformation,

Knox's English prose, and the Authorised Version of the Bible. Use of English as opposed to Scots was the result of a tradition which also made Latin an attractive language. Such an internationalist outlook was also one of the inspirations behind indigenous developments in professional and university training, which frequently aimed to set up a domestic equivalent of the educational standards available in Holland or France.

Mackenzie's first published work was a contrived novel called *Aretina, or the Serious Romance*, derivative of the French genre of Mme Scudery, although its title page emphasized that it was an original composition in English. Sir Thomas Urquhart's *Jewel*, published a few years previously, was the only extant Scottish model for such a work. Possibly earlier, Mackenzie had made an attempt to imitate the poetry of Donne, but after reading 'Ane Apologie for Blacknesse', it is easy to sympathise with the reaction of Mackenzie's uncle and patron Sir John Wedderburn: 'I hug a statesman more than a poet.' Shortly after, Mackenzie wrote a long poem called *Caelia's Country House and Closet*, which is in effect a neoclassical description of his personal iconography at the time: Cato, Montrose, Jonson and Waller, Pompey and Cleopatra. Mackenzie recommended Waller to his fellow-royalist Dryden on first meeting him in 1679. *Religio Stoici*, Mackenzie's first moral essay, was a 'sedulous aping of Sir Thomas Browne'[2] which praised a 'Stoicall Indolency and Christian Repose', later to be translated as professional leisure and political security. A conventional controversy with John Evelyn over the relative merits of solitude and public employment developed these themes, and essays on *Happiness* and *Moral Gallantry* confirmed that he felt classical morality and English courtly style were equally means of increasing the reputation and learning of his own country.

However, throughout his early works Mackenzie's later identification of Scottish intellectual excellence with his own profession is visible. In *Aretina*, he analysed four literary modes of the mid century and decided that the University mode was too dry, the philosophic too strong, the courtly too exaggerated, while the legal was superior to the others. His essay on *What Eloquence is fit for the Bar* introduced the patriotic element into this argument, praising the 'Scottish idiom of the British tongue':

> English is fit for haranguing, the French for complimenting, but the Scots for pleading. Our pronunciation is like ourselves, firy, abrupt sprightly and bold; their greatest wits being employ'd at Court, have indeed enricht very much their language as to conversation, but all ours bending themselves to study Law, the chief Science in repute with us, hath much smooth'd our language, as to pleading . . . their language is invented by Courtiers . . . but ours by learn'd men, and men of businesse, and so must be more massie and significant.

Mackenzie's mastery of English literary styles did not prevent him from seeing that Scottish traditions were different. In his eyes the line of continuity in intellectual achievement stretched from the Renaissance Court to the Restoration Bar. The support given by his profession to the Faculty of Advocates Library shows he was not isolated in these ideals, and helped to make their influence felt through the next two centuries.

As an accomplished Latinist, Mackenzie shared in another distinctive strand in Scottish culture between the Restoration and the Union, one which also had Renaissance origins and patriotic motives. Actual writing in Latin was coming to the end of its development, but the content of humanist study—'liberal education'—remained a central source of ideal and image to educated Scots. Mackenzie wrote that the Scots exceeded the English as far in Latin as the English did the Scots in their own language, and elsewhere reiterated a widely used parallel: that the Scots had set the physical bounds to the Roman Empire by their bravery, and bounds to Roman eloquence by the brilliance of Buchanan, Barclay and Blackwood. Mackenzie's praise of Buchanan, however, was directed towards his Latin style, and he remained, like all royalists, an enemy of Buchanan's politics; such an attitude towards Buchanan remained typical of Scottish Latin writers throughout the seventeenth century, from the Renaissance Court to the post-Revolution Jacobites. In reality the Latin achievement of the Scottish Renaissance Court had declined into mere epigrammatic, elegiac—as in Sibbald's Latin funeral inscriptions to the Jacobite general Dundee, and to Dr Pitcairne—and occasional writing, a 'wit' which was admired by many Jacobites between the Revolution and the Union. And even in the universities, academic dissertations in Latin with their stiff logical forms can be seen as hindering an effective use of Scots or English.

Nevertheless, the influence of Latinism, and of the humanist tradition with which it was closely bound up, remained an inspiration to a wide range of Virtuosi. Mackenzie's essays, Gregory's education proposals and Fletcher of Saltoun's political arguments—such as the benefits of national service and republican virtue—were all derived from classical models. Thomas Ruddiman's publishing work after the Union, though continuing the Jacobite Latinist tradition by attempting to justify Scottish pride in native authors, aspired to the highest standards of international scholarship, and thus also made available to the eighteenth-century Scottish public accurate editions of classical authors. Although it might be hard to prove that Scots intellectuals after the Union discovered civic humanism in Scots Latinism, they certainly found there a nationalist humanism which proved to be an equally stimulating example.

Whereas law and medicine were rapidly developing their institutional and intellectual influence in late seventeenth-century Scotland, the traditional centres of learning, the universities, had a more uneven history They did not before 1707 modify their central role as the seminaries of a godly clergy, or their system of regenting, whereby one teacher took a group of students through all four years of the course. Modifications to these traditional features of university life were clearly influenced by the political history of Scotland: before the Revolution, royalist political patronage led to piecemeal extension of their intellectual preoccupations, and in the 1690s, a lengthy Presbyterian visitation attempted to define a fixed academic course.

Soon after the Restoration, specialist professorships were established at the College of Edinburgh in particular. James Gregory, for example, was 'bought' from St Andrews to become Professor of Mathematics in 1674, and his nephew David succeeded to his chair in 1683. Other new professors included James Sutherland in Botany in 1676 and the three doctors mentioned above in 1685, though these last had no teaching role. Principal Leighton in the 1660s and Laurence Charteris, Professor of Divinity from 1675 to 1681, set high standards in theology. Of particular interest, however, is the influence of the professions on the College as its status began to change before 1688. James Gregory was required to give two public lectures a year; Sutherland's appointment was 'much desired be sevrles of the nobilitie, gentrie and physitianes and chirurgeons.' In 1675 the Lords of Session asserted the rights of lawyers to vote in the election for the Humanity professorship. The doctors' appointments recognised both their professional standing and the status of the college as a university, specifically empowered to appoint specialist professors. Finally, in 1688, the College was promised a new charter by James VII, which combined political control through the Town Council with permission to erect professions, 'faculties and societies' 'for further promotion or advancement of learning.'

Before 1689, royalist patronage of the universities had been a piecemeal reaction to political pressures and extramural initiative; for the Presbyterians in the 1690s the production of a godly clergy was a vital means of national regeneration, especially after thirty years of Episcopalianism and a consequent shortage of ministers to replace those ousted from parishes or universities. The Commission for the Visitation of the Universities first met in 1690 with the task of removing unreliable regents on moral, political or intellectual grounds. In 1693 it was planned to introduce a new professorship of divinity and ten bursaries in theology for every university. Then in 1695 the reactivated Commission revived the idea of 1647 that a complete and standardised philosophy course should be drawn up, under pain of deprivation. The visitors also made conservative suggestions in relation to the teaching of philosophy—for example, the rejection of Descartes' rationalism as giving no account of traditional medieval philosophy. The universities' reluctance to comply with this task was shown by their failure to complete by 1700 the course originally demanded for 1696. New Committees for Visitation were chosen in 1699, and the following year the Principals met in Edinburgh to discuss the course but failed to agree on a final version. In 1702 the professorship of Greek was established, but the entire exercise had effectively ground to a halt on the death of Principal Rule of Edinburgh, who had become responsible for most of its aspects.

It was not until 1708 that the old regenting system was replaced by fixed professorships. This was largely the work of William Carstares, a major figure in the re-establishment of Presbyterianism since 1689. He had recommended to his brother-in-law, Principal Dunlop of Glasgow, as early as 1691, that foreign professors might be imported; and in 1703 he had become Principal of Edinburgh University himself. Yet the reorganisation of the universities had been prefigured by proposals put to the Commission in its first period of activity by David Gregory and Lord Stair. Gregory had proposed a national system of higher education which emphasised classical studies for those following a 'liberal education':

> by which not only these languages may be attained and made familiar to the Youth, but that the Virtue, learning, knowledge of the World and politeness, which are originally to be seen in those languages, may have the due impression and effects.

Teachers of classics might thereby retrieve their subject from its inferior status to metaphysics. Gregory also demanded an abbreviation of the philosophical part of the course, as it was of such little use 'either in the affairs and knowledge of the world, or in the great professions of Divinity, Law and Physick.' He called for professorships of the last two subjects, encouragement of mathematical skills applicable to trade, manufactures and invention, and cross-fertilisation with foreign universities.

Gregory's plans were addressed to the Commission but ignored; those of Stair were written from within its broad intentions. His proposals included a third year course on ethics and morals, including 'the particular vertues of the members of families and the members of civil societies', and a fourth year course based upon practical experiments in natural philosophy. Both Gregory's and Stair's proposals revealed a desire for change in the traditional institutions of learning which was as yet held back by political circumstances.

Stair, like Gregory, had already made a crucial contribution to contemporary Scottish thought through his own profession. His *Institutions of the Laws of Scotland* were published in 1681 but had probably been circulating in manuscript since he became Lord President ten years earlier. In his work of the same name, Mackenzie tried to minimise the differences between Scots and Roman Law, but Stair was happy to change the order of his work from that of Justinian. Moreover, Stair presented obligations not as rights but as limitations on liberty; he argued that obligations precede property, that the first obligations were obediential and the first obedience was due to God. This Calvinist perspective, based on Stair's lectures as regent at Glasgow University in the 1640s, is also visible in his rejection of the orthodox medieval rationalism which lay at the root of Mackenzie's legal and social philosophy. Stair preferred the voluntarist view: that law is founded on the will of God, repeated reasonably at an indefinite number of points. Both men were trying to write practical and logical legal handbooks, but Mackenzie, who had 'travelled no further in theology than a sabbath day's journey' had a more immediate political purpose. He feared the logical development of Stair's principles into limitations on royal prerogative and thence social disorder. Conversely, Stair objected to royal

interference in personal religious belief and emigrated after the Test Act of
1681, not returning until 1689.

The main intellectual influence of Calvinism in the period was through
Scottish law, where even Jacobite advocates followed Stair rather than
Mackenzie in court. Calvinism also contributed to academic style, espe-
cially to the dialectic disputations of the older universities, though those of
Aberdeen had a different tradition; Rutherford at St Andrews before 1661
had maintained this influence, as had Stair at Glasgow.

The debate between Presbyterianism and Episcopalianism over the
forms of church organisation—the struggle which occupied most of the
political energies of the Scottish people between 1660 and 1707—might
have been expected to produce a parallel intellectual debate of equal
intensity. In fact Episcopalianism's lack of a well-defined liturgy and any
non-Calvinist theological tradition meant that the debate lacked
philosophical depth. Similarly, though 'godly debate was as forensic as any
lawyer could desire', and a contemporary was much impressed by the
'commonalty capable of arguing', the quality of ecclesiastical pamphlets
has attracted such descriptions as 'windy scoldings', 'entangled scrupulos-
ity', and 'authoritarian and uncritical'.[3] Only glimpses survive of such
visionary inspiration and demotic wit as the wind scattered from the
mouths of Restoration field preachers such as Kirkton, Cameron and
Peden, though an example such as this: 'Sirs, I'll tell you where the Kirk of
God is, wherever there is a praying lass or lad at a dyke-side in Scotland'—suggests the vigour of what has been lost.

Of the printed debate, the Episcopalian side produced the better literature. Mackenzie's defence of the Episcopalian establishment was continued in opposition after the Revolution. Ex-Principal Monro of Edinburgh wrote of the 'new opinions' with bitter wit, and John Sage, formerly
a minister in Glasgow, argued forcibly against the *Fundamental Charter of
Presbytery*, in 1695. Neither could match the venomous caricature of
Presbyterianism in Pitcairne's unpublished play *The Assembly*. Episcopalian and Jacobite writers had the advantage of being able to draw on
the moral as much as the political tradition of their party's writings before
1688. Robert Leighton was the outstanding figure in this tradition. He had
helped to develop a new style of preaching which discoursed on a common
subject rather than offering a close textual analysis. As Professor of Divinity
at Edinburgh he was a moral inspiration to Sibbald and a classical one to
Pitcairne. On his death in 1684 he left a large library in Dunblane to be
used by young Episcopalian ministers, a professional parallel to those of
the doctors and lawyers. As an ecclesiastical adviser to Charles II, Leighton had played a reluctant part in the periodic attempts at tolerant accord
with the Covenanters; his *Modest Defence of Episcopacy* is interrupted by
the cry: 'Oh who would not long for the shadows of evening, from all these
poor childish contests.'

A similar longing for the end of religious conflict runs significantly through much Episcopalian writing into the eighteenth century. It derived from the 'Aberdeen Doctors' of the 1630s and had been fully developed in the Quietism of Henry Scougall's *Life of God in the Soul of Man*, 1677. James Garden, an overseer of the library Scougall left to King's College, Aberdeen, was influenced by the French mystic Mme Bourignon in his *Comparative Theology*, 1707. Garden's brother George continued the Quietest tradition and in 1710 the synod of Aberdeen complained he was influencing 'some of the better sort' including local gentry. This distinctive theology of the North-East led many Jacobites there to build a high wall between the garden of reflection and the wilderness of conflict after the political dislocation of 1689–90.

George Garden, however, was a correspondent of both Sibbald and the Royal Society on 'curious' subjects. Indeed, in their secular intellectual interests many Episcopalian ministers resembled the Presbyterian Moderates of the following century. Before the Revolution, their work had been inspired by Sibbald and his Edinburgh colleagues in the image of the professional Virtuoso. Rev Andrew Symson, tending a reluctant flock in Galloway, 'judged it not excentrical to my profession' to comply with Sibbald's request for local information. The contributions of Wallace of Kirkwall and Gordon of Rothiemay outreached the limitations of the finished *Scotia Illustrata*. John Cockburn, brother-in-law of the Gardens and cousin of Scougall, edited *Bibliotheca Universalis*, made up of translations from Dutch learned journals, published at Edinburgh in 1688 in a single edition before censorship suppressed it. Robert Kirk's *Secret Commonwealth of Elves, Fauns and Fairies*, 1691, was a repository of folk belief. Andrew Symson became a bookseller and printer in Edinburgh in the 1690s. Alexander Edward worked with the architect William Bruce on Hopetoun House. John Sage edited Ruddiman's edition of Drummond's works in 1711.

It is noticeable even from this brief list that the varied and geographically widespread secular achievements of the Episcopalian clergy, while losing their professional structure in 1688, retained a focus for intellectual communication in the form of the capital city. For in the late seventeenth century Edinburgh itself was becoming a major institution for learned intercourse in Scotland. Urban society was developed interdependently with professional institutions. The amenities which the city provided for the aristocracy and gentry by 1689 included transport, luxury goods, specialised education, recreation, formal societies and a more spacious fabric. The quantity and quality of printers defied the monopoly of Mrs Anderson, widow of the King's Printer; coffee-houses were added to taverns as meeting places; libraries, previously a clerical or private privilege, were now provided for doctors and lawyers as well as academics.

A country-house circle comparable to that which had emerged in England did not yet exist. The Court last formed a centre for Scottish society in 1681–3, and Parliament in the years before the Union. In their absence, the legal term of the Court of Session provided a substitute focus for formal social life, conspicuous expenditure and intellectual discussion. But it was in the city itself that these activities were actually carried out. Hence a major element in the rise to intellectual leadership of the Scottish professions was the fact that the city could recreate a modified version of the cultural life of the Court.

By 1718 this could be described as a truism by Allan Ramsay, in *Edinburgh's Address to the Country*, where Edinburgh refers to the law courts as the 'dearest image' of the long departed royal court, and goes on to describe its linked social and intellectual pleasures in these terms:

> My witty Clubs of Minds that move at large
> With every Glass can some great Thought discharge,
> When from my Senate, and the Toils of Law
> T'unbend the Mind from Business you withdraw.

The city's earliest clubs—such as Allan Ramsay's 'Easy Club'—which looked back to the conviviality of Pitcairne and the Jacobite taverns of the 1690s, also helped to fill the gap left by the removal of Court and Parliament. Such clubs played a social as well as an intellectual role. Young lawyers and doctors were concerned with politeness as well as professional qualifications: John Spottiswoode's 'College of Law' intended to teach history and philology, and he told prospective students 'You, being Gentlemen, entitles you to good manners.' A similar concern with the rules of polite behaviour was characteristic of most contemporary clubs. Intellectually, these new centres of culture admired both the Scottish Virtuoso tradition and the polite learning of contemporary England. Robert Hepburn praised 'the Force and Beauty, the Elegancy and Propriety of the English Tongue' in his translation of Mackenzie's essay on forensic eloquence in 1711. Such praise was characteristic of the contemporary intellectual tone, and stood in contrast to the ideals, if not the practice, of the original author. By the imitation of London, Edinburgh might create a replacement for the lost Court culture: Spottiswoode reminded himself to follow 'ceremonies of civility and court breeding', 'acts of civility and Courtesie' and 'the rules of behaviour' and teach them to the young professional classes.

Yet the linguistic situation of Scottish culture at the start of the eighteenth century was more complex than Hepburn's straightforward endorsement of English might suggest. Vernacular Scots survived in common speech and in the oral tradition of ballad and song which Ramsay and others were soon to 'rediscover'. It was this oral tradition that formed the mainstream of culture for the mass of the Scottish people, while for the literate three-quarters of the artisan and tenant farmer classes the 23,000 religious works and 30,000 bibles left by Mrs Anderson provide enough indication of their staple reading diet.

Among professionals, tension between Scots and English can be found in Mackenzie's praise of forensic Scots, Leighton's reputed limitations as a preacher due to his English accent, the distinction in other preachers between English exegesis and Scots anecdote, and finally the contempt with which Pitcairne treated his Scots-speaking characters in *The Assem-*

bly. There was a link between the emphasis on the imitation of English and the lack of a development of an easy style in the language. This was why Mackenzie turned from a courtly to a professional style in 1672. Forensic Scots provided him with a contemporary patriotic cultural idiom, yet, like all seventeenth-century Scots professionals, though he thought and spoke in Scots, he wrote in English. That he found it easier to do so as a lawyer than as a poet or philosopher suggests one explanation of the difference between Scottish and English intellectual traditions in the seventeenth century.

There are other indications of an ill-defined relationship between popular and polite culture during this period. The ballads—thought some were written down from 1650 onwards—continued to be transmitted orally and recomposed orally. This was essentially a regional or international rather than a national process, and it was not halted by the first publication of the ballads as part of a national culture. Ramsay and his contemporaries collected popular verse as an object of national pride rather than sociological enquiry, for the intelligentsia and professional classes shared a language of speech with the whole country. Folk belief and oral evidence in general were treated with a similar mixture of interest and credulity by many Virtuosi. For example, Rev Robert Kirk became obsessively involved with the superstitions of Aberfoyle, Rev Andrew Symson wrote a treatise on second sight, and Viscount Tarbat sent Sibbald a description of St Kilda 'as he had it from an intelligent person dwelling on the place.' In some cases, however, popular belief and learned information were firmly contrasted. For instance, Sibbald himself used sixty-two popular names for birds in the ornithological section of *Scotia Illustrata*, yet named a third of his species in Latin only; Tarbat wrote to the Royal Society about discovering molucca beans washed up on the shore:

> which the Common People supposed to be sea-tangles, and laughed at me, when I said they were land beans.

Scots and English were of course not the only languages to be found in seventeenth- and eighteenth-century Scotland. Gaelic remained the language of large sections of the north of the country, though its culture was far from wholly isolated from that of the Anglo-Saxon Lowlands. In Gaelic poetry individual writers such as Niall MacMhuirich and Roderick Morison were beginning to modify the traditional role of the bard and manipulate the received forms of the classical tradition of Gaelic verse. In particular Ian Lom became involved in Lowland politics, as the chiefs were, being made poet laureate in 1660 and writing laments for Montrose and denunciations of the 1688 Revolution and the Act of Union. Since in this period the Highlands did not pose a political threat to the rest of the country, the Lowlands were not yet concerned to assimilate Gaelic culture. Indeed, in this relatively peaceful period of Highland history the chiefs were looking to the Lowlands for status, educating their sons there as suggested by the Statutes of Iona, 1609, and not only cadies were speaking Gaelic in

Edinburgh: it was there in 1681 that the Chief of the Macleods met the 'blind harper', Roderick Morison, whom he took back to Dunvegan as bard.

The printing and selling of books in Scotland expanded steadily between the Restoration and the Union. The will of the bookseller John Calderwood in 1683 mentioned trade with the College of Edinburgh, a bishop, three nobles, a gentleman, four schoolmasters, nine university regents and forty ministers. These classes formed the general reading public, on whose behalf the editor John Cockburn complained in 1688 that neither the 'Stationer's Trade' nor 'Private Stock' could import many foreign works, though a trade with London and the continent existed. James VII when in Edinburgh had personally intervened to limit the Anderson monopoly, and in the 1680s a number of more complex new works were executed by Scottish and Dutch printers, such as *Scotia Illustrata* and David Gregory's *Exercitatio Geometrica*. Both Privy Council, who could grant monopolies on books, and the Court of Session, who dealt with disputes, were involved in bibliographical patronage, and they were both prepared to take the advice of professional experts.

During the reign of James VII Catholic printers in Edinburgh enjoyed royal patronage. But both Mackenzie and Pitcairne had works printed in 1688 by the Protestant John Reid. However one of the Catholic printers, James Watson, maintained his career after the Revolution by changing his religion; his son James published a *History of Printing* in 1713 whose introduction described continuing government interference and a long fight for rights over Mrs Anderson's monopoly in the 1690s. The economics of the book trade may well have benefited from the expiry of the 1662 Licensing Act in 1695, and suffered from the 1696 import duties on paper and pamphlets. However, Watson's account of the revival of printing in Scotland was as much a statement of cultural identity as his famous and pioneering *Choice Collection* of Scots poems of 1711. Watson associated from 1706 with Pitcairne's protégés Ruddiman and Freebairn, who, with Henry Maule's *History of the Picts*, had begun to publish works of relevance to Scotland's past. By the Union this group of Jacobite printers, working together in the Virtuoso tradition, effectively formed a further professional institution.

What this account suggests once again is the pervasiveness of the Jacobite Episcopalian tradition in Scottish culture even though 1688 marked the failure of that tradition in political terms. In the 1690s Jacobite Virtuosi such as Pitcairne and Sibbald remained influential. Pitcairne's example inspired both printers and the members of Ramsay's Easy Club, and Sibbald maintained a wide correspondence even though nothing came of his Royal Society of Scotland, the list of whose potential members included few Whigs. In the 1690s the medical, legal and academic institutions of Scotland retained a Jacobite bias. However the Jacobite tradition was probably too conservative in intellectual terms to survive, even if it had retained a political power base. Its lasting influence was worked out through institutional organisation among the professions, and individual example and patronage. After the 1702 Act of Indemnity, though the years of severe Presbyterian reaction were over, Jacobite intellectual influence became fragmented. Though men such as the Virtuoso politician the Earl of Cromarty and David Gregory worked with the government, the greatest official intellectual innovation of the early eighteenth century, the reorganisation of Edinburgh University, was the work of the Whig Carstares. By the time of the Union, moreover, the terms of reference of the debate had changed from those of 1660–1700, the Episcopalian Sibbald for example being firmly Unionist and the nationalist Fletcher firmly Presbyterian.

The tensions and uncertainties over Scotland's future between 1688 and 1707 produced an unprecedented maturity of political life. A tradition of historiography or of memoirs or diaries had not existed previously, and political writing had been taken up with ecclesiastical issues, or their political implications, as in Mackenzie's memoirs. The advocate John Lauder of Fountainhall and Gilbert Burnet, later bishop of Salisbury, both wrote readable and comparatively detached descriptions of Restoration political life, but neither's work was published till long after their death, despite their eminence in Whig circles. However, the standard of secular, public political argument was raised by the development around 1700 of parties, newspapers, clubs and oratory, all applied to issues relating to the Union.

Two leading writers in favour of the Union came from pre-Revolution Virtuoso backgrounds: William Seton of Pitmedden and the Earl of Cromarty, formerly Viscount Tarbat. But the outstanding political writer of the pre-Union period was its most famous opponent, Andrew Fletcher of Saltoun. His political discourses of 1698 discussed economic and social issues, and put forward his plan for national regeneration through a militia, which would teach moral and intellectual improvement to help protect Scottish liberty. These ideas can be compared to contemporary Presbyterian ambitions expressed in the societies for the reformation of manners, with which Defoe became involved on his visit to Scotland in 1705, in the Visitation of the Universities, and in the 1696 Education Act which, though of no immediate impact, was the first to suggest ways of financing the Reformation ideal of a school in every parish. Such patriotic intellectual ideals were very different from those of the Jacobite Virtuosi with their emphasis on aristocratic and professional cultural obligations.

Both Presbyterian and Jacobite however helped to provide Scotland with a cultural identity which allows George Davie to describe the Union as 'unity in politics combined with a diversity in what may be called social ethics', where there was a 'distinctive life of the country not in its religion alone but in the mutual interaction of religion, law and education.'[4] The Presbyterian church and education system were preserved in the Act for Securing the Protestant Religion, 1706. Articles XVIII and XIX of the Act of Union itself allowed the Scottish law and courts to continue in most areas. The survival of these professions has been described as 'recognition of the sources of political power in Scotland',[5] but that power in fact had lain largely in the old parliament, which was incorporated. The distinctive identity which allowed the Scottish professions to survive the Union lay rather in their recently developed intellectual institutions and cultural role. Hence those areas of public life that were left untouched by the Union guaranteed the continued independence of Scottish culture. In the long term the Union meant increased prestige and authority for the Scottish professional classes, and in so far as these classes provided the social and cultural context out of which the Scottish Enlightenment emerged, they eventually allowed Scotland the kind of cultural 'union' of equals which Fletcher had wanted politically.

NOTES

Details of primary printed and manuscript sources may be found in the author's article: 'James VII and the Patronage of Learning in Scotland, 1679–1688' in J Dwyer, R Mason, A Murdoch (eds), *New Perspectives on the Politics and Culture of Early Modern Scotland* (Edinburgh, 1982).

1   William Ferguson, *Scotland: James VII to the Present* (Edinburgh, 1968) p 283.
2   Andrew Lang, *Sir George Mackenzie* (London, 1909) p 312.
3   David Reid, *The Party-Coloured Mind* (Edinburgh, 1982) pp 9, 13.
4   G E Davie, *The Democratic Intellect* (Edinburgh, 1961) p xiv.
5   P H Scott, *The Union of Scotland and England* (Edinburgh, 1979) p 53.

FURTHER READING

LITERARY HISTORY

Craig, David, *Scottish Literature and the Scottish People* (London, 1961)
Jack, R D S, *Scottish Prose 1550–1700* (London, 1971)
Reid, David, *The Party-Coloured Mind* (Edinburgh, 1982)
Watson, Roderick, *The Literature of Scotland* (London, 1984)

POLITICAL HISTORY

Buckroyd, Julia, *Church and State in Scotland 1660–1681* (Edinburgh, 1980)
Donaldson, Gordon, *Scotland: James V to James VII* (Edinburgh, 1965)
Ferguson, William, *Scotland: 1689 to the Present* (Edinburgh, 1968)
—— *Scotland's Relations with England* (Edinburgh, 1977)

CULTURAL SURVEYS OF THE PERIOD

Chitnis, Annand, *The Scottish Enlightenment* (London, 1976)
Cowan, Ian B, *The Scottish Covenanters* (London, 1976)
Daiches, David, *The Paradox of Scottish Culture* (London, 1964)
Davie, George E, *The Democratic Intellect* (Edinburgh, 1961)
Henderson, G D, *Religious Life in Seventeenth Century Scotland* (Cambridge, 1937)
McElroy, Davis D M, *Scotland's Age of Improvement* (Washington, 1969)
Meikle, H W, *Some Aspects of Late Seventeenth Century Scotland* (Glasgow, 1947)
Mitchison, Rosalind, *Lordship to Patronage* (London, 1983)

BIOGRAPHIES AND MONOGRAPHS

Brown, I Gordon, *The Hobby-Horsical Antiquary* (Edinburgh, 1980)
Campbell, A H, *The Structure of Stair's Institutions* (Glasgow, 1954)
Craig, W S, *History of the Royal College of Physicians, Edinburgh* (Oxford, 1976)
Cruickshanks, E (ed), *Ideology and Conspiracy: Aspects of Jacobitism* 1689–1759 (Edinburgh, 1982)
Duncan, Douglas, *Thomas Ruddiman* (Edinburgh, 1965)
Henderson, G D, *Mystics of the North-East* (Aberdeen, 1934)
Houston, R A *Scottish Literacy and the Scottish Identity* (Cambridge, 1985)
Mackenzie, W C, *Andrew Fletcher of Saltoun* (Edinburgh, 1935)
Marshall, Rosalind K, *Virgins and Viragos* (London, 1982)
Walker, D M (ed), *Stair Tercentenary Studies* (Edinburgh, 1981)

Chapter 2

Modern Rome and Ancient Caledonia: the Union and the Politics of Scottish Culture

IAIN GORDON BROWN

The theme of this chapter is nationalism and antiquarianism in eighteenth-century Scotland after the Union of 1707 and before the age of the Enlightenment. The notion of a post-Union national identity-crisis, the cultural paradox of eighteenth-century Scotland in general, and the explanation of how eighteenth-century Scots came to terms with their world, are now almost commonplaces of cultural historiography. But here I hope to look at the problem and the paradox in a different way, and to show that there was a solution to the crisis alternative to that offered by a purely literary antiquarianism. This approach may be regarded as a counterpart, or a complementary study, to the work of David Daiches on literature and nationalism. The theme and purpose are the same; but the argument adduced depends not largely on literary evidence but on that of archaeological and classical scholarship. 'This is the historical Age and this is the historical Nation' was David Hume's opinion in 1770;[1] and the literati in general were preoccupied by history, with the consideration of processes of historical evolution, progress and change. This chapter will highlight an earlier interest in the explanation of the current circumstances of Scotland through the study of the past.

It has been well said that Scottish nationalism in the eighteenth century is inevitably associated with antiquarianism.

> The effect of the passing of the Act [of Union] was in general traumatic on the Scottish people. They did not quite know what had happened to them, or what they now where. It was in this atmosphere that some Scotsmen turned to Scotland's cultural past to comfort themselves with a sense of Scotland's nationhood.[2]

Opposition to the Union produced an intensified patriotism which found cultural outlets, for example in the general cultivation of antiquarianism as an expression of patriotic sentiment. This cultural nationalism secured an identity for Scotland. Men appealed to the past to discover a solution to the problems of the present. Scottish antiquarianism, in its widest sense, stemmed from the uncertainty and self-doubt prevalent after the Union. In both historical studies and literary scholarship, patriotic Scotsmen sought consolation rather than the truth. Ultimately the Union was responsible for making nostalgia the most characteristic emotion in the Scottish national psyche.

Cultural nationalism found its most celebrated expression in the revival of vernacular literature. However, literary antiquarianism in general provided an outlet for patriotic assertion of national prestige as some form of consolation for the loss of political identity. Patriotic nationalists reacted to the Union by forging links with the past literary greatness of an independent nation with a flourishing courtly culture. And as some men sought the anodyne of literary antiquarianism, so did others find comfort and consolation in archaeological and classical studies. To the literary-based cultural nationalism of James Watson and Allan Ramsay, and to the tradition of patriotic publishing of Thomas Ruddiman and the vernacular humanism of the exponents of a Scottish Latin culture, must be added a further and fascinating response to the Union: the political antiquarianism and patriotic archaeology of Sir John Clerk and his circle.

Clerk of Penicuik (1676–1755) exemplifies in a particularly interesting way several of the paradoxes which are apparent in the careers of prominent cultural figures in the history of early eighteenth-century Scotland. He is the outstanding example of that school of thought which attempted, first through the medium of archaeology, and secondly (and more generally) through cultural leadership, to rationalize the contemporary position of Scotland in relation to her southern neighbour by appealing to the memory of past greatness, and in the process to offer a solution to the identity-crisis which Scotsmen faced after 1707. Clerk would not merit much more than a few paragraphs in a history of Scottish literature if we were to take him simply as a literary figure in his own right, even though he was a significant patron and something of a poet. But he may legitimately be allowed to loom large because of the singular instructiveness of his attitude to post-Union cultural problems: as an interpreter of these he is without peer.

Clerk is now generally regarded as one of the most significant figures in Scottish cultural history between the Glorious Revolution of 1688 and the age of the literati after the 1750s.[3] Like Sir Robert Sibbald before him, he was a cultural leader in the Virtuoso tradition. He was, between about 1720 and 1750, the leading Scottish patron of arts and sciences, and to call him the Lord Burlington of Scotland is to equate him quite properly with great contemporary leaders of taste and patronage. Given his limited financial resources, his less elevated social position, and his more remote and provincial situation, he played Burlington's part of an 'Apollo of the Arts' north of the border, and his contemporaries recognized the fact: the antiquary Alexander Gordon described him memorably as 'a Treasure of Learning and Good Taste'. As a virtuoso his concerns embraced both arts and sciences. He was interested in geology, astronomy, chemistry and medicine, as well as agricultural improvement and industrial development. He was the leading amateur architect and landscape gardener in Scotland;

an important collector and connoisseur; a very talented musician (he had been a pupil of Corelli in Rome when on his grand tour): he was generally known as the Maecenas of Scotland. Life at his country seats—Penicuik and Mavisbank—preserved the tradition of Scottish great-house culture into the eighteenth century, and Allan Ramsay was not the only man of letters to praise what Alexander Gordon described as Clerk's 'hospitality to the mind'.

Clerk's own literary life is an example of the eighteenth-century cultural paradox. He was the intimate friend, patron and critic of Ramsay. He made his contribution to the song-culture of the day, and enjoyed the tradition and the broad humour of vernacular poetry. But he also wrote in Latin—antiquarian tracts, and a six-volume history of the Union in the style of Livy and Sallust—and as an Augustan who bought from Ramsay's bookshop the poems of Pope on publication, he wrote, too, in a high-flown English didactic idiom. His long, unpublished work entitled *The Country Seat* won the acclaim of Anglo-Scots poets James Thomson and David Mallet: 1,600 lines on how one should build and decorate a country house and lay out a park. In *The Country Seat*, Clerk's interest in poetry and the visual arts were united with his advocacy of *improvement*, improvement which was to be such a keynote of the Scottish Enlightenment.[4]

Above all else Clerk was an antiquary. His antiquarianism had three facets. As a field archeologist, he was a pioneer in the discovery and elucidation of Roman remains in Scotland. He also lived the past, in that his whole existence was in some way modelled on a Roman pattern, whether in his professional gravity as a judge, or in his use of leisure (*honestum otium*), or in his cultivation of the antique life at his Plinian villas. Moreover, there was his idiosyncratic political and patriotic use of the past: the application of the study of material remains in the construction of a political philosophy—or what might be termed 'applied antiquarianism'. Archaeological evidence was used for patriotic ends, and to advance moral arguments. In this too, Clerk is a paradoxical figure. A staunch advocate of the Union, and a Roman antiquary, he employed Roman archaeology in Scotland in such a way as to manifest a nationalism that drew its strength from ancient Caledonian resistance to Rome. This argument, projected forward into the eighteenth century, was deployed in resolving problems of post-Union culture and identity. Clerk sought thereby to find a greatness and a purpose for the smaller nation in face of the political, economic and intellectual power of a Roman England. He wished, para-doxically, to be part of a wider world, and yet to retain the essential character of an independent nationality. He was at once a Roman and a Caledonian, a North Briton and a Scot.

As a young man Sir John Clerk had been a member of the last Scottish Parliament, and after serving as a Commissioner for the Treaty of Union, he had sat in the first Parliament of Great Britain. His belief in the Treaty which he had helped to negotiate was absolute. Looking back in 1744 he could write: 'I rejoice very much that it has been my Fate to be an instrument of so great a benefite to this Island . . .'. Scotland had been 'a poor Antient Matron in Rags'; after the Union she could share 'such power and majesty' as the two separate kingdoms had never known. The Union was the 'summum bonum' of both countries: some of the Articles should be 'written in Letters of Gold'. Clerk saw a Scotland

> in great peace and unity with her nearest neighbours . . . the old maxim of vis unita fortior can never be better applied . . . Therefore sooner ought the old Heptarchy of England to be restored, and the antient kingdoms of the Scots and Picts again divided, than the Union of England and Scotland dissolved . . . Nothing but the influence of Heaven cou'd have carried it on, and I hope the same influence will protect and defend it for ever.

Nonetheless Clerk did not cease to be a Scot. His latent patriotism and nationalist sentiment, though frequently suppressed by the exigencies of holding legal office, could find expression in his intellectual life, and the vehicle for it was the study of the material remains of the past. He cultivated patriotic archaeology, and used material evidence as literary antiquaries might depend for their argument on documentary sources. For Clerk, antiquarian research was not 'speculation entirely useless'; and though not unconcerned with scholarly detail, he preferred to concentrate on the historical and moral implications (as he saw them) of the archaeological evidence. In 1739 Clerk prepared for the Edinburgh Philosophical Society a paper on Hadrian's Wall in which he wrote of the patriotic interest of antiquity-study. The great mathematician Colin MacLaurin told him that he had read the essay 'with equal satisfaction from the learning . . . and pleasure from the patriotism'.

Clerk's investigations into the archaeology of Roman Britain led him to see the greatness and nobility of the native inhabitants: antiquities were interpreted in a way that did honour to the Caledonians. He looked at Roman remains and saw in their grandeur the reflected glory of Scotland's past. Clerk was anxious to find Roman antiquities because of the way he could interpret them. He wanted to believe, for example, that all ancient bronze weapons were Roman rather than native. The Roman attribution provided evidence of imperial interest and effort at conquest—a sort of tribute to the Scotland of old. By contrast, an English antiquary like Roger Gale could afford to take a different view: weapons thought Roman were evidence of Roman conquest, those believed native were evidence of Caledonian defeat—'they being found near a Roman praetorium is not an absolute proof of their being Roman; they may have been left and lost there by an enemy upon a repulse in attacking the Roman camp . . .'. As a Scottish antiquary, Alexander Gordon was determined that swords found near Bannockburn should *not* be thought medieval: the evidence he could assemble 'takes away all doubts of their not being genuine Roman'. What was clearly evidence of a later victory against the English on this site was not sufficient for a patriotic antiquary in the 1720s: proof had to be found of attempted conquest and of conquest repelled in the Roman past.

Gordon's concern was to amass evidence that would 'redound to the honour of our Predecessors and our Patria'. Gordon and Clerk, however, men of classical education, had an ambivalent attitude to the Roman conquest of Scotland. For a short period their land had been part of a wider civilized world. In their own day they valued an equivalent level of culture and progress; yet they mourned the loss of nationhood. Their appeal to the martial glory and moral integrity of a past Scotland—even their use of such words as 'predecessors', 'progenitors', 'Patria', etc—seems to echo the sentiments expressed by Lord Belhaven in his famous speeches against the Union, especially his emotional evocation of 'our Antient Mother CALEDONIA'.[5] But if Belhaven had founded a tradition of appeal to the past at a time of present political distress and national discomfiture, then that weapon was greatly developed for use in the cultural arena by Gordon and Clerk.

The ambivalence of attitude was clearest when Scottish antiquaries looked at Hadrian's Wall. Clerk's friend William Stukeley typified an Englishman's view of the Wall:

> I saw enough to make me admire at the grandeur of thought, the discipline, the invincible perseverance of that victorious people who could perform so vast a work . . . under arms, with the pickax, the trowel, the sword and buckler in hand all at once . . .

Certainly Clerk subscribed to the view of the greatness of the achievement:

> . . . there is no work of the Antients now extant of more magnificence, labour and expence . . . At the same time I must acknowledge that our forefathers the Caledonians received very great honour by the pains which the Romans took to defend this part of Britain against them.

The real meaning of the Wall, that it reflected the glory of old Caledonia, had been overlooked; for it 'did us more honour than all our warlick actions put together'. To call it 'vallum barbaricum' rather than 'vallum Romanum' suggested more accurately where the achievement lay. To fail to see the monuments in this light was to ignore the possibility that Caledonia had preserved an independent noble savagery, and that the Roman military and architectural achievement was a response to the vigour of their opponents.

Clerk's interpretation of the monuments anticipated the work of others. His ideas were incorporated by Gordon in the *Itinerarium Septentrionale* of 1726, where they mingled with Gordon's own brand of nationalist antiquarian response to the Union. This influential work continued to be the vade-mecum of Scottish antiquaries right down to the days of Mr Jonathan Oldbuck himself: Walter Scott was keenly aware of the antiquarian inheritance of the laird of Monkbarns. Indeed the ambivalent and paradoxical attitude to the Roman past of Scotland was never more tellingly or more wittily illustrated than by Scott in *The Antiquary*. Oldbuck was made to suggest a subject for an epic poem to be written by Lovel. This was to be entitled 'The Caledoniad; or, Invasion Repelled'.

Lovel protested that Agricola's invasion had *not* been repelled. A poet, replied Oldbuck, need not be bound to truth or probability: 'You may defeat the Romans in spite of Tacitus.' Yet Oldbuck, with his 'auld-warld stories', his 'tales of folk lang syne', his tireless searching for Roman forts, and his anxiety to find on his ancestral acres the site of Agricola's camp before Mons Graupius, betrayed a powerful desire to forge a link between his remote corner of northern Europe and the romance and splendour of the classical world of his education and youthful reading.

Clerk had first expressed his views fully in 1724: 'There are no remains of antiquity we ought to boast of so much . . .'; for Hadrian's Wall represented a Roman failure of nerve. Far from being, as the historians of later antiquity asserted, the 'maximum decus' [greatest glory] of the reign of its builder, it was, in truth, the 'maximum dedecus' [greatest dishonour]: the 'decus' belonged to the Caledonians because of the quality of their opposition that made the work necessary. In *The Country Seat* Clerk wrote of the dishonour of the Roman aggressor forced back—'meanly shrunk behind his Walls and Towr's'—and he confessed to Stukeley his amazement at Roman efforts against the 'insults of the naked Caledonians'. Englishmen found excuses for the building of the Wall: at a point where

> the ambitious bravery of the Romans had so enlarg'd their Conquests on all sides, that they began to be jealous of their own greatness; the Emperors thought it most advisable to set some bounds to their Dominions . . .[6]

English antiquaries suggested that the Romans did not consider it worthwhile to conquer Scotland; Clerk that they were not able to do so.

Hence there were patriotic reasons for the preservation of antiquities. To destroy an ancient monument was to fail to respect those memorials of Roman tribute to the formidable bravery of the Caledonians. Roman ruins were eloquent of a past of invasion, and of world-conquerors expelled. Edward I's destruction of ancient monuments in Scotland was particularly resented because he aimed at 'extirpation of our memorie . . . all the marks of our antiquity and independency'.[7] In like manner Clerk was enraged by the destruction in his day of the celebrated building known as Arthur's O'on. He saw in this enigmatic structure a symbol of attempted Roman conquest, a monument to the effort Rome had made to advance so far north: it was a temple to Terminus, the boundary of Empire, erected when the Romans could go no further.

As a member of William Stukeley's antiquarian club of the Roman Knights, Clerk adopted the pseudonym 'Agricola', after the Roman conqueror of the Caledonians in AD 84. Alexander Gordon, more unguarded in his nationalism (he was not a Whig Baron of Exchequer, of course), took the name 'Calgacus', after the Caledonian leader at Mons Graupius. Clerk's choice was significant, and indicative of his cultural and nationalist confusion. As Agricola, Clerk was the man of Roman inclinations, in eighteenth-century terms a north Briton: pro-Union, a seeker for the strength, security, place in the world, and the cultural benefits of Augustan civilization which union with England—as incorporation in the Roman

Empire—brought. Togeter, England and Scotland would make an Empire greater than the Roman. Clerk was a patriotic Scotsman who could nevertheless readily sublimate his Scottishness into a comprehensive Britishness. When discussing the Romans in Britain, he used the terminology of the Hanoverian state of his own day, and in thinking of the Roman occupation in the past he was led to consider the contemporary benefits of a united country. Yet despite Clerk's theoretical argument of a state of mutual subjection in a joint equality, there was in fact an inescapable sense of dominance by the stronger party. He saw the English, in their dealings with Scotland, playing the Roman role, both in their desire for union in the interests of their own security, and in their cultural supremacy. So, as a Scotsman, valuing national identity, he too was in antiquarian terms Calgacus the Caledonian.

Clerk and Gordon recognized the cultural attractions of England. Their feelings about the advantages of contact with the south closely resemble what their friend Roger Gale believed were the benefits Rome conferred on a subject people: 'they tended only to the civilizing them, reducing them under their own laws and Government from their wild and savage way of life' to 'a better way of living under theyr kind and instructive conquerors . . .'. This in turn was similar to what Gale detected as happening in Scotland as a result of the Union: 'I think learning in all sciences is travelling northwards apace, such improvements do we hear of every day from Edenborough.' Gale, as an Englishman, saw the benefits that would have been conferred on Caledonia by the Romans in the same light as the advantages that would increasingly be conferred on Scotland by the English. With the calm superiority of a member of the dominant party—Roman or English—he discounted the disadvantaged feelings of the Caledonians or Scots facing the loss of liberty as the price of civilization. Clerk and Gordon, as Scotsman, saw the penalties, and though Roman in their culture, remained Caledonian in their patriotism. Clerk remarked on an interest in Roman antiquities on the part of English scholars which was attributable to their identification with Rome. These were the very men he labelled the 'blind Admirers of the Roman power and Grandeur', who regarded Hadrian's Wall as 'no more than a Wall of Separation between the Humanity of the Romans and the Barbarity of our forefathers'. A Scot, he believed, would regard it rather as the 'Great Boundary of the British Liberty and Servitude', and that liberty had been maintained solely by the Caledonians, who kept it in trust, as it were, for the other peoples of the island. Clerk criticized those who accepted unequivocally Rome's civilizing mission: 'The Caledonians would not understand the Roman yoke in this sense . . .'. Likewise, Gordon, who had written a thick folio on the subject of Roman antiquities, still felt impelled to smite the people who had obligingly left behind the objects of his study (a study which he hoped would make him a tidy sum in subscriptions): he lambasted 'the griping (sic) Tallons of the grand Plunderers of the World'.[8] Clerk transposed the ancient state of Scotland, subject to the all-pervasive influence of a powerful neighbour, into the present. He wondered

'how far the present successors of the Caledonians have ane interest in the
Virtues and Warlike Disposition of their forefathers . . .', and concluded
that nothing could diminish the honour that post-Union Scots should
derive from the actions of their progenitors.

Antiquarian patriotism was paralleled by a wish to see a revival of Scottish
national greatness, and a strengthening of moral character and cultural
vigour sufficient to resist complete domination by England. Roman civilization had been bought only at the expense of freedom. The poet Samuel
Boyce once sent Sir John Clerk a translation of the celebrated speech of
Calgacus from Tacitus's *Agricola*, a piece of rhetoric which had a particular
appeal for Scotsmen torn between their political interest and their patriotic
conscience:

> See from their Hands what Mercy will ye find
> Those civiliz'd Destroyers of Mankind . . .
> With specious arts has veil'd its horrid face
> Call'd Rapine, Virtue; and Destruction, Peace! . . .

Although Clerk argued that the Union meant an end of economic warfare
and political suspicion, and the beginning of real freedom for both countries, and accepted that English Augustan civilization could be obtained
(as he put it at the very beginning of his Latin history) 'non armis sed
animis'—not by spears but by spirit—yet he felt that Scotland might still be
overborne by southern ways and customs to the diminution of her native
character. He sought consolation in the knowledge that in antiquity the
peoples of Italy had joined with Rome, yet retained their individuality. He
hoped that the eighteenth-century Scots would be to the English as the
Sabines and Albans were to the Romans, joining in incorporating union
with the stronger people in such a manner that their 'Posterity were no less
remarkable for Honour and Antiquity, than they were before; tho' they
cou'd not act any more in a separate way from the Nation they had united
with'. He quoted lines from Virgil (*Aeneid*, XII. 189) as sentiments
applicable to Anglo-Scottish union: 'Let the two nations, each still unsub-
jected, enter upon an everlasting compact under equal terms.' But the
post-Union uncertainty that afflicted many Scots is illustrated in Clerk's
constant concern to eulogize the Union, as if he had to convince himself
that there was indeed equality of opportunity in these Virgilian terms,
when in reality he suffered and resented discrimination. He protested too
much, insisting that there was no distinction made on grounds of nationality—and that if Englishmen occupied the best jobs it was because of better
qualifications or more adroit soliciting for office. For his own part, Clerk
had hoped for years to be Lord Chief Baron of the Exchequer, his small
ambition only to be king of his own castle. But in fact he realized that 'no
Scotsman was to be trusted with this office. This observation is indeed
injurious to our whole country . . .'. He begged his masters 'not to suffer us

to be choaked with some Bully from London who will be a perfect stranger to our affairs'. On Clerk's last bid for the office (in 1741) the Earl of Galloway wrote: 'As for your disappointment, though I'm sensible you have for several years had the burden of managing the business of the Exchequer, yet I'm of the mind that you are at the height of your promotion . . . noe Scotsman will ever be honoured with being Chief Baron so long as they can have anie English atturnie to ask for it . . .'. The Duke of Queensberry had told the last session of the last Parliament of Scotland that the members there gathered must needs 'become one in Hearts and Affections, as we are inseparably joyn'd in Interest with our Neighbour Nation'. Clerk saw the interest, even if the difficulty of securing it was real; but his heart and affection, like those of countless others, were still fixed on the sentimental idea of an independent Scotland. There was a constant battle between reason and Britishness, sentiment and Scottishness.

Reacting to the smothering pressure exerted by the civilization of the south, Clerk saw it as his duty to improve Scotland and Scottish culture. The Caledonian spirit was invoked in the peaceful struggle with the modern Romans. When he communicated his thoughts on ancient funerary practices (in a paper based on his own archaeological investigations), their recipient, Alexander Gordon, a Scot on the loose in the scholarly whirl of London societies and coffee-houses, was delighted. Gordon revealed his nationalist pleasure: 'I have many reasons to be rejoised at yr sending it, and blessed be God I've by this been able to shew the English what kind of men of learning Caledonia has yet reserved for herself: as Calgacus said, "Quos sibi Caledonia seposuerit" '. Those for whom Clerk acted as patron frequently advanced his name as representative of Scottish learning and taste (especially in antiquarian matters); and when, in 1726, Allan Ramsay wrote his 'Scots Ode to the Society of British Antiquarians', Clerk was presented as an equal competitor in the lists with the 'first Rate' of all Britain. Ramsay begins by offering homage to these English luminaries:

> To Hartford and his learned Friends,
> Whase Fame for Science far extends,
> A *Scottish* Muse her Duty sends,
>   From Pictish Towers . . .

Then, at a climactic point in the poem, Clerk is wheeled out:

> Nor want we *Caledonians* Sage . . .

claims Ramsay, who might entitle his ode 'the *British* Antiquarians' but who did his best to magnify any possible Scottish contribution to the scholarly endeavour of a united kingdom.

Ramsay, Gordon and Clerk all, in their different ways, betrayed a fascinating ambivalence towards England. Their craving for improvement and wider intellectual horizons drew their tribute to 'Apollo's favourite Residence' (as Gordon described London); yet they indulged in the antiquarian patriotism which we have been examining. The cultural nationalism of Gordon's campaign to cry up Scottish intellect in the south marched in step with his admission to Clerk of the cultural superiority of London. Attending, for instance, a meeting of the Society of Antiquaries, he would be anxious to show the Scots as great scholars. When writing home to Scotland, on the other hand, he admitted the attraction of London intellectual life, and could ill-conceal his discontent at Scottish parochialism and his fervent hope that his countrymen might emulate southern cultural life. As Gordon wrote:

> Indeed, Baron, 'tis not here as in Scotland that men of Fashion and Quality are ashamed to talk of Antiquity, for the honour of learning and good taste prevails so here, that the greatest ornament a man can have is to know and be able to converse upon them . . . Great is the difference 'twixt the way of thinking in this Country and ours in Scotland with regard to Virtuosoship, for no Conversation here is more cultivated nor esteemed so much as learning and the sciences.'

And Clerk, for his part, revealed his hope thus: 'A good time may come for our countrymen's improving in taste and encouraging such labours as doe point out to mankind how to live and relish life . . .'.

The Country Seat was regarded by its author, and those Scotsmen who read it—whether London Scots or home-based amateurs of the arts—as something of a national manifesto of taste. They considered that here was a digest of the Augustan rules as absorbed by a sensitive Scot and codified by him for the improvement of his countrymen. Thomas Blackwell, Professor of Greek at Marischal College, Aberdeen, hailed it as a national triumph, a 'glorious Monument . . . raised to yourselfe and your country'. Blackwell pointed the contrast between a man like Clerk, who had absorbed the best of the taste and culture available and was now ploughing it back, as it were, into his native heath, and many of the Scottish nobility and gentry who failed as patrons, or whose patronage was active only in the south. 'The cares of ambition and money', lamented Blackwell, 'or the lazy pleasure of sauntering and drinking, swallows up the whole time of those who shou'd taste and encourage literature most.' And Clerk himself recognized the loneliness of his cultural crusade, for the last lines of *The Country Seat* read

> But others are on whom these Rules ye waste
> For Goths will always have a Gothick Taste.

In the *The Gentle Shepherd* (Act IV, Sc. ii, 49–52), Ramsay makes Roger speculate upon the imminent departure of Sir William Worthy and Patie for London and the great world. Ramsay was here touching a raw nerve in the post-Union national consciousness. He had already seen, in reality rather than in the fictional world of a Pentland pastoral, his two painter friends John Smibert and William Aikman set their faces towards London—'the great Town of Lud'—and fame and fortune. In more than one poem he lamented the call of patronage by emigré Scots which drew such men, the ornaments of the Edinburgh artistic world, southwards. Clerk, Aikman's own cousin, noted how the south had become a lodestone for Scottish 'quality'. He accepted the necessity of being familiar with the English language as a prerequisite for a public career in the United Kingdom; but he recognized 'that there was this bad consequence from an English education, that Scotsmen bred in that way wou'd always have stronger inclination for England than for their own Country'. The insidious tendency was to despise Scotland. English culture could be bought too dear. A manuscript poem among his papers includes the lines:

> But England gains their talents and their toil
> Which ought to ornament their native soil.

Yet, ambivalent as ever, Clerk sent his eldest son to Eton.

Thomas Blackwell hinted at the degeneracy of Scots living the good life in the south; and Clerk himself, in a penetrating analysis of the manners and tastes of England, written in 1733 on his return from a London season, saw immorality and corruption as the price of keeping up with English standards of luxury. The notion of national degeneracy produced by English influence led post-Union Scots of an antiquarian turn of mind to ponder on how this situation had (supposedly) been anticipated in Britain during the Roman period. Tacitus's celebrated passage on the insidious softening of the Britons by Roman luxury (*Agricola*, cap. 21), the moral conquest following military and political victory so that the trappings of 'civilization'— good living (the baths, etc.), dress and language—became the subtle bonds of a more far-reaching subjection, was a favourite one with Scottish writers. Archaeologists from Sir Robert Sibbald to General William Roy commented upon the Tacitean diatribe, though it is interesting to note the different conclusions drawn by Sibbald and by Gordon. The former, writing at the time of or just after the Union, took only a favourable view of romanization.[9] Gordon, by contrast, wrote of 'the Blandishments of Vice and Effeminacy' which 'at the Bottom were nothing but the Baits of *Slavery*'.[10] For his part, Allan Ramsay made patriotic appeal to the dress of old Caledonia, in the simplicity of which (by contrast with the foppery of modern fashions) he seemed to find a parallel with ancient virtue and courage. The relevant poem is called 'Tartana, or the Plaid', the very title coyly Augustan and suggesting again the deep-rooted ambivalence of the age:

> 'Twas they could boast their Freedom with proud *Rome*,
> And arm'd in Steel despise the Senate's Doom;
> Whil'st o'er the Globe their Eagle they display'd,
> And conquer'd Nations prostrate Homage paid,
> They only, they unconquer'd stood their Ground,
> And to the mighty Empire fix't the Bound.
> Our native Prince who then supply'd the Throne,
> In Plaid array'd magnificently shone:

>Nor seem'd his Purple, or his Ermine less,
>Tho cover'd by the *Caledonian* Dress.

Ramsay's sentiments were echoed later in the century by Sir Henry Erskine's lines 'In the Garb of Old Gaul' (later set to music by General John Reid, to become the slow march of many Scottish regiments).

Alexander Gordon contrasted the moral strength of ancient Caledonia with contemporary Scotland. From London he wrote of his aim to do justice to Scotland

>in applying these Monuments of Roman Antiquity in order to shew them as lasting trophys of the invincible valure of our noble predicessors and by them shame the growing degeneracy we're involv'd in with southeren luxury. If therefore I meet with discouragement (as I have done here) from Scotsmen, I don't wonder, since how much the more I shall illustrate our forefathers Grandeur; they will be stings to so many corrupted and degenerate sons.

Yet even Gordon, the ardent modern Caledonian, was, as ever, ambivalent in his way, and betrayed the contemporary obsession with 'politeness' which he had derided in the age of his progenitors: he was embarrassed by the 'Scotch speech' of Clerk's second son when escorting him in virtuouso circles in London. Ramsay of Ochtertyre was to highlight the obsession of eighteenth-century Scots with 'polishing their periods and dropping their Scotticisms'.[11] Contemporary concern for gentility in language, which so preoccupied Scotsmen later in the century, early caused Clerk to search for historical parallels. He was led to study the language of the ancient Scots because of changes in that of the modern, which (as he argued in a lengthy 'Enquiry into the Antient Languages of Great Britain about the time of the first Invasion by the Romans', 1742) were the result of political and cultural dependence. He defended the 'beauty and energy' of the old literary language of medieval Scotland against that spoken 'pollished . . . to make it more comfortable to our neighbours in England'.

The desire to maintain a distinct national character—or to avoid losing that national spirit irrevocably—arose from the post-Union identity-crisis. Clerk, as we have seen, believed in the maintenance of a Scottish patriotism within a wider Britishness. Through archaeology, Clerk sought in the valiant Caledonian past for that strength and national integrity which he sensed Scotland was losing in the present. In the Roman monuments of northern Britain he found that greatness: they were eloquent of Scottish resistance. When, later in the century, men adjusted to the Union, and Scots, as North Britons, found in intellectual and literary fields new realms in which to compensate for their lost nationhood, so the need for the patriotic application of archaeology was modified. In the year of Clerk's death, Alexander Wedderburn noted:

The memory of our ancient state is not so much obliterated, but that, by comparing the past with the present, we may clearly see the superior advantages we now enjoy, and readily discern from what source they flow.

North Britain was guided on its course of improvement by 'the more mature strength of her kindred country'. When Alexander Carlyle saw Hadrian's Wall in 1762 he noted that it had been

> constructed to prevent the inroads of the barbarians on the Roman provinces or the defenceless natives . . . and while it demonstrates the art and industry of the Romans, brings full in our view the peace and security we now enjoy under a government that unites the interest and promotes the common prosperity of the whole island.[12]

Thirty years later the young Walter Scott conveyed to Clerk's grandson only the 'stupendous idea of the perseverence of its founders' that the Wall aroused in him.[13]

David Steuart Erskine, eleventh Earl of Buchan, however, was one who adhered to the tradition of the political use of the past which Clerk and Gordon had developed. The Society of Antiquaries of Scotland (founded 1780) was described as 'that Altar erected by [Buchan] *Genio Caledoniae*'. The Earl declared: 'I consider the elucidation of the first dawn of History in my Country as no mean or frivolous employment adapted to the plodding Antiquary only, but to the Historian and the Patriot.' The Society, and antiquarianism in general, became an outlet for his patriotism.

When Sir John Clerk looked at Hadrian's Wall he recognized that Rome had 'wall'd out humanity from us'. It had been a victory for Caledonia in that the Romans had been forced to concede the impossibility of permanent subjection, but it was a Pyrrhic victory. The Scots remained free but uncivilized. As he put it in *The Country Seat*:

> How glorious was the Cause of Liberty
> Tho' founded in a gross barbarity.

Clerk saw no intrinsic merit in Caledonian savagery; indeed he did not claim blindly for the Caledonians a culture which was not in reality their due. He mocked the efforts of a contemporary to prove that Latin was descended from Gaelic: 'the poor man is just now sweating upon it and dayly making new discoverys for the honour of the ancient Caledonians'. All he admired was their stand for independence, which he could appreciate in the context of the post-Union Scotland of his own day.

Clerk's attitude to the Caledonia of old was a sentimental one. He had a romantic vision of Scottish prehistory, and of a land peopled by noble savages on the eve of the Roman invasion. All this he opposed, following Tacitus, to the cruel decadence of Rome. In his Latin history he contrasted the mood of Roman jubilation after the victory of Mons Graupius with

Caledonian dejection amid the slaughter: a fine illustration, in his imagination, of making a desert and calling it peace. He could afford to take this attitude of mourning for noble savages because their world did not touch him. The Caledonians were the creation of romantic sentiment, and their remoteness endowed them with mystic virtue. For the modern equivalents of the Caledonians, the Highlanders, Clerk had only contempt: 'a parcel of idle, vain mortals. The Highlanders where I passed are a race of men who will not merit any regard from the rest of mankind unless they change their manners.' Their dishonesty was legendary. 'Never send or lend your monie beyond the River of Tay' was his advice to his sons. The clansmen were real. Their stand against Hanoverian law and government, in defence of what they saw as their liberty, or in the interest of an older order, threatened Clerk's world. Gordon commented on the danger posed to the Romans by the unsubdued tribes of the north:

> ... seeing it was always in the power of these People to join with the Malcontents in the subdued Province, and thereby excite a general Rebellion, whereby the Romans might be liable to lose the whole Island ...[14]

There is here a clear parallel with the threat of the clans joining with English Jacobites to upset the peace in England. The eighteenth-century Highlanders were to the English and the Scottish Whigs what the Caledonians had been to the Romans and British provincials.

Clerk's Caledonian patriotism, founded as it was upon Roman archaeology, was emotional and nostalgic. Nor had it anything whatsoever to do with Jacobitism. When his own security and peace were threatened, he was a Roman. Thomas Blackwell, an enthusiastic volunteer on the Government side in 1745, expressed the *debellare superbos* view of a Hanoverian Scotsman: we can picture the Romans, with Cumberland as some latter-day Severus, and the Lowland Whigs as his auxiliary troops. Clerk's contemporaries were urged to adopt a Roman attitude to solving the problem of 'the pungent stings of a Bloodsucking Bosom Enemy'. A remarkable Latin inscription by Clerk, designed to be cut on a pillar by the highway on Loch Lomondside, paid eloquent tribute to the subjugation of the Highlands by the British Army after the Forty-five and looked forward to a time when the wild Clans would submit themselves to the arts of peace.

The prerequisite for civilising the Highlands by that economic and industrial development of which Clerk was an advocate, was the pacification of the region. Sir John described an early Government fort as 'a bridle on the Highlanders'. He wrote of the Hanoverian barrack at Ruthven as if he thought it should have been stronger to be more effective in its deterrent role. If the later massive fortifications like Fort Augustus and Fort George were maintained, the 'Highlanders [would] never have it in their power to give disturbance'. In the construction of such forts, and the associated system of roads, there was an obvious parallel between the Hanoverian pacification of the Highlands and that attempted by Rome. In fact, interest in the archaeology of the Roman invasions of Scotland—in the field monuments, and in the artefacts of war—was stimulated by the similarity of the Hanoverian conquest, and indeed by the actual work necessary to ensure the success of the latter undertaking. The surveying connected with the network of roads and forts led to many and celebrated discoveries of Roman Scotland,[15] while reading of the *Agricola* encouraged enquiry in the field. This is the background to the world of Scott's *The Antiquary*. Tacitus had mentioned Agricola's programme of public works, by which the influence of civilization was to be introduced. The antiquaries of later eighteenth-century Scotland were led to search for those physical remains. They read in the *Agricola* (ca. 46) of how the ancients fell into oblivion. Their exploration of the past was designed to give life back not only to Agricola and the Roman invaders, but also to Calgacus and their own forebears. Thus something of the spirit of Sir John Clerk's archaeological enquiry survived into the world of the Scottish Enlightenment, and on into the Scottish romantic movement which followed.

NOTES

This chapter is based very largely on material in the Clerk of Penicuik Muniments in the Scottish Record Office, H M General Register House, Edinburgh. Detailed information on sources, including manuscript references, may be found in my 'Sir John Clerk of Penicuik (1676–1755): aspects of a virtuoso life' (Cambridge PhD thesis 1980), especially chapter 5. (A copy of this is in the National Library of Scotland, MS.Acc 7944.)

1   J Y T Greig (ed), *The Letters of David Hume*, 2 vols (Oxford, 1932), II, p 230.
2   David Daiches, 'Scholarship, Literature and Nationalism in 18th Century Scotland', in *Literary Theory and Criticism: Festschrift presented to René Wellek*, Joseph P Strelka (ed), 2 vols (Bern, Frankfurt am Main and New York, 1984), II, p 748.
3   J M Gray (ed), *Memoirs of the Life of Sir John Clerk of Penicuik . . . extracted by himself from his own Journals*, Scottish History Society XIII (Edinburgh, 1892). A biographical and critical study, founded on the thesis mentioned above, is in preparation by the present writer.
4   I have in hand an edition of *The Country Seat* with a detailed introduction and commentary.
5   *The Lord Beilhaven's Speech in Parliament, Saturday the Second of November on the Subject-matter of an Union* (n.p. 1706); John Robertson, *The Scottish Enlightenment and the Militia Issue* (Edinburgh, 1985), pp. 43–6.
6   E Gibson, *Camden's Britannia*, 2nd edn (London 1722), II, col. 1142, account of Hadrian's Wall by Robert Smith.
7   James Anderson, *Historical Essay, showing that the Crown and Kingdom of Scotland is Imperial and Independent* (Edinburgh, 1705), p 49
8   Alexander Gordon, *Itinerarium Septentrionale . . .* (London, 1726), p 138
9   Sir Robert Sibbald, *Historical Inquiries Concerning the Roman Monuments and Antiquities in the North Part of Britain Called Scotland* (Edinburgh, 1707). p 51; id., *The History, Ancient and Modern, of the Sheriffdoms of Fife and Kinross* (Edinburgh, 1710), pp. 31–32.

10   *Itenerarium Septentrionale*, p 32.
11   A Allardyce, (ed), *Scotland and Scotsmen in the 18th century from the MSS. of John Ramsay of Ochtertyre*, 2 vols (Edinburgh 1888), I, p 139.
12   John Hill Burton (ed), *The Autobiography of Alexander Carlyle*, (Edinburgh, 1910), p 447.
13   H J C Grierson, (ed), *The Letters of Sir Walter Scott*, 12 vols (London 1932–37), I, p 23.
14   *Itinerarium Septentrionale*, p 137.
15   William Roy, *The Military Antiquities of the Romans in North Britain* (London, 1793), Prefatory Introduction, pp i–vi.

FURTHER READING

GENERAL HISTORIES

Ferguson, William, *Scotland: 1689 to the Present* (Edinburgh, 1968)
Mitchison, Rosalind, *Lordship to Patronage: Scotland 1603–1745* (London, 1983)
Smout, T C, *A History of the Scottish People 1560–1830* (London, 1969)

THE UNION

Daiches, David, *Scotland and the Union* (London, 1977)
Riley, P W J, *The Union of England and Scotland* (Manchester, 1978)
Smout, T C, 'The Road to Union', in *Britain After the Glorious Revolution*, G S Holmes (ed), (London 1969)

INTELLECTUAL AND CULTURAL BACKGROUND

Brown, Iain Gordon, *The Clerks of Penicuik: Portrain of Taste and Talent* (Edinburgh 1987)
Phillipson, N T, 'Culture and Society in the 18th Century Province: the Case of Edinburgh and the Scottish Enlightenment', in *The University in Society*, Stone, L (ed), 2 vols (Princeton, 1975), II, pp 407–48.
Phillipson, N T and Mitchison, Rosalind (eds), *Scotland in the Age of Improvement*, (Edinburgh, 1970), esp. essays by John Clive and Janet Adam Smith

LITERARY BACKGROUND

Brown, Iain Gordon, *Poet and Painter: Allan Ramsay, Father and Son, 1684–1784* (Edinburgh, 1984)
Craig, David, *Scottish Literature and the Scottish People* (London, 1961)
Daiches, David, *The Paradox of Scottish Culture: the 18th-century experience* (London, 1964)
Duncan, Douglas, *Thomas Ruddiman: a Study in Scottish Scholarship of the Early Eighteenth Century* (Edinburgh, 1965)

ANTIQUARIAN BACKGROUND

Brown, Iain Gordon, *The Hobby-Horsical Antiquary: a Scottish Character, 1640–1830* (Edinburgh, 1980)
'Critick in Antiquity: Sir John Clerk of Penicuik', *Antiquity*, LI (1977), pp 201–10
Piggott, Stuart, *Ruins in a Landscape: Essays in Antiquarianism* (Edinburgh, 1976)

FURTHER READING

Chapter 3

Scholarship and Politeness in the Early Eighteenth Century

DOUGLAS DUNCAN

With their general interest in how societies progress from a 'rude' to a 'polished' state, Scottish men of letters in the later eighteenth century were struck by how their own country's culture seemed to have emerged in the course of their lifetimes from barbarous obscurity to international fame. One of them, John Ramsay of Ochtertyre, attributed this sudden flowering to warm winds blowing from the south since 1707. The seeds had been planted by 'the appearance of *Tatlers, Spectators* and *Guardians* in the reign of Queen Anne' which 'prepared the minds of our countrymen for the study of the best English authors, without a competent knowledge of which no man was accounted a polite scholar.' There had been a fusion of modern with ancient learning, of 'the best English authors' with 'the Greek and Roman classics, which were still universally read and admired.'[1] Ramsay's explanation neglected the modern French and Italians but might otherwise have satisfied most of his contemporaries, the 'polite scholars' of the Scottish Enlightenment. It was confirmed by Scott's novels of eighteenth-century life, where 'civilized' Scots, in touch with southern as well as native values, tend to be marked off from half-educated pedants whose whole secular culture is expressed in Latin tags. And it survived into the twentieth century in the influential historical studies of Henry Gray Graham. Linking cultural to economic poverty and isolation, Graham saw in Scotland in the first quarter of the eighteenth century 'destitution of scholarship' and 'a dreary stagnation of all intellectual life.'[2] In that gross darkness the only ray of hope was that young readers were silently assimilating the values of Addison and Steele.

But in the last thirty years these views have been challenged, first as part of a political reappraisal of the Union and secondly through a search for Scottish origins of the Scottish Enlightenment. The present orthodoxy, while not of course denying external influence, is to trace back the Enlightenment less to the Union than to earlier causes within Scotland itself: perhaps to the Presbyterian Whig Settlement of 1690, where Scotland's Age of Transformation begins for T C Smout, or to the Episcopalian royalist culture of the 1670s and 1680s, with its emphasis on learned foundations like the Advocates' Library, or even to the late survival in Scotland of a still earlier classical humanist tradition. The late seventeenth and early eighteenth centuries, previously shunned as barren wastes, have suddenly become a focus of specialized scholarly investigation, most of it aimed at those autonomous areas of the nation's life—education, the established church, and the study of law—which immediately affected Enlightenment thinkers. Detailed examination of the school system has suggested that Knox's ideal of universally accessible education had not collapsed as totally as Graham implies, and that, in addition to Latin and English, 'modern' subjects such as French and mathematics were increasingly becoming available. There have been studies of how the Church, unaffected by Union, painfully forced itself in the following years to face the challenges of secular thought. Its suspicion of what Davie Deans calls 'carnal-witted scholars' never quite eclipsed respect for learning, which remained more widespread in Scottish society than in English. The charge of cultural isolation has been answered by reminders that well-to-do Scots, who went to foreign (usually Dutch) universities to study medicine or law until well into the eighteenth century, brought back ideas, such as the natural law theories of Grotius and Pufendorf, that proved seminal to later Scottish thinking. As for the Scottish universities themselves, the myth that they entered the century still shrouded in scholastic fog has been banished by evidence that they accepted Newtonianism with remarkable alacrity. The founding of new chairs, and especially of a medical faculty at Edinburgh in the 1720s, has been cited as evidence of progressive policies by academic and civic authorities working together. Also, although the Scottish universities were slow to abandon Latin as the medium of instruction, it has been argued that they were quicker than their English counterparts to care about improvement in teaching. When specialist professors lecturing on their own subjects began to displace the old system of regents (who had each single-handedly guided a class through its whole course in arts), the aim was not to promote specialization among students but to strengthen the effectiveness of the broad arts curriculum. And the fact that this included mathematics and natural philosophy (or science) in the final year is seen to have prolonged the life of the Renaissance concept of unity of knowledge in a way that proved fruitful for Hume and his successors. Their conscious application of Newtonian method to moral and social subjects has often been linked to the success of an integrated, well-taught curriculum unavailable at Oxford or Cambridge. Finally, convincing disproof of intellectual stagnation has been found in the overflow of academic interests into extracurricular clubs and societies such as the Rankenian Club at Edinburgh, founded in 1716 by young academics, advocates and ministers with the object of 'mutual improvement by liberal conversation and rational enquiry.'

Research along these lines is adding much to our knowledge of a neglected period, and those who wish to explore native roots of Enlightenment should consult recent titles listed at the end of this chapter. But the orientation of such research carries with it some dangers. Graham's dark view of the state of Scottish learning in the early eighteenth century may be over-corrected if we look only for the first signs of dawn. Conversely, valuing all scholarly activity by the degree to which it anticipated a later standard can lead to neglect of much that was good in itself and characteristic of its time: scholars who swam against the tide of the century but whose interests and attitudes were never submerged and remained part of the total Scottish scene. Another danger threatening us here is that histories of scholarship tend to dehumanize their object. Since the present chapter presupposes readers with no first-hand knowledge of the scholars discussed, it will try to avoid the kind of summary charting of 'movements of thought' which reduces individuals to argumentative data. It offers instead, at some risk of incoherence, introductory glimpses of eight or nine variously representative figures, linking them only by considering their responses to the pervasive eighteenth-century concept of politeness.

When Ramsay of Ochtertyre referred to his friends as 'polite scholars' he was joining, conventionally, terms which at the start of the century in Scotland had been almost mutually exclusive. They had not always been so. The Renaissance-humanist ideal of a polite (i.e. polished) scholarly culture, suited to courtiers and gentry, had inspired Gavin Douglas to turn Virgil into Scots. It survived even after the Court moved south in 1603, and in spite of the wedge between scholarship and courtliness driven by populist Reformers. When the turmoil of the seventeenth century subsided, Scotland still had its own kinds of gentleman-scholar. But by then a stronger influence was the Anglo-French court culture which had dominated the south since 1660. This encouraged learning but infused it with standards of social propriety set in Paris and London. Certain habits of thought and uses of scholarship—traditional in Scotland—ceased to be gentlemanly. Pedantry, dogmatism, religious 'enthusiasm' became social as well as intellectual taboos. Whole nations and their languages, notably the Scots, were marked down as less polite than others like the French and Italians with their heritage of sceptical thinking and artistic achievement. And a well-mannered tone was prescribed for all kinds of learned discourse, a tone which quickly appropriated standards of 'reasonableness' and later 'good taste'. This socially-oriented refinement of learning did little to disturb the best English scholars: scientists at Cambridge and the Royal Society, antiquarian scholars in Oxford and the diocesan libraries. But on Scotsmen made conscious of cultural inferiority it was soon to have a mesmerizing impact, as transmitted through the elegant writings of the Earl of Shaftesbury, or as offered for bourgeois emulation by the periodical writers. It is not surprising that Scots in our period often thought of politeness in relation to their English prose style, but the problems it posed for them were of deeper origin.

Around the time of the Union of 1707 few Scots could be at ease with the notion of politeness apart from members of the highest nobility who were prevented by their rank from being practising scholars. To lesser members of the nobility and gentry professional careers were open, and in this class a striking attempt to unite scholarship and southern courtly standards had been made earlier by the royalist advocate, Sir George

Mackenzie. His father was the brother of an earl, his mother an academic's daughter. As romance-writer, poet and moral essayist he had passed muster in London; at Edinburgh he made his mark as a scholar by codifying the criminal law. But though he mastered both fields he did not connect them. He banned from his Advocates' Library the reflective, imaginative kinds of writing he had earlier practised. In doing so he made a then-normal distinction between books as the fruit of contemplation and retirement and books as equipment for the active life—between what would soon be called 'belles-lettres' and the traditional scholarly disciplines. But it was eighty-four years before his idea of a learned library was formally challenged by the Faculty of Advocates, when it noted in its Minutes in 1773 that its collection was 'remarkably deficient in the modern Classicks.' A reason for this conservatism is that the Edinburgh advocates had been influenced by a Scoto-Dutch concept of learning different from the Anglo-French. Holland, where most of them had studied because of the shared debt to Rome of Scots and Dutch law, was Protestant, republican and classicist, resistant in the main to the more modern courtly culture spreading out of Catholic France. It preserved the distinction between scholarship and belles-lettres which the French and English were subtly breaking down. And its universities, though open to developments in science, kept up the humanist policy of concentrating on the ancient world as a base from which to study the new. The Dutch connection must help to explain why Scotland in the early eighteenth century, without being insular, restricted to the natural sciences its interest in that obsessive Anglo-French topic, the quarrel between ancients and moderns. If we look at the catalogues, not only of the Advocates' Library in 1742 but of the private libraries of individual scholars in the period, we find a formidable array of international learning of traditional kinds but also a dearth of what Englishmen had come to recognize as 'modern classics'. The French and English essayists, dramatists and poets (except for Milton's religious epics) rarely appear.

In 1704 an anonymous writer published *Proposals for the Reformation of Schools and Universities*, deploring Scotland's failure to educate its gentry. He complained that the policy of ensuring access to poor students had dragged down academic standards, and that the 'vulgar' character of the nation's universities had brought learning into social contempt, tending to 'unfitt a Scholar for a Gentleman and to render a Gentleman asham'd of being a Scholar.' 'Till we Reconcile the Gentleman with the Scholar,' he declares, "'tis impossible Learning should ever flourish.'[3] The writer may sound like a spokesman for Anglo-French politeness, but the model for his proposals was if anything Dutch. By raising fees, paying higher salaries to attract better teachers, and lengthening the period spent at university, his primary aim was to give the sons of gentry a more thorough grounding in classical authors (though natural philosophy was also to be stressed). It would be good if the ascription of this pamphlet to Andrew Fletcher of Saltoun could be proved, since it reinforces several features of his thought. Fletcher (1653–1716) was unquestionably a scholar as well as an original thinker and patriot. Our knowledge of him, however, is still shamefully limited: we do not even know where he studied, though in view of his republicanism Holland is the likeliest guess. From his political writings we know that he valued the gentry as an educated élite, and that he habitually approached contemporary issues through classical precedents. He also, like Mackenzie, makes nonsense of the notion that Scotsmen of his time could not write fine English prose, but the style of his essays and speeches shows no trace of southern politeness. Sinewy and trenchant, it was a highly-crafted instrument built on Roman models to display not only his own cast of mind but also (one suspects) how a Scottish gentleman could differ from an English one. The most intimate glimpse we have of his mind comes from letters he wrote to his nephew when the latter was a student at Leyden in 1716.[4] These show him ordering for his library learned volumes in the humanist tradition: works of juridical and historical scholarship, critical editions of the classics and collections of neo-Latin verse. His own example as a gentleman-scholar was plainly not that which Addison and Shaftesbury transmitted to the Scottish Enlightenment.

To read Fletcher's vigorous, hastily-scribbled letters is to see that his distance from Anglo-French politeness was due as much to native temperament as to traditional loyalties or standards of scholarship. The same is true, in different ways, of two of his contemporaries, Sir Robert Sibbald (1641–1722) and Dr Archibald Pitcairne (1652–1713), who separately affected the course of scholarship in our period, although their most important work was done before it.

Sibbald is now rightly treated with respect as a scholar of remarkable industry and versatility: botanist, natural historian of his country, prime mover in founding the Royal College of Physicians of Edinburgh, antiquary in touch with leading figures of the English antiquarian movement. Pitcairne, too, is remembered for his brief international celebrity as an applier of mechanistic views to anatomy, for his impact on medical teaching in Scotland, his virulent anti-Presbyterian satires and his distinction as a Latin epigrammatic poet. The professional rift between these medical colleagues was wide and long-lasting, but one episode in the story will point to their essential difference. In 1696 Pitcairne published *Dissertatio de Legibus Historiae Naturalis*, laying down scientific principles for the writing of natural history and using Sibbald's *Scotia Illustrata* (1684) to show how much they were needed. He advances four axioms: the writer must rely on sound mathematical principles; he must describe only what he himself has seen; he must be qualified to describe things accurately; and he must not generalize on the basis of incomplete evidence. On the first of these, which underlies the others and refers to a basic understanding of Newtonian method, he finds Sibbald defective at all points. He then goes on to criticize Sibbald for relying on published authorities and correspondents' reports instead of investigating Scotland for himself. (Why would he hand on an old wives' tale about a cow giving birth to a hare, or say 'he has been told' that there are eagles in Scotland, or that 'he does not know' if there are bisons? His job was to ascertain facts). Sibbald's qualifications as

Geographer Royal are queried in the light of his alleged ignorance of hydrostatics, optics, gravity, tides; he might as well (Pitcairne says) have described Greenland, which would have afforded him more scope for his imagination and less danger of being proved wrong. And on the matter of generalizing without proof Pitcairne cites Sibbald's favourite theory of Scotland's self-sufficiency: how can he assert this while admitting he does not know if the properties and creatures he describes are to be found there? The self-sufficiency theory irritated Pitcairne as profoundly unscientific, not only because it encouraged patriotic falsehoods—Sibbald claims a walrus for Scotland—*tanta ... mentiendi pro patria libido* ('so great his eagerness to lie for his country')—but because based on a theological presupposition. The dedication of *Scotia Illustrata* to Charles II had reflected the Stuart view of the divine order. Scotland lays at the feet of her king the natural resources which Providence had endowed her with in total fulfilment of her needs. In particular, Sibbald's interest in herbal medicine had led him to assert that the divine Dispenser had provided each region of Scotland with remedies for the diseases infesting it, thus making it unnecessary to import foreign drugs. Aware that this theory had been turned into an economic argument against international trade, Pitcairne argues that a doctor must get what he needs where he can find it. And he insists that the naturalist must first use his reason to establish what the laws of nature are before interpreting them as evidence of a divine purpose. *Ego ... imprimis quid verum sit exquiro, & tum demum Deo Adjutori gratias ago* ('I seek truth first, and give thanks to God after').

In 1710, hearing that Pitcairne's dissertation had been reprinted in Holland, Sibbald published a belated vindication of *Scotia Illustrata*, blandly pointing out that his work had appeared before Newton's *Principia* and had been modelled on Pliny. He had collected the reports and opinions of others as interesting in themselves and had not felt obliged to vouch for their veracity. Sibbald, it should be said, did make some effort to adjust to new methods, but it is clear that in their sympathies he and Pitcairne stood on opposite sides of the Newtonian divide. In his later years Sibbald's main interest was national antiquities: Roman Scotland, local history, ancient records, fields in which his influence contributed much to the vast body of patriotic work put out by Scots before and after the Union in response to their threatened sense of nationhood. He gave practical help to many but was chiefly influential through the general character of his writings: painstaking, often valuable research shot through with intellectual naiveté and expressed, whether in Latin or English, with an indifference to style which he freely admitted. He was the leading Scottish example in his day of what was then called a Virtuoso, but he never paraded his interests as those of a cultivated gentleman, evidently sensing that the Scottish scholar must be true to his own light. Pitcairne reached the same conclusion by a different route; if Sibbald's light was honestly dim, his burned with hectic brilliance. Over-hasty in his faith that mathematics could explain the body's mechanisms, he none the less served Scotland well by strenuously promoting Newtonian method. He was equally whole-hearted in pushing rationalism to the theological conclusion that Newton fought shy of. As one of his adversaries noted, having turned the 'conjectural art' of medicine into a 'certain science' by the power of mathematics, he used the same principle to turn biblical certainties into conjecture:

> This learned Man holds, that nothing is infallibly certain, but a Demonstration; and that all other Certainty, even that which depends on the faith of History, is nothing but Probability and meer Conjecture; and consequently all the Infallible or Indubitable Certainty we can expect from any History, tho never so well attested, is That it is infallibly uncertain; because all History whatsoever supposeth . . . some things that cannot be demonstrat.[5]

Perhaps, though this cannot be 'demonstrat' either, Pitcairne's radical scepticism helped to make Hume possible in Scotland, or at least to facilitate the metaphysical enquiries of young Edinburgh intellectuals in the Rankenian Club soon after his death. But if he was 'modern' in those respects, in others he was strongly conservative and reactionary. His roots were in royalist Restoration Scotland, whose heroes he commemorated in fine Latin poems, and its collapse in 1690 as he approached his peak years of achievement made him a satirist for the rest of his life. His mastery of Latin was not a foretaste of balanced eighteenth-century classicism but a weapon of his humanist élitism which he flourished in the face of Presbyterian illiteracy. And the same tradition led him in scholarly argument to adopt the caustic, arrogant, wholly 'impolite' tone that we sensed in his attack on Sibbald. Several of his Scottish medical friends went south to London and grew rich by imitating the English gentlemanly manner. One was John Arbuthnot, Pope's good-humoured mentor. Another, George Cheyne, renounced the style of writing he had learned from Pitcairne as 'unbecoming Gentlemen, Scholars and Christians.'[6]

In that linkage of terms we sense willing acceptance of an English standard of politeness that Pitcairne, Sibbald and Fletcher could afford to defy. For the next generation of scholars that politeness mattered rather more, even for those, not gentlemen themselves, who found it alien to their deepest convictions.

Robert Wodrow (1679–1734), Church of Scotland minister at Eastwood, then a village near Glasgow, responded to Pitcairne's death in 1713 with shocked comment on his drinking and his mockery of religion, and concern to know if he 'had remorse at his death.'[7] The passage is typical of many in his *Analecta* that historians enjoy quoting to illustrate the narrow Calvinist anti-secularism soon to be countered by the Moderate wing of the Church. How, though a cause of scholarship in others, could this gossiping provincial moralist be a scholar himself? But Wodrow, after graduating at Glasgow where his father was a divinity professor, had for six years managed the university library for John Simson, the Moderate theologian, and fallen under the spell of Sibbald and the Virtuoso movement which crossed denominational and national boundaries. He accumulated a huge library,

strongest in divinity ('practical' and 'polemical') and history ('civil' and
'ecclesiastic'), but also containing a solid collection of Latin and Greek
authors in cheap editions, Hobbes, Locke and the *Tatler*, and 145 French
titles including the *Journal des Scavants*. Even the *Analecta*, not meant to
be published, is scholarly in a sense. 'My wife tells me,' a typical entry
begins, 'that she heard her mother frequently tell that Mr John Campbell
. . . frequently told her . . . .' Scholarly? But what Wodrow was doing, over
thirty years in six closely-written manuscript volumes, was, like Sibbald, to
collect reports for their own sake; in this case reports of the workings of
God, 'Materials for a History of Remarkable Providences.' The result is
gossip with a scholarly purpose and a scholarly value not wholly accidental:
it reveals in detail the spiritual perceptions of the writer and his circle. But
in the work he reluctantly wrote for publication, his massive two-volume
*History of the Sufferings of the Church of Scotland, from the Restauration
to the Revolution* (1721), it was not sufficient to report, he had also to
convince. Especially he aimed to convince English readers that the proceedings of the Royalists against the Presbyterians had involved religious
persecution and denial of civil liberties and not been (as Sir George
Mackenzie, for example, alleged) a legitimate suppression of rebellion. So
Wodrow's greatest strength as a historian, his commitment to tell a story
which he knew to be true, brought him directly up against his
dilemma—that those he aimed to convince were the least likely to listen.
He discusses his problem in terms of prose style. As a country minister he
had no need of good English. 'I write just as words offer,' he admits to an
adviser in London; 'no corrections will make anything I write answerable
to the English taste. Could I get it good grammar, and free of obvious
Scotticisms, so as people might fully understand it, I should be easy as to its
politeness.'[8] Let the facts do the talking. Yet he certainly knew that his
subject (religious zeal), his heroes (simple men and women), and their
reported speech (Scots, 'which must not be altered') would offend against
politeness as much as his style. His recourse was to rely as far as possible on
the records of dignified bodies, the judiciary and privy council, which he
transcribed faithfully, even when their matter was heavily slanted against
his cause. Modern historians complain of his distortions, because he also
relied on the partisan evidence of the 'sufferers' themselves. But it is this
which gives his *History* conviction, its truth of spirit, if not always of fact.
He argued acutely in his preface that the 'prevailing Humour of searching
Records' could 'degenerate into Scepticism, Incredulity, and a groundless
calling in question such Things as . . . we cannot expect to meet with in
Records'—that is, the spiritual motives of the sufferers, which were not
documented and could not be explained in terms of contemporary rationalism, but which he rightly saw as his central concern as a historian.
Wodrow's was a difficult task, telling a story which needed to be told and
most readers wanted to forget. Neglect or disparagement of his achievement today reflects badly on Enlightment-worship.

A less heroic but more professional scholar, whose work brought him
more into contact with the gentry, was Thomas Ruddiman (1674–1757). It

was Pitcairne who had lured him in 1699 to leave schoolteaching at Laurencekirk and come under his patronage to Edinburgh, where he soon found work in the Advocates' Library. Unlike Wodrow, Ruddiman remained a librarian for almost fifty years, his classical and historical interests reflecting and to some degree shaping the traditional character of that library as it grew into a national collection. By the time he handed over the Keepership of it to David Hume in 1752 the kinds of scholarship he stood for had become outmoded.

Whereas Wodrow was a product of the covenanting West, Ruddiman had grown up in an Episcopal, Jacobite culture that was strong in the North-East, especially at King's College, Aberdeen where he graduated. Along with it he imbibed, as a crofter's son, a feudal respect for his social superiors, to whom he always remained obsequious, though he stood on the dignity of his academic degree—he liked to be called 'Master Thomas'. In his early career he found little conflict between his scholarship and the tastes of those he served, since many of the promoters of learning in Edinburgh were then Jacobite-Episcopal too. He was quick to assimilate Sibbald's interest in records—he became expert in those in the Advocates' collection and later published many—and Pitcairne's faith in reason as a guide to truth, which he soon found reflected internationally in Bentley's principles of textual criticism, Mabillon's tests of the authenticity of charters, and more generally in neoclassic standards of literary judgment. When the entrepreneurial Jacobite printer Robert Freebairn organized the support of the gentry for large-scale re-editions of early Scottish humanist classics—Gavin Douglas's *Aeneis* (1710), George Buchanan's *Opera Omnia* (1715)—Ruddiman gladly contributed most or all of the scholarly labour. It is only after the 1715 rebellion, when the Jacobite appropriation of Scottish culture became suspect and the tastes of the gentry began to change, that his scholarly convictions start to isolate him. Chief among these was his belief in Latin as the gateway to higher knowledge. This led him to insist that its grammar must be thoroughly mastered, a view that was rapidly losing ground to Locke's, that a gentleman could gather what he needed from Roman authors without fretting over grammatical niceties. When Ruddiman dedicated to the Advocates his finest and most enduring work of scholarship, *Grammaticae Latinae Institutiones* (1725, 1731), he acknowledged that they might find it trivial, yet slyly gave it a title which evoked comparison with their own revered bible, Stair's *Institutions of the Law of Scotland*. His lifelong adherence to the 'ancient' point of view that the classical tongues were 'the only sure Channels through which all useful Learning did and should run'[9] is of interest not merely as a cultural anachronism in mid-century Edinburgh but for the loyalty it suggests to the old humanist concept of learning that is 'useful' by promoting the moral good of the individual and the state. The new, more socially-oriented view—that the goal of learning was to enable gentlemen to show polite familiarity with authors and their views—embarrassed him much as it did Dr Johnson, who not surprisingly held Ruddiman in high regard.

Ruddiman is sometimes credited with another humanist policy, that of fostering literature in the vernacular, but this proposition needs more careful treatment than it usually gets. The spirited Glossary he compiled of Douglas's Scots did in fact stimulate interest in the language, but there is no sign that Ruddiman meant it to encourage a revival of Scots vernacular poetry. On the contrary, his commitment to the neoclassic code made him stress the 'incorrectness' of Douglas's language. Later, he did print Allan Ramsay's works but such evidence as there is suggests that this was a commercial partnership which involved no meeting of minds between poet and printer. Whatever he may have felt, he never risked his status as a scholar by endorsing poetry in Scots. On the other hand, he often professed loyalty to the tradition of Scottish writing in Latin. Nurtured by the example of North-East poets like Arthur Johnston, and latterly Pitcairne, this brought his learning and his patriotism together. Although English critics were now scorning the Renaissance Latinists as 'incorrect', Scotsmen after the Union needed to take pride in their only writers of international fame. So Ruddiman's edition of Buchanan was encouraged by gentry of all parties, by Fletcher and Pitcairne as well as the Whigs. Insofar as his aim was to confirm Buchanan's fame by submitting his Latin to the test of pure classical usage, Ruddiman had all Scotland behind him. But in his notes to the political writings, especially the *History of Scotland*, he applied (with naive or disingenuous confidence) the much more divisive test of historical truth. Like Johnson on the subject of Milton, Ruddiman hated Buchanan's politics as much as he revered his art. As a result, his edition prolonged and intensified the period's saddest misuse of scholarship on angry disputes over the authenticity of texts and records to prove that the early Scottish monarchy had often been elective (Buchanan and the Whigs) or always hereditary (their Jacobite opponents). To study these controversies is to understand why the new clubs and societies springing up in Edinburgh often banned political discussion. Some of the writers, like Ruddiman himself, showed knowledge of French standards of polite historiography, but on such explosive topics in the Scotland of their day the pretence of dispassionate, impartial truth-seeking could deceive nobody.

Only one contributor to the Buchanan controversy emerged with credit. Thomas Innes (1662–1744) came from a poor Catholic family in Aberdeenshire. In his mid-teens he followed his elder brother Lewis to study for the priesthood in France, where both rose to high positions in the Scots College at Paris. His *A Critical Essay on the Ancient Inhabitants of the Northern Parts of Britain* (London, 1729) was therefore the product of a French-trained mind, though Innes had returned to Scotland at least twice: for a long spell of dangerous mission-work at the turn of the century, and in 1724 on a research-trip to the Advocates' Library which Wodrow was curious to hear about from Ruddiman ('He is . . . a Monkish, bookish person, who medles with nothing but literature'). His essay presents, for the first time systematically, the evidence then available about the earliest history of Scotland, but its main thrust lay in a 'critical' assessment of Scottish historians up to Buchanan, showing how and why they had invented patriotic myths and manipulated them in support of their political views. That Innes himself had political views was not to be doubted—his college's links with the Pretender's court were known, and a letter he wrote to 'the King' survives which acknowledges his aim to discredit Buchanan. His achievement therefore was not impartiality but a persuasive appearance of it. His cool style, careful method, scrupulous respect for evidence, and above all his ubiquitous scepticism, constituted a 'tone' in the best French manner which itself seemed to guarantee objectivity, and enabled him to make a case which no resident Scot was equipped to answer.

In 1738 Innes wrote a letter on behalf of his college to the University of Glasgow in reply to a courteous request for a copy of a charter. It gave him satisfaction, he wrote, before he died, to find that the 'aversion' to members of his communion was wearing away in that city, 'at least among the more learned and more polite inhabitants.'[10] The compliment was conventional enough, but Innes's own example reminds us that politeness, as a quality of mind and style, did not need to carry with it those awkward social overtones which it generally had for early eighteenth-century Scots, those of the English gentleman with his easy manner and tolerant outlook, the representative of a richer, more spacious, more modern culture than their own. His background made him unique, however, and for the forbears in Scotland of Ramsay of Ochtertyre's 'polite scholar' one is bound to look to the ranks of the Anglophile Whig gentry, and in particular to Sir John Clerk of Penicuik (1676–1755). Clerk inherited what we loosely called the Scoto-Dutch cultural tradition; it is well represented in the surviving catalogue of his father's library, and he himself, in the 1690s, had studied at Glasgow and Leyden. But then came his adventure-tour of Italy, vividly described in his *Memoirs*, and a period of hobnobbing with the nobility in London while he helped to negotiate the Treaty of Union of 1707. With his skill in music and poetry, his knowledge of painting and architecture, his friendship with the Earls of Pembroke and Burlington, above all in the ease of his letter-writing style, he was by any standard a polite gentleman. And his scholarship, too, especially in the field of Roman artefacts, was warmly praised by English Virtuosi who made him a corresponding Fellow of the Royal Society. Clerk was a Virtuoso of a different stamp from Sibbald. Yet the scholarship and the politeness still did not quite fuse. The former drove him back to his Scottish roots, and so led him not only to Roman remains but to the Roman tongue: he wrote a six-volume History of the Union in Latin. On the other hand, his sense of what was proper for a gentleman always made him chary of publishing. It was probably vanity that impelled him, aged seventy-one, to ask Ruddiman to print his *Dissertatio de Monumentis quibusdam Romanis*, written many years before. Ruddiman, seventy-three, kept him waiting for a reply while he wrote an anti-Whig pamphlet and then offered to correct Clerk's Latin. But Ruddiman could not resist a gentleman's commission on such a subject and finally even humoured the author with a fictitious preface (in translation: 'When I saw this work negligently cast aside in his library, time and again I implored him to publish'). Thus, while Enlightenment dawned, two old men warily negotiated common ground in ancient Rome.

The fusion not quite reached in Clerk was achieved by young men who had read Addison and Steele in boyhood. Some achieved it gracefully. Colin MacLaurin (1698–1746), who like many of the Enlightenment masters whom he taught at Edinburgh was a minister's son, effortlessly overlaid his mathematical genius with a social self-assurance and wide range of interests which made him prized in polite circles on both sides of the border. But literary scholars were more self-conscious when they donned polite dress. Thomas Blackwell (1707–1757), Professor of Greek at Marischal College, Aberdeen, had also been reared in a household of old-fashioned, pious learning but soon mixed with the Rankenians, was befriended by Berkeley, and earned his place among the new Scottish intelligentsia, for whom he helped to make Greece as instructive a subject as Rome. His *An Enquiry into the Life and Writings of Homer* (London, 1735) is deservedly a milestone in the history of criticism, the first detailed attempt to explain a major author as a product of his social and geographical background. What is awkward, however, in its blend of scholarship and politeness, is that both are ostentatiously paraded. Vast tracts of Greek as well as modern languages are given untranslated in the notes, while the text, addressed to a nobleman who had commissioned the enquiry, is punctuated throughout with 'my lord' and 'your lordship' to the relative detriment of Homer. Blackwell's self-image appears in his opening pages when he cites Horace as the ancient writer who 'made the happiest union of the *Courtier* and the *Scholar*;' the influence of Shaftesbury, which he acknowledged to Sir John Clerk, suffuses his literary tone. His letters to Clerk also betray what is blatant in the work, a calculated attempt to impress and reap social rewards. This clever chameleon Scot, scorning his Aberdeen colleagues and fastening on the image of the polite scholar, highlights a changing view of the uses of learning. His interest in the past is not primarily in words, like Ruddiman, or in objects, like Sibbald or Clerk, or in fact, like Wodrow or Innes, but in whatever can contribute to speculative theory. In Blackwell we see literary scholarship ceasing to be a self-contained discipline with its own rewards and becoming an accomplishment to be used as a base from which gentlemen can exchange ideas.

The scholars we have glimpsed here were various in their interests, came from different regional and social backgrounds, and differed in their religious and political loyalties. Yet all felt obliged to define their positions by embracing or rejecting, wholly or in part, an Anglo-French cultural code which, in the total context of Scottish intellectual history, appears strikingly anomalous in the way it subjected the mind—the *praefervidum ingenium Scotorum*—to values associated with rank and good breeding. We need not conclude that all who adopted it were false to their origins or ceased to think like Scotsmen; rather, they had to synthesize their intellectual heritage with a new notion of what it meant to think and write like gentlemen. To lament the transition to Enlightenment values would be even more foolish than to applaud it automatically, and also unnecessary, since most of the interests of the old scholars were to be revived in Scotland within the next hundred years. This chapter has merely tried to suggest how difficult the transition was. Historical hindsight can show that it was inevitable and long prepared for, and that the shedding of sclerotic disciplines and provincial obsessions was necessary for the nation's return to the mainstream of European thought, and in fact gave new energy to it. But for the individual scholars themselves there was nothing self-evidently right about change that required them to discard traditional sanctities and think in a wholly new way, to adopt an alien and pretentious vocabulary and a tone of voice not their own. However they responded, they command our interest. Their predicament was one that recurs.

NOTES

1   *Scotland and Scotsmen in the Eighteenth Century*, A Allardyce (ed), 2 vols (Edinburgh, 1888), I, pp 6–7.
2   *The Social Life of Scotland in the Eighteenth Century*, 2nd edn (London, 1901), p 449.
3   Quoted by Donald J Withrington, 'Education and Society in the Eighteenth Century', in *Scotland in the Age of Improvement*, N T Phillipson and Rosalind Mitchison (eds) (Edinburgh, 1970), pp 169–99 (p 172).
4   'Letters of Andrew Fletcher of Saltoun and his family, 1715–16', Irene J Murray (ed), in *Miscellany*, X, Scottish History Society (Edinburgh, 1965, pp. 143–73.
5   'A Discourse of Certainty', pp 10–11, appended to *Apollo Mathematicus* (Edinburgh, 1695).
6   *An Essay of Health and Long Life* (London, 1724), p vii.
7   *Analecta: or Materials for a History of Remarkable Providences*, Maitland Club, 4 vols (Edinburgh, 1842–3), II (1842), p 255.
8   *The Correspondence of the Rev Robert Wodrow*, Thomas M'Crie (ed), Wodrow Society, 3 vols (Edinburgh, 1842–3), II (1843), p 295.
9   *A Dissertation upon the Way of Teaching the Latin Tongue* (Edinburgh, 1733), p 31.
10 *Miscellany of the Spalding Club*, 2 vols (Aberdeen, 1842), II, p 369.

FURTHER READING

(excluding titles cited in text and notes)

Brown, Iain G, 'Critick in Antiquity: Sir John Clerk of Penicuik', *Antiquity*, LI (1977)

—— The Hobby-Horsical Antiquary (Edinburgh, 1980)

Campbell, R H and Andrew S Skinner (eds), *The Origins and Nature of the Scottish Enlightenment* (Edinburgh, 1982)

Chalmers, George, *The Life of Thomas Ruddiman* (London, 1794)

Davie, G E, *The Democratic Intellect* (Edinburgh, 1961)

Duncan, Douglas, *Thomas Ruddiman* (Edinburgh, 1965)

Emerson, Roger L, 'Conjectural History and Scottish Philosophers', in *Historical Papers*, Guelph 1984, Canadian Historical Association

Fletcher, Andrew, *Selected Political Writings and Speeches*, David Daiches (ed), (Edinburgh, 1979)

Hont, Istvan and Michael Ignatieff (eds), *Wealth and Virtue* (Cambridge, 1983)

McElroy, D D, *Scotland's Age of Improvement* (Washington, 1969)

Phillipson, N T, 'Culture and Society in the 18th Century Province: the Case of Edinburgh and the Scottish Enlightenment,' in *The University in Society*, II, Stone, Lawrence (ed), (Princeton, 1974)

Rae, Thomas I, 'Historical Scepticism in Scotland before David Hume,' in *Studies in the Eighteenth Century*, Brissenden R F (ed), (Toronto, 1973)

Rendall, Jane, *The Origins of the Scottish Enlightenment* (London, 1978)

Simpson, A D C, 'Sir Robert Sibbald—the Founder of the College', *Proceedings of the Royal College of Physicians Tercentenary Congress 1981* (Edinburgh, 1982)

Starkey, A M, 'Robert Wodrow and the *History of the Sufferings of the Church of Scotland,' Church History*, XLIV (1974)

Wodrow, Robert, *Early Letters of*, Sharp, L W (ed), (Edinburgh, 1937)

Chapter 4

Allan Ramsay and Literary Life in the First Half of the Eighteenth Century

ALEXANDER M KINGHORN and ALEXANDER LAW

Recent extensive research on Ramsay exposed a formidable body of unpublished material, including poems, correspondence, attributed writings and, most significantly for his editors, the *Journal of the Easy Club*, all printed in the Scottish Text Society's edition of the poet's *Works*, completed in 1975. Since then further factual data and one important poem have been added. In this essay we shall try to place Ramsay in his context as eighteenth-century makar, in Scotland the best-known writer of verse in his day, author of a memorable dramatic pastoral and editor and populariser of songs and poems that recalled and revitalised old Scots traditions.

First his background. Ramsay was born in Lanarkshire into a rural Scots-speaking community and passed the first fifteen years of his life on his stepfather's smallholding. He learned to understand the speech and daily habits of shepherds together with other intimacies of rural society as other contemporary writers of pastoral, notably Pope and Prior, never did. Born in the lead- and gold-mining village of Leadhills, forty-six miles from Edinburgh, on 15 October 1684 or 1685, young Ramsay's formal education was limited to the 'three Rs' and bible knowledge but may have included the rudiments of Latin—a subject not uncommon in the parish schools of the time. Early rustic images and impressions were to remain with him for the rest of his life, as they did with Burns.

Ramsay's mother was English of Derbyshire stock. His father, a supervisor in the Earl of Hopeton's lead mines, died when Allan was a baby and his mother remarried. His status as stepchild probably lent encouragement to his romantic claim to kinship with the Earls of Dalhousie. The poems *To the Whin-Bush Club* and *To Mr William Starrat* recall those formative years when Ramsay's education came out of nature rather than from books, though the MS *Life*, an unsigned account in his eldest son's handwriting, claims that his father's knowledge of Scots history and literature, the cultural spring of his nationalism, was acquired before he left Leadhills for Edinburgh, in about 1700. For a decade after that Ramsay's career is obscure. He became an apprentice wigmaker in 1704, and six years later master wigmaker and burgess of Edinburgh. In 1712 he married Christian Ross, daughter of a lawyer's clerk, and of their five children, the eldest became a noted artist, given the title of 'One of His Majesty's Painters in Ordinary' by George III.

Between 1712 and 1715 the budding poet was a founding member of a coterie of young men affecting nationalist leanings born of hostility to Scotland's role in the 1707 Union. Called the Easy Club and modelled on Addison and Steele's Spectator Club, this society kept a journal. (Its discovery in an Edinburgh bookshop in 1907 was fortunate since the manuscript disappeared some years later but not before it had been transcribed.) From this journal, (printed in *Works*, V), the Club's activities may now be reconstructed. The members discussed verses they had composed, argued about what they meant by 'Easy', invented replies to letters received, resolved to read a copy of Addison's *Spectator* at each meeting, and debated Anglo-Scots relations. As was the practice in other Edinburgh social clubs they assumed pseudonyms such as Isaac Bickerstaff, George Buchanan, Sir Roger l'Estrange and Tom Brown, but later decided to adopt Scots patrons only. Ramsay himself changed his Club name from Isaac Bickerstaff to Gavin Douglas 'sometime bishop of Dunkeld and a famous old Scots poet'.

Several of Ramsay's earliest verses were contributed to the Easy Club. His fellow members were so delighted with *Poem To The Memory Of The Famous Archibald Pitcairne, MD* that they had it printed at the Club's expense. This poem, the first of Ramsay's to be published, came to light only recently. Pitcairne, a notable physician, Latin poet, dramatist and opponent of religious bigotry who supported the Stuart kings, had died on 20 October 1713. A month later Ramsay's elegy was read to the Club.

Its theme is Pitcairne's arrival in paradise, on the way to which he

> . . . Observ'd a pool of boyling gold,
> On which did float, those who their country sold.
> They howl'd and yell'd, and often curs'd the gods,
> Who had not made them vipers, asps, or toads.

The shades of Bruce and Wallace appear. Wallace regrets the absence of liberating heroes like himself and yearns to return 'once more to lead the valiant clans'. The narrative ends with Pitcairne's welcome to paradise by Bruce, Wallace, Douglas, Graham and other Scots champions. The iambic pentameters flow easily if without distinction, and the patriotic sentiment, claiming that English gold had bought the Union, is echoed in two later poems, *A Tale of Three Bonnets* and *The Vision*. Ramsay's first volume of collected poems included several in this vein, for example, *Edinburgh's Address to The Country, Wealth Or The Woody* and *The Prospect Of Plenty*, attesting to his conviction that Scotland, poor as she was, would expand and prosper, with or without the benefits promised by Union.

In a doggerel verse dated 6 June 1712 a member of the Easy Club referred to what must have been Ramsay's first poem in Scots, *Elegy on Maggy Johnston, who died anno 1711*. Maggy Johnston had kept a tavern on the road to Morningside beyond Bruntsfield Links, where Edinburgh's citizens played golf. The poem's attraction lay not only in the intensity of the Scots vocabulary but also in the stanza-form.

Whan we were weary'd at the gowff,   [golf]
Then Maggy Johnston's was our howff: [meeting place]
Now a' our gamesters may sit dowff   [mournfully]
     Wi' hearts like lead.
Death wi'his rung rax'd her a yowff   reached out and hit her
     And sae she died.   with his cudgel]

Ramsay found the stanza, which he called 'Standard Habby' (standard because frequently used), in James Watson's *Choice Collection of Comic and Serious Scots Poems, both Ancient and Modern* where it occurs in Robert Sempill of Beltrees's *Life and Death Of The Piper Of Kilbarchan* (Habby Simson). Watson's volumes, which included *Christ's Kirk On The Green* among other poems by sixteenth- and seventeenth-century Scotsmen, inspired young Ramsay with a lifelong enthusiasm for the old *makars*. In 1718 he published an edition of the anonymous *Christ's Kirk*, adding cantos in his own version of Middle Scots. Not only was he fascinated by the language and vocabulary to which Watson's compilation introduced him but he also savoured the various metres and the elaborate, often traditional, stanzas in which these 'good old Bards' experimented. Poems in Scots by Ramsay started to appear in broadsides or in small collections together with a number in English, modelled on the style of Pope and his contetemporaries.

In 1721 Ramsay collected his poems and issued them to four hundred and sixty-four subscribers including influential literary figures in England (Pope, Steele, Burchet and Arbuthnot among them) and many from aristocratic families in Scotland. This approach may be thought calculating on present-day standards but in the eighteenth century, patronage and dependence upon sound public and private relations with people who might aid his advancement was a recognised necessity for an ambitious poet or artist. A number of Ramsay's subscribers had houses in Edinburgh, or were connected with the Law Courts there, and a select number owned country estates close to the city. His list also included members of the Town Council, prominent merchants and professional men. Sir John Clerk of Penicuik, Baron of the Exchequer, Duncan Forbes of Culloden, later Lord Advocate, his nephew John Forbes of Newhall and Lord Somerville of The Drum, to name four of the more distinguished, took a lively interest in painting, architecture and antiquities, agricultural reform and the theatre, and their spacious country houses became centres for gatherings of congenial like-minded friends. Ramsay was a welcome visitor. It cannot be said that his relations with Edinburgh's upper classes were one-sided or sycophantic and his long, intimate correspondence with Clerk and others, such as his friend of later years, Sir Alexander Dick of Prestonfield, makes it clear that their enthusiasms were genuinely shared and their friendships unqualified.[2]

Ramsay's wider reputation began to spread on the publication of the 1721 collection. His fame rests on it and on the 1728 volume of *Poems*, on *Ever Green, Tea-Table Miscellany* and especially on his pastoral drama *The Gentle Shepherd*, first published in 1725, though its conception dates from

1720 or even earlier. A third volume, including all other poems published during his lifetime, some posthumous verses, and a number of compositions never before printed, appeared under our editorship in the Scottish Text Society series. Ramsay classified the content of his 1721 *Poems* as being 'Serious, Comick, Satyrick, Pastoral, Lyrick, Epistolary and Epigrammatick', a description which also fits the 1728 volume; like Dunbar he exhibited great versatility in 'making' on any subject that attracted him.

In the fashion of his time, Ramsay introduced the 1721 volume with a Preface, justifying the inclusion of English verses like *The Morning Interview* and *Content* by saying that 'good Poetry may be in any language' and that these poems differed from the others only in spelling so that 'tho' the Words be pure English, the Idiom or Phraseology is still Scots'. The poet in Scots, he explained, could draw on richer resources and should write in the manner natural to him. This statement begs several questions relating to contemporary usage of Scots. Writers hoping to reach a public beyond Scotland thought that, as far as possible, they should avoid Scots, though the majority of Ramsay's Scottish subscribers spoke Scots-English, and were familiar with and enjoyed using Scots phrases. In *The Gentle Shepherd*, the laird, Sir William Worthy, uses both Scots and English and is meant to represent his class, a class whose national identity was retained by a preferred though necessarily selective use of Scots. Scots was a living speech at all levels of social contact and the vocabulary and phrases of Ramsay's *Elegies* or of the *Familiar Epistles* between Hamilton of Gilbertfield and himself were cast in a heightened form of contemporary idiom. Thomas Ruddiman, who published Gawain Douglas's *Aeneid*, probably helped Ramsay with the glossaries appended to both 1721 and 1728 volumes. Ruddiman was one of several writers who thought that Scotland's living speech was in great part a survival of old Scots and Sir John Clerk held to the same opinion. Ramsay's joy on first discovering the language of Henryson and Dunbar was not that of an antiquary for a relic of the past, but of a poet confronted with a vocabulary which he could claim as his own. Critics of his editing, notably Hailes and Pinkerton, pointed out that Ramsay was ignorant of Middle Scots forms but this did not impair his ability to use its surviving vocabulary. Any stanza from the *Elegies* or *Familiar Epistles* will furnish examples of that intimate colloquy, light, amusing and inventive, through which both Fergusson and Burns later brought their vignettes of town and country to life. This stanza from Ramsay's first *Answer* to Hamilton

May I be licket wi' a Bittle,	[beaten] [club]
Gin of your numbers I think little;	
Ye're never rugget, shan, nor kittle,	[untidy] [pitiful] [vague]
But blyth and gabby	[fluent in speech]
And hit the Spirit to a Title,	
Of Standard Habby	

is the work of a genuine pioneer, for the Scots verse epistle, later so brilliantly employed by Burns, originated with these exchanges between Ramsay and Hamilton. Their purpose was to show friendship, and bestow good-natured criticism in a rustic diction, employing a mode of self-conscious burlesque which, without loss of dignity, could mock the pretentious and over-serious.

The impression of venturesomeness is heightened by the varied stanza forms. As well as 'standard Habby', Ramsay experimented with light octosyllabics and the *Christ's Kirk* verse pattern, recalled the dignified movement of Montgomerie's *Cherrie and the Slae*, and deftly caught the elusive lilt of the traditional song, as in *Up in the Air*:

> Now the sun's gane out o' sight,
> Beet the ingle and snuff the light: [kindle the fire]
> In glens the fairies skip and dance:
> And witches wallop o'er to France,
>   Up in the air
>   On my bonny grey mare.
> And I see her yet, and I see her yet

In his 1721 Preface Ramsay calls his subscribers' attention to 'his imitations' of Horace's Odes. Ramsay's attempts to relate Scots to a Latin original were, as he said, 'only to be reckoned a following of his Manner'. He made ten such versions, of which five were printed in the 1721 volume. Of these the best is *To The Phiz*, from *Odes* I, ix, which begins:

> Look up to Pentland's towring taps,   [peaks]
> Buried beneath great wreaths of snaw
> O'er ilka cleugh, ilk scar and slap,   [shelter between rocks] [bare patch
> As high as ony Roman wa'.   [wall]   on a hillside] [gap]
>
> Driving their baws frae whins or tee,   [golf balls]
> There's no ae gowfer to be seen,   [not a single golfer]
> Nor dousser fowk wysing a jee   [more prudent people] [directing
>   in a curving course]
> The byas bouls on Tamson's green   [bowls with a tendency to curve]

—a complex set of images which brings Edinburgh and Rome into conjunction. The opening stanza conjures up a familiar scene, for the Pentland Hills, walked over by generations of Edinburgh people, are only an hour's distance on foot from the city. Newhall, thought to be the locale of *The Gentle Shepherd*, is just beyond them. Soracte, near Horace's Sabine home which Ramsay alludes to in the poem's epigraph, is twenty-six miles from Rome but visible from the capital. Correspondence of imagery is sometimes close but, as Ramsay admitted, he understood Horace 'but faintly in the original' and his model was itself a translation. Nevertheless, his transmutation of the Odes lost little by not being academically inspired and no contemporary translator could have achieved the striking effect of this sketch of Edinburgh life, as Ramsay conveyed it through his vivid picture of 'gowfers' and 'dousser fowk' barred from their outdoor sports by the harsh, merciless northern winter. What Ramsay communicates is an urgent realism in the tradition of Henryson and Douglas, whose impressions of inclement weather were charged, as Ramsay's were, from the same local experience.

The 1728 volume, dedicated to all Ramsay's subscribers, contains a number of celebratory verses in English, marking his acquired social connections. By this time the poet had been welcomed into polite society at a high level and his lines praising the Royal Company of Archers responded to his own election as 'Bard to the Royall Company'. The tone of the 1728 Preface is far more self-assured than that of his 1721 introduction and should be counted a manifesto of Ramsay's claim to importance in the history of Scottish literature. In it he observed that, through his novel presentation of examples of the old makars' writings.

> ... the most part of our Gentlemen, who are generally Masters of the most useful and politest *Languages*, can take pleasure (for a Change) to speak and read their own.

Ramsay's labours as gatherer and imitator of older forms of Scots speech and writing defined his ambition to reveal their rich literary tradition to his fellow-countrymen by printing as many examples as he could find of pre-1600 Scots poetry. In *Ever Green* (1724)—dedicated to the Royal Company of Archers—Barbour, Henryson, Dunbar, Douglas, Alexander Scott, Montogmerie and others were transcribed from the Bannatyne manuscript of the sixteenth century and revived for Ramsay's own and later generations, but Ramsay's editing was to be subjected to harsh criticism, verging (in the case of Pinkerton) on abuse. His conifident statement that he had published the works of the makars

> ... neat, correct and fair,
> Frae antique manuscripts, with utmost care

drew the fire of later and more expert editors, who criticised his glossary, his editorial practices, his mis-transcriptions, alterations of originals, and general lack of fine scholarship, preferring to disregard the pioneering character of *Ever Green* and its popularising aim, which compelled Ramsay to make concessions to fastidious contemporary tastes. Certain of the problems which confronted him, for example, in connection with pronunciation and metrics, are still puzzling and the positions of present-day linguists are less firm than their authoritative statements imply. Ramsay's texts betray his inability to recreate in his own mind the sound of Middle Scots. 'This fals warld is bot transitory', from Dunbar's *Lament For The Makars*, is not to be turned into 'This world false and transitory' without changing both meaning and aural effect. His glossary of Middle Scots was indeed inadequate but it is less than fair to describe it, as Hailes did in his

Preface to *Ancient Scottish Poems* (1755). as 'redundant, erroneous and imperfect'. Ramsay's editing, like Watson's, must be judged in its context and though *Ever Green* was not definitive it was undoubtedly superior to Watson's *Collection*, which relied upon printed sources, not manuscripts. Unfortunately *Ever Green* was reprinted only four times, unlike *Tea-Table Miscellany* which went through twelve reprints during Ramsay's lifetime and set the seal on his reputation as a collector of songs.

One of his early verses, *To The Music Club*, praises local enthusiasm for native rather than imported tunes but Ramsay aimed at an English as much as, or more than, a Scottish audience.[3] English taste for Scots song was by then well established since Tom D'Urfey's *Wit and Mirth*, *Pills To Purge Melancholy* had set the fashion going in 1699; it was reprinted twenty years later. The first important Scots song book, published in London, William Thomson's *Orpheus Caledonius*, (1725) included a group of songs by Ramsay with new words set to old melodies. Scots living in London, like Arbuthnot, as well as Gay, Pope and Swift, were, we are told, ready 'to unite their strength and abilities in the composition of a song;[4] and this movement, growing in the salons of London, Bath and other places claiming sophistication, popularised a number of Scottish tunes for which words had been composed. In *Tea-Table Miscellany* Ramsay offered his public the best-known and the most 'Scottish' of collections obtainable at that time. Until Herd's *Ancient and Modern Scots Songs, Popular Ballads &c* appeared in 1769, the *Miscellany* had no real rival, though many publications of the kind had been issued; Ramsay's helpers, who included Sir John Clerk, Robert Crawford, Hamilton of Bangour, Hamilton of Gilbertfield and David Mallet, among others, were thus able to communicate their own patriotic enthusiasm to several generations of amateur musicians. In the Preface to the 1730 edition of this four-volume collection, Ramsay justified the *Miscellany* by its wide distribution:

> The Fifth Edition in four Years, and the general Demand for the Book by Persons of all Ranks, wherever our Language is understood, is a sure evidence of its being acceptable. My worthy friend *Dr Bannerman* tells me from *America*,

> > Nor only do your Lays o'er *Britain* flow,
> > Round all the Globe your happy sonnets go;
> > Here thy soft Verse, made to a *Scottish* Air,
> > Are often sung by our *Virginian* Fair . . .

Since he particularly wished his collection to appeal to the 'the fair Singer' and his 'Dear Lasses' who would sing round their tea-tables, Ramsay was not greatly concerned with retaining the original words of old melodies, and changed phrases as he saw fit. His versions of *Clout The Caldron* and *The Generous Gentleman* show the limitations of his method and his cavalier treatment of oral sources. Even so, his shortcomings as editor are less serious here than in *Ever Green*, where he was aware of the special literary and historical importance of his material. His aim was to entertain and please, and his flexible standards were governed by the interests of his audience who sought to make their own music, and cared little about the accuracy of Ramsay's transcripts.

The songs which Ramsay wrote himself include the lyric *My Peggy is a young thing*. It opens his finest achievement, *The Gentle Shepherd*, described as 'a pastoral comedy' and set in a Scotland of sixty years earlier. The play takes its beginnings from two earlier eclogues, *Patie and Roger* and *Jenny and Meggy*, and was apparently written for the Grammar School of Haddington, whose Head Master, John Lesly, encouraged his pupils in dramatic exercises. The play's first version contained only four songs but the Haddington boys seem to have been sufficiently inspired by a performance of Gay's *Beggars' Opera* (which had sixty songs) to ask Ramsay to convert the original into a 'ballad-opera'. In public performance this modified *Gentle Shepherd* included twenty-one songs, reprinted in subsequent editions of *Tea-Table Miscellany* and in other collections. It was as a ballad-opera that Ramsay's pastoral achieved its greatest popularity and in view of this success it is unlikely that he regretted the change as much as the *MS Life* claims he did.

The period of the play is the Restoration, when the local laird, Sir William Worthy, returns from exile. The imaginary setting is his estate on the south side of the Pentland Hills; in fact, the details are of Newhall, the country house of Ramsay's friend John Forbes. Ramsay's first-hand knowledge of rural life and the actual ways of shepherds decided the type of pastoral he would write. Historically, his play comes towards the end of the long-drawn-out debate on pastoral which grew out of the 'Ancient versus Moderns' quarrel conducted in literary circles both in England and France. Ramsay's dedication to the Countess of Eglintoun hopes that he 'be class'd with Tasso and Guarini, and sing with Ovid' but he was really no 'Ancient'. He brought something novel to the *genre*: his characters reflect near-contemporary customs and attitudes and command far more attention than the simple plot requires. Long established pastoral conventions provided the framework, but Ramsay's Lowland peasants live realistic lives. They are not figures of the kind associated with Pope or Phillips, nor survivors from the whimsical comedy which presented country-folk as buffoons. In Act I Roger tells Patie 'I'm born to strive with hardships sad and great', and Bauldy, the clown of the play, bewails his unrequited love for Peggy—'tis war (worse) than Hell', he complains—while Jenny tells Peggy of the actual effects of poverty and bleak climate on the wedded state in one of the most poignant passages in the whole of Scots literature (I,ii,128–41). Symon refers to a shepherd who buys 'books of history, sangs or sport' and Glaud, another old shepherd, recalls the cheerful hospitality of the dispossessed laird who used to invite all the cottars to share his board and to drink till they could no longer stand up by themselves. These scenes, recreating not only the homespun conviviality which Ramsay himself valued so much, but also emphasising the unlovely side of the peasant's life, could not have been conceived without personal experience.

Acts IV and V are, if not the most original, certainly the most animated. The 'supernatural' elements, gradually introduced from Act II onwards, are represented mainly in the character of Mause, thought by Bauldy to be a witch who will help him get the love of Peggy, and in the 'spaeman' or fortune-teller disguise adopted by the returning laird. Act IV opens with a scene of rough comedy, when Glaud's sister Madge gives the hapless Bauldy a bloody nose and puts him to flight, crying triumphantly,

I think I've towzl'd his harigalds a wee;   [shaken up his guts a little]
He'll no soon grein to tell his love to me.   [be anxious to]

She plots with Mause to punish Bauldy further by dressing up as a ghost while Mause plays the witch. Bauldy's account of his terrifying ordeal anticipates Burns's *Tam o'Shanter*, but while Burns's supernatural is both real and comic, Ramsay's is induced by a practical joke; the effect of the verse in conveying the impression of rapid movement controlled by an unseen force is, however, much the same in both instances. Some of the best lines in the play are to be found in scenes wherein Ramsay recollects places which his audiences knew and habitually visited. One example must suffice, from Act I, scene ii:

Go farer up the burn to Habby's How,   [farther]
Where a' the sweet's of spring and summer grow;
Between twa birks, out o'er a little lin   [birch trees] [pool]
The water fa's, and makes a singand din;   [falls] [singing]
A pool breast-deep beneath, as clear as glass,
Kisses with easy whirles the bordring grass

—a rural vista very similar to the one visible today between Habby's How and Carlops, later to be finely illustrated by David Allan's coloured drawings in the 1788 Foulis edition, greatly admired by Burns.

The original character of *The Gentle Shepherd*, not a 'romantic' so much as a naturalistic work, was praised by the *literati* of a later day, who, while understanding that Ramsay's representation of peasant manners was authentic, nevertheless charged him with using Scots to depict only low-life characters and subjects so that the success of his pastoral came to be regarded as potentially damaging to the language. This was the opposite of the effect at which the poet aimed and the long-term result of such criticism did not help his reputation. Unfortunately, little contemporary comment is recorded, though Sir John Clerk of Penicuik did write to Ramsay praising the work and offering advice on possible improvements.[5]

The play's success speaks for itself. Twenty editions of *The Gentle Shepherd* appeared in Ramsay's lifetime and a further forty-five before 1800. A Drury Lane performance, reduced to two Acts and with many cuts, was given by Theophilus Cibber in 1731, but until 1751 the play was put on in Scotland only by amateurs, who spoke Scots naturally. When touring companies offered it their adopted 'cottar' accents they were greeted with mirth. Long after Ramsay's death, misguided attempts to rewrite the pastoral in English throughout were treated with derision by reviewers who thought that audiences could follow the original, even in London.[6] The *Gentle Shepherd* was a dramatic experiment, national in character, touching a responsive chord in Scots people and appealing to audiences in both England and America, the latter mainly immigrants drawn by nostalgia. Ramsay's 'home-bred' Muse was not to be denied and twentieth century judgements, developing from J W Mackail's 1924 article in *Essays and Studies*, claim Ramsay as an innovator and even as a precursor of the romantic movement. But, though *Ever Green* and *The Gentle Shepherd* may seem to point towards that new dawn, Ramsay himself was no visionary. His patriotic zeal fired him to idealise the past while his urge for practical improvement regarding the present was neither revolutionary nor innovative by design.

In the 1720s Ramsay published *Fables and Tales*, modelled on Gay's *Fables* and consisting of thirty stories, the majority inspired by the French fabulists La Motte and La Fontaine. His first source was an English translation but he informed his readers that he had endeavoured to make the French authors 'speak Scots'. The *MS Life* states that Ramsay was a master of French, no doubt an exaggeration, though Edinburgh did contain teachers who may have given him lessons. Comparisons show a more consistent word-for-word accuracy than in his Horace versions, but the situations and idiom are cruder and an earthy vitality takes the place of the elevated sophistication of his models. Even the best of his renderings, *The Twa Lizards* and *Jupiter's Lottery*, entirely lack the Gallic sharpness of wit required for such a task as he set himself in the *Fables and Tales*, though in *The Twa Lizards* Ramsay, like Henryson and Burns, reveals a fine touch when he describes small creatures:

> Beneath a Tree, ae Shining Day
> On a Burn-bank twa Lizards lay
> Beeking themsells now in the beams,   [warming]
> Then drinking of the cauller Streams.   [fresh]

Elsewhere the poet's vocabulary of about 1,500 Scots words proved adequate in relatively short poems, e.g. *The Function Of Satiric Poetry*, the fragment commencing 'Like twa fell flesher Tikes inured to Quarell' and more rarely in narratives like *The Monk and The Miller's Wife*, based on the anonymous fifteenth century *Freris Of Berwick*, well told in swiftly-moving humorous Scots. His early biographer, Woodhouselee, said that this 'would of itself be his passport to immortality as a comic poet', even comparing him with Chaucer and Boccaccio in native strength. In serious works he found it more difficult to sustain the language; *Keitha*, a pastoral lament on the death of the Countess of Wigtown, moves awkwardly and fails to fulfil the promise of its opening lines.

Throughout his creative period Ramsay prospered in business, giving up his wig-making in favour of bookselling, for him a more appropriate trade. In about 1725 he founded, in his bookshop, the first circulating library in the United Kingdom. Situated in the middle of Edinburgh's old town near the Law Courts, this establishment became a recognised meeting-place for persons of literary and artistic interests. Ramsay was able to get his patrons the volumes they wanted and his correspondence records the range of classical and foreign books which formed the basis of his stock.

Ramsay's views on the arts were enlightened and in 1729 he helped to found the 'Academy of St Luke' to encourage painting, sculpture and architecture, and an essay attributed to him, *Some Few Hints In Defence Of Dramatical Entertainments*,[7] sums up his style of thinking on the theatre, an institution which had long met with opposition in Edinburgh. Inevitably, he came into conflict with the more parochially-minded members of the Edinburgh Presbytery when he himself opened a theatre in Carubber's Close in 1736, showing Dryden's *The Recruiting Officer* and a ballad-opera by George Farquhar, *The Virgin Unmask'd*. This venture was impeded by Walpole's 1737 Licensing Act and eventually, after a long battle, Ramsay's theatre was closed in 1739[8] Contemporary verses with threatening titles like *The Flight of Religious Piety from Scotland Upon the Account of Ramsay's lewd Books &c and the Hell-bred Play-House Comedians who debauch all the Faculties of the Souls of our Rising Generation* indicate the prejudice with which Ramsay had to contend. The library and bookshop were not suppressed and both survived for nearly a century.[9]

One of Ramsay's last significant poems, *The Marrow Ballad* (1738), a subtle attack on clerical hypocrisy and the 'unco-guids', merits special mention. This barbed satire mocks at the brothers Ralph and Ebenezer Erskine, leaders of the evangelical party in the Church of Scotland, who espoused the narrow sectarian doctrines embodied in Edward Fisher's *Marrow of Modern Divinity* (1646, re-issued in 1718). Even in its unpublished state, *The Marrow Ballad* is a small masterpiece. Set to the well-known tune *Fy let us a' to the bridal*, this is an open-air poem, in the tradition of *Christ's Kirk* and *Peblis, to the Play* and indeed recalls the latter's crude sexuality:

> And there will be blinkan eyed Bessy
>   blyth Baby and sweet lipet Megg[10]
> and mony a rosie cheek'd Lassie
>   with coats kiltet to their mid-legg   [petticoats]
> to gar them gang clever and lightly
>   we'll carry their hose and their shoon   [shoes]
> syne kiss them and clap them fou tightly   [very]
>   as soon as the sermon is done
>
> The sun will be sunk in the west
>   before they have finished the wark   [work, action]
> then behind a whin Bush we can rest
>   ther's mekle good done in the dark.   [much]
> There Tammy to Tibby may creep
>   Slee Sandy may mool in with Kate   [fornicate with]
> while other dowf sauls are asleep   [sad, dull]
>   we'll handle deep matters of State.

With unerring accuracy, Ramsay, in one of his most inspired moments, has exposed the homespun hypocrisy surrounding such furtive frolics.

In his early fifties, Ramsay issued another volume, *A Collection of Scots Proverbs* (1737) of which the only original part was his *Dedication*, addressed 'To the Tenantry of Scotland, Farmers of the Dales and Storemasters of the Hills'. His stated aim was to preserve the 'wise sayings and observations' of Lowland tradition so that his audience, recalling 'the Spirit of their bauld Forbears', might pass on these pithy phrases to the next generation. The whole compilation testifies to the sharp, bitter and contentious farm and village life of the times. Ramsay arranged, in alphabetical order, 2,522 proverbs mostly from other collections, and supplied a glossary. Their idiom, rooted in rural Scotland, was the very spring of Ramsay's literary vocabulary, though his contribution lay in the spelling, hardly at all in the substance of the proverbs themselves, which had parallels in England and other European countries. Many of them are still current and others were formulas used or recognised by Scots of all classes until recently, e.g. *Make a kirk and a mill o't: Keep your ain fish guts to your ain sea maw: He that will to Cowpar will to Cowpar*, and *Biting and scarting* [scratching] *is Scot's Fowk's Wooing*. The *Dedication*, Ramsay's only composition in Scots prose, resembles the language of *The Gentle Shepherd*, and, like most of Ramsay's Scots, is best read aloud:

> As nathing helps our Happiness mair than to have the Mind made up with right Principles, I desire you for the thriving and Pleasure of you and yours, to use your Een and lend your Lugs (ears) to these good auld Saws, that shine with wail'd [choice] Sense, and will as lang as the Warld wags

and he asks his readers to make their children learn them by heart.

No contemporary challenged Allan Ramsay's supremacy as a poet in Scots and his warm personality encouraged other poets to lend active assistance or give advice, as in the case of *Tea-Table Miscellany*. He probably made himself known to Pope's circle in London through Clerk's cousin William Aikman and must have encountered Steele and Gay during their respective visits to Edinburgh, for in a letter to Clerk, Ramsay confessed: 'I am the more pleasd with my self when you tell me of my general likeness to Gay' and anticipated a personal introduction.

Descriptions by Ramsay himself and others support the image which his works create—that of a benevolent soul 'mair to Mirth than Grief inclin'd', largely self-educated, possessed of a considerable variety of literary and light artistic talents, imaginatively patriotic and intelligently practical in conceiving schemes for improving Edinburgh's cultural life. Ramsay was no genius, like Burns or the young Fergusson, but he was clever and independent, dedicated to versifying inventively and editing as well as he knew how. His last dated poem, *An Epistle to James Clerk, Esq of Pennycuik* (1755) looks back at fifteen years of leisure in his oddly-shaped house, the Goose Pie, still standing on the Castlehill in Edinburgh, where he kept his cow and hens. His wife had died in 1743 and the poet is ruminating on his last years, 'frae schochling [troublesome] trade and danger free', aware of death's approach but sure that his poetic voice would not sink into silence:

> Sir, I have sung, and yet may sing,
> Sonnets that o'er the dales may ring,
> And in gash glee couch moral saw,   [sensible song]
> Reese virtue and keep vice in awe;   [praise]
> Make villainy look black and blue,
> And give distinguish'd worth its due;
> Fix its immortal fame in verse,
> That me till doomsday shall rehearse.

Ramsay died on 7 January 1758. In a 1756 letter to Sir Alexander Dick he refers to himself as 'a philosopher and lover of all the calm and social virtues'. Glimpses of the poet in these declining years show him assured, confident that he had justified his own existence and won for himself a modest place in the pantheon of poets in Scots. Without him literature in Scotland would have taken a different road. He ensured that the native Muse would survive and flourish.

The place accorded Ramsay by literary historians has, however, been always far too modest.[11] No named poet marked his passing and the obituary notice in the *Edinburgh Evening Courant*, which mentioned 'that noble and elegant Scots pastoral' and spoke of 'his merit as a collector, as well as a poet', was brief. Yet he was praised by the minor poet Alexander Ross, whose *Helenore*, a poem inspired by *The Gentle Shepherd* begins with an 'Invocation' to Ramsay and in a later generation his name and fame were admired by Burns who, in his First Commonplace Book, praises 'The excellent Ramsay and the still more excellent Fergusson'. Like theirs, Ramsay's ideals were those of the classic Scottish poet.

NOTES

1   Text of the poem by F W Freeman and Alexander Law in 'Allan Ramsay's first published poem; the poem to the memory of Dr Archibald Pitcairne', *The Bibliotheck*, 9, no 7 (1979), pp 153–60.

2   For more detail see *Works*, IV, pp 43–6 and Ramsay's correspondence with Clerk in the same volume.

3   Ramsay's letter to Andrew Millar (Letter 31 in *Works* IV) reveals that the 1732–3 edition of *Tea-Table Miscellany* was not to be produced in Edinburgh and that Allan Ramsay the Younger, who had recently gone to London to study under Hyssing, was to act as his father's agent in making arrangements for publication there.

4   From the poet Cowper to the Rev William Unwin; quoted in James Kinsley, 'The Music of the Heart' *Renaissance and Modern Studies*, VIII (1964), p 882.

5   Copy of letter supplied by Dr Iain Brown of the National Library of Scotland.

6   Vanderstop's version 'done into English' (1777) was described as 'undone into

English' (*Monthly Review*, 57). The same journal, reviewing *Select Songs of The Gentle Shepherd* at the Theatre Royal, Drury Lane, referred to 'the beautiful and dramatic Scotch pastoral of Allan Ramsay', but went on to say that 'the alterations are altogether for the worse' (65, 1781) *See also* vols 76 (1787) and 86 (1791).

7   This piece and the preceding fragment 'In Defence of an Edinburgh Theatre' were probably connected with an earlier visit by Tony Aston's troupe of actors, which ended in Aston's hasty departure under Presbytery pressure. Ramsay ridiculed the situation in *Prologue for Aston* (*Works*, II, p 197).

8   A full account of Ramsay's management is given in *Works*, IV, pp 33–40.

9   See *Works*, IV, p 64, n 74, and p 65, n 82, for details of Ramsay's shop and subsequent history of the library.

10 *blinkan-eyed Bessy . . . sweet lipet Meg* recalls Ramsay's earlier poem *Lucky Spence's Last Advice*. Ramsay's elegy on this well known Edinburgh 'madame' refers to 'black-ey'd Bess and Mim-mou'd Meg' as amateurs whom she procured.

11 See *The Library of Literary Criticism of English and American Authors*, ed C W Moulton (1902: repr Gloucester, Mass. 1966, 5 volumes), III, pp 403–11 for a gathering of comments on Ramsay by nineteenth-century *literati*.

FURTHER READING

Martin, B, Oliver, J W, Kinghorn, A M and Law, A (eds), *The Works of Allan Ramsay*, (Scottish Text Society, Third and Fourth Series, 6 vols, Edinburgh and London 1954–75). This edition is cited throughout the chapter

Kinghorn, A M and Law, A (eds), *Poems by Allan Ramsay and Robert Fergusson* (Edinburgh and London, 1974, 1985)

Crawford, Thomas, *Society and the Lyric: a Study of the Song Culture of Eighteenth-Century Scotland* (Edinburgh, 1979), chapter V ('*The Gentle Shepherd*', pp 70–96) and Mr Crawford's 'The Vernacular Revival and the Poetic Thrill: a Hedonistic Approach' in *Scotland and the Lowland Tongue*, McClure, J Derrick (ed), (Aberdeen, 1983)

Freeman, F W, 'The Intellectual Background of the Vernacular Revival Before Burns', in *Studies in Scottish Literature*, XVI (1981) pp 160–87

MacLaine, Allan H, *Allan Ramsay*, (New York, 1985)

Chapter 5

James Thomson and the Anglo-Scots

MARY JANE SCOTT

James Thomson, author of *The Seasons*, was but the best known of the many Anglo-Scottish poets of the eighteenth century. Yet twentieth-century Scottish critics have shown the Anglo-Scots little sympathy; they have too often banished them to a bleak literary borderland for being too English, and not quite Scottish enough. Thomson's achievements can help us appreciate the potential and positive contribution of these Anglo-Scots; for most had more complex, and indeed more noble, motives for adopting English as their literary language than the pathetic, social-climbing Boswellian stereotype might suggest. They knew, for example, that writing in English, already the practical language for the business of Britain, would allow them to reach a wider audience. Again, writing in English was not necessarily a pro-Union political statement; nor did using English make these poets any less Scottish. Writers could, if they so wished, move to London, lose their accent and even change their name to a more English-sounding one (like David Malloch/Mallet). They could master the mechanics of Augustan English verse (like William Hamilton of Bangour). They could loudly proclaim their 'British' patriotism in poetry and song (like Thomson himself). But they could not will themselves to be other than Scottish, even if they wanted to—and most, deep down, did not.

For Scottishness is a stubborn thing. It is not simply a matter of language or locale. It takes more than a Scottish birth-certificate, or a vocabulary sprinkled with Scotticisms, to make a Scottish poet. It is all those intangible influences—religious, historical, educational, aesthetic, geographical, linguistic, literary, and broadly cultural—which work together to determine national and individual character. Such potent influences can scarcely be disguised in a 'foreign' language; indeed those Anglo-Scots who tried the hardest to become 'English' poets were the very ones who gave Anglo-Scots a bad name. Most, like, Thomson, were proud of their Scottishness and, far from trying to conceal their nationality, paid explicit tribute to their native parts of Scotland. In their poetry we find affectionate references, for example, to Smollett's Leven Water, Armstrong's Liddell, Mallet's Invermay, Grainger's Grampian Hills, John Wilson's Clyde, Mickle's Eskdale Braes, Beattie's unnamed but lovingly described Dee Valley and Kincardineshire, and Thomson's own Tweed, Jed and Cheviots.[1]

While the relatively unfamiliar formal English medium was a problem for many Anglo-Scots, it was not an insurmountable obstacle; Thomson overcame the limitations of language, and he did so not by trying to fit his poetry into an intractable English language, but by daring to fit the English language to his own—Scottish—poetic voice. He saw the great potential of English as a viable medium for a true *Scottish* poetry. So it is particularly ironic that he, foremost among Anglo-Scottish poets, has been so efficiently appropriated into the 'English' canon, while only the Anglo-Scots of lesser vision and achievement have been left exclusively to Scottish literary posterity.

Who, then, were the Anglo-Scots? Simply stated, they were Scottish poets who chose to write in English rather than in Gaelic or Scots. Some stayed at home to practice their art, including the Rev Mr Robert Blair (*The Grave*, 1743), William Hamilton of Bangour, William Falconer (*The Shipwreck*, 1762), William Wilkie (*The Epigoniad*, 1757), the Rev Dr Thomas Blacklock, James Beattie (*The Minstrel*, 1771, 1774) and John Wilson (*The Clyde*, 1764). Others, like Thomson himself, went to England or farther afield to seek their literary fortune. These include Thomson's friends David Mallet (*The Excursion*, 1728), Joseph Mitchell, and Dr John Armstrong ('Winter', c. 1725; *The Art of Preserving Health*, 1744), and, in the next generation, poet and novelist Tobias Smollett, James Macpherson (*Ossian*, 1760–63), Dr James Grainger (*The Sugar-Cane*, 1764) and William Julius Mickle (*The Lusiad*, 1771, 1776). These eighteenth-century Anglo-Scots were by no means uniformly bad, and they should not be lumped together as a group of inferior poetasters. True, their poetry was often conventional, and uneven in quality, yet this was not merely a matter of their writing in the 'wrong' language. Some other Scottish, and to an extent culturally-determined, qualities which most shared—their relentless and rather humourless compulsion to preach and teach, their propensity toward high-flown rhetoric, their dogged thoroughness, their sense of moral and social duty—while no doubt admirable qualities, were not conducive to poetry of a high, imaginative order.

Other Scottish characteristics, however, were more positive forces in their poetry, at least potentially, and Thomson expressed these best: their skill at accurate and loving natural description, especially of wild nature; their empirical impulse, which prompted new poetic themes and perspectives; their intimacy with a living classical culture; their native themes and traditions—the Scottish landscape itself, both Highland and Lowland, the elements of the supernatural, folk life and lore, and more subtly or even subconsciously, the sound-effects and suggestive power of the Scots language itself. Rather than trying too hard to suppress these Scottish strengths, Thomson allowed them into his English-language poetry. At first with näiveté, then with canny confidence, Thomson bent the Augustan English rules, to forge a uniquely Anglo-Scottish poetry.

James Thomson grew up in the Scottish Borders, in Southdean, Roxburghshire. His father was an austere minister of the old-style Church of Scotland. Thomson grew up speaking Scots, though he knew the English Bible well, and his first formal reading language was English. Latin was his second formal, literary language; he had the traditional Scottish humanistic education at Jedburgh's Latin Grammar School. The boy was eager to enjoy English polite letters, too, and English books were beginning to arrive in quantity in Scotland after the Union, but his father disapproved of such pursuits. He found friends in the Borders who did approve—Sir William Bennet of Grubbet, himself a Neo-Latinist poet; the Sir Gilbert Elliots of Minto, Jnr and Snr; and the boy's learned tutor Robert Riccaltoun, farmer and nature-poet who became a Moderate Presbyterian divine. These early companions were deeply involved in Scottish cultural, religious and political life, and all were Scottish patriots, yet they were also receptive to English influences, and encouraged Thomson in his Anglo-Scottish poetical ambitions.

In the Borders, too, Thomson absorbed the native tradition of ballads and songs; these would influence the color, pace and process of his descriptive poetry. He also learned the local lore, particularly the superstitions and fears of the supernatural, which would continue to haunt his poetry. Thomson shares this theme with Robert Blair, author of *The Grave*. Blair was morbidly obsessed with such supernatural themes, while Thomson was always careful to qualify them, distancing them from his rational self; yet one senses the same credulity in both Scottish poets about the sinister spirit world. Mallet, Armstrong, Beattie, Mickle, and especially Macpherson, would exploit this theme, which would become a major Romantic motif.

The most significant Scottish influence on young Thomson was the Border landscape itself—both the wild and isolated 'rough Domain' shadowed by bare, bleak hills near Southdean, and the refreshingly pretty setting around Jedburgh, by

the *Tweed* (pure *Parent-Stream*,
Whose pastoral Banks first heard my *Doric* Reed,
With, silvan *Jed*, thy tributary Brook)

('Autumn', 11. 889–91) which inspired his first verses. He would adopt the Border landscape in its many aspects, sublime as well as beautiful, both literally and symbolically, as a central theme for his poetry. The distinctive ways of seeing, thinking and feeling which he acquired in Scotland would stay with him for life. The poet's nature and nurture were thoroughly Scottish.

At the time of the Act of Union of 1707 James Thomson was only seven. Yet as a poet he shared in the national identity crisis intensified by that political settlement. Like those of so many of his contemporaries, his emotions on this issue remained an often painful mixture of nostalgic Scottish nationalism and a true desire to do whatever would be best for Scotland—even if that meant joining with England. For Thomson, being a good Scot finally meant patriotically and politically supporting the Union. One symbolic national identity he respected and adopted for his poetry was that 'Scoto-Roman' ideal[2] whereby Scotsmen drew an analogy between the ancient Roman Empire and the new Augustan Empire of Great Britain, and saw Scotland as a proud province of that Empire. In the juvenile verse entitled 'Poetical Epistle to Sir William Bennet of Grubbat, Baronet,' young Thomson thus compared himself with his poetical model Virgil, the rural, northern provincial poet of the Roman Empire, and his first patron Bennet with Virgil's patron Maecenas. The Anglo-Scots, however, were not exclusively pro-Union and Hanoverian—Hamilton of Bangour, for example, would join the Jacobites. When the Jacobites threatened Edinburgh and the Borders in 1715, the year he went up to Edinburgh University, the Whig Thomson certainly supported the government against the rebels; yet even then he probably felt (as did Allan Ramsay) a strain of sentimental Jacobitism, or nostalgia for another, more ancient Scottish identity, a mixed emotion he would have to reckon with again in 1745.

Thomson studied Arts at Edinburgh University (1715–19), where he strengthened his command of Latin and Greek, and was introduced to natural philosophy, and notably the new science of Newton. Edinburgh University was an early center for the study of Newtonianism. The poet's lifelong fascination with Newton's laws informs his descriptions as well as his religious and moral thought. His early encounter with empirical science also provided an important impetus for the new sort of accurately-descriptive poetry he would write. The spirit of empiricism particularly characterises Thomson's own poetry, and to an extent, that of the other Anglo-Scots; Thomson's greater willingness to experiment in large measure helped him to succeed where other less imaginative Anglo-Scots sometimes failed.

Thomson found education also in Edinburgh club life, and joined various literary societies; he was associated with the Worthy Club and with Joseph Mitchell's Athenian Society. Mitchell was a minor Anglo-Scottish poet and playwright; after 1720 he went to London, where he later fell out with Thomson, but in these early years he was encouraging to the younger poet. The avowed mission of the zealous Athenians was to promote Anglo-Scottish poetry. They published several volumes of new Anglo-Scottish verse, including *Lugubres Cantus* (1719), a collection of poems, some by Thomson's friends. Supportive dedicatory verses by English Athenians Ambrose Philips and Edward Young testify to a close relationship between such poets of pastoral and meditative poetry in England and their Scottish counterparts. Philips acknowledged,

> That we must own the *English* Muse is yours,
> With as much Right and Liberty as ours.[3]

The most important Athenian publication was *The Edinburgh Miscellany* (1720) where Thomson's first published poems appeared. The *Miscellany* poems show surprising diversity of forms and themes. Many are conventional pastoral, religious or meditative pieces; some are poems of natural description, such as Thomson's germinal 'Of a Country Life', a native georgic hinting at *Seasons* themes as well as the poet's creative use of language. His other contributions were the undistinguished 'Verses on receiving a Flower from his Mistress' and the ambitious Neoplatonic allegory 'Upon Happiness' (which has much in common with Ramsay's Anglo-Scottish *Content: A Poem*, published 1721). David Mallet ('DM') had several verses in the volume, and there are also poems attributed to Robert Blair ('B') and Henry Home, later Lord Kames ('Mr Hume'). Politically, the *Miscellany* poems are heterogeneous; among them are militantly Scottish nationalistic and even Jacobite poems. Yet the unifying purpose of the volume itself is its insistent and optimistic Anglo-Scottish patriotism expressed, for instance, by John Callender:

> In spite of our hereditary Snows,
> Our Winds and Ice a noble Fervour glows
> In *Scottish* Breasts, which, if improven, vyes
> With *English* Warmth produc'd in clement Skies.

Thomson's juvenile poems[4] (*c.* 1714–21) are mostly trite Anglo-Scottish apprentice pieces, but occasionally a glimmer of good poetry appears. They also anticipate the themes, modes and styles which recur in the mature poetry, and show great variety. A number deal with specifically Scottish subjects, such as tributes to Sir William Bennet and his Border estate, a witty mock-heroic picture of Edinburgh town life, some Scottish patriotic pieces modelled on Ramsay's *Tartana*, and Aesopic animal-fables recalling the fables of Henryson and Ramsay. One odd but intriguing verse is Thomson's only extant poem in Scots vernacular, 'An Elegy Upon James Therburn in Chatto', in the Scots mock-elegy tradition. The poem is coarse and crude, yet revealing; in the poet's own emendations to the MS, he can be seen deliberately trying to make the Scots diction more dense, representing a conscious effort to Scotticize his basically English literary language; *written* English was actually the more natural and familiar language for him, whereas *written* (as distinct from spoken) Scots had to be learned, copied from Ramsay and other Scots poets. (Ramsay and his Scots colleagues, incidentally, met many of the same problems as the Anglo-Scots as they learned their chosen literary language, trying to balance colloquial with formal and English Augustan elements to discover the appropriate level of language for their audience, which included many readers in England.)

English as a written medium thus came more readily to Thomson than did Scots—and Latinate English particularly so. Thomson's Latinate language has always come in for harsh criticism; insensitive readers even today find it distasteful, even comical. What they rarely acknowledge is that both written and spoken Latin, as well as Latinate English, were comfortable, natural idioms for the educated Scot in Thomson's day—more natural even than written Scots. Thomson drew from Latin diction (frequently directly, even before the words had been filtered through poetic English) to expand the range and flexibility of his formal English diction. This practice also demonstrated the poet's instinctive etymological curiosity, his interest in the origins of words, and their evolving meanings. Thomson, especially in *The Seasons*, used Latinate English to achieve greater descriptive precision as well as to exploit classical connotations. Such creative use of Latinisms compared with the aureation of the Middle Scots Makars, notably Gavin Douglas's expansion and enrichment of literary Scots. Only when Thomson's Latinate English becomes too far removed from the reality of natural description, does it sound pompous or ponderous (this was one problem with *Liberty*). Thomson also used Scots and northern or Scots-related words to stretch his poetic English vocabulary; this use of Scots analogues and archaisms, giving his English a distinctively Scottish accent, likewise reflected his historical linguistic sense. The sounds of Scots proved a significant if subtle influence on the language of *The Seasons*, while the influence of written, literary Scots (mainly Middle Scots) would gain importance later where it would complement the poet's Spenserian archaic language in *The Castle of Indolence*.

The Edinburgh literary society to which Thomson certainly belonged was called (for reasons unknown) the Grotesque Club. Another member was David Mallet, Thomson's lifelong friend who preceded him to London to write descriptive poetry in the manner of *The Seasons* (*The Excursion*) as well as lyrics and plays. Mallet, who ridiculed Thomson for being the club's clown, was an unlikeable and unprincipled man; Dr Johnson called him, 'the only Scot whom Scotchmen did not commend', and others could not understand Thomson's loyalty to him.[5]

Thomson's goal was first to become a minister of the Scottish Church; he aspired to the dual career of poet-clergyman, writing poetry of an acceptably religious nature. Role-models were rare in Scotland, but he admired Isaac Watts in England, who had successfully combined both careers. Thomson entered Divinity Hall in Edinburgh in 1719, under Professor William Hamilton, a learned, open-minded divine who hovered precariously close to the brink of Moderatism and inspired his students to think beyond the narrow bounds of old-style Calvinist theology. Hamilton prepared his pupils for the pulpit, stressing in his class assignments a clear, straightforward rhetorical style; Thomson reportedly benefited from Hamilton's kind yet candid criticism.[6] Hamilton also fostered Thomson's interest in Physico-theology—the revelation of God in His Creation; *The Seasons* is motivated by just such a religious perception of the natural world. Thomson early learned that religion and science could happily co-exist, even as fit subjects for poetry.

At Divinity Hall, Thomson almost certainly knew fellow-student Robert Blair, who was practising poetry at the time, though he was reluctant to present his work to the public until much later; his gloomily descriptive and meditative blank-verse *The Grave* was not published until 1743, when the religious climate in Scotland was more congenial to art-literature (especially that written by a minister). In Edinburgh, Thomson probably also met William Hamilton of Bangour. Thomson's friends Mallet and Joseph Mitchell went down to London before him, while Hamilton remained in Edinburgh to write his polite Augustan verse until he was exiled as a militant Jacobite in 1746. Thomson may also have met the boy John Armstrong in Edinburgh or the Borders, and Armstrong's juvenile verse 'Winter', which may have been inspired by Thomson's 'Winter', would in turn influence Thomson's own revisions. Armstrong became a physician, and soon followed Thomson south.

Thomson completed his Divinity course in 1724, but did not take the degree. Instead he made plans to go to England, where he could pursue his poetic vocation free of the strictures of the Scottish Church, live a more comfortable life than that of a clergyman in Scotland, and reach a wider and more appreciative readership for his poetry. Thomson did not literally carry a draft of 'Winter' with him when he sailed from Leith (as popular myth has it), yet in every other sense he did bring his poem with him from Scotland, to England and to English poetry. For *The Seasons*, its English language notwithstanding, is a profoundly Scottish poem, and it proves how much an Anglo-Scot could achieve.

Thomson published 'Winter', his first *Season*, in 1726. This brief edition was an immediate success, so the poet decided to complete a poetical year. 'Summer' (1727) followed, then 'Spring' (1728) and finally 'Autumn' (1730). In his Preface to 'Winter' (June, 1726) Thomson proclaims his poetic priorities and professes his calling as poet of religion and nature. He compares the 'DIVINE ART' of poetry with Revelation itself. He insists that poetry be 'once more restored to her antient Truth, and Purity' to warm the contemporary 'Wintry World of Letters'; the 'winter' image is apt and prophetic, reflecting his Scottish cultural perspective and predicting his own 'seasonal' achievement. He likewise calls for a 'Native POETRY' on his favorite theme, the '*Works of Nature*', echoing Ramsay's plea in his Preface to *The Ever Green* (1724) for a native Scottish pastoral. Thomson also praises his two chief models of nature-poetry, Job (and ultimately, the 'Almighty Author' Himself) and Virgil; these would continue to inspire not only his nature-imagery and language, but also his broader spiritual, moral and humanistic values.

Why did Thomson choose nature as his subject? In one sense, it was an outgrowth of his early religious vocation and education; he had learned that to study Creation was to study its Creator, and now he could praise as well as preach through nature-poetry. But there was another significant reason for Thomson's choice of nature for his 'native POETRY'. Realistic natural description had been a special province of the Scottish poets, both Gaelic and Scots (and more recently, of Anglo-Scots such as William Drummond of Hawthornden) long before it became a major poetic theme in England. Even the Scottish ballads frequently displayed an immediacy and drama of description. Scotland was still a rural society, and its poets have always been in close touch with the natural world; they seemed to see with acute sensitivity, to be aware of the psychological and emotional effects of nature on man, to feel strong sympathy with all creatures, and to be able to describe these perceptions with extraordinary realism. Thomson took up this long tradition of Scottish nature poetry as the vehicle for his fundamental religious purpose in *The Seasons*. Yet his more immediate inspiration was the Border landscape itself; specifically Scottish scenes abound in

The Seasons, recalled with nostalgia and love from where he made his home in England.

A favourite natural subject for Scottish poets was 'winter'—for them, the season of strongest and most direct impact. Winter description seems to have survived in Scotland along with the late-medieval northern alliterative poetic tradition. Scottish poets such as Henryson, Dunbar and Douglas traditionally had tended to describe winter with denser vernacular diction, stronger alliteration, and far more realistic visual imagery than they chose for more temperate scenes. For spring and summer description, they frequently resorted to borrowed 'Mediterranean' conventions, a practice Ramsay sharply criticized in his *Ever Green* Preface. Thomson inherited this Scottish descriptive—and winter—poetic pattern and passed it on to English poetry through *The Seasons*.

Thomson chose blank verse as the most appropriate and flexible form for his poetry portraying dynamic nature-in-process. His blank verse reflected important influences of Milton and the Authorized Version and, free from the restraint of rhyme, it was probably also the least-intimidating English verse-form for a Scotsman to master. As the poet strove for comprehensiveness within the seasonal scheme, he revised his poem many times, losing some vitality of language as he added much geographical, historical, philosophical, socio-political and scientific material. This heavy freight of added information sometimes obscured the clarity of the poem's vision, but happily did not destroy the strong and pure descriptive core of the nature-poem.

'Winter', written in Thomson's first year of acute homesickness in London, best illustrates the Scottish aspects of the miscellaneous *Seasons*. The poet greets the familiar season, and recalls his apprenticeship in 'wintry' Scotland:

> . . . Welcome, kindred Glooms!
> Cogenial Horrors, hail! With frequent Foot,
> Pleas'd have I, in my chearful Morn of Life,
> When nurs'd by careless Solitude I liv'd,
> And sung of Nature with unceasing Joy,
> Pleas'd have I wander'd thro' your rough Domain . . .
>
> ('Winter', 11. 5–10)

The sequence of three native storms which follows is a prime example of Thomson's descriptive skill, and introduces important Thomsonian and Scottish themes: energetic portrayal of the violent processes of nature; preoccupation with the supernatural; sympathetic involvement in peasant life; concern for all creatures, suffering together in a harsh environment; the urge to preach the moral lessons taught by nature; abundant use of Latinate language, including accurate Virgilian periphrasis; close attention to sound effects, especially alliteration, assonance and consonance, to capture the sounds, movement and moods of the natural world; and the choice of diction close to Scots words in sound and sense to enhance descriptive connotations.

The very realistic, wild winter rainstorm recalls, and may have been inspired by, Robert Riccaltoun's Border poem 'A Winter's Day'. The wind storm follows, arousing fear of the 'Demon of the Night'. Thomson linked such superstitions with the unenlightened religious belief still prevalent in the Borders; here, he proclaims his personal faith in God, 'Nature's KING,' who calms the storm. Despite the poet's obvious awareness of ideas of Pantheism and Deism and his generally eclectic beliefs, Thomson's Deity is the One he depicts here, all-powerful, immanent, active and providential—fundamentally, the orthodox God of Scottish Calvinism. The storm provokes a sermon attacking vanity (11. 209 ff.), resounding with that Scottish pulpit-rhetoric which echoes throughout *The Seasons*. The third storm in 'Winter', the snowstorm, describes a beautiful but deadly Border scene. Here Thomson appeals to 'Shepherds' to be kind to their 'Charges'; the poet's characteristic sympathy toward animals as fellow-creatures under the watchful eye of 'PROVIDENCE' is an attitude traditionally strong in Scottish literature.

Thomson typically reveals a deeper awareness of the evils of the fallen world than do such English optimists as Shaftesbury. He confronts the full horror of 'Winter'; the tragedy of the swain frozen to death in the blizzard ('A stiffen'd Corse, / Stretch'd out, and bleaching in the northern Blast,' 11. 320–1) is almost ballad-like in its fatalism, its chilling directness of expression. Even when the poet travels to remote or imaginary foreign scenes, as in his grisly Alpine description of wolves, 'hungry as the Grave! / Burning for Blood! bony, and ghaunt, and grim!' (11. 393–4) he is drawing on Scottish folk-memory (wolves were still a terrifying presence in early eighteenth-century Scotland), as well as on the Scottish 'grotesque' descriptive tendency; here, too, he echoes the persistent northern alliterative poetic line. Thomson added such sensational scenes (much as Mallet would do, with less discretion, in his *Excursion*) to expand his descriptive range and enhance the sublime impact of each *Season*. Foreign as well as domestic scenes thus draw strength from Thomson's recollected emotion for his native Scotland.

Foreign scenes in *The Seasons* also help to illustrate the important sociological debate, which runs right through Thomson's works, of Primitivism *v.* Progress. This neoclassical theme is highly relevant to Thomson's own situation; he himself came from Scotland, still a primitive land in many ways, and though he loved it he was painfully aware of the dire need for Progress there.[8] In 'Winter' he contrasts the unhappy, primitive Siberians with the happy Laplanders, who have adapted well to their Arctic environment (Beattie in *The Minstrel* would also make the Lapps an example of positive primitivism). Thomson also recalls, in a 'Winter' village scene of folk-dancing to 'native Music' and telling the 'Goblin-Story' (11. 617–29), the sort of wholesome rural primitivism he knew in Scotland; he contrasts this simple convivial scene with the glittering, artificial life of City and Court, and also with the prosperous, progressive Russian cities under Peter the Great. So his solution is not the simple Augustan stereotype of the honest country as opposed to the corrupt city; primitivism *per se* is not his ideal, nor is sophisticated urban life. A Virgilian, relativistic nostalgic progressivism is the closest Thomson comes to an answer, as he promotes a progress firmly grounded in georgic rural life and labour, characterised by healthy adaptation to and improvement of nature, and benefiting the whole of society. His seems the most appropriate solution for an enlightened Scotsman in the eighteenth century.

'Winter' thus exemplifies, like each *Season*, Thomson's pervasive neoclassical worldview. His roll-call of the 'Mighty Dead' (11. 424 ff), political and cultural heroes of the ancient world, is one instance where he links that familiar world with his own, and shows special regard for Roman—both Republican and Imperial—values of patriotism and social virtue; these classical values were impressed upon the poet at an early age, and provided his best models for the British national destiny, including that of its northern province Scotland. Among other noteworthy Augustan passages which are part of *The Seasons*' neoclassical vision are the pompous panegyric to 'BRITANNIA' in 'Summer' (11. 1438–1619) where again he parallels the Roman Empire with contemporary Britain, and an encomium to British 'INDUSTRY' in 'Autumn' (11. 43–150). These passages, in contrast to descriptive scenes, tend to be elevated, inflated and abstract, anticipating the declamatory rhetoric and bombastic pro-British patriotism of *Liberty*.

Violent 'Winter' ends with a dynamic description of a Border thaw and flood (corresponding to a similar 'Autumn' scene). Such pictures of nature's destructive power frequently provoke stern Calvinistic sermons; and the homily which follows could almost have come from Blair's *Grave*, as the poet warns 'fond Man' of the imminence of wintry death. Job-like, however, Thomson holds out hope of the 'SPRING' of eternal life for the virtuous and patient soul.

'Summer' represents the opposite seasonal and poetic extreme. 'Summer', along with 'Spring', are the more 'British' (and English), public and conventional *Seasons*, in contrast to the more personal, Scottish and realistic 'Winter' and 'Autumn'. 'Summer' is replete with imagery of light and colour—both Neoplatonic and Newtonian. In 'Summer' Thomson set out to describe an ideal summer's day (as did his Scots predecessor in nature poetry, Alexander Hume, in the lovely 'Of the Day Estivall', *c*. 1599). He added to his descriptive framework, over the years, numerous digressions and exotic foreign descriptions, many based on reports of tropical flora and fauna sent to him by his friend in Barbados, Anglo-Scottish playwright William Paterson. Relying on such second-hand descriptive material and evocative place-names, in 'Summer' Thomson portrays the tropics as a lush but violently primitive, uncivilized realm. Closer to home are descriptions of hay-making and more realistic (Scottish-inspired) sheep-shearing, and also the dramatic thunderstorm raging over British peaks including 'Heights of heathy *Cheviot*' (11. 1103 ff).

In 'Summer' a thunderstorm introduces the first of *The Seasons*' three interpolated tales, the story of Celadon and his beloved Amelia, who is struck by lightning (11. 1169–1268). The tale, while in pastoral guise, is a revealing instance of Thomson's lingering Scottish Calvinist determinism, even fatalism, in the face of nature's cruelty. The grotesque 'blacken'd

Corse' is evidence of the intervention of Providence ('Mysterious Heaven!' l. 1215), which man should not presume to question, demonstrating Thomson's life-long intense insistence on the limits of human reason to comprehend God's ways. The second pastoral tale, 'Damon and Musidora' (11. 1269–1370), is a sensual story of Damon's spying semi-clad Musidora as she bathes, recalling a scene where Patie peeks at Peggy and Jenny washing in the stream in Ramsay's *Gentle Shepherd* (I.ii).

In another revealing, native 'Summer' descriptive sequence, Thomson evokes a border scene, as 'His folded Flock secure, the Shepherd home / Hies, merry-hearted . . .' (11. 1664 ff). The shepherd, however, betrays his superstitions of the 'Fairy People' and 'yelling Ghost'; Thomson typically dismisses these fears ('So night-struck Fancy dreams,' 1. 1681) which were nonetheless so real to him. The amazing, accurately-observed 'Comet' in 'Summer' (11. 1693–1729) likewise raises 'superstitious Horrors', yet those 'enlightened Few, / Whose Godlike Minds Philosophy exalts' (among whom the poet hoped to be counted) welcome the cosmic event. A description on the same pattern of 'Meteors' (properly, the Aurora Borealis) occurs in 'Autumn' (11. 1103–37); again, Thomson blends scientific and descriptive detail with genuine awe, and draws the distinction between ignorant masses and 'Man of Philosophic Eye'. 'Summer' concludes with a paean to saving 'serene Philosophy', couched in conventional symbolism of the Neoplatonic 'rising Mind' which often recurs in *The Seasons*. This concept appealed to the poet's empirical sense, compelling continuing discovery of nature's truths, and leading ever closer to God. Yet his understanding of God is limited—here (as throughout his works) 'PROVIDENCE' remains too remote for the human mind to know. Thomson confirms this Calvinist awareness of man's earthly limits, and affirms his own deep religious faith, in the 'Hymn' which concludes *The Seasons*.

'Spring' is the poet's love song, ascending the scale of all Creation. It is also Thomson's personal love song, to the tune of his unrequited love for his compatriot, Elizabeth Young ('Amanda'). In 'Spring' is the most pervasive *Georgics* influence; Thomson's descriptions here, and throughout *The Seasons*, enhance Virgilian scenes and images with details from his own observation and experience. In 'Spring' he especially focuses on the 'regulated Wild' of garden and improved landscape. Thomson enjoyed, from his Border youth, a keen interest in landscape gardening, an art closely akin to his own art of descriptive poetry (and he shares his considerable knowledge of horticulture and husbandry a good deal more poetically than, for one, Grainger in his *Sugar-Cane*). In this mild *Season*, too, appears the 'SMILING GOD', a softer, more benevolent and Moderate countenance than that of the stern, Calvinistic God who shows His face elsewhere in the poem.

The Eden-Fall-Deluge sequence of 'Spring' is but one illustration in *The Seasons* of the parallel Christian and classical traditions, the Christian humanism, to which the poet was educated. The emblem of God's Covenant with man is the famous 'Rainbow' ('NEWTON . . . thy showery Prism', 11. 209–10). The Rainbow (and a corresponding, colorful description of

'Gems' in 'Summer', 11. 140–59) demonstrate the poet's enthusiastic knowledge of Newtonian science; Mallet shows similar Newtonian interest in *The Excursion*. Like Thomson's Comet and Meteor passages, his Rainbow illuminates his extraordinary ability to combine scientific accuracy, descriptive accuracy, implicit religious perception and his own true wonder at observing the beautiful phenomenon. As in his 'Poem Sacred to the Memory of Sir Isaac Newton' (1727), Thomson here defines and brings into harmonious relationship both the poetic and the scientific imaginations.

With 'Autumn', Thomson perfected his poetical seasonal cycle, and completed the first collected *Seasons* edition. 'Autumn' has special Scottish significance; here, Thomson comments most fully on Scotland's history and civilization, her people and prospects. 'Fading', fallow autumnal description clearly symbolizes Scotland's own barren contemporary situation, her need for renewal, fruition and harvest.

'Autumn' is the *Season* of 'INDUSTRY', and the poet illustrates his abstract paean with a pastoral, Virgilian parable, the third interpolated tale of 'Palemon and Lavinia' (11. 177–310). Palemon represents Art, improving Nature in the person of Lavinia; the tale follows closely the plot of *The Gentle Shepherd*. 'Autumn' is also a season of violence; after a description of a destructive storm (11. 311–431) comes a lively sequence on the autumnal cruelty of hunting, where the poet's sympathy with animals typically prevails. But a good-natured mock-heroic satire on the drunken huntsmen swiftly turns into another austere harangue on the evils of debauchery, the 'social Slaughter' (1. 561). In 'Autumn', Thomson's contemporary social concerns are perhaps most evident, and these embrace his profound concern for Scotland.

The central Scottish sequence of 'Autumn' opens in a wild, mountainous and very Scottish landscape enveloped in fog (11. 707 ff); upland mists eerily magnify a shepherd to gigantic size (a phenomenon also recorded in Hogg's *Confessions of a Justified Sinner*). Thomson delighted in describing mountains, and sorely missed such dramatic topography in the gentle, monotonous English landscape.[9] The poet's nostalgia leads him to the proud prospect of 'CALEDONIA, in romantic View.' He depicts a Hebridean scene of the well-adapted, primitive St. Kilda natives, then boasts of Scotland's many resources, her 'airy Mountains', 'waving Main', 'Forests huge, / Incult, robust, and tall', 'azure Lakes', 'watery Wealth', 'fertile Vales', and most of all, her 'manly Race, / Of unsubmitting Spirit, wise and brave . . .' (11. 800 ff). Here, too, he praises Scottish heroes: William Wallace, John Campbell, Duke of Argyle, and the poet's close friend Duncan Forbes of Culloden. He eloquently pleads for a true 'Patriot' dedicated to the improvement—indeed salvation—of Scotland. These personal reflections prompt a bitter-sweet autumnal mood of 'Philosophic Melancholy', as the poet contemplates the ideals of 'Autumn': the joyous harvest-home (a Scottish rural scene), the emblem of the happy, virtuous and productive life of nostalgic progressivism.

Several basic—and in a sense, Scottish—themes thus emerge from the vast and miscellaneous *Seasons*. The poem's central religious message was much influenced by both old-style and Moderate Calvinist beliefs. Its detailed and sensitive natural description places Thomson within the Scottish tradition of nature poetry, and represents his chief contribution to English literature. The poem's eclectic philosophy was related to Hutchesonian (as distinct from Shaftesburyian) benevolism and Christian Stoicism, and would also find parallels in the Common Sense ethics and aesthetics of his friend, the philosopher George Turnbull (Thomas Reid's teacher). Thomson's considerable knowledge of science, his empirical spirit, were stimulated at Edinburgh University; his related passion to acquire a wide range of information and experience, and his practical and generous urge to share it, linked him with several other Anglo-Scots. His social goals of Improvement and nostalgic progressivism held special significance for an eighteenth-century Scot, and were likewise ideals of the nascent Scottish Enlightenment. Thomson's humanitarian sympathy was not simply an abstract, Augustan sentiment, but grew from his own Border countryman's experience. His British patriotism was the positive patriotism of a Scot who hoped his native land would share in the general prosperity of united Britain. Classical ideals of Virgilian adaptation and rural industry, as well as Roman patriotism and social virtue, inform the poem, and native Scottish and classical images reinforce one another in this native georgic. *The Seasons*, then, is many kinds of poem. It is a religious poem, a nature poem, a philosophical and empirical poem, a socio-political poem, a scientific poem, and a neoclassical poem. As a Scottish miscellany, it brings the strengths of the poet's Scottish heritage together with a great variety of English and other influences, to prove a rare Anglo-Scottish success.

Liberty (1735–36) was not so successful. First intended to be a '*Portrait-painting of Nature*,'[10] based on Thomson's experiences on the Grand Tour, it evolved instead into an inflated neoclassical epic charting the fortunes of the Goddess of Liberty through the rise and fall of civilisations, to her current reign in Britain. This historical-allegorical scheme may have been suggested by David Lindsay's *The Monarche* (*c*. 1550); Thomson's idea of history was potentially interesting, but he found himself unable to turn the vast theme into good poetry. The least pleasant aspect of *Liberty* is its dominant tone of pro-British chauvinism. This tone is, to an extent, the voice of a Scot (and Opposition Whig) on the defensive; Scots in England suffered strong prejudice and scorn throughout the century, aggravated by the current threat of Jacobitism. In *Liberty* Thomson launches a vituperative attack on the Stuart monarchy, probably to protect himself from charges of Jacobitism as well as to emphasize his Hanoverian allegiance. There is a similar anti-Stuart statement in the patriotic pageant *Alfred, A Masque* (1740) which Thomson wrote with Mallet.

Even in its patriotic bombast, however, *Liberty* reveals Thomson's growing ambivalence about 'Augustan' Britain—and its recurrent symbol, Imperial Rome. Now, the poet shows greater respect for Roman Republican virtues of independent spirit and national integrity (recalling the 'Republican' sentiments of anti-Union Scots) along with a growing disgust with the dissolute Roman Empire (corresponding to his own disillusionment with the English Augustan Age, and specifically Walpole's corrupt, anti-Scottish regime). At the same time, Thomson invokes an alternative model for 'liberty': Gothic or northern liberty, which he admires and implicitly associates with the 'manly Race' of Scots.

Liberty, as epic and as art, was a failure. Other Anglo-Scottish attempts at epic poetry, like Wilkie's Homeric Epigoniad and Mickle's translation of Camöens' Lusiad, fared no better; all were too abstract, too rhetorically overblown, too ambitious. Liberty lacked natural description (and with it, the poet's versatile descriptive language). The poem also largely lacked religious purpose (except implicitly, through social and ethical pronouncements). Liberty finally lacked life—the life of the poet's Scottish personal experience and perspective.

During the 1730s and 1740s, Thomson wrote a number of plays. Some were set in the neoclassical world where he was so much at home, such as Sophonisba (1730), Agamemnon (1738) and Coriolanus (published posthumously, 1749); the others, love-stories like Edward and Eleanora (1739) and his best play Tancred and Sigismunda (1745), introduced an innovative, more subjective and romantic element. These plays did well in their day, though they are mostly, if unjustly, forgotten now. Each contains some fine heroic, and occasionally descriptive, blank verse, but for the most part they were better suited to being read than acted; they tend to be over-rhetorical and under-dramatic. Thomson's weak dramatic sense was surely rooted in his Scottish upbringing, where the Church had long suppressed the drama, and where Latin school plays provided probably the only 'live' theatre he had known as a boy. But while Thomson's tragedies were not very memorable in themselves, they did accomplish two things: first, they signalled a revival of serious Scottish drama after a long silence (most Scottish plays of the period were comedies or light pastorals);[11] and second, they revealed much about the contemporary British political scene, from Thomson's Anglo-Scottish stance.

Several of Thomson's plays bear an alternative Scottish interpretation along with their more obvious Opposition Whig propaganda. Sophonisba shows Thomson's increasing sympathy with the smaller, independent nation in the face of Rome's power. Sophonisba's Carthage was ultimately defeated, but she herself displayed great courage, patriotism and integrity; while the heroine died rather than submit to Rome, her Carthaginian lover Massinissa joined the Romans and brought his manly virtues to that union (though not without terrible emotional turmoil). Parallels with Scotland's relationship to England, and Thomson's own ambivalent feelings about national allegiance, seem clear. In Agamemnon, the theme of usurpation is relevant, not only to internal, ministerial abuse of authority, but also to the Jacobite crisis; Thomson shows some sympathy for the exiled King and his threatened son in the classical drama—might this represent a trace of sentimental Jacobitism on Thomson's part? At the least, it hints at his own awareness of the complexity of the political situation, particularly from a Scottish point of view. *Tancred and Sigismunda* is on the surface a statement of reconciliation between Whig factions after Walpole's fall, but its political message is more complicated than that. *Tancred* appeared in March, 1745, just before Prince Charles Edward Stuart's invasion of Britain; the play was a subtle attempt by Thomson, both to satisfy the Hanoverians of his continued loyalty, and to placate the restless Jacobites. He did this by cleverly sustaining ambiguity in his treatment of themes of dynastic rivalry, threat of civil war, and legitimate royal succession—themes which could apply equally well to either the family of Frederick, Prince of Wales, or the family of Charles Edward Stuart (though Tancred's support for ancient lineal succession has undeniable Jacobite overtones). Thomson thus avoided censorship, and at the same time entertained audiences of both persuasions; his personal insecurities about nationalism, in this case, lent depth and complexity to the drama. In *Coriolanus*, the broken hero's ineffectual encampment outside the City of Rome recalls the Young Pretender's march on Derby and silent retreat; the play evidently celebrates Thomson's relief at the failure of Prince Charles Edward's English campaign in 1746. Ultimately, of course, he had to acknowledge that this turn of events was best for Great Britain.

Thomson's last poem was *The Castle of Indolence* (1748), a delightful allegory in the manner of Spenser. It ranks with *The Seasons* as an Anglo-Scottish masterpiece. Spenserian imitation had special appeal for the Anglo-Scots, perhaps because of its supernatural element and exaggerated description, and probably because of its archaic language, so closely akin to Middle Scots. Thomson made the Spenserian form his own in *The Castle*, creating a complex religious and social allegory and transcending strictly realistic natural description to explore extremes of the supernatural, both idealized and grotesque. Beyond Spenser, Thomson also drew from the Middle Scots tradition for his allegorical mode, his striking 'hellish' scenes, and his archaic diction. An especially significant influence was probably Gavin Douglas's *The Palice of Honour*.

Canto I of *The Castle* sets the idealized (ultimately false) scene; in Canto II come the more grotesque descriptions, along with the poem's serious message. *The Castle* is both a Calvinistic parable of spiritual and moral regeneration through divine grace (The Knight of Arts and Industry is, in one sense, a Christ-figure) and a social allegory of Progress and Improvement (the Knight is also an energetic secular leader, embodying archetypal Whig values). On a personal level, *The Castle* is animated by witty self-irony as the poet satirizes himself (the amiable, indolent 'bard . . . more fat than Bard beseems,' I. lxviii.1) and his friends—he caricatures mostly Scots, including John Armstrong and William Paterson—for vainly wishing to remain passive and safe within the Castle. There, they would not have to face the immediate danger of the Jacobites, nor the longer-term duty of Improvement. Eventually the slothful Scots are roused to responsible, pro-British action—action which also corresponds to Calvinistic interpretations of the so-called work-ethic, and action which parallels Thomson's personal initiative in moving from primitive Scotland to progressive England. The Scottish Moderate clergy actually saw the Forty-five rebellion as God's punishment on a sinful British, and Scottish, society, and preached the need for a regeneration to restore the nation to spiritual, social and moral health. This is the very regeneration (or Calvinistic 'begun recovery') which Thomson envisages in *The Castle*.

The Castle is Thomson's most consciously artistic work, and demonstrates the facility and elegance he had attained by this stage in the use of formal English poetic language, enriched with Spenserian and Scots language, in an intricate verse-form. Beattie, Mickle, Hamilton of Bangour and other Anglo-Scots, though with considerably less skill and grace, would also imitate Spenser and indeed Thomson's Spenserian poem.

As Thomson's caricatures of the lazy but likeable *Castle* inmates indicate, the poet was at the centre of a loyal Scottish circle of compatriots in London, some of whom he had known since college days; among them were Armstrong, Paterson, George Turnbull, and sometimes (though he was not popular with the others) Mallet. Thomson also kept contact with Joseph Mitchell, was acquainted with Smollett, and once even invited the Jacobite Hamilton of Bangour to dinner. For all of his contemporary Anglo-Scots (even those ungenerous ones like Mallet and Mitchell who resented his success), Thomson was something of a model and hero. He had proved that an Anglo-Scot could succeed—and what is more, could do so on his own terms and without sacrificing his Scottishness.

The Anglo-Scots who emulated Thomson, while most were not gifted with his genius or sheer gumption, did have much in common with him. Most shared, in the Scottish democratic tradition, similar educational advantages. Many were drawn to description as a poetical theme; Blair, Mallet, Armstrong, Beattie, Falconer, Smollett, John Wilson and Macpherson all contributed to the Scottish tradition of nature poetry. Related to this descriptive sensibility was their empirical enthusiasm, their desire to accumulate information so as to achieve a comprehensive vision. They were often obsessed with accuracy of detail, in an almost scientific sense—examples are found in the poetry of seaman Falconer and physicians Grainger and Armstrong. The Anglo-Scots were experimental in the forms they attempted (although unlike Thomson most did not experiment very imaginatively within those forms). One of their favourite modes was the didactic; they took their teaching responsibility seriously, and set out to 'improve' both individual and society. As Scots, many could identify with Thomson's ideals of nostalgic progressivism, and they, too, debated the central Primitivism *v*. Progress question: Beattie was ambivalent, but his *Minstrel* opted for an enlightened primitivism, or rather nostalgic progress, while Macpherson's Ossianic heroes remained in the misty realm of Celtic primitivism.

The Anglo-Scots were also deeply serious about their religious and moral responsibilities. They loved to preach, and indeed some were ministers (Blair, Blacklock) or had studied for the ministry (Mitchell, Thomson). Blair in particular represented the traditional Scottish Calvinist mindset. Along with this spiritual concern, the Anglo-Scots also showed a metaphysical tendency, not unrelated to their lingering fascination with supernatural themes. The Anglo-Scots were classicists so thoroughly grounded in vernacular humanist culture that its language, themes and forms would inevitably determine their ideals of life and literature; Hamilton of Bangour (who translated Horace), and later Wilkie and Blacklock especially strove to keep the Scottish Latinist legacy alive. The Anglo-Scots were likewise preoccupied with the art and science of Rhetoric (sometimes to the degree that their overwrought language stifled sense—even Thomson was sometimes guilty of this). Yet early on, Thomson was bold enough to practise in poetry what the next generation of Anglo-Scottish rhetoricians would formulate, that is, a new rhetoric based on traditional rules but also admitting of more subjective standards. Beattie, Macpherson and later-eighteenth-century Anglo-Scottish poets would take these freer literary aesthetics to even greater, pre-Romantic lengths.

Indeed the Anglo-Scots embodied, in varying degrees, the ambitions and ideals—if not always the real achievements—of the Scottish Enlightenment itself. They shared the Enlightenment's optimistic vision of an improved and cosmopolitan North British civilization. Their work should be wholeheartedly accepted into the canon of legitimate Scottish literatures, along with Gaelic and Scots. The best of them, like Thomson, deserve to be considered not just as footnotes to the broader history of English Literature, but as central to the Scottish literary tradition.[12]

NOTES

1 A M Oliver, 'The Scottish Augustans', in *Scottish Poetry: A Critical Survey*, James Kinsley (ed), (London, 1955), pp. 136, 139.
2 Douglas Duncan, *Thomas Ruddiman: A Study in Scholarship of the Early Eighteenth Century* (Edinburgh and London, 1965), pp 148 ff.
3 Joseph Mitchell, John Calendar [Callender of Craigforth] *et al.*, *Lugubres Cantus: Poems on Several Grave and Important Subjects, Chiefly Occasion'd by the Death of the late Ingenious Youth John Mitchell* (London, 1719). Philips and Young were associated with the Athenian Society of London. Ambrose Philips, 'To the Author of the First Part of the Lugubres Cantus' [Mitchell], *Lugubres*, n.p.
4 Most of Thomson's juvenile poems are in the holograph 'Newberry MS'. (*c.* 1720–21); the MS was at the Newberry Library, Chicago until it was lost in 1970 (a photostat survives).

The new edition of *Liberty, The Castle of Indolence and Other Poems*, ed James Sambrook (Oxford: Clarendon Press, 1986) appeared after this chapter went to press, but is now the standard edition of the juvenilia. Earlier printed editions badly mishandled the juvenile poems.

5   Samuel Johnson, 'Mallet', in *Lives of the English Poets*, 3 vols, George Birkbeck Hill (ed) (New York, 1967), III, p 403.

6   Hamilton reprimanded Thomson for an extravagant homily, and 'told him, smiling, that if he thought of being useful in the ministry, he must keep a stricter rein upon his imagination, and express himself in language more intelligible to an ordinary congregation'; recalled by Thomson's classmate, Anglican clergyman Patrick Murdoch, (ed), *The Works of James Thomson*, 2 vols (London, 1762), I. v–vi.

7   Edition of *The Seasons* quoted here is: *James Thomson: The Seasons,* James Sambrook (ed), (Oxford, 1981).

8   John MacQueen, *Progress and Poetry: The Enlightenment and Scottish Literature*, 2 vols (Edinburgh, 1982), I, pp 63–7.

9   Thomson, Letter 'To William Cranstoun', [*c*. 1 October 1725], in Alan Dugald McKillop (ed), *James Thomson: Letters and Documents* (Lawrence, Kansas, 1958), p 16.

10   Thomson, Letter 'To George Dodington' (27 December 1730), in *Thomson: Letters*, pp 77–8.

11   Terence Tobin, *Plays by Scots, 1660–1800*, (Iowa City, Iowa, 1974), p 132; one example is Joseph Mitchell's *The Highland Fair*.

12   Full reference to the sources from which I have drawn in writing this chapter may be found in my *James Thomson, Anglo-Scot* (Athens: University of Georgia Press, 1988).

FURTHER READING

Bushnell, Nelson S, *William Hamilton of Bangour: Poet and Jacobite*, with bibliography (Aberdeen, 1957)

Campbell, Hilbert H, *James Thomson* (Boston, 1979)

——*James Thomson: An Annotated Bibliography* (New York and London, 1976)

Cohen, Ralph, *The Art of Discrimination: Thomson's 'The Seasons' and the Language of Criticism* (London, 1964)

Grant, Douglas, *James Thomson: Poet of 'The Seasons'* (London, 1951)

King, Everard H, *James Beattie* (Boston, 1977)

McKillop, Alan Dugald, *The Background of Thomson's 'Seasons'* (Minneapolis, 1942)

Spacks, Patricia M, *The Poetry of Vision* (Cambridge, Mass., 1967)

——*The Varied God: A Critical Study of Thomson's 'The Seasons'* (Berkeley 1959)

Thomson, James, *The Plays*, Adams, Percy G (ed), (New York and London, 1979)

For additional biographical and bibliographical information on the Anglo-Scottish poets the following should be consulted:

Aitken, W R *Scottish Literature in English and Scots, A Guide to Information Sources*, (Gale Research Company, Detroit, 1982)

Foxon, D F, *English Verse, 1701–1750*, 2 vols, (Cambridge University Press, 1975)

Royle, T, *The Macmillan Companion to Scottish Literature*, (London, 1983)

Watson, George (ed), *The New Cambridge Bibliography of English Literature*, Vol 2, 1660–1800, (Cambridge, 1971)

Chapter 6

The Importance of Tobias Smollett

KENNETH SIMPSON

The following is the description of Crabshaw as he appears to Dr Fillet after his rescue from the river at the start of Smollett's *The Life and Adventures of Sir Launcelot Greaves* (1760–61):

> His stature was below the middle size: he was thick, squat, and brawny, with a small protuberance on one shoulder, and a prominent belly, which, in consequence of the water he had swallowed, now strutted out beyond its usual dimensions. His forehead was remarkably convex, and so very low, that his black bushy hair descended within an inch of his nose: but this did not conceal the wrinkles of his front, which were manifold. His small glimmering eyes resembled those of the Hampshire porker, that turns up the soil with his projecting snout. His cheeks were shrivelled and puckered at the corners, like the seams of a regimental coat as it comes from the hands of the contractor: his nose bore a strong analogy in shape to a tennis-ball, and in colour to a mulberry; for all the water of the river had not been able to quench the natural fire of that feature. His upper jaw was furnished with two long white sharp-pointed teeth or fangs, such as the reader may have observed in the chaps of a wolf, or full-grown mastiff, and an anatomist would describe as a preternatural elongation of the *dentes canini*. His chin was so long, so peaked and incurvated, as to form in profile with his impending forehead the exact resemblance of a moon in the first quarter (p 10).[1]

That could only have been written by someone in whom, as in Smollett, a knowledge of Cervantes, Le Sage, Fielding, Shakespeare, and Jonson was complemented by the legacy of the older Scottish literary tradition.

One of the characteristics of that tradition is an acute sense of physicality, and especially physical incongruity, that verges on the absurd or grotesque; this is often represented by means of animal analogies. While these features are to be found in other medieval literatures, they are more prominent and endure longer in Scottish literature. Indeed one of the foremost hallmarks of the Scottish literary tradition is its ready accommodation, even its relishing, of the grotesque. There is substance to Agnes Mure Mackenzie's claim that whereas 'the Englishman is swept off his feet by the grotesque, the Scot smacks his bonnet on his head and plunges overboard'.[2] Like the Makars, Smollett notes but also celebrates the comically grotesque qualities of human beings. In the novel in English it is only in the work of Dickens that there is anything remotely comparable and in his portraits some of Smollett's uncompromising bite has been softened. Obviously it would be extravagant to cite Smollett as a link between the Makars and Dickens, but there is validity in the contention that he is instrumental in assimilating these features of medieval literature into the English novel.

This essay will also argue that the nature and the extent of Smollett's influence have been under-rated and that, as novelist, he is much more experimental and modern than has been recognised. Likewise, his originality has been under-estimated. While it is undeniable that he reproduces several of the stock elements of both the Elizabethan comic dramatists and his English and European predecessors in the novel—interpolated anecdotes and memoirs, the social masquerade, the misanthrope, farcical misunderstandings in inns, conversations in stage-coaches—his techniques and much of his material mark him out as an original talent. Certainly Smollett is undervalued if, as has often been the case, he is regarded as the poor relation of the eighteenth-century English novelists—Defoe, Richardson, Fielding, and Sterne. His work is appreciated most readily by taking cognisance of his identity as Scot. Much of his originality derives from his roots in the Scottish literary tradition and his prose techniques reflect the integration of features of the Scottish tradition into English fiction. Principally these are a sense of physicality; breadth of social observation; an interest in the grotesque, the fantastic, and the demonic; and a stylistic verve.

The first page of Smollett's first novel, *Roderick Randon* (1748), exemplies his skill in the creative conflation of previously separate literary modes. For a paragraph Roderick's account adheres to the formula for autobiographical fiction as represented in, for example, the opening of *Robinson Crusoe*. What follows thereafter, however, becomes almost as bizarre as the start of *Tristram Shandy*, but when Sterne allows his hero to commence his account from the circumstances of his conception the principal target is the fictional mode, whereas, with Smollett, it is simply the subject-matter itself which is unusual. Troubled by a dream during pregnancy, Roderick's mother has sought the advice of a Highland seer as to its meaning:

> She dreamed, she was delivered of a tennis-ball, which the devil (who to her great surprize acted the part of a midwife) struck so forcibly with a racket, that it disappeared in an instant; and she was for some time inconsolable for the loss of her off-spring; when all of a sudden, she beheld it return with equal violence, and earth itself beneath her feet, whence immediately sprung up a goodly tree covered with blossoms, the scent of which operated so strongly on her nerves that she awoke. The attentive sage, after some deliberation, assured my parents, that their first-born would be a great traveller, that he would undergo many dangers and difficulties, and at last return to his native land, where he would flourish with great reputation and happiness (p 1).

Here is epitomised Scottish literature's tendency to mingle contraries, to unite the factual with the unusual or fantastic. Realistic observation and wild exaggeration are twin sides of the same Scottish coin. Those bizarre details in Roderick's account have their ancestry in the world of the ballad. Noting Celtic literature's fondness for the grotesque, Kurt Wittig singled out for particular attention a 'grotesque exaggeration . . . a reckless irreverence, an eldritch imaginative propensity'.[3] Yet, as John Barth observed, Roderick's narrative proves that 'the dream means exactly and unironically what [the seer] says it means: that Roderick will travel a great deal, suffer adversity, return, and flourish'.[4] The sequence of events in *Roderick Random* suggests the unfolding of a pattern—bizarre, certainly, but a pattern nonetheless. Again the antecedents are in the Scottish culture of earlier centuries. Wittig has remarked upon 'the sheer grotesque absurdity' of those Scottish poems which give 'intellectual delight by tracing a fantastic but logical pattern that forms a comic counterpart to the complex traceries of Celtic carved stones, or, in fiddle music, the intricate rhythms and wicked tunes of many strathspeys and reels'.[5]

In the world of Smollett's novels the logic is that of Providence. For Smollett Providence represents not God's benevolent care but rather the random operations of fate and coincidence. In a letter to Garrick he wrote,

> I am old enough to have seen and observed that we are all playthings of fortune, and that it depends upon something as insignificant and precarious as the tossing up of a halfpenny whether a man rises to affluence and honours, or continues to his dying day struggling with the difficulties and disgraces of life.[6]

For Smollett's characters it's a small Scots world. In London seeking a post as a naval surgeon, Roderick is referred to one Mr Cringer as a man of influence. Cringer, who as it transpires is of no assistance, had served Roderick's grandfather as footman. Later, however, Providence favours Random: in Buenos Aires he encounters the wealthy Don Rodrigo who happens to be his father and whose wealth facilitates Roderick's marriage to his beloved Narcissa.

The supremacy of Providence in the world of Smollett's novels helps account for the frantic pace of the action. Given the primacy of Providence, Smollett's interest is in the sequence of events rather than the characters' responses to them; people are acted upon, rather than being the initiators of events. As a consequence, Smollett's characterisation is largely concerned with externals and, in the early novels at least, there is little scope for individual development or psychological investigation. In Smollett's world (with the qualified exception of *Humphry Clinker*) the alternatives are either acceptance of one's given condition (the normal response) or defiance of the hegemony of Providence, which leads invariably to the extreme, the bizarre, the grotesque. Roderick is recommended as valet to a learned lady by Mrs Sagely who describes her thus:

> Being by this visionary turn of mind, abstracted as it were from the world, she cannot advert to the common occurrences of life; and therefore is so absent as to commit very strange mistakes and extravagancies, which you will do well to rectify and repair, as your prudence shall suggest (p 217).

The abstraction which her mental pursuits engender has taken its toll of her physical appearance, and the incongruity which the lady exemplifies is compounded by the nature of Roderick's response in that, besotted with her niece Narcissa, he is blind to all else. Such is the lady's capacity for empathy that 'affected with the notes of the hounds in the morning . . . she actually believed herself a hare beset with the hunters and begged a few greens to munch for her breakfast' (p 221). Roderick's account continues,

> . . . I was summoned by the bell to my lady's chamber, where I found her sitting squat on her hams, on the floor, in the manner of puss when she listens to the cries of her pursuers. When I appeared, she started up with an alarmed look, and sprung to the other side of the room to avoid me, whom, without doubt, she mistook for a beagle thirsting after her life. Perceiving her extreme confusion, I retired, and on the stair-case met the adorable Narcissa coming up, to whom I imparted the situation of my mistress: she said not a word, but smiling with unspeakable grace, went in to her aunt's apartment, and in a little time my ears were ravished with the effects of her skill. She accompanied the instrument with a voice so sweet and melodious, that I did not wonder at the surprizing change it produced on the spirits of my mistress, which were soon composed to peace and sober reflection (p 222).

Such a concatenation of contraries and such a marked flux of emotions identify Smollett as a descendant of the older Scottish literary tradition. A raw and robust physicality recurs throughout *Roderick Random*. Physically ill-treated by his schoolmaster, the young Roderick takes revenge in kind. Acknowledging that in the late sixteenth and early seventeenth centuries satire involved punishment, James L Clifford asks pertinently, 'Could Smollett's heroes, then, be essentially fictional representations of the satiric persona, with the physical punishment of sinners as their principal function?'.[7]

One of Smollett's particular strengths is his ability to use language dynamically for pictorial representation. In London Roderick and Strap visit a Scottish linguist who specialises in teaching the pronunciation of English. Here, uncharacteristically for Smollett, the incongruous aspect of the individual's situation precedes the caricature itself, Roderick admitting that 'three parts in four of his dialect were as unintelligible to me as if he had spoke in Arabick or Irish' (p 67). The short caricature follows the standard formula of representation of physical features, dress, and speech:

> He was a middle-size man, and stooped very much, though not above the age of forty; his face was very much pitted with the small-pox, his eyes blear'd, and his mouth extended from ear to ear. He was dressed in a night-gown of plaid, fastened about his middle with a sergeant's old sash, and a tie-perriwig with a fore-top three inches high, in the fashion of king Charles the second's reign.

This typifies Smollett's skill as a visual artist. He uses the vigour of language to focus upon specific visual elements, creating through the dynamism of words something that approximates to a series of arresting slides. In suggesting that the essence of caricature lies not in imitation but in configurations of clues, E H Gombrich observed, 'Expression in life and physiognomic expression rest on movement no less than on static symptoms, and art has to compensate for the loss of the time dimension by concentrating all required information into one arrested image'.[8] In his dynamic representation of the pictorial Smollett achieves precisely the effect that Gombrich so described, and again one of the antecedents is the poetry of the Makars. In their lively renderings of the predominantly visual, G Gregory Smith found that 'the completed effect of the piling up of details is one of movement, suggesting the action of a concerted dance or the canter of a squadron'.[9] This comment might be applied even to the speech of Mr Bowling, Roderick's sea-faring uncle. Here he confirms that Roderick's grandfather is dead:

'Dead! (says my uncle, looking at the body) ay, ay, I'll warrant him as dead as a herring. Odd's fish! now my dream is out for all the world. I thought I stood upon the Fore-Castle, and saw a parcel of carrion crows foul of a dead shark that floated alongside, and the devil perching on our sprit-sailyard, in the likeness of a blue bear—who, d'ye see, jumped overboard upon the carcase, and carried it to the bottom in his claws' (p 13).

The grotesque, impressionistic, but sustained physicality of the dream renders the reality of the situation more effectively than statement of fact could have done.

Smollett's expressive energy is part of his inheritance from the older Scottish tradition. There such energy at its most extreme found expression in the *flyting*. Smollett informs his writing in standard English with a comparable vigour. When Roderick complains of his early ill-treatment he sounds very like Smollett protesting in his letters about his reception in London. Likewise when, in the last and generally mellower novel *Humphry Clinker* (1771), Matt Bramble fulminates against the mob, he is close to representing the views of his creator. Now it is undeniable that in such passages in Smollett the nature of the prose indicates the nature of the man. From Smollett came this self-characterisation: 'I am an unfortunate Dog whose Pride Providence thinks proper to punish with the Tortures of incessant Mortification; and I resent my Lot accordingly' (*Letters*, p 18). However it is less than accurate to attribute the vehemence of much of Smollett's prose to the nature of his personality and in particular to his irascibility and acute sensitivity to insult and injustice. Certainly it is one source, and so too is the suspicion and hostility which, like other Scots who thrived in the south, he prompted in some Englishmen. Smollett's letters reflect a combination of naive confidence and combative energy which, together with his association with the widely unpopular ministry of Lord Bute by virtue of his editing *The Briton* from 29 May 1762 to 12 February 1763,[10] aroused some personal opposition. But it is unjust to Smollett to characterise him, as Jery does Matt, as 'a man without a skin' and to account for the indignant force of his writing in terms of personality and temperament. Too much has been made of Smollett's prickliness. It is worth noting, as Lewis Knapp does (*Letters*, p 104, n 1), that when the friendship between Smollett and Wilkes foundered as their divergent political opinions found expression in *The Briton* and *The North Briton*, it was Wilkes who first resorted to personal insult.

In Smollett's vigorous denunciation of social ills the prime motivating force is the genuine concern of the satirist (which had prompted his two early verse-satires, *Advice* (1746) and *Reproof* (1747)). By vividly depicting social conditions Smollett argues convincingly the need for improvement. Of Rowlandson's illustrations V S Pritchett writes, 'we see the nightmare lying behind the Augustan manner' and of Smollett he comments, 'He enjoyed being the shocking surgeon who brings out horrors at the dinner-table; but because he was shocked himself. Smollett's sensibility is close to Swift's'.[11] Like Swift's, Smollett's shock is that of a high idealism that is confronted by the often-terrible reality of human behaviour. Smollett acknowledged, 'I have such a natural Horror of Cruelty that I cannot without uncommon Warmth relate any instance of Inhumanity' (*Letters*, p 69). Miss Williams's description in *Roderick Random* of her experiences in Bridewell is one manifestation of this, and it compares favourably with Moll's account of life in Newgate in *Moll Flanders*. Miss Williams's formal Augustan prose serves, by contrast, to underline the horrible actuality of conditions. This technique of effective contrast of manner and matter is developed in Roderick's reports of his experiences on board the 'Thunder' (partly based on Smollett's service as a naval surgeon in the Caribbean in the winter of 1740–41). Here Roderick recounts faithfully his experience of battle:

> . . . I concealed my agitation as well as I could, till the head of the officer of Marines, who stood near me, being shot off, bounced from the deck athwart my face, leaving me well-nigh blinded with brains. I could contain myself no longer, but began to bellow with all the strength of my lungs; when a drummer coming towards me, asked if I was wounded; and before I could answer, received a great shot in his belly which tore out his intrails, and he fell flat on my breast. This accident entirely bereft me of all discretion. I redoubled my cries, which were drowned in the noise of the battle; and finding myself disregarded, lost all patience and became frantick; vented my rage in oaths and execrations, till my spirits being quite exhausted, I remained quiet and insensible of the load that oppressed me (pp 167–8).

If Smollett shocks, it is because the realities of war shock. The same unflinching realism of observation informs the accounts of the treatment of the injured and the disposal of the casualties, and conveys the author's sense of outrage. If such descriptions share with the ballads a stark recognition of life's physical dimension, at the same time they anticipate the way in which the enormities of two world wars led such writers as Sassoon, Owen, Heller, and Vonnegut to register their protest against the carnage by reporting conditions as they were.

In *Roderick Random* various literary influences merge. Smollett was familiar with the works of the Latin satirists, for whom *satura* was a medley, and he was thoroughly conversant with the picaresque with its loose episodic structure. As Ronald Paulson noted,[12] the fusion of these modes led to the recording of some of the less creditable aspects of human behaviour, and this was done with a candour which occasioned charges of tastelessness against Smollett. In charting the literary ancestry of this strain in Smollett account should also be taken of the breadth of social realism which was one of the principal features of the older Scottish tradition.

Roderick is followed through a succession of experiences wherein the discrepancy between appearance and reality is highlighted. What particularly distinguishes Smollett's treatment of this standard theme of satire is the acerbic edge to his observations, which locates him within the Scottish tradition of sceptical rationalism as typified by David Hume. In *Roderick Random*, as throughout Smollett's fiction, the over-riding note is that of a rationalist realism. Superstition, the potentially Gothic, the excesses of sensibility, and the self-indulgence of the sentimental lover—all are reduced by Smollett's presiding rationalist sense. It is paradoxical that Smollett's energetic and vibrant prose, which has its origins in a tradition noted for its propensity to the bizarre, the extreme, and the fantastic, should be set so effectively to the service of upholding reason. At the root of this paradox is the co-existence of fact and fantasy in the older Scottish tradition. While Smollett may resemble Fielding at times in terms of the situations of their novels, he has affinities at least as marked with major Scottish writers of the time, and pre-eminently Robert Fergusson. In the *flytings* of Fergusson Kurt Wittig found grotesque extremes of logic, but contended that they are controlled by reason into social satire.[13] The similarity to Smollett's method and achievement is striking.

Smollett's second novel also reveals him as both social historian and master of imaginative invention. *Peregrine Pickle* (1751), which Dickens preferred to *Tom Jones*, demonstrates on a greater scale Smollett's ability to unify various otherwise distinct literary modes and sources. There is abundant evidence of specific influence: as ever in Smollett's novels there are distinct echoes of Shakespeare in both characteristation and language; the 'Entertainment in the Manner of the Ancients' seems likely to have been inspired by Trimalchio's banquet in the *Satyricon* of Petronius; the misanthrope, Crabtree, bears a resemblance to the Man of the Hill in *Tom Jones*; and on one occasion Smollett mimics Fielding while repudiating his technique, as follows:

> I might here, in imitation of some celebrated writers, furnish out a page or two, with the reflections he made upon the instability of human affairs, the treachery of the world, and the temerity of youth; and endeavour to decoy the reader into a smile, by some quaint observation of my own, touching the sagacious moralizer: but, besides that I look upon this practice as an impertinent anticipation of the peruser's thoughts, I have too much matter of importance upon my hands, to give the reader the least reason to believe that I am driven to such paultry shifts, in order to eke out the volume (pp 682–3).

Though hybrid, Smollett's technique and mode are highly successful. After speculating as to whether the pattern of *Peregrine Pickle* is satire, realism or melodrama, James Clifford contends, quite rightly in my view, that

> What gives Smollett his own particular flavour is the mingling in his novels of so many diverse traditions—the picaresque, classical formal satire, comedy, melodrama, the new sensibility, and at times stark realism. Yet his fertility is so great, his vigour of presentation so appealing, that the reader simply does not care. The story drags him headlong through every slough and side road.
>
> (*PP* pp xxv–xxvi)

This is not to imply that to read Smollett's novel is to be propelled at great speed on a tour of his literary influences and sources. *Peregrine Pickle* exemplifies not just the characteristic verve and momentum of Smollett's narrative but also his considerable imaginative fertility.

For evidence of the latter one need look no further than the early chapters which are dominated by that striking original, Commodore Trunnion. A succession of incidents in which he is involved bears testimony to the extent to which Smollett inherited Scottish literature's fondness for the incongruous and grotesque. For instance, Hatchway and Pipes play a trick on Trunnion which involves lowering down his bedroom chimney at midnight 'a bunch of stinking whitings' (p 33) while yelling through a speaking-trumpet, ' "Trunnion! Trunnion! turn out and be spliced, or lie still and be damned" ', all of this producing the desired effect of arousing Trunnion's superstitious fear. Later, involved in a fracas with an attorney, Trunnion grasps a whole turkey and uses it as a weapon. In the use of bizarre detail this resembles the point in Fergusson's poem, 'The King's Birthday in Edinburgh', where a wig, inadvertently set alight by a stray firework, is doused by being struck by a drowned cat. Behind both of these examples lurks more than a hint of Hume's scepticism about man's capacity to relate cause and effect, means and end.

Probably the most memorable and sustained manifestation of Smollett's imaginative ingenuity is his description of the progress of the Commodore to his wedding. On land as on sea Trunnion believes that the way to advance is by tacking. Unfortunately both he and Hatchway are mounted on hunters and, the sound of fox-hounds reaching the ears of their horses, they have no choice but to participate. The account of Trunnion's wild flight, predominantly comic-epic in manner, culminates in the truly epic achievement of Trunnion, still mounted, flying over the top of a passing carriage and, after a two-hour, twelve-mile chase, being first at the death of the deer. This episode's place in the genre of 'The Wild Ride', and its affinity with 'Tam o' Shanter' are worth noting.

The legacy of Scottish literature's interest in the bizarre is reflected also in the gallery of originals that comprise Smollett's characters. They served as a major source of inspiration in characteristation for such novelists as Scott, Galt, and, above all, Dickens, who derives much in this area from the example of Smollett. Playing variously upon peculiarities of physique, appearance, and speech, Smollett created in his first novel, *Roderick Random*, vivid caricatures such as Launcelot Crab, Captain Weazel, Lavement the apothecary, and Lieutenant Bowling. Caricature has obvious attractions for a fertile imagination constrained by a cultural tradition which encourages breadth of social observation but does nothing to stimulate in-depth investigation of the individual as such. But in a number of his characters—principally Trunnion in *Peregrine Pickle* and Lismahago in *Humphry Clinker*—Smollett's imagination transcends such limitations and creates beings who progress beyond their starting-point in caricature and end up achieving a stature as characters far greater than that of any caricature. Trunnion's individuality of personality and values is both richly comic and highly impressive; our response as readers combines amusement and wonder in equal measure. Suggesting that, 'like Dickens with Mr Micawber, Smollett could compound genuine human traits with powerfully overwrought humours to form memorable characters which both embody and transcend life itself', Clifford makes the useful comment that 'artistic distortion . . . rather than caricature, may be a better term to use for Smollett' (*PP*, p xxviii).

It is significant that it is in the context of Trunnion that Smollett first proposes that man's emotional state is complex, a compound of various constituents. Hatchway, Pipes, and Peregrine have been unremitting in playing a succession of tricks upon Trunnion, whereupon Smollett remarks,

> Howsoever preposterous and unaccountable that passion may be, which prompts persons, otherwise generous and sympathising, to afflict and perplex their fellow-creatures, certain it is our confederates entertained such a large proportion of it, that not satisfied with the pranks they had already played, they still persecuted the commodore without ceasing (p 72).

Their next scheme involves forging a letter to Trunnion from a much-hated uncle. Appropriately, Trunnion's response to it is a hybrid:

> It would be a difficult task for the inimitable Hogarth himself to exhibit the ludicrous expression of the commodore's countenance, while he read this letter. It was not a stare of astonishment, a convulsion of rage, or a ghastly grin of revenge, but an association of all three, that took possession of his features (p 75).

Despite the fact that he does not always make the point through his characters (Trunnion surpasses most in terms of emotional complexity), for Smollett the truth of the human condition is that emotions are composite and the flux of the passions is continuous. The indulgence or the prolongation of any single emotion is absurd. Smollett distances himself from Peregrine's behaviour as romantic lover which, like that of Roderick, is subjected to comic reduction. Flux of experience—courtesy of Providence—and flux of response, are central to Smollett's view of the human condition. On receiving a warrant for his arrest, Pickle beats the bailiff, only to succumb to the melancholy prospect of being 'doomed to the miseries of a jail', and Smollett comments, 'What would become of the unfortunate, if the constitution of the mind did not permit them to bring one passion into the field against another? passions that operate in the human breast, like poisons of a different nature, extinguishing each other's effect' (p 678). For Smollett it is reason only which can bring any control to this tumult of the passions. The clearest pointer to this lies in his account of the visit of Peregrine and his acquaintances to 'the temple of excess, where they left the choice of fare to the discretion of the landlord, that they might save themselves the pains of exercising their own reason' (p 582).

Two years after *Peregrine Pickle*, in February 1753, appeared *Ferdinand Count Fathom*, which is certainly Smollett's most complex and most disturbing novel. In his dedication Smollett ventured this definition:

> A Novel is a large diffused picture, comprehending the characters of life, disposed in different groupes, and exhibited in various attitudes, for the purposes of an uniform plan, and general occurrence, to which every individual figure is subservient (p 2).

And he referred to his 'attempts to subject folly to ridicule, and vice to indignation; to rouse the spirit of mirth, wake the soul of compassion, and touch the secret springs that move the heart' (p 4). While his motives seem to be mixed, the plan derives its uniformity from Smollett's rationalist sense.

Smollett's breadth of social vision—with which may be compared that of Ramsay, Fergusson, and Burns—offers a licence for stylistic variation, and *Ferdinand Count Fathom* is Smollett's most radical and experimental novel in terms of both subject-matter and technique. Hazlitt found 'more power of writing occasionally shown in it than in any of his works'.[14] In the *Monthly Review* Ralph Griffiths termed *Ferdinand Count Fathom* 'a work of mixed character',[15] noting that it combined affecting scenes with humorous, and mixed realism with extravagant fancy. And David Masson's contrasting of Smollett's style with that of Fielding serves to identify those properties which find most acute exemplification in *Ferdinand Count Fathom*:

> There is . . . a rhetorical strength of language in Smollett which Fielding rarely exhibits; a power of melodramatic effect to which Fielding does not pretend; and a greater constitutional tendency to the sombre and the terrible. There was potentially more of the poet in Smollett than in Fielding; and there are passages in his writings approaching nearer, both in feeling and rhythm, to lyric beauty.[16]

Despite the vigour of Smollett's writing in these various veins it should be acknowledged that even here the reductive rationalist note is still present.
    The technique which Smollett develops to most immediate effect in

Ferdinand Count Fathom is that of the comic-epic. He had experimented with this mode intermittently in *Peregrine Pickle* but here he sustains its use throughout his account of Fathom's birth and early life. With great dexterity Smollett employs the apparently grand manner and the trappings of the epic for the representation of low subject-matter. His mastery of the mode is evident from, for instance, his introduction of Fathom's mother:

> Certain it is, the count's mother was an Englishwoman, who, after having been five times a widow in one campaign, was, in the last year of the renowned Marlborough's command, numbered among the baggage of the allied army, which she still accompanied, through pure benevolence of spirit, supplying the ranks with the refreshing streams of choice geneva, and accommodating individuals with clean linnen, as the emergency of their occasions required: Nor was her philanthropy altogether confined to such ministration: she abounded with 'the milk of human kindness', which flowed plentifully among her fellow-creatures; and to every son of Mars who cultivated her favour, she liberally dispensed her smiles, in order to sweeten the toils and dangers of the field (p 7).

Smollett's exuberant use of the inflated style of the comic-epic in his account of Fathom's mother's attack on the Turkish leader, and her subsequent death, may owe an immediate debt to Fielding's description of the battle in the churchyard in *Tom Jones* (Book IV, chapter viii), but there is at least an equal debt to the comic use of aureate diction in the poems of Dunbar, Lynsday, Alexander Scott, and Alexander Montgomerie. Smollett sounds a note which recurs throughout Scottish literature—that of reduction, which is the great social leveller. He typifies that Scottish realist sense which feigns grandiloquence only to undermine it. When Smollett relates that the resumption of war between the Austrians and the Turks had important implications for the young Ferdinand, not least his witnessing 'that famous victory, which, with sixty thousand men, the imperial general obtained over an army of one hundred and fifty thousand Turks' (p 11), his reductive juxtaposing of world and individual anticipates the use of such a device by Burns (as, for instance, in 'Elegy on the Departed Year, 1788') and by Galt (most obviously in *Annals of the Parish*).

Contrast is integral to the comic-epic. It is also central to Smollett's technique and thought in *Ferdinand Count Fathom*. In his dedication he explains that he created 'a virtuous character [Renaldo], in opposition to the adventurer [Fathom], with a view to amuse the fancy, engage the affection, and form a striking contrast which might heighten the expression, and give a *Relief* to the moral of the whole' (p 3). A brothel-keeper is depicted as follows:

> . . . age had bent her into the form of a Turkish bow: her head was agitated by the palsy, like the leaf of the poplar-tree, her hair fell down in scanty parcels, as white as the driven snow: her face was not simply wrinkled, but ploughed into innumerable furrows: her jaws could not boast of one remaining tooth; one eye distilled a large quantity of rheum, by virtue of the fiery edge that

surrounded it, the other was altogether extinguished, and she had lost her nose in the course of her ministration. The Delphic sybil was but a type of this hoary matron, who by her figure might have been mistaken for the consort of chaos, or mother of time (p 93).

But the narrator approves of her appearance as offering 'an agreeable contrast with the beauty and youth of the fair damsels that wantoned in her train. It resembled those discords in musick, which properly disposed, contribute to the harmony of the whole piece' (p 93). Similarly, the sensuous description of Monimia includes the observation that

> ... one half of [her eyes'] vivacity was eclipsed by a languishing air of melancholy concern; which, while it in a manner sheathed the edge of her beauty, added a most engaging sweetness to her looks: in short, every feature was elegantly perfect; and the harmony of the whole ravishing and delightful (p 201).

For Smollett, such a natural union of diverse elements cannot be created. When Fathom demonstrates his skill as musician to the extent that his playing was 'ravishing', a lady listens 'as with rapture to the harp of an angel', and all were 'transported by the harmony which our hero produced' (pp 248–9). Smollett emphasises that this is unnatural; part of Fathom's attraction derives from his ability as illusionist, and the single, all-consuming note which he creates is unnatural and false. Smollett's is a world that is characterised by plenitude. Such diversity is to be welcomed: just a little later Plato is cited to the effect that 'contraries are productive of each other' (p 280).

In *Ferdinand Count Fathom* the character of the hero and the nature of his experiences combine to permit of the fullest expression of Smollett's plentitude of vision. Smollett employs the picaresque model to investigate a wide range of subjects that includes the allegedly demonic and the supernatural. The criticism of values is effected through not only the social encounters of the itinerant hero but also his behaviour. Fathom is an opportunist extraordinary and a compulsive role-player. In the masquerade which Smollett shows fashionable society to be, Fathom triumphs: at Bristol 'Fathom, as usual, formed the nucleus or kernel of the beau monde . . . [he] was the soul that animated the whole society' (p 165). This is probably Smollett's most telling indictment of false social values, and the point is more subtly and more effectively made than when conveyed through the harangues of Matt Bramble in *Humphry Clinker*.

At the 'soul' of society in *Ferdinand Count Fathom* is a master charlatan. This affords Smollett considerable licence, a licence which embraces range of technique as well as range of subject-matter. Fathom is instrumental in Smollett's critique of the excesses of both romance and the Gothic, both of which—however vividly they are evoked—are subsumed ultimately within Smollett's reductive rationalism. Just as Smollett had been at pains to distinguish genuine suffering from false (in *Roderick Random*, for instance, Jack Rattlin bears appalling hardship with great fortitude whereas

Roderick is the earliest of Smollett's several characters who endure the self-induced anguish of the romantic lover), so he is concerned to differentiate between true and false feeling.

In his introduction to *Ferdinand Count Fathom* Damian Grant refers to 'the typical inadequacy of Smollett's language when describing heightened emotions' (*FCF*, p xii). While there is plainly some substance to this objection, it is important to recognise that Smollett was anything but insensitive to emotion. In a letter to Samuel Richardson Smollett complimented that author on his 'amiable Benevolence, sublime morality and surprizing Intimacy with the human Heart, which must ever be the objects of Veneration among People of good Sense and Integrity' (*Letters*, p 48). Now, as V S Pritchett noted, 'the vogue of sensibility, the first shoots of the Romantic movement, spring from the pool of Richardon's pious tears'.[17] While appreciative of Richardson's understanding of human emotions, Smollett as satirist has as his prime concern the identification of false feeling and excessive feeling; these are shown to be absurd and even grotesque. Richardson's knowledge of the human heart Smollett respects, but he chooses not to reproduce it, concentrating instead on demonstrating what potential ludicrousness lies in the vogue of sensibility which Richardson's emotional bias engendered.

Such a perspective recurs throughout Smollett's novels and John Barth has aptly termed it Smollett's 'antisentimental candour'.[18] Thus if the language used by Fathom as romantic lover is overwrought, this is quite deliberate on Smollett's part (and the point is underlined by the fact that Fathom's amorous adventures are shown to be aspects of his opportunist charlatanry). Similarly, the nature of his prose shows that Smollett is equally detached from his account of the behaviour of Renaldo. Recollection of his beloved Monimia induces in Renaldo a 'pleasing anguish' and he visits her grave with his soul 'wound up to the highest pitch of enthusiastic sorrow' (p 317). So enthusiastic is his sorrow that his friends contrive a reunion of the lovers. Smollett exploits to the full the potential theatricality of the situation, and he takes care to point out that reason has no place in Renaldo's response. When Renaldo is conducted to the grave at midnight 'his imagination began to be heated into an extasy of enthusiasm, during which he again fervently invoked the spirit of his deceased Monimia' (p 323). At the unexpected sound of notes from the church organ, Renaldo 'was roused to the keenest sense of surprize and attention: reason shrunk before the thronging ideas of his fancy, which represented this musick as the prelude to something strange and supernatural'. When the scene is suddenly illuminated Renaldo's reaction is described thus: 'What passed within his mind on this occasion, is not easy to be described: all his faculties were swallowed up by those of seeing and of hearing' (p 324). And as the following indicates, the account of the reunion between the lovers typifies the extent to which Smollett uses style as a distancing mechanism:

> In the midst of these ejaculations, he ravished a banquet from her glowing lips, that kindled in his heart a flame, which rushed thro' every vein, and glided to

his marrow: this was a privilege he had never claimed before, and now permitted as a recompence for all the penance he had suffered; nevertheless, the cheeks of Monimia, who was altogether unaccustomed to such familiarities, underwent a total suffusion; and madame Clement discreetly relieved her from the anxiety of her situation, by interfering in the discourse, and rallying the count, upon his endeavours to monopolize such a branch of happiness (p 326).

The joys of grief, the pleasures of benevolism, sensation uncontrolled by reason, and the indulgence of romance—all are taken to a ludicrous extreme in the concluding section of *Ferdinand Count Fathom*.

One of the most significant features of Smollett's novels is the extent to which he appears to exemplify current vogues only, by distortion and exaggeration, to demonstrate comically their dangers and limitations. Like the conventions of the vogue of sensibility, the trappings of the Gothic are taken to extremes. Smollett employs a typically Scottish interest in the supernatural and the demonic for the purpose of exploring, and indicating the limitations of, the Gothic. In his dedication to *Ferdinand Count Fathom* Smollett asserts that 'the impulses of fear which is the most violent and interesting of all the passions, remain longer than any other upon the memory' (p 3). His earliest representation of fear in this novel is that experienced by Fathom during the 'Gothic interlude' in chapters 20 and 21. What emerges clearly from that episode is that the imagination can exacerbate responsiveness to fear. Since Fathom is the exemplar of this, he is identified as manifestly human in his limitations—a point that has to be established to counterbalance his alleged diabolism (He has, for instance, been mistaken for 'Satan *in propria persona*' (p 52)). As his deviousness and his fear demonstrate, Fathom, far from being the devil incarnate, is a real human being. Thus, while one of the roles he adopts is that of the devil, the quasi-diabolism is entirely subservient to his opportunism. Meeting the lovely Celinda, Fathom wishes 'to banquet his vicious appetite with the spoils of her beauty' (p 158). Detecting her 'superstitious fear', he plays upon 'such sensibility'. By means of music he soothes her sense of hearing 'even to a degree of ravishment, so as to extort from her an exclamation, importing, that he was surely something supernatural' (p 159). Habitually Fathom succeeds in his aims by overcoming the power of reason in others. As suggested by the recurrent analogy with the Garden of Eden and the identification of Fathom with the serpent (e.g. 'the biter is bit' (p 178)), Fathom is a variant upon the over-reacher: he is the man who, for his own purposes, would play, not God, but the devil. And for long such a man prospers in a society whose values are awry. Thus the rich fertility of Smollett's imagination has served his aims as satirist. Perhaps there is a certain irony in the fact that in the course of communicating his predominant rationalist sense Smollett has created a central character who epitomises in heightened form the chameleon quality that typified so many Scottish writers in the century after the Union.

In *Humphry Clinker* (1771) the trappings of the Gothic are prominent in the account of Lismahago's sojourn with the American Indians. Plainly Smollett's intention was to parody the adventure-tale. In the description of the torturing of Lismahago horror is undermined by absurdly exaggerated detail. It is worth noting, as evidence of the different stances of the two authors, that Henry Mackenzie was soon to offer similar material, but without the comic undermining, in *The Man of the World* (1773). Smollett, as well as parodying a popular literary genre, is casting typically sceptical doubts on the quest for noble savagery. But he does more: it is a tribute to the subtlety of Smollett's satire that through the figure of Lismahago he links the squaw Squinkinacoosta and Tabitha Bramble. Hearing of the former's epic achievements in savagery, Tabitha, all vanity and pretension, is interested only in the details of the wedding finery of the first Mrs Lismahago: two societies and their respective values have been neatly juxtaposed.

Humphry Clinker highlights an aspect of Smollett which seems to foreshadow a major emphasis in twentieth-century writing: the recognition, even the celebration, of the subjectivity inherent in human perception. This is achieved in two main ways—by showing how individuals in a group react variously to the same event, and by means of ironic self-revelation, especially through distinctive use of language. The former technique is not, of course, peculiar to Smollett and when, for instance, in *Roderick Random*, he presents the range of responses to the appearance of a highwayman the debt to *Joseph Andrews* is evident. But Smollett's fertility of invention is to the fore in *Peregrine Pickle* when he describes the range of behaviour at Trunnion's death-bed. In *Sir Launcelot Greaves* (1760–61) the interest in multiplicity of viewpoint finds fuller expression in that the novel, inspired in part by *Don Quixote*, is largely concerned with the individual responses of the group of characters who form around the hero in his travels. *Humphry Clinker* sees this technique reach full maturity. Matt, Tabitha, Jery, Lydia, and Win make the same tour of Britain but their responses to the shared experiences are separate and distinct. For the impressionable young Lydia, Bath is 'a new world . . . an earthly paradise' (p 39). The contrasting of her response with that of her irascible uncle is redolent of the exchange between Miranda and Prospero in *The Tempest* V, i. Matt, here a mouthpiece for Smollett, has misgivings about the hygienic aspect of the wells, and he is offended by the breakdown of the hierarchical social structure which he so values. For his nephew Jery, throughout the amused observer of life's farce, it is in precisely that same social heterogeneity that the attraction of Bath resides. Each response is valid for the individual concerned. According to Hume, 'a thousand different sentiments, excited by the same object, are all right; because no sentiment represents what is really in the object'.[19] When Smollett juxtaposes individual responses in this way he is maintaining a tradition of subjective impressionism which Wittig, finding it exemplified in such writers as Dunbar, Henryson, Hogg, and Stevenson, deemed distinctly Scottish.[20]

In this context the device of ironic self-revelation is especially significant. The way in which Matt is allowed to portray himself unwittingly through his letters may stand comparison with Galt's sustained use of the technique in *Annals of the Parish* where the annalist, Micah Balwhidder, reveals much more about himself than he realises. Self-revelation is a feature also of Scottish poetry from, for example, Dunbar's 'Testament of Mr. Andro Kennedy' to, at its most merciless, Burns's 'Holy Willie's Prayer'. When Matt writes of 'that fantastical animal, my sister Tabby' and continues, 'I vow to God, she is sometimes so intolerable, that I almost think she's the devil incarnate come to torment me for my sins; and yet I am conscious of no sins that ought to entail such family-plagues upon me' (p 12), he offers a view of his sister, says something about himself (He has fathered Humphry, but seems here to choose to overlook the fact), and in his choice of terms reflects several of the preoccupations of his author's cultural background.

The other characters, too, are subject to ironic self-revelation. The terms of his first letter reveal Jery as the self-consciously urbane impresario, intent on entertaining. Lydia writes as if she were one of the heroines of romance, all naive joyful innocence as she enthuses on Gloucester in terms drawn from her reading:

> The air is so pure; the Downs are so agreeable; the furze in full blossom; the ground enamelled with daisies, and primroses, and cowslips; all the trees bursting into leaves, and the hedges already clothed with their vernal livery; the mountains covered with flocks of sheep, and tender bleating wanton lambkins playing, frisking and skipping from side to side; the groves resound with the notes of black-bird, thrush, and linnet; and all night long sweet Philomel pours forth her ravishingly delightful song (p 27).

Likewise, hearing a particularly strident vocalist at Vauxhall, Lydia cannot find it in her nature to criticise; hence,

> Among the vocal performers I had the happiness to hear the celebrated Mrs —, whose voice was so loud and so shrill, that it made my head ake through excess of pleasure (p 93).

Smollett had developed as a dimension of caricature his talent for rendering distinctive use of language as an index to personality and values. Across a range of examples in his fiction oddities of speech relate chiefly either to nationality or occupation. In the travesty of legal language which flows from the mouth of Mr and Mrs Gobble in *Sir Launcelot Greaves*, he achieves a richness of invention worthy of Dickens. Here, for instance, is Mrs Gobble's rebuke to Greaves:

> 'Sirrah! sirrah! (cried she) do you dares to insult a worshipful magistrate on the bench? Can you deny that you are a vagram, and a dilatory sort of person? Han't the man with the satchel made an affidavy of it? If I was my husband, I'd lay you fast by the heels for your resumption, and ferk you with a primineery

into the bargain, unless you could give a better account of yourself—I would (p 94).

It is not just the nature of the language but also the character of the errors in the use of language that reveals the personality of the speaker. In the idiosyncratically flawed use of language as an index to values, Smollett anticipates not only Dickens but, especially where the terms bear a psycho-sexual significance, James Joyce.

Self-revealing diction is brought to a pitch of perfection in the letters of Tabitha and Win in *Humphry Clinker*. Here Tabitha laments some problems of household economics, but in terms which inadvertently betray some of her other, more private, concerns:

> Gwyn rites from Crickhowel, that the price of flannel is fallen three-farthings an ell; and that's another good penny out of my pocket—When I go to market to sell, my commodity stinks; but when I want to buy the commonest thing, the owner pricks it up under my nose; and it can't be had for love or money—I think everything runs cross at Brambleton-Hall (p 44).

Win begins a letter to Molly Jones with the assurance, 'Heaving got a frank, I now return your fever, which I received by Mr Higgins, at the Hot Well' (p 42). Her terms are rampantly physical: 'I defy the devil to say I am a tail-carrier' (p 71); 'O Mary! the whole family have been in such a constipation!' (p 155); 'and you would be surprised, Molly, to receive a bride's fever from your humble sarvant—but this is all suppository, dear girl' (p 307); 'Young squire Dollison and Miss Liddy make the second kipple; and there might have been a turd, but times are changed with Mr Clinker' (p 338); 'Now, Mrs Mary, our satiety is to suppurate' (p 352). This is the way in which she heralds the arrival of evangelical Methodism in the person of Humphry:

> O Mary Jones, pray without seizing for grease to prepare you for the operations of this wonderful instrument, which, I hope, will be exorcised this winter upon you and others at Brambleton-hall (p 156).

Such exuberantly Freudian use of language compares with Joyce's inventive word-play in *Ulysses* and *Finnegan's Wake*.

This is one respect in which Smollett's technique points forward to the twentieth century, but its origins may well lie in the Scottish cultural background. An interest in both language and rhetoric characterised Scottish education. Moreover one of the effects of the Union of 1707 was to make educated Scots acutely aware that Scotticisms in their language, spoken and written, might make them figures of fun outwith Scotland. David Hume, for example, lamented that '[we] speak a very corrupt dialect of the tongue we make use of',[21] and he was in the habit of sending his manuscripts south to David Mallet so that any Scotticisms might be identified and removed. In *Humphry Clinker* Matt is used to convey Smollett's awareness of the problem:

> . . . I think the Scots would do well, for their own sakes, to adopt the English idioms and pronunciation; those of them especially, who are resolved to push their fortunes in South-Britain. I know, by experience, how easily an English-man is influenced by the ear, and how apt he is to laugh, when he hears his own language spoken with a foreign or provincial accent (p 231).

One beneficial effect of this situation may well have been to sharpen Smollett's linguistic sense, with the verbal anarchy of Tabitha and Win the happy outcome.

There are other respects, too, in which Smollett and his achievements may be regarded in terms of the specific features of Scottish culture in the aftermath of the Union. The range and the diversity of Smollett's writing reflects the energetic response of Scots to the challenge which partnership in the Union—cultural as well as economic—presented, and the oppor-tunities it afforded. Even granting that Smollett collaborated with others in some of the translations that bear his name, the sheer range of his literary output is impressive. On the basis of a handful of poems in English which were widely anthologized ('The Tears of Scotland', 'Ode to Leven Water', and 'Ode to Independence') Smollett achieved considerable fame as a poet. But he was renowned also as historian, travel-writer, editor and literary journalist; and one of his letters refers to his 'extensive Plan . . . for a sort of Academy of the belles Lettres' (*Letters*, p 46).

By virtue of his *Complete History of England* (1757–8) and its *Continua-tion* (1760–5) Smollett shared with David Hume and William Robertson the pre-eminence that Scots achieved as historians in the mid-eighteenth century. Reasons for this success can be traced to both the central concerns of the Scottish Enlightenment and the pattern of events in Scotland in the eighteenth century. Common to the diverse activities of the major figures of the Scottish Enlightenment was a concern with man in society (on the practical level Smollett typifies this in, for instance, his *Essay on the External Use of Water* and, in his fiction, in his presentation of Bramble's reform of Baynard's estate management in *Humphry Clinker*). If rational-ist values were constant, then the purpose in examining human experience was to establish what were for Hume the universal principles of human nature by identifying the purely circumstantial or contextual. Both Hume and Smith tried to delineate the origin and the development of social and political institutions as an integral part of an attempt to understand the advance of civilisation in terms applicable to all people and cultures, and explicable in terms of the principles inherent in the processes. This evolutionary sense and the general concern of the Scottish Enlightenment philosophers with social progress helped stimulate historical research and interpretation. Moreover, after the Union, when Scottish independence ceased to be a possibility, the national spirit in Scotland tended to focus on Scotland's past. As David Daiches has pointed out, Scottish nationalism in the eighteenth century inevitably became associated with antiquarianism, and even before the defeat of the Jacobite cause there was already a vogue of sentimental Jacobitism.[22] Of Smollett's poems, 'The Tears of Scotland' and, to a lesser extent, 'Ode to Independence', originate in a sentimental nationalism which is to be found in the writing of various Scots—in no way excluding those who, like Smollett, had sought literary fame in London—who were publicly supportive of the Union and the Hanoverian dynasty. The 'Ode to Leven Water' sees Smollett expressing his nostalgia for his homeland in the most formal and stereotyped of English poetic diction. Such paradoxes are not rare in literature written by Scots in the eighteenth century.

In their quest for what they might deem cultural respectability for Scotland the Edinburgh *literati* sponsored a programme which resulted in William Wilkie, Thomas Blacklock, and John Home attempting to prove Scottish eminence in, respectively, epic, lyric, and tragic modes. Writers of no great originality, they allowed the traditions of genre to dictate the terms in which they wrote without their possessing the expressive ability to match them. In each case the writer was overwhelmed by the conventions of the medium. In contrast, Allan Ramsay and, even more so, Robert Fergusson, were prepared to employ actively, rather than merely defer to, or mimic, traditional forms. By means of a creative conflation of elements of the Scottish and English traditions they breathed new life into forms such as the pastoral, the epistle, and the elegy, employing them for distinctive purposes. Smollett is their counterpart in the novel. Like Ramsay, Fergusson, and also Burns, Smollett had the confidence and the ability to experiment with modes and techniques, achieving a cross-fertilisation of features of previously separate literary traditions. No slavish adherent to rules, Smollett was more ready to experiment than, for instance, Fielding, for whom the traditions of decorum and genre had much more meaning.

Here again one is confronted by one of the most strikingly paradoxical aspects of Smollett: the readiness for technical experimentation accompanies a strong endorsement of both the supremacy of reason and the hierarchical social order. In his *Essay on the Principles of Translation*, Lord Woodhouslee wrote that

> Smollett inherited from nature a strong sense of ridicule, a great fund of original humour, and a happy versatility of talent, by which he could accommodate his style to almost every species of writing. He could adopt, alternately, the solemn, the lively, the sarcastic, the burlesque, and the vulgar.[23]

The chameleon capacity of such eighteenth-century Scottish writers as Boswell and Burns is also exemplified in Smollett. Like Burns, Smollett occupies a pivotal position in the history of Scottish literature: both are poised between the comprehensive social vision of much medieval Scottish literature, and that dislocation and multiplicity of voice which have characterised so much Scottish writing since the Union. Probably the persistent pleas voiced in Smollett's fiction for social conservatism function as a counter-balance to the stylistic experimentation. In the crisis of Scottish identity in the eighteenth century may lie the principal source of the pace, the stylistic medley, and the multiple voices of Smollett's writing, with the habitual recourse to reductive rationalism representing an attempt to introduce a controlling agent into such diversity.

NOTES

1   References are to the Oxford University Press editions of the novels of Smollett: *The Adventures of Roderick Random*, edited with an introduction by Paul-Gabriel Boucé (Oxford, 1979); *The Adventures of Peregrine Pickle*, edited with an introduction by James L Clifford (London, 1964); *The Adventures of Ferdinand Count Fathom*, edited with an introduction by Damian Grant (London, 1971); *The Life and Adventures of Sir Launcelot Greaves*, edited with an introduction by David Evans (London, 1973); *The Expedition of Humphry Clinker*, edited with an introduction by Lewis M Knapp (London, 1966).
2   Cited by Kurt Wittig, *The Scottish Tradition in Literature* (Edinburgh, 1958), p 120.
3   Wittig, p 71.
4   *Roderick Random*, with an afterword by John Barth (Signet, New York, 1964), p 469.
5   Wittig, p 120.
6   Lewis M Knapp (ed) *The Letters of Tobias Smollett*, (Oxford, 1970), p 98.
7   Clifford, (ed), *Peregrine Pickle*, p xiii.
8   E H Gombrich, *Art and Illusion: A Study in the Psychology of Pictorial Representation* (London, 1959), p 292.
9   G Gregory Smith, *Scottish Literature: Character and Influence* (London, 1919), p 15.
10 In a letter of 18 May 1770 Smollett wrote of 'the absurd Stoicism of Lord Bute, who set himself up as a Pillory to be pelted by all the Blackguards of England, upon the Supposition that they would grow tired and leave off' (*Letters*, p 137).
11 V S Pritchett, *The Living Novel* (London, 1954), p 20.
12 Ronald Paulson, 'Satire in the Early Novels of Smollett', *Journal of English and Germanic Philology*, July 1960, 381–402.
13 Wittig, p 174.
14 William Hazlitt, *Lectures on the English Comic Writers*, R Brimley Johnson (ed) (London, 1907), p 153.
15 *The Monthly Review*, viii (1753), p 203.
16 David Masson, *British Novelists and their Styles* (London, 1859), p 144.
17 Pritchett, p 9
18 *Roderick Random*, with afterword by Barth, p 476.
19 David Hume, *Four Dissertations* (New York, 1970), p 208.
20 Wittig, pp 125, 248–50.
21 J Y T Grieg (ed) *The Letters of David Hume*, (Oxford, 1961), i, p 255.
22 David Daiches, *The Paradox of Scottish Culture* (London, 1964), p 27.
23 Cited by Sir Walter Scott, *The Lives of the Novelists* (London and New York, 1910), p 85.

FURTHER READING

Alter, Robert, 'The Picaroon as Fortune's Plaything', *Rogue's Progress* (Cambridge, Mass., 1964), pp 58–79

Bold, Alan, (ed), *Tobias Smollett: Author of the First Distinction* (London and Totowa, N.J., 1982)

Boucé, Paul-Gabriel, *The Novels of Tobias Smollett* (London and New York, 1976)

Bruce, Donald, *Radical Dr Smollett* (London, 1964)

Giddings, Robert, *The Tradition of Smollett* (London, 1967)

Goldberg, Milton A, *Smollett and the Scottish School* (Albuquerque, 1959)

Grant, Damian, *Tobias Smollett: A Study in Style* (Manchester, 1977)

Kahrl, George M, *Tobias Smollett, Traveler-Novelist* (Chicago, 1945)

Knapp, Lewis M, *Tobias Smollett, Doctor of Men and Manners* (Princeton, N.J., 1949)

Martz, Louis L, *The Later Career of Tobias Smollett* (New Haven, 1942)

Paulson, Ronald, *Satire and the Novel in Eighteenth-Century England* (New Haven and London, 1967), pp 165–218

Preston, Thomas R, *Not in Timon's Manner: Feeling, Misanthropy, and Satire in Eighteenth-Century England* (Alabama, 1975), pp 69–120

Spector, Robert D *Tobias Smollett* (New York, 1968)

Chapter 7

Lowland Song and Popular Tradition in the Eighteenth Century

THOMAS CRAWFORD

Ballad editors, antiquarians and song-writers from Tom d'Urfey through Francis James Child and Cecil Sharp to A L Lloyd have recently come under embattled and polemical scrutiny in Dave Harker's *Fakesong*: (Milton Keynes, 1985).[1] For Harker, there is in Britain a workers' culture (he fights shy of terms like 'peasantry' and 'people') which we know largely from the records of non-worker mediators (i.e. collectors and editors), and which has been fairly consistently falsified by those who have used and indeed robbed it, just as in the economic sphere they have appropriated the workers' surplus labour-power. In the eighteenth and early nineteenth centuries the worst offenders were the Scots, and they included not only Lord Hailes (provider of key ballad texts for Percy's *Reliques of Ancient English Poetry*, 1765), Walter Scott, Charles Kirkpatrick Sharpe, and Robert Jamieson; not only such a notorious fabricator as John Pinkerton—but the queen of ballad recorders herself, Anna Gordon (Mrs. Brown of Falkland), as well as the 'upwardly mobile' Allan Ramsay and Robert Burns.

Although Harker does not like the word 'folk', there is much in common between his basic position and Gramsci's view that the essence of folksong is that it is a 'separate and distinct way of perceiving life and the world, as opposed to that of "official" society'.[2] I prefer to retain 'folk' for orally transmitted material: to speak of Gramsci's distinct ways of seeing as 'plebeian'; and to see unity as well as division in the song culture. No-one would wish to deny the truth of another often quoted statement by Gramsci: 'the people is not a culturally homogeneous unit, but it is culturally stratified in a complex way'.[3] In lowland Scotland in the eighteenth century, however, that complexity meant that strata (regional, urban, rural, or class) were not completely isolated from each other, and that there was much cross-fertilisation. It was thus possible for the upper classes, if they wished, to be aware of almost the whole culture, and for an 'upwardly mobile' genius like Burns to use popular culture for the highest creative purposes, as Bartók and Kodaly were to do for music in twentieth-century Hungary.[4]

It is my contention then that the eighteenth century from Ramsay to the death of Burns saw the rise and maturity of a lyric culture in which practically everybody took part. On this view popular song is a genus:

folksong, broadside and chapbook song, and what Francis Collinson, adapting a nineteenth-century term, has called 'national songs'[5]—i.e. literary creations specially composed or cobbled together from older songs with publication in mind—are species of the genus. But among the populace at large there was no absolute division between 'folk' ballads and street songs. Broadsides and chapbooks circulated in Scotland throughout the century; they were sold at country fairs and hawked around villages and farms by pedlars, as well as in the towns by street singers like the whore in Fergusson's *Auld Reikie* (lines 87–97). In practice, however, balladmongers sold sheets that might contain folk ballads, pastorals, lamentable ditties about betrayed maidens, atrocity stories, tales like 'The Babes in the Wood', and national songs like 'My Peggy is a young thing' or 'In the garb of old Gaul'. Only a part of the broadside repertoire proclaimed 'the vigorous anti-heroic realism and hearty sensuality' which have been seen as the essential qualities of the street ballad,[6] and which seem to fit in with Gramsci's 'separate and distinct way of perceiving life and the world': the rest was much more like the sensational or sentimental matter of modern popular newspapers. In addition to 'national song' itself, the narrower term 'artificial song' is helpful, applied to a peculiar sub-class associated with the 'polite' and having an idea-content linked to the mid and late century cult of sentiment. These categories continually overlap; 'Ae fond kiss' and 'A rosebud by my early walk', in spite of their Scots-English language, manage to be artificial and national at one and the same time.

The model which sees folksong as just a species of the broader genus popular song has the merit of being able to accommodate what actually happened in Scottish popular culture during the century. Scots tunes and songs had been known and liked in England from the late sixteenth century (a 'Scotch jig' is mentioned in *Much Ado about Nothing*, II. 1. 70–1): in the late seventeenth century they were being adapted and even manufactured, both words and music, and published by such classical composers as Purcell, or the hugely successful versifier and editor Tom d'Urfey, whose *Pills to Purge Melancholy* (four editions between 1699 and 1719–20) contained a few genuine Scottish airs and a very large number of fakes. Some of these came back over the border to be re-Scottified and sung at least by the middle classes. The most important effect of d'Urfey's *Pills* in Scotland, however, was to stimulate Allan Ramsay to follow up his minuscule *Scots Songs* of 1718, 1719, and 1720 with the four little volumes of *The Tea Table Miscellany* between 1723 and 1737, which speedily became the most popular collection of song-words, not just in Scotland but throughout the British Isles. It contained some genuine folk pieces, some d'Urfey songs with the phoney Scots 'corrected', and a larger number of freshly written words to old tunes, with the aim of making them more acceptable to the 'refined', particularly the ladies of polite Edinburgh. In his preface to the 1733 edition Ramsay said that in the first two volumes he had supplied his own new verses for 'above sixty' tunes, and 'about thirty more by some ingenious young gentlemen', such as David Malloch (Mallet) and Robert Crawford. Ramsay and his young gentlemen consolidated the practice of writing new words to old tunes, which was continued later in the century by men like Alexander Ross and the Reverend John Skinner, whose 'Tullochgorum' was termed by Burns 'the best Scotch song ever Scotland saw' (*Letters*, I, 167); by women like Alison Cockburn, Jane Elliot, and Lady Nairne; and above all by Burns himself.

Ramsay's *Miscellany* stimulated the production of other song books. Most were without music, but William Thomson's *Orpheus Caledonius* (London, 1726, 1733) is an important exception: David Johnson judges some of its settings 'extremely tasteful', with 'delicately ornamented' vocal lines (p 140). Some seventy-four song books are known to have been published in Scotland before 1786 (*SL*, pp 216–9), containing between them about three thousand separate songs, the majority being of English origin; and of course miscellanies printed south of the border would be sold by Scottish booksellers. The pieces in the song books are broadly speaking the same sort of songs as those in the chapbooks, slips, broadsides, and manuscripts that have been preserved, though they print a larger number of art songs than the other vehicles. David Herd's *Ancient and Modern Scots Songs, Heroic Ballads, &c.* (Edinburgh, 1769, 1776) is rather different: the predominant language is Scots, and it contains a high proportion of plebeian material, especially in the 'fragments of comic and humourous songs' in the 1776 edition. All these sources record an active song culture; the printed ones furthered the activities of singing and composing in everyday life.

The role of printed song books as distinct from oral tradition in the daily living of a gifted young plebeian can be seen in Burns's account of the unnamed 'select Collection of English songs'[7] which was his 'vade mecum.—I pored over them, driving my cart or walking to labor, song by song, verse by verse; carefully noting the true tender or sublime from affectation and fustian' (To Dr Moore, *Letters*, I, 138–9). The upper and middle classes had been involved with both Scots and English songs from the beginning of the century: Ramsay of Ochtertyre, for instance, tells us that in the 1720s 'persons of wit and fashion . . . attempted to write Scottish poetry', and he makes a telling point when he says that 'a song in the dialect of Cumberland or Somersetshire could never have been generally accepted in England, because it was never spoken by people of fashion'.[8] In the burgh schools where upper and middle-class children were educated alongside working-class 'lads o' pairts', they took part in plays in Latin, English, and even Scots (the first recorded performance of Ramsay's *Gentle Shepherd*, which of course included songs, was by schoolboys, and it was actually the pupils of Haddington Grammar School who asked Ramsay to make a ballad opera out of it). Nor were the actors always boys. Sir William Bennet copied out in a manuscript notebook a dramatic lyric written for a school play, a translation of Terence's *Eunuchus*, 'as it was acted by the scholars of Kelso' on 18 August 1727. The lyric was inserted into the prologue and 'spoken by a young Lady, fam'd for a fine voice, followed by a set of others, all habited like Amazons, with gully knives in sheaths, hanging at their Girdles'. After the first stanza of the prologue 'and betwixt all the stanzas following the Lady's did draw their gullys and flourished the same, round their heads, singing the Chorus to the Tune of, geld them, Lasses, geld them'.

The Clerk papers in the Scottish Record Office seem to provide an instance of that almost legendary 'folk' activity, group composition, dating from c. 1708; but it is by a highly cultivated, not an illiterate group. It is 'The Pennicuick Song . . . about Nanse Weston . . . composed by John Clerk, younger, of Pennicuick, Dr. John Clerk, and Dr. Arthure . . . To its proper tune composed by the same hands First part for a grave tune in common time'.

The manuscript is set out just like a printed broadside and the piece is written in broadside style, colloquial in idiom though not in vernacular Scots. The rather English-sounding chorus almost sings itself:

> Come sit thou down my Nanse
>   thou art my only fancy
> The Lily & Rose thy cheeks compose
>   and thy breath's sweat like a Tansy.   [sweet]

The interest of this family in Scots song is seen in the rather stilted vernacular of Stanzas ii–iv of 'O merry may the maid be / That marries with the miller' added by Sir John Clerk to the traditional first stanza (*LLL*. pp 42–3).

A key document for the way songs and ballads aided and indeed expressed the social life of at least some Scottish Enlightenment families is the St Clair manuscript (also known as the Mansfield MS) in Broughton House, Kirkcudbright.[9] Its compiler, Elizabeth St Clair, was for most of her life a friend of Alison Cockburn, author of one of the two main sets of 'The Flowers of the Forest'. Her MS includes twenty texts of traditional ballads and many orally transmitted folksongs and fragments (some overlapping with texts in the MSS of the antiquarian and editor David Herd), as well as songs copied from print and—what is of most interest here—songs composed by Mrs Cockburn, other members of the Dalrymple-Cockburn circle, and also, it would seem, of the Hamilton family.

There is one particularly choice item—a delightul parody on 'Willie's gane to Melville Castle', where the protagonist throws all the lassies into confusion when he is forced to leave for a watering place. The women are all mentioned by name in the succeeding stanzas—the Duchess of Ross, Miss Ross, Jeany Hamilton, Betty Ross, Betty Dalrymple, Betty Graham and Lady Betty Montgomerie. They all 'greet' when Billy leaves, then 'dry up their e'en' and give him a loud Huzza. The last two stanzas read:

> O Lady Ross sat knotting by
> And wondered at them a'
> Dear lasses trust in providence
> And ye's get Husbands a'.   [you'll]
>
> But what care we if he come back
> Or he return at a'
> For a' our Lasses shall be wives
> Or Billy comes frae spaw.   [spa]
> (p 122)

Another song, definitely by Alison Cockburn, applies the street-singer's style to an aristocratic occasion—a ridotto at Holyrood House (pp 198–201). Certain persons are mentioned, and a peculiarity of each is detailed, just as in that most plebeian of forms, the nineteenth-century bothy ballad. An example is Stanza xii on the writer of the manuscript herself:

> Bess St Clair was there so charming & gay
> As red as the morning & bright as the day

or the malicious Stanza xiv:

> Seven virgins laid hold of one man woes me
> Alas for the Ladies Monboddo was he.

The songs I have quoted from the St Clair MS are occasional pieces by the women of a small in-group who knew all about folk ballads, and indeed collected them, and for whom it was the most natural thing in the world to write their own 'lyrics of action'.

One person who produced lyrics for music throughout his life was James Boswell.[10] He wrote on his amours ('A Crambo Song on losing my mistress'): on his own and other legal cases, like the famous Douglas Cause, which he celebrated in a Scots song beginning 'Gif ye a dainty mailing [small-holding] want / And idleseat prefer to working'; on that most fascinating of beings, himself ('B[oswell], a Song; To the Tune of "Old Sir Simon the King"', an English tune used in *The Beggar's Opera* and by Burns for the merry-andrew's song in *Love and Liberty*); and, satirically, on the characters of others, like those in his broadside-type concoction 'The Justiciary Garland' of 1776, featuring the luminaries of the Scottish law-courts in exactly the same way as Alison Cockburn treated aristocratic women, mentioning each by name and briefly indicating their peculiarities: Auchinleck (Boswell's own father), Macqueen (later Lord Braxfield), Kames, Hailes, Dundas and Monboddo are only a few of the names that crop up. Among the Boswell papers at Yale are plans for a ballad opera on a Scottish law theme, with songs assigned to many of the same characters; it is clear that the Garland records a considerable part of this 'Justiciary Opera'; and the extraordinary thing is that some of the songs, from the tory Boswell, exhibit attitudes which Dave Harker might be disposed to see as typical of workers' culture, or a follower of Gramsci as expressing the philosophy and modes of feeling of the oppressed. The following 'Song in the Character of Lord Kames' is a case in point:

>   Of all the judges in the land
>   I surely must be held the chief,
>   For, none so cleverly can hang
>   A bloody murderer or thief . . (Stanza i)

Considerably more radical are the implications of the 'Prisoners' Chorus',

>   O send us owr the wide seas   [over]
>   Our ain kind Lordies   [own]
>   To the Plantations where you please
>   Our ain kind Lordies;
>   For gang this trial as it will   [go]
>   Our ain kind Lordies
>   In Scotland we can fare but ill
>   Our ain kind Lordies.

Among the Yale MSS is one song in Boswell's hand, separate from 'The Justiciary Opera', which may yet be connected with it. Entitled 'Cut him down Susie', it conveys all the horror of the public execution system with a marvellous dramatic economy:

>   Cut him down Susie,
>   Haste ye wi your gully knife   [large knife]
>   Ye'se get him for your ain Gudeman   [you shall]
>   Gin ye contrive to save his life.   [if]
>
>   Cut him down and take him hame
>   And send for folk to dance and sing
>   And pit your arms about the neck   [put]
>   That on the gallows tree did hing.

I have already said that the Clerk family's 'Pennicuick Song about Nanse Weston' seems to have been produced in an extraordinary outburst of group spontaneity. Some at least of 'The Justiciary Opera' was written in the same way, for Boswell notes on 17 March 1778: 'Crosbie and I amused ourselves at times during this journey with making more of *The Justiciary Opera*, adapting the proceedings of the Criminal Court to tunes and putting them in rhyme, with much merriment produced by parody and ludicrous contrasts of various kinds'. Three persons were originally involved in its composition—Andrew Crosbie, John Maclaurin (later Lord Dreghorn), and Boswell, the occasion being the acquittal of certain clients of theirs (Journ. 4 March 1776). Now the tunes to which the songs in 'The Justiciary Opera' are directed to be sung are in the main Scottish—proof positive, one would think, of the legal profession's familiarity with both the words and music of their country's popular song.

Burns has left us two excellent accounts of the role of popular song in the lives of farmers and country workers—the story of how he composed his earliest song, and his description of how he first heard of John Lapraik. Burns wrote 'O once I lov'd a bonie lass' when he was about fifteen, for Nelly Kirkpatrick, his fourteen-year-old neighbour in the harvest field. Nelly provided the stimulus by singing a song written in the locality by 'a small country laird's son, on one of his father's maids, with whom he was in love; and I saw no reason why I might not rhyme as well as he' (To Dr Moore, *Letters*, I. 137–8). It was an incident in a courtship ritual where young people were expected to sing to each other, and although the pieces were not labour but leisure songs, they were yet sung on the fringes of economic activity: further, the tune to which Burns's words were to go 'was her favorite reel to which I attempted giving an embodied vehicle in rhyme.' Almost all the features of Burns's mature writing for Johnson's *Scots Musical Museum* and Thomson's *Select Collection of Original Scotish Airs* are here present in a 'folk' or 'workers' context; yet that song, as preserved by Burns, contains such artificial tea-table lines as 'But it's innocence and modesty / That polishes the dart' (lines 23–4).

The Lapraik incident took place at a sort of *celidh* of neighbours on Shrove Tuesday evening, 1785, where everybody sang a song in turn. One song pleased him above the rest, 'When I upon thy Bosom lean', which was so refined, so anglified

> Thought I, 'Can this be Pope, or Steele,
>   Or Beattie's wark?'   [work]
> They tald me 'twas an odd kind chiel   [told]   [agreeable fellow]
>   About Muirkirk.   [near]

('Epistle to J Lapraik', lines 21–4)

Lapraik had once been a small laird, and what may have been a first version of his song was printed in Ruddiman's *Weekly Magazine* for 14 October 1773. The occasion provides further evidence of the spread of artificial lyric by this time: a piece reminiscent of Pope or Steele could be presented in what was still almost a 'folk' cultural context.

There is nothing really surprising about the interpenetration of the cultures of the upper and lower classes in Scotland; it is merely a special case of a general European phenomenon (Burke, pp 60–3, and *passim*). In protestant countries there was higher general literacy than in catholic ones, with the result that oral transmission was strongly reinforced by print; in Sweden there was a breakthrough to majority literacy about 1700, and in some parishes a literacy rate of 98 per cent by 1714 has been claimed (Burke, p 252). Although comparable results were not achieved in Scotland till somewhat later, 'between them, the parochial schools and the adventure schools of the Lowlands were able to maintain a rural society in which almost everyone seems to have been able to read and write from at least as early as the mid-eighteenth century'.[11] The development towards literacy was necessarily patchy and uneven, and it may well be that in the areas of the traditional ballad communities of the North-East and the Borders majority literacy was not achieved before the very end of the century. The laird's children mixed with the cottar's in the parochial schools, and would no doubt learn their songs, dances and tales, as well as the rudiments of Latin, which was mentioned in the Old Statistical Account of Scotland as taught in 185 parishes by the end of the century (Scotland, I, 67). It seems to me that the following song in the folk mode (perhaps it accompanied a children's game) illustrates perfectly how the different classes and their cultures may have come together at school level:

> There was a pretty maiden & she was dress'd in satin
> And she was dress'd in satin,
> And she sat down upon the ground
> Cried kiss me Jacky Latin.
> Kiss me Jacky, kiss me Jacky,
> Kiss me Jacky Latin
> Won't you kiss your pretty maid,
> Altho' she's dress'd in satin
> (St Clair MS, p 14)[12]

The community also shared in popular processions and games. At Scone in the early eighteenth century, for example, 'every man in the parish (even the gentry) was expected to turn out to the annual Shrove Tuesday football game between married men and bachelors, which began at two in the afternoon and lasted until sunset' (Scotland, I, 68). When such close contacts between persons of differing status are borne in mind, it seems the most natural thing in the world that small lairds like the Sempills of Beltrees should have been the pioneers of a new *vernacular* poetry in the seventeenth century. ('The Life and Death of Habbie Simson', ascribed to Robert Sempill, deals with folk life if ever a poem did; its subject is the town piper, who played to rouse the townsfolk at break of day, or before a hunt or a shearing, or at fairs, dramatic performances, horse races, weddings, and feasts).[13] Nor does it seem altogether far-fetched that literate persons in the countryside or even the burghs may have been among the creators of at least some of the traditional ballads, writing in a mode whose structure was originally determined by the process of oral composition and transmission.

It is the same story with music proper. David Johnson's major premise is that there were two 'distinct types' of music, folk and classical (p 3); he is well aware that the folk tradition in eighteenth-century Scotland was available to all classes, but it is his strategy to 'temporarily separate folk and classical music from each other, and consider them as different cultures' (p 19), with the implication that it is sometimes possible to see them as parts of a single whole. Sometimes they are in confrontation, sometimes united. The complexities of the process are well illustrated at the material level by the development of musical instruments, and also from the history of dance. To take instruments first: the violin had been used to play folk tunes as early as 1680 (Johnson, p 101) and had become the predominant instrument in the lowlands by the beginning of the eighteenth century. It was not a direct descendant of the sixteenth-century rebeck or its medieval predecessors, but an *upper-class* importation from Italy, *via* England. In an incredibly short time Scottish craftsmen's copies of the Italian baroque violin had in the lowlands driven all earlier folk instruments into the background; even in the highlands and islands it made inroads against the bagpipe, while over the country as a whole it became the main vehicle for a new type of dance music. Its repertoire was not so much transmitted aurally, like that of the folk instruments of earlier centuries, as passed on in manuscript and print by players in the mainstream—'the dancing-masters, the village and town craftsmen, and professional men such as schoolmasters and doctors' (Johnson, p 112)—that is, by the same sort of *literate* people as wrote vernacular poetry.

Fiddle music went hand in hand with dancing mania. If we accept the probability that 'many current steps and figures have their origins in both the medieval Lowlands and Highlands',[14] then it seems plain that the Church had been quite unable to suppress these prototypes—the dances for which Habbie Simson and his ilk provided the music. In the early eighteenth century there was a positive explosion—what might be called 'the dance revolution', summed up in the title of a manuscript written in Edinburgh by David Young in 1740: 'A collection of the newest Countrey Dances Perform'd in Scotland'—no less than forty-eight of them, all with their steps and movements explained in detail (Johnson, p 121). Now the instrument which accompanied these dances, the violin, could also be used to play Corelli, Handel, Haydn, and the music of such native composers as the Earl of Kellie. Once again there is juxtaposition and blending of 'higher' and 'lower' cultural strands, an intermingling formalised in the practice of the Musical Societies of Edinburgh and Aberdeen, at whose concerts Scots tunes were regularly played and Scots songs sung, sometimes after and sometimes in the middle of the main classical programme.[15] These songs were not performed in a 'folk' style, but with instrumental, harmonised accompaniment, and the words were generally as supplied by Allan Ramsay or some of his ingenious young gentlemen. In purely instrumental music, there were further types of fusion, like Disblair's set of variations on 'John Anderson my Jo', with sections entitled 'Vivace', 'un poco Largo' etc., or Alexander Munro's 'Scots Sonatas' in *A Collection of the best Scots Tunes* (Paris, 1732).[16] The best effects were obtained where classical techniques were absorbed 'but the result still has a folk identity', in the style associated with the composer and music publisher James Oswald (Johnson, p 119). Neil Gow (1727–1807) was merely the best known of a number of virtuoso professional fiddlers, thoroughly conversant with classical modes and techniques, who played and composed Scottish dance music; and it is significant that when Burns wrote new words to existing tunes for *The Scots Musical Museum* they came as often as not from recent collections of fiddle music that already bore the marks of cultural fusion in the purely musical sphere.

Listening to songs and sonatas at the Musical Societies, and to professional singers at the theatre, was of course a passive pleasure; but music in Scotland was on the whole an active pursuit, with men playing mainly recorder, flute, violin, and cello, and ladies mainly keyboard instruments and the cittern (English guitar), while the bulk of both semi-professional and amateur string playing accompanied that most active of social enjoyments, the dance. Burns comments ironically on the musical synthesis in his rendering of the presumably illiterate pigmy gut-scraper in *Love and Liberty*:

> Wi' hand on hainch, and upward e'e,   [haunch] [eye]
> He croon'd his gamut, ONE, TWO, THREE,
> Then in an ARIOSO key,
>   The wee Apollo
> Set off wi' ALLEGRETTO glee
>   His GIGA SOLO (lines 123–8)

Let us now return to song. Popular lyrics had three social functions: they transmitted past attitudes and emotions (some of rural origin, some urban-plebeian, some upper class and even, ultimately, courtly) to the younger generation; they provided a medium in which people of all ages could share such experiences as love, tragic emotion, 'social glee', and bacchanalian abandon; and they could be used, sometimes by gifted writers like Ramsay and Burns, more often by ordinary people in everyday life, to body forth perceptions differing in some degree from those of their neighbours.

Tragic and wondrous emotion were conveyed primarily by such of the 'big' heroic and romantic ballads as remained in oral circulation or were printed in broadsides—like 'The Twa Sisters' and 'Lamkin' in Anna Gordon's repertoire.[17] Her text of 'Lamkin' has three stanzas whose class consciousness would surely appeal to both Hacker and Gramsci:

> 'O sall I kill her, nourice,   [shall] [nurse]
>   or sall I lat her be?'   [let]
> 'O kill her, kill her, Lamkin,
>   for she neer was good to me.'

> 'O scour the bason, nourice,   [basin]
>   and mak it fair and clean,
> For to keep this lady's heart's blood,
>   for she's come o noble kin.'

> 'There need nae bason, Lamkin,
>   lat it run through the floor;
> What better is the heart's blood
>   o the rich than o the poor?'
> (Stanzas xx–xxii)

Though there were differences between the drinking songs of the upper and lower classes, they need not detain us, for the sentiments are naturally very similar. Plebeian pieces like 'Todlen Hame' and 'The Four Drunken Maidens/Down i' the Nether Bow' are far more energetic than the average (English) catch in the Scottish song books, but they cannot equal the vigour of Robert Fergusson's (also English) Cape Club song 'Hollo! keep it up, Boys', with its

> How all things dance round me!—'tis life, tho' my boys
> Of drinking and spewing how great are the joys!
> (lines 11–12)

or Burns's superbly Scottish 'Rattlin, roarin Willie' and 'Willie brew'd a peck o' Maut'.

There is one class of song which by definition the upper classes could not produce—the song of physical labour, and if relatively few of these have come down to us as compared with the orally transmitted waulking, rowing and reaping songs of the Gaelic-speaking areas, that is no doubt because they lacked interested 'mediators'. Most Lowland songs connected with work that have survived concern the praise of a trade or, as with many ploughman songs, with the sexual prowess of its practitioners, and quite a few are written from a woman's point of view, like the version of 'Hey ca' thro [Hey work with a will]' in the St Clair MS:

> We have sheets to shape
> And we have beds to make
> And we have corn to shear,
> And we have bairns to bear.
> (p 106)

The most remarkable of all these women's songs from the world of labour is to be found in *The Universal Scots Songster* (Edinburgh, 1781). It is 'My yellow-mou'd [jaundiced] mistress, I bid you adieu' to the tune 'Sodger Laddie', which Ramsay had used for some insipid patriotic verses in *The Tea Table Miscellany*, and Burns in 1785 for the martial chuck's song in *Love and Liberty*. Its way of perceiving life and the world seems quite different from the establishment's. It is about a maidservant who is fed up with her tyrannical mistress, though the revenge she craves is not a bloody one like the nurse's in 'Lamkin'. The last straw is when she goes to the well and loses her pitcher—'And when I came home, she kicked my doup [behind]'. There is nothing for it now but to go off and be a camp-follower:

> In heat of battles, I'll keep on the flank,
> With a stone in a stocking, and give them a clank.
> If he be knock'd down, though he be my daddy,
> I'll bring all his clink to my sodger laddie.   [cash]   [soldier]
> > *My sodger laddie, my sodger laddie,*
> > *The kisses are sweet of a sodger laddie.*
>
> For robbing the dead is no theivish trick,
> I'll rifle his breeches, and then his knapsack,
> But yet on a friend I'll not be so ready,   [likely to]
> If he's been acquaint with my sodger laddie.
> > *My sodger laddie, etc.*
> (Stanzas ix, x)

And when she comes home overflowing with riches she'll

> ... ask my old lady if she's found her burn stoup,   [pitcher]
> And all my days after, I'll live like a lady,
> On the gold I've got from my sodger laddie.
> (Stanza xi)

The servant girl in 'My yellow-mou'd mistress' is a younger, more innocent sister-under-the-skin of Burns's martial chuck, a superb example of the type I have called 'the independent heroine' of folk and popular song, who either expresses simple and overwhelming delight in getting the man she loves instead of some wealthy fool her parents want to foist on her, or else is bent on venturing all for love, perhaps choosing to live in sin with her lover when her father refuses to give the necessary tocher (examples are quoted in *SL*, pp 23–5). When married, she is the singer in the high-kilted version of 'John Anderson, my Jo', a plebeian beauty of gargantuan desire, who will give her man 'the cuckold's malison' if her demands are not satisfied—as she says in Stanza vii of the *Scots Nightingale* text (Edinburgh, 1778), not found in Burns's *Merry Muses* version:

> I'll study my ain conveniency,
> John Anderson, my jo.

She even found her way into the drawing-room fare of *The Tea Table Miscellany*, as in this courtship dialogue (II, 1740, p 70, Stanza iv):

> Jeany said to Jocky, gin ye winna tell,   [if]   [won't]
> Ye shall be the lad, I'll be the lass my sell.   [self]
> Ye're a bonny lad, and *I'm a lassie free*   [my italics]
> Ye're welcomer to tak me than to let me be.

When ladies sang or listened to songs like the above, they presumably—by partially identifying with a compliant peasant girl—experienced an imaginary and vicarious sensation of freedom. It is, after all, one of the pleasures of pastoral.

If the themes of upper and lower class love song were often the same, the differences in treatment were significant. 'She delays too long' and *carpe diem* are not merely private emotions for ordinary folk, but are almost always presented in a social context, for example in the dreadful prospect of life-long celibacy that might confront the coy girl in Ramsay's 'The Bob of Dumblane' should she once more refuse her wooer's offer:

> [dress in your finery]
> Busk ye braw, and dinna think shame;   [don't be ashamed]
> Consider in time, if leading of monkies
> Be better than dancing the *Bob of Dumblane*.
> (lines 7–8)

(An old folk belief was that after death old maids led apes in hell; the Bob of Dumblane is both the name of a dance and in this context a synonym for sexual intercourse). On the other hand, love-melancholy and despair, perhaps the commonest feelings expressed in the love lyric, are by their very nature individual, and are common to both sectors of the song culture. Lyrics that delight in the ups and downs of courtship are found in upper-class as well as lower-class song, and pastoral makes its way into every nook and cranny—not just *The Gentle Shepherd*, which at one time seems to have been just as popular as Burns' works were to be in the next century, but thoroughly artificial pieces like 'The Shepherd Adonis being weary'd with sport' (*TTM*, II, 114), generally attributed to Sir Gilbert Elliot of Minto. As the century wore on this song, felt as completely Scottish despite its formal English language, was even assimilated into the urban popular repertoire. It was printed in an Edinburgh chapbook of 1776, and expanded in an undated broadside from forty-eight to eighty lines. Its inclusion in 1788 in *The Scots Musical Museum* (No. 159) acknowledged it as one of the standard national songs of the century.

The lyric medium could be employed to further a cause, or for political and social satire, or as an integral part of a play like *The Gentle Shepherd*, or within a basically narrative form like *Love and Liberty*. The last two works, masterpieces that *use* the song culture, body forth what Raymond Williams called 'structures of feeling'—the one an ideologically orthodox, partly realistic pastoral condemning luxury, superfluity, and superstition in the interests of social integration, the other using songs of a plebeian sort (basically, broadside and 'chap' songs) to unite a root and branch critique of all orthodox society with a 'world-upside-down' celebration of energy and instinct. Though love songs often contain incidental social criticism (e.g. those centring in the love-money antagonism), social satire is largely the preserve of broadside balladry.

The causes furthered in lyrics of a partisan sort were upper-class and bourgeois ones like Jacobitism; the Hanoverianism of the whigs and 'cits'; and Freemasonry, whose celebration of fraternity looked forward to at least one of the ideals of the French Revolution. But there was little commitment to democracy until the end of the century, and only Burns's libertarian songs like 'Scots Wha Hae' and 'A Man's a Man for a' that' made any lasting impact; even his own most revolutionary song, 'The Tree of Liberty', was never in print till 1838, and was excluded as of doubtful authenticity from most editions of the poet's works throughout the nineteenth and early twentieth centuries.[18] As in England, there were election ballads in support of parliamentary candidates, of which once again Burns's are the best example (Kinsley, Nos. 491–4): these, as befitted their genre, were first printed as broadsides—vigorous, ephemeral pieces, with lines like the following:

> Yon beardless boy comes o'er the hills,
>   Wi's uncle's gowd, and a' that: [gold]
> But we'll hae ane frae 'mang oursels
>   A man we ken and a' that.—
>   For a' that and a' that,
>   Here's Heron yet for a' that;
>   We are na to the market come
>   Like nowt and naigs and a' that.   [cattle] [horses]
> (491, Stanza v)

In this essay I have been at pains to stress the unity of the lowland song culture in the eighteenth century, rather than its divisions. Gavin Greig, perhaps the greatest of all Scots song collectors, had a different view. In the last of the 180 articles on folksong he contributed to the *Buchan Observer* between 1907 and 1911 he stated a position that can easily be reconciled with those of Harker and Gramsci:

> The fact of the matter is that we have been wrong about our native mins-
> trelsy—wrong all the time. We have taken it to be the body of lyrics written by
> Ramsay, Burns, Hogg, and the rest of the Scottish bardic fraternity, and set to
> so-called Scottish airs—all as per the books; whereas the true native minstrelsy
> of Scotland—what our peasantry have really sung all down the generations, is
> just the traditional songs and ballads set to traditional airs which we have been
> bringing to light.[19]

It is possible, however, to interpret the data in a slightly different way. 'The true traditional minstrelsy' did not exist in a separate compartment sealed off from national and art song, but interpenetrated with it—an intermingling which was of crucial importance in the entire Scottish achievement. As James Kinsley once put it, 'the most striking feature of eighteenth-century Scottish culture, philosophy and historiography aside, is the cultivation of folk-song and traditional music.[20] Folk-song and traditional music were not pre-existent and statically 'given' from the start, but two sides of a developing medium created by individuals, known and unknown. In the paragraph already quoted Gavin Greig went on to say: 'We must not be taken as disparaging our Scottish Song as per the books. Of its kind and class we believe it to be the finest in existence'. But when we go on to ask *why* it is the finest in existence, we come up with the reason that the activities of a Ramsay, a Skinner, or a Burns in setting new words to pre-existing tunes were not in principle different from those of the unknown authors of 'Binnorie' or the original 'Ay, waukin O'. The making of new tunes, dances and lyrics by both upper and lower classes went hand in hand, in the age of the Enlightenment, with the impulse to record and preserve, so that often creation was disguised as antiquarianism, as in some of the pieces in Ramsay's *Ever Green* or Macpherson's Ossianic 'epics'. A recent parallel is the establishment of the School of Scottish Studies for the academic study of traditional culture, and such related creative activities as the songs of Hamish Henderson and Adam Mac-Naughton, or the lyrics in the 7:84 Company's *The Cheviot, The Stag and the black, black Oil*. Each resurgence of the creative spirit in Scotland since 1707 has been associated with renewed interest in popular culture and with something of a 'folk revival'; each has felt the need to tap the popular tradition which is, perhaps, the most abidingly *national* part of our culture.

NOTES

1   The following short titles are used in references within the text and in the notes:
   Burke: Peter Burke, *Popular Culture in Early Modern Europe* (London, 1978)
   Harker: Dave Harker, *Fakesong: the manufacture of British 'folksong' 1700 to the Present Day* (Milton Keynes, 1985)
   Johnson: David Johnson, *Music and Society in Lowland Scotland' in the Eighteenth Century* (London, 1972)
   Journ.:   Boswell's MS Journal, Yale University Library
   Kinsley: James Kinsley (ed), *The Poems and Songs of Robert Burns*, 3 vols (Oxford, 1968)
   J de Lancey Ferguson and G Ross Roy (eds), *The Letters of Robert Burns*, 2 vols (Oxford, 1985)
   LLL: Thomas Crawford (ed) *Love, Labour and Liberty: the eighteenth-century Scottish Lyric* (Cheadle, 1976)
   Scotland: James Scotland, *The History of Scottish Education*, 2 vols (London, 1969)
   SFM: David Johnson, *Scottish Fiddle Music in the eighteenth century* (Edinburgh, 1984)
   SL: Thomas, Crawford, *Society and the Lyric: a Study of the Song Culture of eighteenth-century Scotland* (Edinburgh, 1979)
   TTM: *The Tea Table Miscellany* [edited by Allan Ramsay], 4 vols (Edinburgh, 1723–?1737; London, 4 vols in 1, 1740); references are to the 1740 edition.
2   Antonio Gramsci, *Opere*, VI (1950), 215f, as translated and quoted in *The People's Past*, E J Cowan (ed) (Edinburgh, 1980), p 14.
3   Gramsci, loc. cit., as translated and quoted in Burke, p 29.

4   For some comparison of Bartok's theory with Burns's practice, *see* Thomas Crawford, *Burns: a Study of the Poems and Songs* (Edinburgh, 1960), pp 343–5.

5   Francis Collinson, *The Traditional and National Music of Scotland* (London, 1966), p 2.

6   V de Sola Pinto and A E Rodway, *The Common Muse* (Harmondsworth, 1965), p 45.

7   The most convincing attribution is *The Lark* (Edinburgh, 1765). *See* Hans Hecht, 'Burns' lyrisches Vade mecum: The Lark, 1765', *Archiv für das Studium der neueren Sprachen*, 143 (1922), 176–83.

8   John Ramsay (of Ochtertyre), *Scotland and Scotsmen in the Eighteenth Century*, ed A Allardyce, 2 vols (Edinburgh, 1888), I, 19.

9   Quotations by kind permission of the E A Hornel Trust.

10 For Boswell's songs, see *SL*, pp 168–72; quotations by kind permission of the Yale Editions of the Private Papers of James Boswell.

11 T C Smout, *A History of the Scottish People* (London, 1969), p 455.

12 The tune *Jackie Latin* is found transposed for flute in a music book of 1768 (*SFM*, p 10), and Burns wrote 'The Lass of Ecclefechan' for 'Jack Latin' (Kinsley, III, 1505).

13 For the text of 'The Life and Death of Habbie Simson, the Piper of Kilbarchan', see *The Oxford Book of Scottish Verse*, John MacQueen and Tom Scott (eds) (Oxford, 1966), pp 305–8.

14 R M Goss, 'Dance', in *A Companion to Scottish Culture*, David Daiches (ed) (London, 1981), p 90.

15 H G Farmer, *A History of Music in Scotland* (London 1947: repr New York, 1970), p 316.

16 David Johnson prints four 'variation sonatas' in *SFM*, including Alexander Munro's on 'Bony Jean of Aberdeen' (pp 170–79) and an anonymous one on 'The Lea Rig' (pp 183–85).

17 *A Scottish Ballad Book*, David Buchan (ed) (London, 1973), pp. 18–20, 56–9.

18 *See* Thomas Crawford, 'Political and Protest Songs in eighteenth-century Scotland II: Songs of the Left', *Scottish Studies*, 14 (1970), 105–31.

19 Gavin Greig, 'Folk-Song of the North East' No. 180, 'Valedictory', in *Buchan Observer*, 6 June 1911.

20 James Kinsley, 'The Music of the Heart', in *Critical Essays on Robert Burns*, D A Low (ed) (London, 1975), p 131.

FURTHER READING

Brown, Mary Ellen, *Burns and Tradition* (Urbana and Chicago, 1984)

Buchan, David, *The Ballad and the Folk* (London, 1971)

—— *A Scottish Ballad Book* (London, 1973)

Crawford, Thomas, *Society and the Lyric: A Study of the Song Culture of Eighteenth-Century Scotland* (Edinburgh, 1979)

—— ed, *Love, Labour and Liberty: the eighteenth-century Scottish Lyric* (Cheadle, 1976)

Davie, Cedric Thorpe, *Scotland's Music* (Edinburgh, 1980)

Elliott, Kenneth and Frederick Rimmer, *A History of Scottish Music* (BBC Publications, London, 1973)

Emmerson, George S, *A Social History of Scottish Dance* (Montreal and London, 1972)

Johnson, David, *Music and Society in Lowland Scotland in the Eighteenth Century* (London, 1972)

Kinsley, James, 'The Music of the Heart' in *Critical Essays on Robert Burns*, D A Low (ed) (London, 1975)

McGuirk, Carol, *Robert Burns and the Sentimental Era* (Athens, Georgia, 1985)

Chapter 8

Robert Fergusson: Pastoral and Politics at Mid Century

F W FREEMAN

Robert Fergusson, whom Burns pronounced 'By far, my elder brother in the Muses', Wordsworth greatly admired, and Scott, Stevenson, Muir and MacDiarmid, recognized as one of the foremost of Scottish poets, was dismissed by literary worthies in his own day as 'dissipated and drunken', 'coarse', tending to the representation of 'blackguardism'.[1] He was not an artist to whom one reacted with indifference. The young Edinburgh poet, whose life spanned just twenty-four years (1750–74), was by nature brooding and unsettled. Born of poor Northeast parents, who would endow him more with pride and intellectual interests than financial security or career prospects, he was ill-suited to the world in which he found himself. Neither his artistic aspirations nor his solid academic grounding in the classics and in the philosophy, mathematics and literature of the Enlightment, from study at the Edinburgh High School, Dundee Grammar School and the University of St Andrews, accorded well with the tiresome, frustrating life he was to lead as a clerk for the Commissary Office in Edinburgh, recording testamentary and matrimonial cases.

However, it was not only his occupation which made Fergusson ill at ease in the Edinburgh of his day. Culturally, he was wholly out of step with the Anglicized, Whig, Moderate Presbyterian Scotland of the mid-eighteenth century, however nationalistic it could be in its support of militia movements, Ossianic heroes, or such native literary figures as Thomas Blacklock, John Home, Henry MacKenzie and—Fergusson's friend—William Wilkie. If for MacDairmid in this century 'back to Dunbar' was the slogan pointing the way to the revival of a flagging poetic tradition, it was for Fergusson back to vernacular classicism, to the Scots Renaissance art of Gavin Douglas. Generally, Fergusson aspired to classical cultural ideas and values. He composed town poems and pastorals after the models of Juvenal, Horace and Virgil, and, at some point, planned his own translation of the *Georgics* into Scots. Politically, he was a romantic Jacobite, a Scots Tory, as Dr Johnson would have defined one,[2] a Counter-Enlightenment apologist, and if not a regular member of any church (despite short bouts of religious gloom among the small Presbyterian sect called the anti-Burghers), an artist with Episcopal sympathies, as a letter from his brother cautioning him against 'Church of England' forms implies (8th October 1773), and lines from 'An Expedition to Fife and the Island of

May . . .', referring to the ill-deeds of the Scottish Covenanters and the murder of Archbishop Sharp (11.107–19), fully indicate. He had close ties with his publishers, the Ruddimans, and their circle, whose spiritual home was that Jacobite stronghold, Old St Paul's in Edinburgh's Old Town, and he typified as M P McDairmid aptly describes it, a North-east Episcopal outlook.[3] What is manifest is that he often wrote in the style and tradition of the Scots Episcopal (and Catholic) satirists and elegists, most of whom were published by the Ruddiman press: Samuel Colvil, Archibald Pitcairne, Alexander Nicol, James Wilson (Claudero) and others.

As a Tory traditionalist, Ferguson at his most idealistic upheld a hierarchical view of the cosmos and of society: what the Episcopal royalist, Sir George Mackenzie of Rosehaugh, called the 'Order of nature which God has established':[4] the Stuart king, courtiers and merchants in the town; the laird, gudeman and tenants in the countryside. Expressions of such a view occur in his poems concerning the demise of the old rural order: the displacement of the gudeman by the new capitalist farmer, the creation of an alienated urban poor drawn from the unemployed of the country, the old laird's abandonment of his tenants for a legal career in the town. Certainly in his country verse he espouses the Tory ideal of a well-regulated rural society through the skilful use of pastoral or, more broadly speaking, *la belle nature*, in terms reminiscent of Sir John Denham's 'Cooper's Hill' or Pope's 'Windsor Forest', with its notions of 'Order in Variety' (1.15), 'Rich Industry . . . on the Plains, / And Peace and Plenty' under a 'STUART' (11.41-2).

From his first literary efforts the poet creates and resolves tension between the pastoral world and its opposite, or between nature and art, where the latter represents the agrarian revolution and the forces of change, and the former the traditional way of life. 'Pastoral II. Noon', a rather hackneyed neoclassical lament, written in the style of Cunningham or Shenstone but for its stronger, albeit gentle, political overtones, is the earliest example of this kind of poem. According to the dejected shepherd, Corydon, his Delia no longer enjoys the 'embowering solitary shade' (1.20) but

> . . . wanders o'er the *Anglian* plain,
> Where civil discord and sedition reign.

> (11.23-4)

—a reference to the turmoil between the government headed by Lord North and the Whigs. Later the lover reveals that he and his opponent, Delia's father, are two different men of the soil, he being a subsistence farmer (with 'the weak fences of a scanty fold', 1.45) who has not yet assimilated more widely-accepted techniques of enclosure, and the father ('a thousand fleeces numbers o'er / And grassy hills increase his milky store', 11.43-4) obviously a gentleman farmer, and prosperous Whig laird. Agrarian reforms have driven a social wedge between the lovers. With a contrived happy ending it is left to Corydon's elder friend, Timanthes, the model stay-at-home laird, to save the day, providing ample pasturage for Corydon's flock and—consistent with the natural metaphor—leading him away from the sharp rays of the sun, safe from the ill-effects of change.

The themes of the good and the bad laird and, especially, the survival of the gudeman, a substantial tenant whose existence was doomed by the new class of rack-renting lairds, were common to Fergusson's anti-Improving poems: works written after the fashion of the early vernacular revival protest poems, like 'The Speech of a Fife Laird, Newly come from the Grave', or, later, Alexander Nicol's 'An Elegy on Auld Use and Wont'. In this genre Fergusson characteristically upholds staunchly royalist models of social class, and appears to be propounding a solution to the plight of the subsistence farmers put forward years earlier by the Scots Jacobite, William Mackintosh, who, having been out in the 1715 and 1719 rebellions, published from his prison cell a very un-Whiggish improving guide, *An Essay on Ways and Means for Inclosing, Planting etc . . . Scotland* (1729), which appealed to the landlords for longer leases and fewer services to the landowners so that the tenant could properly enclose his land and survive.

Fergusson's best known and most elaborate pastoral, 'The Farmer's Ingle', is a piece of cosmic Toryism which employs classical and modern (Enlightenment) concepts to idealize the wholly outmoded gudeman system of farming—especially with respect to the techniques of ploughing and winnowing—and of living: the diet, clothing made and worn, the general conditions within the old world thatched cottage which is portrayed. This idealization is effected through neatly fitting the gudeman into the microcosmic scheme of the classical bucolic and, at the same time, into the macrocosmic pattern of *concordia discors*, the ancient cosmology of harmony through balanced opposition which became a cosmic rationale for the Tory ideal.

Evident in the poem is the influence of Virgil's *Bucolics*, from whence its Latin motto is taken, his *Georgics*, and Horace's *Epodes*: idyllic pictures of farm life in the home, before the ingle. There are also strong traces of Milton and Spenser, and, throughout, a primitivist idealization of the gudeman as the classical stoic highlighted in Stanza V which, by implication, places him on par with 'Caledonia's ancestors' (1.38) who, fortified 'On sicken [such] food' (1.37), were victorious over the Danes and Romans. The closing lines both transform modern economic theory, in which the country sustains the town, into a justification of the gudeman's antiquated 'sock and couter' farming methods (1.111), and equate summer, or pastoral, with his lifestyle through rhetorical parallelism: 'May SCOTIA's simmers', 'May a' her tenants' (11.113, 115). The ultimate answer to the opening question, what 'gars [causes] snaw-tapit winter freeze in vain' (1.6), is the perennial summer the gudeman creates and enjoys, bearing in mind the warmth and security of his own dwelling. As the poet says in 'An Eclogue, To . . . Dr William Wilkie',

> The ingle-nook supplies the simmer fields,
> An' aft as mony gleefu' maments yields.

(11.15-16)

At the macrocosmic level the entire rural social unit, through the symbol of the ingle and, by extension, the imagery of heat and light, becomes elemental to life. The association of the household with the inanimate implements that serve it is beautifully encapsulated in Stanza XII which humanizes—by making them part of the social group—the exhausted 'cruizy' [small oil lamp] and ingle (11.104-05), tired from work and, like tacksman and cottar, ready for a night's sleep. *Concordia discors* is fulfilled in the structure of the poem which moves through a complete cycle of light and heat in two opposing directions (underlining the mirror image of the gudeman and nature): from the 'gloaming grey' (1.1) to the 'dawning's ruddy glow' (1.108); and, in reverse, from the 'bleezing fire' of the introduction (1.21) to the 'restit [burnt-out] ingle (1.105). Such topical Enlightenment issues as thrift, division of labour, and maximum productivity, are deftly interwoven into the tight structure, urging the impossible claim that the gudeman system already provides what were seen to be the fruits of agrarian reform. Fergusson uses 'industry', the key word of utilitarian economic philosophy, in various forms (11.29, 73, 101) and, throughout, underlines an exact balance of rest and industry which yields maximum productivity. Everything in and out of doors is neatly ordered and efficiently productive. The servants work until they are fatigued; the old grandmother cares for the children, makes their clothes and does an evening's spinning; the gudewife organizes every detail of the house, feeds the entire household plentifully, delegates tasks to the workers, and provides for the care of the farm animals. The gudeman presides over the efficient running of the farm, assigns the different chores, and maintains his domestic animals at no extra expense: an exact paradigm of what Adam Smith set down, later, in his *Wealth Of Nations* on feeding smaller animals from the 'little offals of their own table'.[5] Even the inanimate objects of the household work at the optimum level. At the end of the day

> The cruizy too can only blink and bleer,
> The restit ingle's done the maist it dow . . .   [can]

(11.104-05)

Historical and cultural continuity within a traditional way of life were of greater concern to Fergusson than utilitarian hypotheses, like those of the economist Sir James Steuart for depopulating the countryside and making the land more productive, which seemed devoid of compassion and overturned the practices of generations. In several places the poet takes issue with the Improvers, often in response to the exuberances of Hume and his associates who insisted that 'men sink into indolence, lose all enjoyment of life' where there is no demand for superfluities.[6] Sir James Steuart went so far as to maintain that increased consumption had 'banished misery from cottages and country villages' while encouraging frugality as the peasants judiciously saved for the luxuries they desired.[7] In a chapter of his *Political Oeconomy* entitled 'Consequences of the Introduction of a passive Foreign Trade among a People who live in Simplicity and Idleness', Sir James avers, for example, that a new demand for brandy will induce the farmer to part with the family loaf of bread and—really the crux of the matter—to labour harder to recoup the loss.[8]

In 'A Drink Eclogue' Fergusson presents this and the opposing position in a flyting, with Brandy arguing from the indolence and profligacy of the Highland poor (11.66-78) (the Whig side), and Whisky countering that delicacies harry the countryside (11.79-88), as ruthless lairds

> hight their tenants rent
> And fill their lands wi' poortith, discontent;   [poverty]
> Gar them o'er seas for cheaper mailins hunt,   [farms]
> An' leave their ain as bare's the Cairn-o'-mount.

(11.65-8)

By contrast, Whisky recalls his heyday before, as Dr Johnson put it, the 'chiefs . . . turned to the improvement of their revenues'.[9] It was a time when (and this is a point Fergusson makes repeatedly) pastoral idealizations of the countryside—here Ramsay's verse—were still imaginable. Whisky reflects that

> Troth I ha'e been 'ere now the poet's flame,
> And heez'd his sangs to mony blythsome theme.   [inspired]
> Wha was't gar'd ALLIE'S *chaunter* chirm fu' clear,
> Life to the saul, and music to the ear . . .

(11.97-100)

Hence the pastoral age belongs to a lost past, with all such an assumption implies socially and politically.

In 'Hame Content. A Satire' we find the 'niggard' (1.11) laird in Italy; an account of new fashions, including the vogue for imitating 'Roman' poetic models (11.76-7); and, again, the devastation of the poetic landscape. From the earlier conceived pastoral scenes (11.17-38) of 'water' playing 'the haughs bedown' (1.22), we move to 'lifeless dowy pools' (1.78); from 'The simple garb o' NATURE here', to 'disguise . . . on Arno's shore' (11.102, 105-06). Uniting social, political and cultural themes, the poem ends, significantly, with a lament for the death of pastoral and for the loss of the noted Jacobite songwriter and poet, William Hamilton of Bangour.

> O BANGOUR! now the hills and dales
> Nae mair gi'e back thy tender tales!
> The birks on Yarrow now deplore
> Thy mournfu' muse has left the shore:
> Near what bright burn or chrystal spring
> Did you your winsome whistle hing?

(11.107-12)

It is the 'laird / Wha quats his ha'-house an' kail-yard' ('On seeing a Butterfly in the Street', 11.59-60) who is similarly discredited in 'An Eclogue', a light satire on the well-worn subject of bridal problems but having undercurrents of the superfluities theme running through it. Reversals in nature are linked with Sandie's wife—her newfound extravagance and neglect—and, by extension, with the man thought by the two purblind bumpkins best-equipped to handle the problem: 'the laird . . . weel vers'd in a' the laws' / who 'Kens baith their outs and ins, cracks and flaws . . .' (11.108-10): hardly a Timanthes setting matters right as in 'Pastoral II. Noon'.

However, we must not make too much of Fergusson's satirical thrust in poems such as 'An Eclogue'. If superfluities are not seen as yielding more prosperity, it cannot be asserted that the poet idealizes the gudeman. The vision is more aesthetic then moral; the theme more about change than the reconciliation of forces into divine harmony. At times in the poetry there is even a gesture towards those twin Enlightenment aims of Industry and Progress. In 'Ode to the Bee', 'Industry can fetch content' (1.34), pastoral returns, and the Muse thinks of cropping 'The winsome flow'rs frae Nature's lap' (11.59-62) with the adoption of new methods of enclosure, using shrubbery, trees and stone fencing (11.47-58). And considering Fergusson's praise of Dr William Wilkie ('Potato Wilkie') and his 'remarkable improvements',[10] we are naturally led to John MacQueen's conclusion that Fergusson 'was not sufficiently a man of the Enlightenment to identify himself with the Improvers; he was too much one to be able to stomach every feature of the older order'.[11]

Fergusson, like MacDiarmid, would 'aye be whaur Extremes meet'. How we view him is in great measure determined by what we choose to look at: the narrow nationalist, bewailing the Union ('The Ghaists') and deprecating foreign influences, whether in the new taste for French delicacies ('A Drink Eclogue'), Italian music ('The Daft Days') or English neoclassical verse ('Elegy, On the Death of Scots Music'); or, the internationalist, friend of the Italian tenor, Tenducci, and admirer of William McGibbon, the noted fiddler and classical composer (who actually wrote in the Italian style); friend of Thomas Mercer, who dedicated his anthology of poetry, *The Sentimental Sailor* to Rousseau; afficionado of the theatre, thoroughly enjoying the Elizabethan revival of the period and especially Shakesperian drama; Augustan man of letters, relishing (and imitating) the poetry of Pope, Gay, Gray and Collins and, equally, the Anglo-Scottish poetry of Drummond of Hawthornden and James Thomson; Fergusson the Counter-Enlightenment artist or, as we have observed, the advocate of industry and industrial reform.

An identical dualism or division occurs in Fergusson's urban poetry: the town poems frequently contain pastoral elements and rhetorical devices used in a political context. Nothing could be more backward-looking than the idealization of a very medieval Edinburgh as rural village in the pastoral sections of 'Hallow-Fair', for example. Its beginning (11.1-27) recalls the first several stanzas of 'Christ's Kirk on the Green' and, before giving way to pandemonium, sketches an idyllic scene of peasants spruced-up for a day's wooing: Fergusson's 'strappin dames and sturdy lads' (1.7), playfully courting under 'clear' skies (1.2), rising sunlight (1.11), and amidst great plenty. The occasion, Hallowmass, the Festival of All Saint or All Hallows, originally a Celtic and later a Catholic or Episcopal holiday of thanksgiving, celebrates the first night of winter, when the crops are in and all farm hands nestle in their winter quarters. The idyll is of a past age conjured up in the solemnity of the opening stanza, with its conscious echoes of John Burel's 'The Discription of Qveen's Maiesties Maist Honorable Entry into . . . Edinbvrgh . . . 1590' (published in Watson's *Choice Collection*).

Rhetorically, and here we see more pastoral elements, the purlieus of Edinburgh call to mind a Scots country cottage, as lads and lasses move from winter's 'nippin cald' (1.3) into the old fairgrounds, with its 'pantries' full of generous portions of 'kebbucks' [cheese] and 'gude ale' (11.15-17): that is, into something approximating the interior world of 'The Farmer's Ingle'. Within this—note the rhetoric—'shelter' of 'Auld Reikie' (1.74); within this clarty, cosy older town are health and plenty, honesty and ingenuousness, clarity of perception and freedom of communication: the same configuration of values as appears in the idealized rural poems.

In the imaginative tension between Auld Reikie and modern Edinburgh, pastoral passages state and re-state the theme: old Edinburgh = shelter = civilization. It is a formula the poet uses often. In 'The Daft-Days', which also celebrates an Episcopal festival, daft-days being the derogatory title the Presbyterians gave to the 'Pisky' Yule, Auld Reikie is a cosy shelter—'the canty [cheerful] hole, / A bield' [shelter] (11.19-20), once again a magnification of a Scots rural cottage, with a snug 'ingle . . . Baith warm and couth' (11.21-2), plenty of festive drink (1.23) and traditional music (11.43-54); it is a defence against invading winter (11.1-18) and, her exact counterpart, social divisiveness (11.35-40). In terms of the definition of Reikie as a 'canty hole', a shelter from wind and cold (winter and war are images or emblems of Whiggism in the Episcopal literary tradition—see, for example, Pitcairne's *Babell*, 11.9, 125), the old town and its culture, in the equation, are seen as civilization. Indeed in the earlier works

Fergusson has very unflattering things to say of the rising northern Athens (e.g. 'The TOWN and COUNTRY CONTRASTED', 11.17-19); like Claudero, an Edinburgh Catholic poet who wrote numerous ruined building poems which voiced the unpopular opinion that the Whigs were building a new Scotland on the crumbling foundations of its traditional past, Fergusson often expresses a strain of pessimism wholly out of step with the forward looking attitude of the Scottish Enlightment.

If in so many of the town poems Auld Reikie is equated with order and tranquility, purity and health, fair weather or indoor warmth, modern Edinburgh is its antithesis: counterpastoral, or, specifically, as in 'Hallow-Fair', 'Babylon' (1.71), an image familiar to the reading public since the days of Roundhead and Cavalier. Modern Whig Edinburgh, was, in the rhetoric of Mackenzie of Rosehaugh, Colvil, Pitcairne and William Meston, the new Babylon: 'Babel', 'Babylon of Confusions', 'Whore of Babylon', 'Whore of Babel', and so on. Archibald Pitcairne, Thomas Ruddiman's boon companion, simply named his satire on the Church of Scotland's General Assembly, *Babell*, and the relation between Kirk and city satire is obvious in moving from *Babell*, or Colvil's *Mock Poem*, with its screeching and buzzing streets, to Fergusson's 'Hallow-Fair', 'Leith Races' or 'The Election'.

One of the Tory bogeymen from the time of the Reformation was the 'mob'. As Smollett's Matthew Bramble put it, in *Humphry Clinker*, it was '. . . a monster . . . a mass of ignorance, presumption, malice, and brutality . . .'[12] In Fergusson, the mob plays a central role in the counterpastoral vision. In the structure of 'Hallow-Fair', built upon the contrast of an ideally ordered past and chaotic present, the pastoral of the introduction dissipates in a long crescendo of obstructed communication and disorienting noise (reminiscent of *Babell*, 11.872-79) as all classes blend into the contemptible mob: 'Sawny cries' (1.37), 'dinlin [rattling] drums' cause 'alarm', the sergeant 'screechs fu' loud' (11.55-6), horses 'prance and nicker' (1.64), mad drunks 'rant an' roar' (1.67), 'gablin' wives and kiddies produce 'yellowchin and din . . . a-kin / To a' the tongues at Babylon' (11.68-71). The mob of 'Leith Races', with its 'dinsome squeel and bark' (1.58), its reeling crowds 'Of ilka trade and station' (1.96), blurring all necessary distinction, are actually pronounced 'Whigs' (1.152), and Stuart law, 'JAMIE's laws' preserved by 'the wise recorder' (11.149-50)—Jacobites like Mackenzie of Rosehaugh—are celebrated as the last means 'To had the Whigs in order' (1.152).

Caricature is used effectively to ridicule the society of modern Edinburgh as the prominent city of the day act out a travesty of the Tory social order. In this caricature, form is all important. At least part of 'Hallow-Fair', and the song of the same title, 'Leith Races', and 'The Election', satirize the brutalized poor as well as the new merchant class through relating their immediate living conditions to those Tory principles regarding the mob, and through making those conditions part of an old literary pattern. All of these poems are cast in the Christis Kirk stanza which was initially—and subsequently—used to burlesque peasant rites and customs, from a royalist point of view: James I, Drummond of Hawthornden, and

Sir Francis Semple are the outstanding writers working in this tradition. A social historian would recognize a consistency of point of view in moving from, say, Drummond's strictures on the fickle commons and lawless multitude in the *History of Scotland*, to his peasant satire, *Polemo-Middinia*. Such consistency was self-evident to the eighteenth-century Jacobite poets who carried on the royalist tradition. For example, William Meston's *Mob Contra Mob* begins with a quote from *Polemo-Middinia*, and Pitcairne's *Babell* depicts the Presbyterian rabble's meeting in the familiar terms of Christis Kirk:

> Such hubbub yet was never seen,
> But in the dayes at Rullion Green . . .

(11.1352-53)

In using this old stanzaic form Fergusson, in part, subtly upholds royalist notions of a debased commons.

Within the Babylon framework some of Fergusson's caricature draws upon the tradition of Episcopal religious satire, especially the idea of mock order, typified by the would-be knight or cavalier, like Samuel Butler's Hudibras or Meston's *Sir John Presbyter*, attempting unsuccessfully to be what he clearly is not. Relevant here is the starving, vermin infested poor of 'The Election' whose pretense of 'order' (1.46) and 'nobility' (11.52, 62) highlights ironical comparisons between nobleman and peasant and reminds us of the Episcopal literary background (e.g. Pitcairne's play *The Assembly*, 'Act III. Scene I'). The caricature is sharper in depictions of the City Guard, an abusive Whig police, formed after the 1715 rebellion for maintaining order, and comprised mainly of dispossessed Highlanders. Fergusson treats of them in the light vein of Dougal Graham, another little known Glasgow poet, but with some intent to show how far they had strayed from the vigorous, militant Highlanders of Ossianic legend (legend which Fergusson probably believed). In Episcopal literature, Whig society was in a 'continual war' (e.g. *Babell*, 11.1337-51); mock heroics were the conventional means of aspersing it. In 'Hallow-Fair' the combatants, the mischievous Jock Bell and the Town Guard, hail directly from Butler's knights and their battles of bruises rather than blood. Overstatement cuts Jock and 'soldiers' down to Lilliputian size as the guardsman's 'stark Lochaber aix' [axe] delivers a *'clamihewit'* [severe blow] that leaves Jock 'sair' (11.79-81), and the second 'Mair weighty' blow makes him 'spew' (11.87, 89). The 'weirlike' soldier (1.95), whose 'deadly weapons nicket' (1.85) and who invokes a *'Highland* aith' (1.93), adds a sober dimension to the droll high jinks of the Christis Kirk form: the last note struck is appropriately one of 'shame that day' (1.117). In 'Leith Races' the incongruity of pretence and reality is captured through a humour of detail which mercilessly reduces the scale of everything and everybody. The microscopic focus on the clean-shaven faces of the marching guardsmen, which burn with 'WHISKY PLOOKS' (1.64), gainsays the cavalier image they wish to project, while claims to valiant soldiering are undercut by the disparity between their redoubtable weaponry and its use in 'birthday wars' inflicting bloody noses (11.79-80).

In 'Leith Races' the City Guard is associated with noise (e.g. 1.154), and their organization, by subtle conjunction, with animals: 'Baith men and steeds are raingit' [drawn up in line] (1.155). Generally, Whig Edinburgh is populated by men become uncommunicative animals according to the humanist principle that only reason and speech make civilization possible. Integral to the new Babylon are beasts and insects, enabling the poet—like Dryden in 'Religio Laici'—to characterize the Whig as a creature of the unthinking mob. 'Vermin' and 'dirt', deflationary substantives common to anti-Whig literature (e.g. 'vermine Impotent and blind', *Hudibras*, 'Third Part', II), are used effectively in Fergusson's humour of scale. For instance, the scene of John's preparation for the corrupt burgh elections, in 'The Election', swarms with buzzing s's, an atmosphere of flies and decay—'gez' [wig]—'friz' [curl]—'Liz'—'I'se be as braw's [finely dressed] the Deacon is' (11.10-18)—which shadow his every action. They are an emblem of the interior man—small, shabby, sycophantic, and complement the very intimate scene inside the home, where we see him close at hand, doing battle with 'the vermin / Menzies [multitudes] o' MOTHS an' FLAES' (11.31-2) which inhabit his best dress coat. In 'Leith Races' the dominant image is again dirt, mainly in relation to water imagery, a standard Tory symbol of societal harmony or disharmony (see, for example, Denham's 'Cooper's Hill', 11.343-58). By contrast to 'the caller springs' of the introductory pastoral vision, 'Foul WATER' (1.107), the noxious ale of the brewster wives, is said to satisfy the thirst of the townsmen. Wild Whigs 'Sae prime this day' (1.153), prime especially in the drunken sense, crown the stagnant water imagery. Significantly, the end of the poem compares tussles between the Guard and the townsmen to debates where the 'dirt' of the streets (1.166) finds its way into the veritable muck slinging language of the Edinburgh debaters. With this conclusion we are very much in the literary world of Pitcairne's *Assembly* or Colvil's *Mock Poem*.

In 'The Ghaists' Fergusson is most resolutely the Scots Tory, Jacobite and nationalist; most openly anti-England, Hanover and Whig; most uncompromisingly the party political artist. The lines subscribed to the title, questioning the blessings of 'Hanover', carry the political message that the poem's dialogue between Watson and Herriot is designed to put across. Technically speaking, two elements are at work in the poem. There is, firstly, a burlesque of the conventional setting and horrors of sentimental and graveyard poetry which Fergusson associated with Whiggish writers. Second, the pastoral device is employed to contrast the two Scotlands, past and present. The two techniques are complementary. Herriot relates the graveyard literary setting (11.19-28), the Scotland in which he awakens, to a changed 'NATURE' (1.25); and, in so doing, implies that modern Scotland is not the natural ideal—while Edinburgh 'Whan royal JAMIE sway'd the sovereign rod' (1.32) was. His nostalgic effusions follow the equation: 'JAMIE (Stuart Scotland = nature = civilization or, rhetorically, shelter ('stately turrets', 1.36), and growth ('flow'rs ilk [each] coming year', 1.40). Conversely, Whiggism = anti-nature = barbarity, the destruction of shelter ('tow'rs are sunk', 1.41) and death ('lands are barren now . . . flow'rs maun dow', [must fade] 11.41-2).

In the passage referring to the unpopular Mortmain Bill, we see the familiar theme of the good and bad lairds applied more broadly, with England as the oppressive landlord, and Scotland the dispossessed tenantry. The Union is said to have brought 'destructive ills' (1.59); Scotland is now full of servile trustees who carry out the demands of the laird, England, who forces them to pay 'gowd in gowpins [gold in handfulls] as a grassum gift' (1.66), the fee paid to the landlords by the tenants. The English are the cruel masters who 'yoke hard the poor' (1.71). Again there are familiar images of the decline which England has brought about: 'stateliest riggins [roofs] bare', stripped 'acres, houses, woods . . . fishins' (11.63-4). Watson reinforces the metaphor, claiming, in a didactic pastoral vein, that 'AULD REIKIE' in the past—'the gowden times' (1.79)—embraced morality and social responsibility. Under the present administration vice prevails: moral values are inverted to serve 'a backgaun [needy] king' (1.84); 'honesty and poortith [poverty] baith are crimes' (1.80); a Hanoverian king connives at 'vice' and, never fretting over the 'price o' sin' (11.85-9), crushes the 'pious' among the poor with—note the beast rhetoric—'ruthless, ravenous, and harpy laws' (11.91-4).

The poem closes, notably, with that recurrent winter image and a suggested antidote to Whig misgovernment. Watson, who first awakened to 'the nippin north wi' angry sough' and 'showers' of 'hailstanes' (11.7-8), threatens to invoke 'some ghaist' (1.116) who will see the unnatural reversals to their ultimate end, should the bribery persist. Herriot's final prescription for the nation's ills is an unequivocal party political statement, for the 'Mackenzie' fam'd' (1.125) to whom they are about to appeal for help was of course the royalist and Episcopalian stalwart Sir George Mackenzie. Mackenzie, known by Presbyterians as the 'Bluidy Advocate' for his prosecution of Covenanters, and as the opponent of Charles II's proposal to unite the two kingdoms, was the author of treatises defending and promoting the House of Stuart; and remained a key representative of those older Scottish traditions to which the revivalists, such as James Watson (publisher of Mackenzie's works), Freebairn, the Ruddimans, and Fergusson turned for inspiration.

Whiggism, in the guise of progress or, more frequently, sentimentalism—'these MEN OF FEELING'[13]—always elicited Fergusson's contempt. 'A Burlesque Elegy on the Amputation of a Student's Hair . . .' and 'The Canongate Play-House in Ruins' are early burlesques, explicitly satirizing the cult of sentiment. Less explicit are the satires on the Whig sentimentalist, employing the mock elegy form and the Habbie Stanza which, I have argued elsewhere, may have political overtones similar to those of the Christis Kirk Stanza.

'The Sow of feeling' and 'Mutual Complaint of Plainstanes and Causey' decry the man of feeling, that genteel literary creation who owed his origins to Hutcheson and Presbyterian Moderate philosophy. 'The Sow' is no more than a well-sustained burlesque of the sentimental elegy (the sort found in Basil Hamilton's *The Mournful Muse*), full of pious expressions and delivered as a homily, by a sow, on the evils of butchering pigs. 'Mutual Complaint of Plainstanes and Causey' belongs to the tradition of anti-Whig legal satire. It pokes fun at the Whig notion of legislating progress and using law as a substitute for action while, at every turn, exposing the man of feeling as a legalist. The poetic structure is built round the Enlightenment philosophy of utility and compromise for the general good, as expressed, for example, in sections of Lord Kames's *Sketches Of The History Of Man*, where the subject is also highways, the weight of traffic on them, and their appropriate tolls. The poem caricatures two Whig personalities: Plainstanes, the man of feeling, whose defence against Causey rests on sentimental claims (he says he is a preserver of love, 11.29-42; 'a weak and feckless creature . . . moulded by a safter nature', 11.71-2; man of affection, 11.79-82; protector of ladies and the elderly, 11.88-92); and Causey, the would-be man of law, cast from the same die as Bull and Frog, in Arbuthnot's *The History of John Bull* (Chapter III), and adopting completely their jargon and manner of handling opposition (e.g. 11.97-102). Plainstanes gradually unmasks himself as uncharitable, calculating, legalistic and snobbish (11.43-8, 63-70, 93-6) while acting like a mechanism of feeling with a set of programmed responses to situations. Causey too acts and thinks as if circumstances were controlled by unintended effects as, for example, in his remark,

> . . . coachmen never trow they're sinning,
> While down the street his wheels are spinning . . .
>
> (11.57-8)

Appropriately, he is a singularly insentient critic of the very cause he wishes to espouse, making ironical comments about the commitment of the provost and baillies (11.133-34), voicing well-aired complaints of Whig maladministration and incompetence regarding the Royal Exchange and the removal of Edinburgh's Mercat Cross (11.107-16). Plainstanes parting suggestion to compromise by dropping the matter— which damns him as a man of sentiment rather than action—is exceedingly close to Butler's *Hudibras* ('First Part', III).

Fergusson's mock elegies in the Habbie Stanza are equally light-hearted and deflative. 'Elegy, On the Death of Mr David Gregory', which follows very closely the tone and style of Robert Sempill's 'Epitaph On Sanny Briggs', chaffs the politico-mathematicians, and their attempt to control destiny through calculations, in the form of Hudibrastic banter (cf. *Hudib-*

ras, 'First Part, Canto I'). A geometrical 'hector' (1.29), able to 'divine' the obvious (11.15-17), Gregory is unable to overcome death despite his 'lang head' (1.22) and awesome intellect. 'Elegy on John Hogg' is a more fully-developed burlesque of the sentimental elegy and a satire on Auld Licht hypocrisy: Hogg emerges as one of those greedy Puritanical merchant types so common to seventeenth-century anti-Whig literature. The poem caricatures the St Andrews University porter whom we see carrying out his duties with a religious fervour, quoting the letter of the law as well as the scriptures (11.33, 39-42, 55-60), outdoing the dominies and preachers in admonishing Fergusson and his cohorts against their evil ways (11.43-8), and debating, like Causey, more for the sake of 'contesting' than for proving a worthwhile point (11.59-60). Above all, John was a 'bien body', as one contemporary described him; a man who

> . . . ay lo'ed to turn the pence,
> Thought poortith was a great offence . . .
>
> (11.79-80)

Moderate Presbyterians fare no better in the 'Elegy on John Hogg' as Fergusson makes light of the rigorous discipline of Thomas Tullidelph, Principal of the University and former Moderator of the General Assembly of the Church of Scotland: 'Pauly Tam', with his 'canker'd snout' face] (1.13), his stringent rules (11.19-24), his formidable railing (1.28), represents the more dour side of even Moderate Presbyterianism. 'To the Tron-Kirk Bell' takes a harder line on the Moderates, linking them with the local government in insidiously restricting the awareness of the masses, and cowing them into submission. The poet makes economic use of the rhetoric of the more fanatical Presbyterian sects in representing Moderate preaching—and associating the church's minister, as in *Hudibras* ('Third Part, Canto I'), with 'Auld Nick' (11.37-48). This is noteworthy. Not only was the Tron a symbol of the Presbyterian ascendancy, the edifice having been completed in 1673 as a classic piece of post-Reformation architecture; but, at the time, John Drysdale was its minister, a staunch disciple of William Robertson and, the following year, himself the Moderator of the General Assembly.

As we have observed, in 'Hallow-Fair' and 'Leith Races' Fergusson makes a clear demarcation between two cities in the pastoral–counterpastoral structures of the poems. Nonetheless one senses that the poet does not fully believe that humanity can be confined within the idealization of a frozen pastoral dream. Within Fergusson the rigid moralist co-exists with the iconoclast. His New Babylon is much like Swift's Dublin or Gay's London, a kaleidoscopic rendering of people and events, possessing moral and amoral dimensions. It is manifestly his intention in the town poems to represent principles of order against which to measure the buffoonery of human activity, but, at the same time, to depict an exciting movement of colour and light, sound and motion which, in its spontaneity, has little regard for order. In this portrayal lies a clash of intentions, as the rhetoric tells us one thing and the energetic movements, something else. It is an inclusive compromise based more on inventiveness and doubt. Characteristically, Fergusson portrays classical models of human behaviour, satirizes their irrelevance to human experience; sketches, like Daumier, the vileness of everyday urban living, and, somehow, allows stumbling humanity, as in 'Auld Reikie', a place in the grand design.

In several of the poems the forces of change and creativity, diversity and unrest, both within the poet and the poem, appear to be forging themselves into a new order. If, for instance, we again find in 'Dumfries' the familiar formula in which pastoral implies anti-Whig (part of the poem satirizes Charles Churchill in these terms), the idyllic portrayal is not of an idealized medieval village but of a technologically and architecturally sophisticated place, a bustling old royal burgh known as the 'Queen of the South'. This must be borne in mind in interpreting Fergusson's pastoral vision of Dumfries as a Scots Eden, a garden of the 'caller [fresh] flow'r', clear 'stream' (11.3-4), 'beauties' (1.8), health (11.21-4) and plenty. It is an ordered ('ilka thing's sae trig and feat' [smart and pretty], 1.11), modern town set in opposition to Churchill's London. Likewise, 'Caller Oysters' focuses on modern Edinburgh as it commends the successful fishing industry which saw Leith merchants selling huge quantities of oysters to London by 1773. In a subtle interlacing of visions Fergusson restates the formula, the traditional culture of Auld Reikie equals pastoral (Luckie Middlemists is a 'hame' with 'gude fare' and life centring on the *'ingle'*, 11.50-3), while attributing the fisherwives' *'top livin'* (1.62), the 'blyth faces' of 'September's merry month' (11.13-14), to commercial prosperity. Progress and tradition, as in 'Ode to the Bee', walk hand-in-hand.

'Auld Reikie' is the most elaborate reconciliation of the two cities. In an emotional and psychological working through *concordia discors*, the town is in turn part of the natural cycle—hence the pastoral muse moves easily from 'SIMMER'S Green (11.7-8) to its sociability (11.3-4) and protection ('whase biggin stands / A Shelter to surrounding Lands', 11.21-2)—and, the city of chaos, home of 'Lies and Clashes' (1.26), dirt, 'stinking Air' INUNDATION BIG' (11.30, 37, 44), darkness and 'DEATH' (1.165). Throughout, the rhetoric of pastoral and shelter is solidly underpinned by an exact architectural balance of themes in harmonious opposition: an interplay of light and dark, sweet scents and stinks, sorrow and joy, growth and death, poverty and prosperity, civilization (rhetorically, shelter, nature, pastoral) and savagery (artifice, false appearance, counterpastoral). In the end Reikie is transfigured into a new pastoral entity, 'tow'ring on thy summit green' (1.362). Conceived in a vision from across the Forth it is like the rural retreat of the opening, but has become a genuine city of the imagination; a heavenly city (11.363-66), and, to use Kenneth Clark's expression, a 'landscape of symbols'. All energy has been reconciled into order by a superior unifying power: as Fergusson puts it in an early poem

That righteous Power, before whose heavenly eye
The stars are nothing, and the planets die;
Whose breath divine supports our mortal frame,
Who made the lion wild, and lambkin tame.

('Pastoral III. Night', 11.29-32)

NOTES

1   Henry MacKenzie *The Anecdotes And Egotisms Of Henry MacKenzie: 1745–1831*, Harold W Thompson (ed) (London, 1927) p 150.
2   This is true if we merely substitute Episcopal Church for 'church of England' in Johnson's dictionary definition: 'TORY— ... One who adheres to the antient constitution of the state, and apostolical hierarchy of the church of England'.
3   *The Poems Of Robert Fergusson*, Scottish Text Society, vols 21, 24, (Edinburgh & London, 1954–56) II, 'Note 107-10', p 300.
4   *'Jus Regium'*, in *The Works Of ... Sir George MacKenzie of Rosehaugh*, James Watson (ed), 2 vols, (Edinburgh, 1716-22) II, pp 459–60).
5   Adam Smith, *Wealth Of Nations*, Alexander Murray (ed), 4th edn (London, 1874) p 181.
6   David Hume, 'Of Refinement in the Arts', in *David Hume: Writings On Economics*, Eugene Rotwein (ed) (Edinburgh, 1955) p 24.
7   *Considerations On The Interest Of The County Of Lanark In Scotland ...*, *The Works ...*, General Sir James Steuart, Bart. (ed), 6 vols (London, 1805) V, p 298.
8   Ibid., p 294.
9   Samuel Johnson, *A Journey to the Western Islands of Scotland* (London, 1775) pp 216–17.
10 *See* McDiarmid *Robert Fergusson*, II, 'Note 70', p 269.
11 John MacQueen *Progress And Poetry* (Edinburgh, 1982) p 120.
12 Tobias Smollett, *Humphry Clinker*, Angus Ross (ed) (Bungay, 1973) p 66.
13 From Fergusson's 'Epilogue to the Prince of Tunis', 'The Sow of Feeling'.

FURTHER READING

Daiches, David, *Robert Fergusson* (Edinburgh, 1982)

Freeman, F W, *Robert Fergusson and the Scots Humanist Compromise* (Edinburgh, 1984)

McDiarmid, Matthew P, *The Poems of Robert Fergusson*, Volume I, 'Introduction' (Scottish Text Society, Edinburgh and London, 1954)

MacLaine, Allan H, *Robert Fergusson* (New York, 1965)

Chapter 9

James Boswell: Biography and the Union

GORDON TURNBULL

Restlessly alive to the cultural currents around him, across the entire social and intellectual range, Boswell left in his copious and candid diaries a record of the debates and diversities of Britain and Europe in the later eighteenth century not in their theoretical abstraction, but lived. Centrally, the great Enlightenment inquiries into the nature of human identity appeared in Boswell as a life-long interrogation of and experimentation with the idea of character, and a fascination with its representation in words. The journals mark a protracted attempt to know himself in written form, as he would try to fix the characters of others in his public biographies. After years of false starts and failed promises to reform his dissolute ways, amid depression in the arduous task of assembling his *Life of Johnson*, Boswell's hopes for a solution to his perplexed state of being—hopes pinned for much of his life variously on filial rebellion, authorial fame, political preferment, illicit sex, wine, the company of the eminent, removal to London—would rest ultimately on a precarious and faintly desperate faith in the next world. But of his erratic life he left nonetheless a remarkable set of written records, out of which as we now know he quarried, at least in part, a contribution to literary biography, the *Life* of Samuel Johnson, of great popularity and continuing influence, discernible still in representations and perceptions of critical, moral and conversational authority.

Aligned with the enterprise of the Scottish Enlightenment historians, Boswell's life-long journal is a kind of memoir of himself, a memoir being in one definition 'personal history that seeks to articulate or repossess the historicity of the self'.[1] In this articulation of a personal historicity, Boswell's massive self-documentation—the autobiographical journals, letters, legal records and their related papers—participates in its odd way in the historiographical endeavour of those historians with references to whom his own writings are dotted: Hume, Sir David Dalrymple (Lord Hailes), Sir John Dalrymple, Robertson, Lord Kames, Burnett (Lord Monboddo), Smith, Adam Ferguson and others, whom Boswell met, and to varying degrees, knew—historians of diverse subjects and styles, but collectively engaged in a great revisionary interrogation of the British identity and its making from the perspective of the post-Union Scot. The journals register the complex interaction of the question of Boswell's relation to Scotland,

and his authorial ambitions as a literary Scot wanting to make his way in London, in his articulation of a personal historicity in the lifelong autobiographical project; and help show—what the twentieth-century recovery of his papers allows us to see—the role in this project of the acquisition of Johnson as a biographical subject, and the psychopolitical needs it addressed. Boswell's perplexed national self-understanding and his attempts to cope with it contribute much to the conduct of his career as a private diarist and public journalist and biographer, and deeply inform his written representations of identity and of his own authorial career.

Boswell loved Edinburgh as his native city, and to its landmarks and monuments was fond of paying ceremonious tributes, but it was of course to London that his hopes constantly turned, his literary and social aspirations issuing from one extreme or idiosyncratic form of those perplexities in the post-Union Scot diagnosed perhaps most tersely as 'cultural schizophrenia'.[2] Now that we know Boswell better, we hear fewer simplistic dismissals of servile Anglophilia. But the ninth Laird of Auchinleck (succeeding at the death of his father on 30 August 1782) had all his life a troubled and complex relation to the fact of his Scottishness. 'I am by birth,' he began a letter to the *Public Advertiser* in a tone equally quizzical and proud, 'a *North Briton*, as a Scotchman must now be called' (6 April 1779). Genuinely regretful of Scotland's loss of national independence, he was nonetheless drawn irresistibly southward by the cultural and social aura of Johnson and, more generally, the emotional, social and sexual freedom of London. For him Edinburgh, despite his affection, was no Athens of the North, but irksome, rough, provincial, constraining, and the chosen colour of dress among gentlemen there was, he once remarked, black, 'law black' (*Later Years*, p 268). London alone, away from what he and his friend George Dempster discussed as 'the sarcastical temper of the Scots', that 'checked all endeavours at excellence' (16 September 1769), could give full release to what in another context he terms his 'English juiciness of mind' (4 July 1782). Dreading social insignificance in the legal career into which his father pressed him, and whose drudgery kept him pining for the excitement of London, he had 'full relish of life' in London, as he wrote once after dining with Johnson and Oliver Goldsmith at General Oglethorpe's: 'I felt myself of some real personal consequence while I made one of such a company' (10 April 1772). The young man who, somewhere near his twenty-first birthday and after only a few youthful literary dabblings, had earned an invitation to join the Select Society of Edinburgh (which then included such figures as Hume, Lord Kames, Hugh Blair, Sir David Dalrymple, and William Robertson), would wait in great anxiety twelve years later for news of his election to The Club in London. This election at the end of April in 1773, sealed, in Frank Brady's words, Boswell's 'emotional transference to London' (*Later Years*, p 52).

But the same man who recorded with pleasure after that occasion Johnson's remark that he was 'the most *unscottified*' of his countrymen was capable of other powerful moods. He would decline to visit the notoriously anti-Scots John Wilkes in prison because: 'I am a Scotch laird and a Scotch lawyer and a Scotch married man. It would not be decent' (20 April 1778). And offended one day by some supercilious treatment from David Garrick, he set the great actor straight: 'I am as proud as Lucifer. I am an old Scot, proud of being descended of ancestors who have had an estate for some hundreds of years' (24 April 1778). Later, Boswell's idealization of Auchinleck and his ancestry would take the form of extravagant devotion to the idea of Family, which he taught his son and heir Alexander by 'catechizing' him on Thomas Boswell's acquisition of the estate from James IV, and the deaths of both ancestor and monarch at Flodden. '"What is your first duty?" "My duty to GOD." "What is your second duty?" "My duty to the family of Auchinleck."' Thomas Boswell, Alexander learns, '"was killed at Flodden Field fighting with his king against the English, for Scotland and England were then two kingdoms"' (6 January 1780).

Again, the Union of Scotland and England, the central political fact of his time, was for Boswell no mere matter of theoretical dispute, or even of simple regret. It entered his muddled life at the core. He felt the allure of a reverential patriotism for a romanticized Scottish past, but found his nation too uncertain of its own identity, 'a country filled with jarring interests and keen parties' (15 August 1773), to help him with his own. A volatile man, disconcerted by the fluctuations in his own sense of self, he was driven instead by ambitions for authorial success to a Johnsonian England which he had come to see as solid, elevated, stable, and culturally central. Agonizing all his life over the choice of where to live, he made the ill-advised but inevitable decision late in 1785 to leave his revered Auchinleck and remove to London, a move as much disastrous for Margaret Boswell's failing health as for his own never sensibly pursued political hopes and not fully serious transfer to the English bar.

The consequences of Union entered too, of course, the language in which Boswell would speak and write. His boyhood tutor, the Rev John Dun, introduced him to *The Spectator*: 'it was then,' he told Rousseau later, 'that I acquired my first notions of taste for the fine arts and of the pleasure there is in considering the variety of human nature. I read the Roman poets, and I felt a classic enthusiasm in the romantic shades of our family's seat in the country (5 December 1764; *Earlier Years*, pp 2–3). In that revealingly simultaneous recollection, Boswell conflates the emergence of his admiration of the English essayistic style (Addison and Steele would remain important pre-Johnsonian models) with a taste for the fine arts, fascination with human character, and enthusiasm both classic and romantic for his 'Roman' Auchinleck: conjoining, that is, Englishness, desirable elegance, the roots of his impulses to biography, and fantasies of lettered and propertied gentlemanly retirement. His later admiration for Thomas Reid's *Inquiry* came not only because with 'strong reasoning and lively humour,' thought Boswell, it countered the challenges of Hume and 'drove to pieces the sceptical cobweb' (19 July 1764), but at least as much because, in the opinion of the actor and elocutionist Thomas Sheridan (who taught Scots to speak English), 'Reid's book was the most correct of any that North Britain had produced, for that he had not found one Scotticism in it.' Hume, in Boswell's opinion, among his other pernicious effects, had 'spoiled the taste of this age' (16 September 1769).[3] Boswell came later to Johnson's essays, and read him with delight, showing an independence, in F A Pottle's account, from his 'critical Mentors, Kames, Adam Smith, and Hugh Blair', all of whom 'disparaged Johnson's writing as heavy and pedantic' (*Earlier Years*, p 112). Boswell's own essayistic ambitions would be gratified later in his series of seventy for the *London Magazine* as 'The Hypochondriack', in an irregular series as 'The Rampager', and in frequent pamphleteering and other miscellaneous journalism. But the range of powerful aspirations Johnson's writing aroused in him would lead to his pursuit and capture of the Great English Moralist in London, profoundly inform the rest of his life, and bring him at length his hoped for authorial fame—but at a time when his dissipations had left him too ravaged to have anything like full relish of it.

'"Know thyself"', twenty-two year old James Boswell began his now famous *London Journal* in 1762. At a time when Scotland itself was engaged in a major repossession of its own historicity in words, in the rich efflorescence of the Scottish Enlightenment, Boswell set about recording his reintroduction (he had escaped to London once before) into the circles of the great, the gay and the ingenious, his life among the high and the low, and, momentously, his long-looked for meeting with Samuel Johnson: 'Don't tell him where I come from,' he begged Tom Davies, in whose bookshop the meeting unexpectedly took place—in a London where anti-Scots sentiment had reached new heights after Lord Bute's administration. His diary entries, given high literary polish and conducted in bouncing good spirits, he sent to his friend and reader John Johnston of Grange. An astute historian of the social conduct of the individual life, especially as it appears in the conversational vignette and the artfully reconstructed anecdote, Boswell would hone to telling power in his biographical writing the recording skills he practised almost daily in his journals and letters. Not for Boswell are the movements of centuries and epochs, or history abstracted to theory and theme: his attitude to national historiography, indeed, we might find illuminated by an entry in his journal for 3 May 1763. Despondent and unable to rest because of the impending execution of some prisoners he had visited in Newgate, Boswell made his barber try to read him to sleep, with David Hume's *History of England*.

Boswell left London in August 1763 for his travels on the continent. For a year he tried, in compliance with Lord Auchinleck's wishes, dutifully to study law in Utrecht, acquire diligence, and remain chaste, and was so miserable that he feared for his sanity. He brightened at the prospect of further travels in Europe in the company of George Keith, 10th Earl Marischal, an 'unexpected felicity', he told Grange, which made him 'quite a new man' (11 June 1764). His European tour produced a constant testing of his Scottishness, a measurement of his national character against others, and the journal he kept was to have formed the basis of a book he was always planning but in his wretched final years could not get himself to write. We might join Boswell in his travels, and compare a conversation he records in Germany with one he had earlier in London, a comparison to point up the deep confusion in the young Boswell's mind in his sense of national and cultural allegiance. In London before he left for his travels, Boswell 'fell upon political topics' with his Scots friends, the Kellie family—their father, the fifth Earl of Kellie, had been a colonel in the Jacobite army in the Forty-Five—and 'all agreed in our love of the Royal Family of Stuart and regret at their being driven from Britain. I maintained,' reports Boswell, 'that their encroachments were not of so bad consequence as their being expelled the throne.' In short, Boswell's journal continues, 'the substance of our conversation was that the family of Stuart, although unfortunate, did nothing worthy of being driven from the throne. That their little encroachments were but trifles in comparison of what Oliver Cromwell did . . . That by the Revolution [of 1688] we got a shabby family to reign over us, and that the German War, a consequence of having a German sovereign, was the most destructive thing this nation ever saw. This,' concludes Boswell, 'was a bold and rash way of talking; but it had justice, and it pleased me' (17 January 1763). A year and a half later, in Germany itself, mingling with Hanoverian royalty and being received courteously in the courts of the Electors, Boswell was discussing Jacobitism again, now with Lord Marischal. Heroic rebel leader in the uprising of 1715 and an intriguer for the Old Pretender in its aftermath, Lord Marischal had grown bitter and disillusioned and had taken no part for Prince Charles Edward in 1745. Though there was something 'pathetic and generous' in Jacobitism, 'as it was espousing the cause of a distressed and ancient royal house', Lord Marischal owned that the Stuarts had deserved to lose the throne of Britain. 'I own so too,' Boswell declares to his journal, the conversation with the Kellie family now forgotten. 'I am sorry for them. I wish to forget them; and I love from my soul "Great George our King"' (23 July 1764). Boswell did indeed, like many of a Tory cast who had shed their Jacobitism, love George III (to whom he justifiably claimed a blood relation), and would later in his life conceive a deep veneration for him; but the Stuarts would never quite relinquish their hold on his emotions. Three weeks later in his German travels, Boswell records an evening's entertainment in terms that gesture implicitly but tellingly towards a resolution of his emotional muddle. He found himself dancing with the Hereditary Princess, Augusta, sister of Great George our King. They made, Boswell wrote, 'a very fine English minuet—or British, if you please, for it was a Scots gentleman and an English lady that performed it. What a group of fine ideas had I! I was dancing with a princess; with the grand-daughter of King George whose birthday I have so often helped to celebrate at Old Edinburgh; with the daughter of the Prince of Wales, who patronized Thomson and other votaries of science and the muse; and with the sister of George the Third, my sovereign . . . It was noble to be in such a frame. I said to the Princess, "Madam, I return your Royal Highness a thousand thanks for the honour you have done me. This will serve me to talk of to my tenants as long as I live"' (13 August 1764). Around the Brunswick ballroom, Boswell and the Hereditary Princess dance a miniature model of the Union, not English but British. Boswell's 'group of fine ideas' trace the history of post-Union Scottishness in an interplay of international political history and the individual, personal record of Boswell's own autobiography. His ideas bring into union the Hanoverian George II (in Boswell's memories of public royal birthday celebrations) and 'Old Edinburgh', his own native city and ancient seat of the Scottish Stuarts; George II's son, the Prince of Wales, with his royal patronage, and James Thomson, whose career as a Scots author achieving great fame in England Boswell would like to emulate; and Augusta, sister of George III (who gloried in being born a Briton), and Boswell's own family estate, in his future vision of the tenants of Auchinleck hearing of this honour in the reminiscences of their Laird. The movement here is consistently away from ideas of an independent Scottish identity now not recoverable, into a complex idea of 'Britain' in which two partners play essential roles. His British minuet with the Hanoverian Princess affords him a subtle inversion of the commonplace 'marriage' metaphor for the Union, such as the one Boswell (after having acquired and read with interest a pamphlet by the Rev William Wright called 'On the Marriage of Fergusia and Heptarchus') would himself use in a public speech on the Articles of Union in 1779, when he 'assimilated the Union between England and Scotland—the stronger and the weaker country—to a contract of marriage' (22 July 1779). Here, Scotland appears in himself and his idealized sense of his ancestral propertied continuity, England in the feminine embodiment of Augusta: a fusion of a romanticized sense of old Highland patriarchy assimilated to Lowland estate succession, and English and European aristocratic culture.

In Germany, he travelled in the company of a Scot who made him proud to be Scottish. He rambled far away from the Presbyterian gloom of studious Utrecht where the weight of his father's wishes oppressed him: when feeling 'exceedingly melancholy' one day and full of 'horrid' thoughts, he thought himself 'just in Scotland' (30 June 1764). Socially successful among the courts of the Electors, accepted by the eminent, he was simultaneously growing into the proud Mr Boswell of Auchinleck, and into aspirations to biographical fame. In Brunswick on an earlier visit in June, Boswell had 'stood with a mind full of the ideas of the last glorious war' as he heard Prince Ferdinand talk of Highlanders who were among the British troops he led in the Seven Years War (28 June 1764). It was, of course, Ferdinand's brother-in-law, Frederick the Great of Prussia, who, having brought his nation through the war as a first rate power, gave Boswell his greatest noble shock: 'Upon my soul, I was struck,' wrote Boswell in a draft of a letter seeking an interview with the King; 'He electrified me. Every time I looked at him, I felt a shock of the heroic' (c. 31 July 1764). Revealingly, the sequence of journal entries covering the two Brunswick visits and his failure (the only one of its kind in his celebrity-hunting career) to secure a meeting with Frederick, chart the growth of his decision to secure the life-long friendship of Johnson, and move away from political and military fantasies of heroism—closely allied to his attachment to an independent Scottish past, and represented as Highland generosity and bravery—into literary and intellectual ones, into an extravagant desire to be contiguous with greatness of a moral and literary kind.

Boswell's letter freely discloses his developing journalistic and bio-graphical aims and methods. He declares himself to be like Socrates, 'who said, "Speak, so that I can see you"'. Boswell was, in one of Pottle's astutest summaries of him, 'a connoisseur of articulate greatness' (*Pride and Negligence*, p 6). The subject *is* what he *says*; the *Life of Johnson* (published first some 27 years after this) would hold its subject forever in the grand spectacle of articulacy. Boswell also frankly concedes in the letter (it is sometimes levelled at him as a supreme insult) that he is not a great man but loves the company of great men, and that there is a boyish or filial quality to this feeling that he would actively seek to preserve: 'I am willing to keep something of the spirit of childhood. Ah . . . it is a pleasant age: one feels then in full force that admiration which to my way of thinking is one of the most agreeable of passions.' The weeks between and around the two Brunswick visits, as he fails in his design to meet Frederick the Great, produce a gradual adjustment of focus in his aspiration to gratify his love of greatness. Away from Scotland and his studious despondency in Utrecht where his father's wishes bore him down, his pained in-junctions to himself to be some other eminent stable man begin to yield to a pleasure in himself as an 'original' character. Reviewing his rather 'too singular' gaiety at a wedding ball in Berlin, 'Why not,' he abruptly asks himself: 'Let me moderate and cultivate my originality . . . Let me then be Boswell and render him as fine a fellow as possible' (20 July 1764). Some time later, 'Why seek to please all? Why fear the censure of those whom I despise? Let me boldly pursue my own plan' (6 August 1764). And most clearly: 'I saw my error in suffering so much from the contemplation of others. I can never be them, therefore let me not attempt it in imagination; therefore let me not envy the gallant and the happy, nor be shocked by the nauseous and the wretched. I must be Mr Boswell of Auchinleck, and no other' (9 August 1764).

At first, excited thoughts of Frederick and Ferdinand kept alive Boswell's heroic Highland soldierly fantasies. 'I find that if I had got a commission in a Highland corps, I should have been as stout a Donald as the best of them' (13 July 1764). Yet his deepening fascination with 'the variety of human nature' (see p 159 above) is troubled by reflecting on the regimentation and mass death that war entails: 'I see such numbers of fine fellows bred to be slaughtered that human beings seem like herrings in a plentiful season. One thinks nothing of a few barrels of herring, nor can I think much of a few regiments of men. What am I then, a single man? Strange thought! Let it go'. But the thought would not quite let Boswell go. In 1777 the

Hypochondriack essayist, recalling his European travels (specifically a visit to the great arsenal in Venice) describes his 'reflections on the horrid irrationality of war.' War, in this essay (December 1777), and the life of soldiering, are now beyond rational explanation, for one of war's chief features is indeed the obliteration of individual value and distinction. In Germany in 1764, Boswell's desire for individual distinction was taking other turns—authorial distinction, an extension of his social distinction as Mr Boswell 'of Auchinleck'. His sense of social identity grows, here, into a complex fusion of the propertied masculine continuity of his family estate, and the glamorous metropolitan literary idea of 'London', embodied in the author of the poem of that name, Johnson. The young Scot would conquer Europe authorially, by winning the Monarch of English Letters as a biographical subject. As these related impulses evolve, Boswell decides to secure from Johnson some articles of this union, a written charter of friendship. On the same day that he decided to be Mr Boswell of Auchinleck, he attended a 'pretty operette' in Brunswick, and 'sat in the Duke's *loge* and was fine with the ladies of the Court'. Amidst all this brilliance, he reports, 'I sent forth my imagination to the Inner Temple, to the chambers of Mr Samuel Johnson. I glowed with reverence and affection, and a romantic idea filled my mind. To have a certain support at all times, I determined to write to this great man, and beg that he might give me a "solemn assurance of perpetual friendship", so that I might march under his protection while he lived, and after his death, imagine that his shade beckoned me to the skies. Grand, yet enthusiastic, idea!' (9 August 1764).

Boswell's terms here are drawn from military and political patronage—he would 'march' under Johnson's 'protection'—but his thoughts of life after Johnson's death show him working already towards immortality. That he would fix this association in the permanence of the written word soon appears: he records his daily attempts to write to Johnson since he 'formed the resolution of demanding a charter of his friendship' (16 August 1764). 'March', 'protection', 'charter': his resolutions are couched in terms that implicitly convert his political and military aspirations to heroic distinction into moral, intellectual and literary ones. Throughout this process, the references to Frederick increase in bitterness: he records remarks that during the war the king 'had no human feeling' (8 August 1764); that he has 'neither religion nor humanity' (9 September 1764); that he is feared 'like a wild beast'. At length: 'I am quite out of conceit with monarchy' (22 September 1764). The thoughts of Frederick the Great that electrified him into fantasies of military greatness yield, then, in time to thoughts of Mr Boswell and Auchinleck, and the conquest instead, in 'reverence and affection', of Johnson—and the deepening of his wishes to become an officer in the authorial corps. It is this portion of his travels that would lead him to heroes of the mind, Voltaire and Rousseau, and then to the Corsican patriot General Paoli whom Boswell would turn into a Plutarchan hero of action and contemplation in his first major authorial success: the *Account of Corsica* (1768). With this book later translated into several languages, the young Scot, his ambitions not at all dissimilar to those of the Edinburgh *literati*, had conquered Europe, not martially, but authorially. And he had accounted to a wider audience for a national struggle for what he himself wanted: filial liberty, cultural transformation.

That letter to Johnson proved troublesome to write, suggestive of the complexities behind it. Eventually, in Wittenberg on September 30, 1764, while bemused spectators gathered around and probably thought him 'a little mad', Boswell lay down upon the tomb of Melanchthon to write his effusive letter: 'At this tomb, then, my very dear and respected friend, I vow to thee an eternal attachment. It shall be my study to do what I can to render your life happy, and if you die before me, I shall endeavour to do honour to your memory'. Boswell did not send the letter until 1777, the biographical association with Johnson already formed, and he published it in the *Life*, the association complete.

In the version of his journal record of the tour to the Highlands and Western Islands with Johnson in 1773, revised with the scholar Edmond Malone's help into a memoir of Johnson after his death, a prelude to the later and larger *Life*, Boswell confronts most fully the connected problems of his filiation (his relation with Lord Auchinleck) and his larger cultural affiliation. He fashions the biographical 'co-partnery' (2 October 1773) as a victorious escape from and triumph over feelings of guilty unworthiness, fostered by the low opinion in which Lord Auchinleck understandably held his erratic son, whom he saw as an inadequate inheritor of Auchinleck. The 'great principle of law . . . on which we all depend,' Boswell informed Lord Mansfield in 1768, explaining his conduct in the great Douglas Cause, is '*filiation*' (20 May 1768). Boswell's vigorously pro-Douglasian activities in the Cause, which turned on the disputed legitimacy of Archibald Douglas and his right to the Douglas estates, originated because the Cause was, in Pottle's words, a symbol of Boswell's own deepest grievance: 'To a Douglasian, the Cause came down to a vicious attempt to prove the true heir a changeling. Metaphorically, that was what [Boswell's] own differences with his father had amounted to: a reiterated and destroying charge that he was not a true son of Auchinleck' (*Earlier Years*, p 313). In his record of the Hebridean journey, Boswell marks the symbolic displacement of Lord Auchinleck (whose actual hold over his son would remain nonetheless strong) by Johnson as the object of his cultural allegiance. And in leaving Edinburgh, travelling through a Highland and Western Island region that stands for the core of Boswell's imaginative Scottishness, the *locus* of his sentimental hankering for the idealized filial and paternal allegiances of the old clan ways of life, Boswell traces in 'the transit of Johnson over the Caledonian Hemisphere' (5 November 1773) the outline of one contained and unified island, beginning and ending where Johnson begins and ends, in London.

Some nine years after dancing his minuet with the Hereditary Princess in Brunswick, Boswell danced a Highland reel on top of Duncaan on the island of Raasay with Malcolm MacLeod of Brae, one of the heroes of the Forty-Five who had helped the Young Pretender elude Government forces and escape to France. Now, in the autumn of 1773, active Jacobitism was no more—yet remained alive as a sentiment—and the Highlands had become for Boswell as for any number of others an idealized focus for old Scots patriotism. In his Hebridean journal, both as written at the time and as revised, Boswell addresses most directly his cultural perplexity, in the relation between himself as a Scot, 'a gentleman of ancient blood, the pride of which was his predominant passion' (18 August 1773) and the ostentatiously English Johnson, 'at bottom much of a *John Bull*, much of a blunt *true-born Englishman*' (*Life* v, p 20).[4] The record of the tour confronts, and in its later published form aims at a complex union in, his divided national self-understanding. As Boswell has shaped them, important moments of the tour turn on paradigms of political union, seen consistently as successful compromise and peaceful resolution after upheaval and rebellion, failure and loss, and Boswell shows both himself and Scotland to have followed that pattern. The Boswell–Johnson 'co-partnery' stands as the personal analogue to the political and cultural link, as it was perceived in idealized and paradigmatic form by the insecure and disoriented Boswell, between Scotland and England. Upon the text of national history, Boswell inscribes his own personal and literary history. The interdependences of biographer and subject represent for the biographer an equality-in-secondariness, a 'generous attachment' (as Boswell words it more than once) that permits a continued survival, in literary immortality, of both partners. The resulting text, a collaborative production of Johnsonian utterance and Boswellian reportage, subtly announces itself as the fruit of the Union.

Back from his European travels, Boswell feels himself entitled to the narrative posture of the cosmopolite, 'completely a citizen of the world', able now to look at both sides of any question, to make judiciously good-humoured appraisals of people and places, undeluded, he believes, by their own self-estimates, aware that even the revered Johnson had a 'stratum of common clay under the rock of marble' (*Life* v, p 20). A happy union of Highland generosity and travelled sophistication, Boswell in his memoir can embrace, contain, but remain unpersuaded by representatives of narrow belief in their own cultural rightness. Johnson 'could not but see in [the Scots] that nationality which I believe no liberal-minded Scotsman will deny'. But Johnson's professed aversion to the Scots produces in Boswell, he says, an inversion of the son–father hierarchy: '. . . when I humour any of them [the English] in an outrageous contempt of Scotland, I fairly own I treat them as children. And thus I have, at some moments, found myself obliged to treat even Dr Johnson' (*Life* v, p 20). Here, as in the later *Life*, Johnson's exaggerated sense of English superiority over all other nations appears as part of a deeper, more complex, and sympathetically registered tenacity about mind and identity; and it is shown to be such by a biographical narrator who represents himself alert to but uncontaminated by questions of narrow 'nationality'—in his own estimate, he is a generous but clear-eyed citizen of the world upon whose perception 'nationality' registers comprehensibly as only part of larger social and cultural definitions of character.

Thoughts and conversations in the early journals report, as we have seen, the competing claims of the Houses of Stuart and Hanover on Boswell's emotions. The Hebridean journal contains accounts from participants in the Forty-Five and its aftermath, notably Malcolm MacLeod and Flora Macdonald, but others too, including, for example, an anonymous 'redcoat' at whose narration of 'the particulars of that unlucky but brave and generous attempt' Boswell 'several times burst into tears' (1 September 1773). These accounts weave in and out of the Boswell-Johnson record to provide a continuing interplay of national history and individual identity. The text of that history seems to him inscribed on the very landscape through which he passes: 'I saw Loch Moidart, into which the Prince entered on his first arrival, and within which is a lesser loch called Lochninua, where the Prince actually landed. The hills around, or rather mountains, are black and wild in an uncommon degree. I gazed on them with much feeling. There was a rude grandeur that seemed like a consciousness of the royal enterprise, and a solemn dreariness as if a melancholy remembrance of its events had remained' (3 October 1773). Establishing Johnson in this setting, recording him in the company of the heroes of the Forty-Five, among the chieftains who represented the little that now survived of the old Highland ways of life, even in the very bed Charles Edward slept in, allowed Boswell boldly to fuse his idealized constructions of the two cultures with claims on his affiliation. For Boswell's generation, initiation into national history had come in the 1750s and 1760s, when Scotland's political and economic relation with England was already an established fact. Without relinquishing his sentimental attachment to the 'pathetic and generous' old cause, Boswell finds in his biographical mission, to record the thoughts and utterances of the Rambler, long-sought participation in the cultural opportunities made possible by Union. Explaining Johnson's Englishness to the Scots even as the journey educates Johnson, who returned from Scotland 'in great good humour, with his prejudices much lessened' (*Life* v, p 20), Boswell socially mobilizes Johnson for his hosts: 'Mr Johnson's immense fund of knowledge and wit was a wonderful source of admiration and delight to them. But they had it only at times; and they required to have interstices agreeably filled up, and even little elucidations of his grand text' (2 October 1773). When Malcolm MacLeod guided Prince Charles Edward in his Highland wanderings after Culloden, he was Boswell's age at the time of the tour to the Hebrides. Military bravery, left behind in the European royal courts, appears here only as sentimental fantasy: Boswell's involvement in Jacobite history is journalistic—he will explain it to the world in words, providing in the published version a sustained account, gathered piecemeal from his informants, of the Pretender's escape. Boswell's heroism is now social, aimed at reconciliation and 'warm union': 'While we were at dinner Mr Johnson kept a close whispering conference with Mrs Mackinnon [Flora Macdonald] about the particulars she knew of the Prince's escape . . . Upon that subject there was a warm union between the soul of Mr Samuel Johnson and that of an Isle of Skye farmer's wife. It is curious to see people, though ever so much removed from each other in the general system of their lives, come close together on a particular point which is common to each' (28 September 1773). Flora Macdonald and Johnson share emotional allegiance to Jacobitism, but to Boswell's approval, such sentiment is expressed verbally and not martially. As the Highland craft and guile of MacLeod, Flora Macdonald and their comrades guided the princely Pretender through the Western Islands to safety, Boswell's considerable social craft and guile guide Johnson, the Monarch of English Letters, into and through spectacular encounters with the Scots. Johnson, massive, static, monumental, requires Boswell's social accommodation and pliability, for with monumentality comes unwieldiness: 'Mr Johnson did not practise the art of accommodating himself to different sorts of people . . . [His] forcible spirit and impetuosity of manner may be said to spare neither sex nor age . . . But I have often maintained that it is better so. Pliability of address I take to be inconsistent with that majestic power which he has, and which produces such noble effects' (5 October 1773). Boswell explains, in the immediate context, Johnson to the Scots, but in the broader biographical one, uses his Scottishness to figure the function of the biographer himself, a credentialled and privileged witness, with the heightened perception of the culturally aware outsider, elucidating the grand Johnsonian text to the audience of the world and posterity.

Boswell's initiation into national history coincided, too, with his own progress to rebellion (a defeated or incomplete one) against the rule of his father, and he reads in the text of national history his own: the history of the Stuarts fascinated him in part because, as Brady has put it, 'they were dramatic in their recklessness and gallant in their daring rebellions. Like himself they had been confined and thwarted by strict gloomy Presbyterians' (*Political Career*, p 30). The inevitable collision between Johnson and Alexander Boswell, Lord Auchinleck, tenacious representatives of the two old cultures with claims on him, marks a decisive episode after the Highland and Hebridean part of the tour. The subjects that brought them into dispute were, not surprisingly, Cromwell and the Commonwealth, Stuart rule, and the merits of Scots Presbyterians. Lord Auchinleck, learned, literate, a classicist and bibliophile, and himself an accomplished talker for victory, 'was as sanguine a Whig and Presbyterian as Dr Johnson was a Tory and Church of England man' (2 November 1773). Boswell declines to 'exhibit my honoured father and my respected friend as intellectual gladiators, for the entertainment of the public', but reports enough of the scene to show his father not at all far from Johnsonian in his shrewd and sophistical argumentative strategies. The contest seems a tie, and a couple of days later the two titans part civilly, but Boswell's final word on the matter shows how he scored it: 'They are now in another, and a higher state of existence; and as they were both worthy Christian men, I trust they have met in happiness. But I must observe, in justice to my friend's political principles and my own, that they have met in a place where there is no room for Whiggism' (8 November 1773).

In his German travels in 1764, Boswell actively sought (and was unlucky not to receive) the Order of Fidelity of the Prince of Baden-Durlach, who had befriended him and listened with evident sympathy to Boswell's wish. 'From my earliest years I have respected the great', Boswell told his journal; 'In the groves of Auchinleck I have indulged pleasing hopes of ambition' (16 November 1764). Nine years later, Boswell's pleasing hopes of ambition have materialized in the form of Johnson in the groves of Auchinleck, and Boswell declares again, now *in actu*, his intention to honour his memory: 'As I wandered with my revered friend in the groves of Auchinleck, I told him that if I survived him, it was my intention to erect a monument to him, among scenes which, in my mind, were all classical; for in my youth I had appropriated to them many of the descriptions of the Roman poets' (4 November 1773). The sketch of himself he wrote for Rousseau in 1764 reported the adolescent dawning of his pleasure in the variety of human nature when his tutor set him reading English essayists, and his 'classic enthusiasm in the romantic shades of our family's seat' as he read 'the Roman poets'. Johnson—monumental, Augustan, Roman, London—has here joined Auchinleck's romanticized groves, and Boswell's monument to him will be a monument in words.

Behind, then, his individual history, Boswell charts at least as seriously as he does playfully the outlines of a national epic, the story of an arduous national quest that ends in 'Britain', the Boswellian version of a story chronicled by the national historians. That Boswell can give his account of the serious cultural disputation between his father and Johnson a nontheless comical cast catches the tone of the whole. Times are now such that cultural collisions are conversational and end civilly; they do not, as they did for the generation who fought in the Pretender's cause, take the form of war. The stage is held not by the Wanderer (Boswell's main designation for Charles Edward) but by the Rambler, a hero of the mind, of the civilized life. The journal record (but not the published memoir) reports Scotland's past as a long history of fighting, of wars with England, and more frequently of dynastic fury among the old clans. Boswell notes, for example, the story of how in violent retributive justice the MacLeods smoked the inhabitants of Eigg to death in a large cave to which they had fled. On Coll, Boswell rummaged through a cabinet full of papers and he copied into his journal stories and letters about the numerous murders and territorial disputes involving that island. Significantly, the next clan fight he records figures in a letter in which the Jacobite writers upraid some Campbells. With this revealing sequence, clear in the manuscript journal but edited out of the published memoir, Boswell implies a direct continuity between the old internecine clan violence, the war in the young Pretender's cause, and its survival in the competing claims on his emotional allegiance.

With his *Account of Corsica*, the young Scot had conquered Europe. With Johnson, he aimed at authorial immortality and his chosen territory was the whole of posterity. In its sustained generic allusion to epic, the Hebridean journal follows not the course of war, but like epic after the *Iliad*, of wandering after war—of Boswell's cultural homecoming. But Boswell's 'epic'—a true national epic, he implies, against which the falseness of Ossian (Johnson, notoriously, denies Ossian both authenticity and merit) is consistently set—can follow the movements of its royal Wanderer only so far. Prince Charles Edward can only fail gloriously and escape with courage and ingenuity into France, and then into romanticized history. Boswell's epic antecedents, more than Homeric, are Virgilian–Augustan, Roman, like monumental Johnson amid Roman scenes in the groves of Auchinleck. (George III's sister, who would come to Auchinleck in the reminiscences of its Laird, bore the Roman name Augusta). Boswell, an authorial Aeneas, is concerned to give shape and definition to a culturally dislocated people, who, though repeatedly baffled and defeated prove (like himself) resilient, and survive through a Trojan/Latin-like fusion with England. But even as the journal aligns itself with the Scottish Enlightenment's historiographical enterprise, to reinscribe the British identity in the post-Union political conditions, Boswell's method departs from the national historians of the Athens of the North with its emphasis on the 'history of manners' as biography, on the individual figure given close attention, on the conversational and anecdotal registration of social life. Johnson's disapproval at one point of Sir John Dalrymple's style produces one of his most frequently quoted pronouncements: '"All history, so far as it is not supported by contemporary evidence, is romance"'—an endorsement, of course, of Boswell's method (20 November 1773). Similarly, Adam Smith is produced to endorse a concentration on particular detail: 'Let me not be censured', Boswell declares, 'for mentioning . . . minute particulars. Everything relative to so great a man is worth observing. I remember Dr Adam Smith, in his rhetorical lectures at Glasgow, told us he was glad to know that Milton wore latchets in his shoes instead of buckles' (*Life* v, p 19). Boswell also finds implied approval from the great historian Principal Robertson (whose contemporary reputation was second only to Gibbon's). In 1762, Boswell wrote to John Johnston of Grange: 'I have read Robertson's *History* for the first time, which has carried me back in Imagination to the ancient days of Scottish Grandeur; has filled my mind with generous ideas of the valour of our Ancestors, and made me feel, a pleasing sympathy for the beautifull accomplished Mary' (13 September 1762). By the end of the Hebridean tour, Boswell has changed his mind somewhat about Mary (more on her presently), and Robertson emerges to provide yet another emphatic endorsement of Boswell's mode. He suggests that a history of the Forty-Five should be written 'in Mr Boswell's way' of gathering reports from witnesses and writing them down, in a spirit of amity and impartiality, as 'both Whigs and Jacobites were now come to talk with moderation' (11 November 1773). The account of the Pretender in the published memoir fulfills Robertson's immediate suggestion; but Boswell's biographical method fulfils it reconciliatory spirit on a much larger scale.

At the ruins of the cathedral at Iona, Boswell's thoughts moved not only to Augustan Rome but to Catholic Rome. Old Scots and Catholic associations had been fused in Boswell's mind at least since the days of his student friendship with John Johnston of Grange. Boswell had long wanted to bring Johnson to this place, as he had wanted to bring him to Auchinleck: '"the great thing is to bring objects together"', Boswell remarks to Johnson, in what could stand as a general summary of his aims and methods. In a letter to David Garrick from Inverness, Boswell had commented on Johnson as a 'permanent London object', and that 'it would not be much more wonderful to me to see St Paul's church moving along where we are now' (*Life* v, p 347). On Easter Sunday in 1779, Boswell went to St Paul's, and his journal entry records explicitly the imaginative union implied here in the Western Isles: 'At altar thanked GOD for uniting Auchinleck and St Paul's—romantic seat of my ancestors and this grand cathedral—"in the imagination which Thou has given me"' (4 April 1779). In the Western Islands, Iona and St Paul's are great objects brought together, as in 'Roman' Johnson, and the Rome of the past and of Boswell's grand tour, where he brought himself close to Cardinal York, the Pretender's younger son, and urged himself to 'think of Grange and old Scots kings and Chapel of Holyrood' (26 May 1765). But St Paul's cathedral is a permanent London object, and Iona is a ruin, coming in the tour after a steady sequence of old Scottish places of worship in decay or collapse, beginning with the Church of St Giles in Edinburgh which 'has lost its original magnificence in the inside by being divided into four places of Presbyterian worship. "Come," said Dr Johnson jocularly to Principal Robertson, "Let me see what was once a church"' (16 August 1773). Ancient Scotland, Celtic Christianity, 'Caledonia', all remain attractive imaginatively, and modern Presbyterianism a less colourful substitute in the mind of the pageant-loving Boswell. In the published memoir, union is enacted in the text itself, as Boswell excerpts from Johnson's own controversially received *A Journey to the Western Islands of Scotland* (1775) his account of the same solemn moment. Johnson concludes this resonant and famous passage: 'That man is little to be envied, whose patriotism would not gain force upon the plain of *Marathon*, or whose piety would not grow warmer among the ruins of *Iona!*' The Boswellian and Johnsonian texts are here the same. All distinctions of time, place, and individual personality, of merely local versions of Christianity, vanish in the sanctity of Iona. Moreover, for Boswell, local versions of nationality, distinctions between Englishman and Scot, are similarly obliterated, cut down by the idea of patriotism on the imaginative plain of Marathon. For Boswell as, he believes, for Scotland, an original magnificence has been lost, but recovery and recuperation follow when great objects have been brought together.

When Queen Mary appears again in the journal, Boswell has lost all interest in her beauty, and she has become instead openly an argument against Stuart claims to the throne of Britain. Despite the 'kind of liking' he and Johnson have for Jacobitism, Boswell cannot find 'the firm feudal hold for which I wish and which my imagination figures. I might fix my eye at the point of James IV, from whom my ancestor Thomas Boswell got the estate of Auchinleck, and look no further, had I a line of males from that Prince. But Queen Mary comes in the way; and I see the sons of Lennox on the throne' (13 September 1773). Mary unluckily violates his 'high notions of male succession', and Boswell accepts George III fully. Idealized

Auchinleck offers a more satisfying succession of male rule than Stuart history—which has now assumed the role of a tale of unworthy filiation: the sons of Lennox do not properly belong on the throne. Both the story of Boswell history and the story of Scotland emerge as tales, like the *Aeneid*, of triumphant recovery after failure and loss. Boswell announced earlier in his journal a plan to write a biography of James IV, or a history of his reign (23 August 1773). It was never written, but its sources of appeal for Boswell are easy to imagine. With this king, Boswell's own personal mythography of Auchinleck originates. This king effected a kind of political union with marriage to the English Margaret Tudor, daughter of Henry VII. Thomas Boswell fell with James at Flodden, but Auchinleck and Scotland recovered, adjusted to new circumstances, and live on.

The biographer, recording the greatness of another, subordinates himself in some senses to his object, but ensures survival, in literary immortality, for both. To read the Johnsonian biographies again in the context of the autobiographical record out of which they in part came is to see the complex historical forces behind them, and the working of those forces in Boswell's repossession in words of his personal historicity. Carving the monumental *Life of Johnson* from his own record, so much a record of failure and loss, Boswell has in his own estimation turned secondariness into success, and, like Scotland, retrieved from a lost original magnificence a rich co-partnery, and a considerable compensatory triumph.

NOTES

Boswell's journals are quoted with the permission of Yale University Library and the McGraw-Hill Book Company.

1 F R Hart, 'Notes for an Anatomy of Modern Autobiography,' *New Literary History* 1 (1969–70), p 491.
2 David Daiches, *The Paradox of Scottish Culture: The Eighteenth-Century Experience* (London, 1964), *see especially* p 10, p 66.
3 Boswell's later anxieties about his English style appear, for example, in the records of the assistance Edmond Malone gave him in revising his Hebridean journal for publication, 'The charge,' as Brady puts it, 'that he had committed a Scotticism always brought Boswell to his knees' (*Later Years*, p 287).
4 Boswell's manuscript journal of the Hebridean tour is quoted (and cited by date) wherever possible. Quotation from the published journal is drawn from the third edition, which appears as the fifth volume of the Hill-Powell *Life*.

FURTHER READING

A multi-volume edition of Boswell's journals, edited and supplemented with other materials (chiefly letters and memoranda) to form continuous narratives, and published by Heinemann in Great Britain and McGraw-Hill in the USA, has been produced by the Yale Editions of the Private Papers of James Boswell. The series begins with F A Pottle (ed), *Boswell's London Journal: 1762–1763* (1950), and the final volume, *Boswell, The Great Biographer: 1789–1795*, is in preparation.

G B Hill (ed), *Boswell's Life of Johnson*, rev L F Powell, 6 vols (Oxford, 1934–50). Vol 5 includes *The Journal of a Tour to the Hebrides with Samuel Johnson, LL.D.* (1785) using the third edition (1786) as the basis of its text
Brady, Frank, *Boswell, The Later Years: 1769–1795* (London and New York, 1984)
—— *Boswell's Political Career* (New Haven and London, 1965)
Clifford, James L (ed), *Twentieth-Century Interpretations of Boswell's Life of Johnson* (Englewood Cliffs, New Jersey, 1970)
Dowling, William C, *The Boswellian Hero* (Athens, Georgia, 1979)
—— *Language and Logos in the Life of Johnson* (Princeton, 1981)
Ingram, Allen, *Boswell's Creative Gloom: A Study of Imagery and Melancholy in the Writings of James Boswell* (London, 1982)
Passler, David L, *Time, Form and Style in Boswell's Life of Johnson* (New Haven, 1971)
Pottle, F A, *The Literary Career of James Boswell, Esq.* (Oxford, 1929)
—— *Boswell, The Earlier Years: 1740–1769* (London and New York, 1966, 1985)
—— *Pride and Negligence: The History of the Boswell Papers* (New York, 1982)
Schwartz, Richard, *Boswell's Johnson: A Preface to the Life* (Madison, 1978)
Siebenschuh, William R, *Form and Purpose in Boswell's Biographical Works* (Berkeley, 1971)
—— *Fictional Techniques and Factual Works* (Athens, Georgia, 1983)
The Hypochondriack: Being the Seventy Essays ... Appearing in the London Magazine from November 1777 to August 1783, edited by Margery Bailey, 2 vols (Stanford, 1928). Reprinted in one volume with briefer annotation, as *Boswell's Column*, 1951

Chapter 10

Gaelic Poetry in the Eighteenth Century: the Breaking of the Mould

DERICK S THOMSON

It was inevitable that the eighteenth century, an era of sharp political and social upheaval in Gaelic Scotland, should also be an era of change in Gaelic literature. It is usual, in the Gaelic literary tradition, for poetry to be the main area of innovation as well as of conservation, and so it is mainly with poetry we shall have to deal.

Changes can be seen from different perspectives. There can be little argument, however, that one of the major processes discernible in the Gaelic poetry of the century is that of emerging from the classical chrysalis, the Gaelic classical chrysalis, that is to say. For many centuries there had been a widely practised tradition of verse-making by professional poets, who had taken lengthy training in bardic schools, wrote in a standard literary dialect which was governed by strict rules of grammar and usage, followed strict metrical practices, and drew on a large body of history, genealogy, legend and exempla. These poets held office (often hereditarily) in the households of clan chiefs, and produced official verse in celebratory, panegyric, historical and legendary modes, with various by-products, such as religious or humorous or scurrilous verses, or poems in the *amour courtois* tradition. This classical tradition, which was closely similar to, and connected with, the Irish Gaelic tradition, was evidently widely disseminated in Scotland. The system depended on both the independence and the Gaelic solidarity of the chiefs who fostered it, and we see the conditions of its survival being undermined in the seventeenth and early eighteenth centuries, and largely disappearing after the Forty-Five Rising. The historical process of the attrition of Gaelic power could take two distinct forms, either the loss of power and position experienced by the Lords of the Isles, or the loss of Gaelic identity experienced by e.g. the Breadalbane Campbells or the Dunvegan MacLeods. For such reasons, and by the gradual shedding of medieval concepts—a shedding that accompanied greater exposure to other evolving societies—the professional poets petered out, in the persons of Niall MacMhuirich who died *c.* 1726, and his less impressive successor Dómhnall MacMhuirich, who was still composing in the 1730s. However, though the professional bardic system was in its death-throes, its effects were far from dead, and a strong case could be made for the survival of many aspects of that classical tradition, in thought patterns, poetic styles, vocabulary, phraseology and metrics, in the vernacular verse of the eighteenth century, and indeed of later centuries.

From a different perspective, some eighteenth-century poetry can be seen as being differentiated from what is found in the oral popular tradition. Implicit here is a correction of the popular misconception that most Gaelic poetry of the period was of or allied to the oral tradition in any case. By not accepting that simplification, we can recognize the contrast between the work of poets who were composing in a more public context and that of the folk poets who express more private and personal emotions although often using shared forms of expression. We can see these contrasting traditions each going their separate ways in both the seventeenth and the eighteenth centuries, but the separation becoming wider in the eighteenth. This divergence is not due to a conscious movement on the part of individual poets, but is rather an effect, again, of changes in society producing a wider gulf between the styles.

These processes of distancing from both the classical and the early folk traditions can be observed in the work of eighteenth-century poets as diverse as Iain MacCodrum (John MacCodrum), Donnchadh Bàn Mac an t-Saoir (Duncan Macintyre), Rob Donn (Robert Mackay), Dùghall Bochanan (Dugald Buchanan), Alasdair Mac Mhaighstir Alasdair (Alexander MacDonald), Uilleam Ros (William Ross) and Eòghan Mac-Lachlainn (Ewen MacLachlan). A few instances will help to clarify the matter. We can see MacCodrum being more successful in his praise of Sir James MacDonald as a warrior (which he hardly was) than as a man of education and other civil gifts, since praise-poetry in his mind would be linked to warrior qualities. The point was made by Donald Archie Mac-Donald in a re-assessment of MacCodrum,[1] and he thinks some of Mac-Codrum's panegyrics are close in spirit to the best of the old professional praise poetry. I would rather describe them as a creditable echo of that earlier poetry, lacking its clear definition and its ampler reference. Where MacCodrum, it seems to me, comes into his own is when he comments on current events, such as the emigration of leading tacksmen and the coming of sheep (which will make poor soldiers in an emergency), or most of all when he brings into play his powers of wit and satire on topics such as a bout of fever, old age, or the bagpipes. Here we see him taking up a more clearly defined new ground, as to subject, and applying a wealth of language and a metrical fluency that are related to the classical tradition but also emancipated from it.

Donnchadh Bàn can stay closer to classical models in his sometimes sychophantic praise of Campbell leaders, but he soars into another element with a poem such as 'Moladh Beinn Dòbhrain' (The Praise of Ben Doran), finding new themes and forms and language. Rob Donn similarly makes new room for himself, though in a very different way, with his detailed and critical, though amused, observation of the rural society he knew. Mac Mhaighstir Alasdair, obviously influenced by the metrics and the language of the classical poems, also is open to influence from Latin and English poetry and this opens up his thematic repertoire. Dùghall Bochanan, in his intense exploration of religious and morbid themes, has a clarity and a concentration that may remind us of the classical bards, but he was strongly influenced by poetry in English too, especially by Edward Young's *Night Thoughts*. Uilleam Ros, allowing emotion and sentiment, and personal love experience, to play an important part in his poetry, is distanced by his more aureate language, and his general sophistication, from the folk poetry on similar themes. And MacLachlainn, translator of the *Iliad* into Gaelic, and Librarian at King's College, Aberdeen, in the early nineteenth century, can write a delicate love poem as successfully as detailed descriptions of the seasons. We shall be returning to several of these poets at a later stage in this chapter.

Besides these—usually regarded as the leading poets of the eighteenth century—there were many other composers or writers of verse, ranging from the formally educated laird to the illiterate folksinger, and representing a considerable diversity of styles. There is Sìleas na Ceapaich, close to the start of the century, with her allegorical religious verse at one end of the scale (e.g. 'An Eaglais', The Church) and her lively exposition of sexual licence at the other ('An Aghaidh na h-Obair Nodha').[2] And the Rev John Maclean, addressing a formal ode in bardic language to Edward Lhuyd, the Welsh polymath, about 1707.[3] Or MacDonald of Dalness, producing a moving love-song in the high style.[4] Or Macpherson of Strathmashie, James Macpherson's collaborator, moving easily from his probable forgery of the Gaelic Book 7 of *Temora* to a hilarious account of a Badenoch wedding.[5] Or Ann Campbell, daughter of a Scalpay (Harris) laird, making her poignant lament for her drowned fiancé ('Ailein Duinn').[6] There was a large crop of Jacobite verse, and a growing fashion for songs and poems about specific localities, often seen in retrospect by people who had moved to a Lowland domicile. And from the eighteenth century we also have an increasing number of songs on local, humorous themes, earlier representatives of the local or village verse which comes so prominently to notice in the nineteenth century. It is probably true to say that eighteenth-century verse offers easily the widest spectrum of any century of Gaelic verse. This is partly because of changing social conditions throwing up new initiatives while the old are still unexhausted: the political upheavals of the Fifteen and Forty-five Risings, the break-up of the clan system, the migration that began to build up from Highlands to Lowlands, and the changing patterns of education, all helped to create new contexts and interfaces which came to be reflected in the literature. The fuller recording of the literature, especially the poetry, opens it up to our view also, for it was largely in the eighteenth century that extensive collection, and preservation in manuscript, of post-classical Gaelic verse, began.

An important factor, in this greatly increased incidence of collection and preservation, was the Ossianic controversy. James Macpherson had collected genuine heroic Gaelic ballads, from both manuscript and oral sources, in the years immediately before and after 1760, and was associated with other collectors of Gaelic verse such as the Rev James McLagan. It is in this context that Gaelic poetry makes contact, in a palpable form, with the luminaries of the Scottish Enlightenment, particularly Adam Ferguson, who was himself a Gaelic speaker and had had a modest acquaintance with the heroic balladry in his Perthshire youth. There can be no doubt that the controversy which followed the publication of Macpherson's alleged translations of 1760–63 also greatly stimulated further collection, partly to show how widespread genuine Gaelic balladry was, but motivated also by a more dispassionate interest in the Gaelic past. There were many collectors, in Perthshire and Argyll, and later in other Gaelic areas, and this movement continued throughout the nineteenth and twentieth centuries. The Rev Donald MacNicol wrote down the poems of Donnchadh Bàn from the poet's own recitation, and it was at this period too that most of the poetry of the seventeenth-century Iain Lom was recorded in manuscript. There were other effects, or adjuncts, of the Ossianic controversy, such as the series of forgeries of heroic Gaelic ballads and/or translations of more epic poems,[7] and the long trail of stylistic influence left by the Gaelic translations of Macpherson's works in the nineteenth century. These are curiosities rather than integral elements of Gaelic literary history.

In the eighteenth century also we can see the influence of university education impinging more clearly on Gaelic writing. Some earlier Gaelic writers, such as John Carswell in the mid-sixteenth century, and various lairds and ministers, had been university-educated. Carswell had wedded his university studies to the traditional kind of literacy that the Gaels had practised, and continued to write in the classical literary dialect. Various parts of the spectrum from high classical to colloquial were used by poets, and occasionally even letter-writers, in the sixteenth and seventeenth centuries, but by the eighteenth we must consider Mac Mhaighstir Alasdair as showing a deliberately antiquarian bent when he writes in the old Gaelic script and copies a medieval Gaelic saga such as *Cath Finntrágha*. Mac Mhaighstir Alasdair was probably a student at the University of Glasgow, where his father had graduated in 1674, and certainly his classical education shows through in his poetry. And something similar can be said of Uilleam Ros and the Jacobite poet Iain Ruadh Stiùbhart (John Roy Stuart), though they had no university connection. The band of collectors of Gaelic verse were mostly clergymen, a prominent group of these St Andrews graduates, and from the 1750s onwards there is a growing series of Gaelic prose publications, most of them sermons or translations of religious works. It was in 1767 that the Gaelic translation of the New Testament was published, and the translation of the Old Testament was gradually completed later in the century. These translators may be said to have been in the van of the movement that recovered Gaelic prose literacy, transforming it in the process from the classical literary dialect (with its associated script) to a more vernacular one. It was still, of course, a 'high' dialect, and a specialised one, which gave Gaelic a proficient register for religious discourse, but it was nevertheless the basis of that greatly increased literacy, resulting eventually in secular prose, which marks the first half of the nineteenth century. Poetry, as we saw above, had made the transition much earlier.

Somewhat hidden behind monoglot barriers was the copious stream of oral prose, with its own differentiated levels, representing for example the survival of medieval and older sagas, the growth of later romances, historical tales and anecdotes, and stories associated with the supernatural or with superstition. Some of this body of prose was already in manuscript, and a little of it was garnered by Edward Lhuyd shortly before 1700, while more came into corporate ownership in the later eighteenth century, some directly through James Macpherson's activities or their sequels. But much had already passed into purely oral circulation, or had never been in manuscript, and that remained to be collected in the nineteenth and twentieth centuries.

The background to Gaelic writing, or composition, in the eighteenth century, is therefore much more complex than is frequently assumed, and it is often illuminating to relate the work of individuals to specific parts of the background. Few of the poets failed to share some of the complexity of that background, and some (Mac Mhaighstir Alasdair in particular) relate to it at many points.

It is salutary to remember that Gaelic was at one time or another the normal speech of practically every part of Scotland, co-existing with British (early Welsh), with Teutonic speech, with Old Norse, and in at least limited contexts with Norman French, and, on the literate plane, with Latin. And we may remember also that the linguistic frontier between Gaelic and Scots or English was a constantly shifting one. That frontier in Ayrshire leaves an echo in the Dunbar/Kennedy flyting in the early sixteenth century, while at much the same time we can observe a more full-blooded co-existence, and see the Latin element in play, in the Perthshire of Dean MacGregor of Lismore, compiler of the trilingual manuscript *The Book of the Dean*. By the eighteenth century there were frontiers in Aberdeenshire, Moray, Inverness and Easter Ross, and the Highland diaspora had begun with a mounting tide of migration to the Central Belt and overseas. Thus there were many levels and periods of possible contact, especially between Gaelic and Scots or English. Some of this shows in religious verse before the eighteenth century, and is continued then, for example in Dùghall Bochanan's verse. In the more sophisticated areas of verse-making, Classical, and especially Latin influence, shows, whether in religious or in secular verse. And in the eighteenth century we see at last quite unequivocally the influence of recent and contemporary work in English on Gaelic poetry.

It will already be clear that Alasdair Mac Mhaighstir Alasdair looms large in any account of eighteenth-century Gaelic poetry. His work spans approximately the period 1720–70. His middle period is by far the best documented, because his associations with the Scottish Society for the Propagation of Christian Knowledge and with the Jacobite Rising of 1745 have left many traces in the records. He was of notable Gaelic stock, with close kinship and marriage links with leading MacDonald families, and these links, and probably his home environment led him to his interest in the classical Gaelic literary tradition. At the same time, it would seem that he saw himself as belonging to a wider literary tradition, which could naturally embrace literature in other languages, and so it is not possible to look on him as a folk poet in any meaningful sense. His exuberance of character led him sometimes to satirical, or even pornographic, themes. Again, during the Forty-five campaign, he played the roles of exhorter and commentator, making his poetry the servant of a political cause, and adapting its style to these purposes. In trying to assess the work of this obviously complex man, we have to take account of such biographical pressures, and to distinguish the intense and creative from the expedient. It was probably in the mid 1720s that he married Jane MacDonald of Dalness, whose family were also involved in Gaelic poetry, and so his 'Oran d'a chèile nuadh-phòsda' (Song to his Bride) is one of his earliest roughly datable poems. The overriding impression here is one of classical control. The lyrical cry comes through in two or three couplets at the centre of the poem, but its incidence is controlled like the rest. There is close, detailed description of Jane's physical appearance, and of her character, with touches of classical comparison (well-formed, ivory-white teeth like Dido), but well-rooted in her native element (she is a female salmon, with the white sheen of the sea still on her), and it was from the Rhymer, i.e. MacDonald of Dalness, he got her. The lyrical cry referred to above is in these lines:

> Fhuair mi mòran, mo thoil mhòr leat,
> Fhuair mi òr na h-Asia.
>
> Fhuair mi òg thu, fhuair mi 'd òigh thu,
> Fhuair mi bòidheach àlainn thu
>
> (I got a great deal, had great pleasure with you,
> I got the gold of Asia.
>
> I got you young, I got you as a maid,
> I got you beautiful and lovely.)

It is probable that only a small group of his surviving poems are early ones, and a likely candidate is his 'Marbhrann do Pheata Coluim' (Elegy for a Pet Dove) which has a Catullan echo, at least in its general theme; he goes on to develop the Biblical theme of Noah's Ark in an attractive way. His 'Guidhe no Urnaigh an Ughdair don Cheòlraidh' (Entreaty or Prayer of the Author to the Muses) is probably early also. In this he addresses each of the Muses separately, appealing for her particular bounty, and ends with a humble assessment of his own poetic skills, apparently thinking in part at least of the rigorous apprenticeship that Gaelic classical poets had to serve, and considering himself an amateur by comparison:

> Tha speuran mo chomais cumhang nas leòr,
> Ge farsaing mo mhiann,
> Gu balla thogail air stèidh cho-mhòr
> 'S clach-shnaighte d'am dhìth:
> Cainnt shnasda d'am dhìth, ge stracte mo thoil
> Tha mi falamh do sgil;
> 'S nì gun susbaint ealain gun sgoil
> Air suibseic mar mhil.

(The orbit of my capacity is restricted enough, / though my desire is expansive, / to build a wall on so great a foundation / lacking chiselled stone: / lacking polished language, though my will be torn (seeking it) / I am empty of skill; / a thing of no substance is art without schooling / though the subject were honey-sweet.)

In these poems, and also in his poem in praise of the Gaelic language, one senses the attitudes of the eighteenth century man of letters rather than the compulsive drive of either the folk-poet or any poet under strong creative pressure. That stance shows up occasionally in other poems too, as in 'Cuachag an Fhàsaich', a song about a milkmaid which is not a love-song but primarily an exercise in observation and careful, detailed, amused description. It might be said that here he is also in tune with the eighteenth-century interest in pastoral subjects, drawing in his own way on the springs of realism and actuality that feed some Scottish writers and painters of the era. And a somewhat similar conclusion may be suggested by the longer and more ambitious poems, 'Moladh Mòraig' (Praise of Morag) and 'Birlinn Chlann Raghnaill' (Clanranald's Galley), the former perhaps dating from the later 1730s or 1740s, and the latter from around 1750.

Formal literary ambition must also lie behind his poems on the Seasons, and such a poem as 'Allt an t-Siùcair' (Sugar Brook), and this brings us face to face with the question of the origin of these poems and their possible relationship to the work of the Border poet James Thomson. Such a relationship has been postulated for a long time,[8] though it is not easy to pin the matter down firmly. Nor would we expect a creative writer of Mac Mhaighstir Alasdair's stature to respond in an obvious or mechanical way to external literary influences. Thomson's *Seasons* were published in 1726–30. These poems, however, were greatly revised and expanded in later editions, as in that of 1730 (reissued in 1738) and 1744. It was probably the 1738 edition that came to Mac Mhaighstir Alasdair's notice. At any rate, it seems likely from an internal reference to the day of the week on which the summer solstice fell, that his 'Oran a' Gheamhraidh' (Winter Song) was written in 1743,[9] and it may well be that his Summer Song was written a little earlier, while his poem 'Sugar Brook' most probably dates from his Ardnamurchan residence (1741–45). The evidence, then, points to this series of poems having been written after Thomson's *Seasons* was readily available to readers. Mac Mhaighstir Alasdair also borrows from the content and metrical pattern of an Allan Ramsay song (on May) to start his Summer Song, but (as Ramsay himself often did) makes no further use of his 'model' after the first stanza. We have the suggestion, then, that the Gaelic poet responded to hints at least in the work of two Scots contemporaries. We can take the matter a little further than this, to show that he also used a series of words that can be regarded as key-words in Thomson's *Seasons*, and picked up sub-themes which occur in the *Seasons*. The close description of bees at work, the categorizing of birds, and the references to the signs of the zodiac, are such common elements, but the evidence of shared key-words is more specific and persuasive. Both poets make repeated use of such words as *planet, globe, sign, tropic, hymns* and *Phoebus*, as Professor John MacQueen notes.[10]

On the other hand, a strong case can be made for the deeper influence of earlier Gaelic models, for natural description is a recurring theme in both Scottish and Irish Gaelic verse, going back to early impressionistic nature poems of the ninth and tenth centuries in Irish, and flourishing in the context of religious verse in late sixteenth-century Scotland. And another context of natural description, Gavin Douglas's *Prologues* to his *Aeneados*, may also have been known to Mac Mhaighstir Alasdair. What emerges from this rich background is, however, a new product, individual and intense, marked by an extraordinarily detailed and close observation and expressed in a rich torrent of language. I give one Gaelic stanza, and a translation of another, to suggest his method and range. The Gaelic one describes May in a series of epithets that create a kaleidoscopic image of the month, showery, sunny, meadowy, milky, frothy, churning, crowdy-ish, lamby, doey, bucky, and so on:

> A' Bhealltainn bhog-bhailceach, ghrianach,
> Lònach, lianach mo ghràidh,
> Bhainneach, fhinn-mhèagach, uachdrach,
> Omhnach, loinideach, chuachach,
> Ghruthach, shlamanach, mhiosrach,
> Mhiodrach, mhiosganach, làn,
> Uanach, mheannanach, mhaoineach,
> Bhocach, mhaoiseach, làn àil.

The short selection of ten translated epithets is culled from the twenty-two in the stanza quoted. It might be thought that there was a danger of overkill in the method, but such is the skill and appositeness in selection, and the variety interwoven into stanzas, that this danger is minimised, so that we are left (as was clearly the intention) with an overwhelming impression of

Nature's variety, fecundity and excitement. Another stanza in translation will give some further insight into the poet's methods and effects:

> Lithe, brisk, fresh-water salmon,
> lively, leaping the stones;
> Bunched, white-bellied, scaly,
> finned, with red-spotted tail;
> speckled skin's brilliant hue
> lit with flashes of silver;
> with curved gob at the ready
> catching insects with guile.

And the birds add a further animation to the scene, intruding their song and colour and movement into the description at many points.

There is a similar fecundity in his 'Allt an t-Siùcair' (Song to the Sugar Brook), which is really a word-picture of Ardnamurchan, and these poems, together with the Song of Winter and the specialized sea-storm-passage of the Galley of Clanranald, establish Mac Mhaighstir Alasdair as a writer of quite outstanding power and delicacy on Nature themes.

His 'Moladh Mòraig' (Praise of Morag) brings similar gifts of vivid, arresting description to a quite different subject, the description of a girl who had aroused erotic feelings in him. Here we have a frank portrayal of eroticism, but without any feeling of satiety. There is a hint that the experiences recounted in the poem are dream experiences, though there is no doubt an element of wish-fulfilment too.

His very positive personality is expressed in a more extreme way in the series of satires, especially of Campbells. Some of these are quite over-done, although always of great linguistic interest, but some have a more balanced interest, as 'An Airc' (The Ark), in which a Campbell (Alexander of Ardslignish) who had fought on the Jacobite side is asked to prepare a new Ark, and to give shelter to selected Campbells, while rejecting others. The reasons for selection, and the manner of rejection, are given in a vivid amalgam of humour and malice.

The decade of the 1740s produced an equally vivid series of political poems. Some of these are frankly exhortatory, as the poet was involved in stirring up enthusiasm before and during the Jacobite campaign. He draws freely on a wide range of techniques and emotions, bringing rhythmical vitality, assonantal richness, figurative variety, into association with appeals to loyalty, nationalism, racial pride, a sense of history, and some-times baser instincts such as greed for booty and blood vengeance. The range of poems includes songs of welcome to Prince Charlie, incitements to the clans, reflections on history, and poems of disillusionment. As an example of the more subtle variety of these, the following may be quoted, from a poem composed in 1746, probably before the defeat at Culloden. The extended stanza, and progressive rhyme of the original, allow a developed statement to emerge where this is needed, as where the poet

recalls the Act of Settlement (1701) and the resulting succession to the
throne of a family not in the direct line:

> Slender the string, O George,
> You played on to three kingdoms;
> guileful the Act used to cloak
> you as King over us;
> there are fifty persons and more
> closer in blood and claim
> in Europe than you are;
> remote and weak and devious
> is the female branch you were plucked from,
> in a distant part of the tree.

From what can be deduced from his poetry, and from what we know of
his life, Mac Mhaighstir Alasdair was a complex, unpredictable and explosive character, yet a man who could steep himself in history and work on
meticulously detailed poems. He had the intellectual strength to forge a
style and a purpose of his own from indigenous and imported elements, yet
combined this with emotional power and also with an earthiness and
coarseness that are equally remarkable.

The work of Donnchadh Bàn Mac an t-Saoir (Duncan Bàn Macintyre)
makes an interesting contrast. A part of it is more conclusively in the
traditional mould than Mac Mhaighstir Alasdair's, but at the same time
probably reveals a lesser critical awareness of that tradition. Another part
takes fire from Mac Mhaighstir Alasdair's innovatory work on Nature
themes and goes on to surpass him in that field. And a third part is cosily at
home in the world of the local bard and entertainer, a role which Mac
Mhaighstir Alasdair hardly bothered to play.

The last of these modes need not detain us for long. Donnchadh Bàn is, in
an essential way, the poet of jollity and good company, whether he is
celebrating the old way of life in Glen Orchy ('Oran Ghlinn Urchaidh') or
life in the Edinburgh Guard or the Breadalbane Fencibles, or composing a
drinking song. Again, his 'Oran don Tàillear' (Song to the Tailor) is
thoroughly in the satirical tradition, but leaning towards humour rather
than malice, as is the manner of the local poet. His political poems, if we
can use that term, are basically an extension of the local bard's repertoire.
He can turn from the anti-Hanoverian sentiment of 'Oran don Bhriogais'
(Song addressed to the Breeks) to the Hanoverian enthusiasm of 'Oran do
Thailbert a fhuaradh o Bhànrigh Màiri' (Song to a Halberd obtained from
Queen Mary). In 'Oran don Rìgh' (Song to the King), addressed to King
George III and dated before 1768, he can say:

> —Chuir e drochaid air gach alltan,
> 'S rèitich e na rathaidean mòra;
> Chuir e sgoil sa' h-uile gleann
> A los gum faigheadh ar clann fòghlam;
> 'S gheibh sinn airm is aodach Gàidhealach
> O 's e 's fheàrr leinn gu bhith spòrsail.

(He put a bridge on every burn, / and smoothed the highways; / he put a school in every glen / so that our children might be educated; and we shall get weapons and Highland dress, / since that is what we prefer to disport with).

One can imagine the contempt with which Mac Mhaighstir Alasdair would have greeted these sentiments.

Donnchadh Bàn's poems about or addressed to various Campbell chiefs and dignitaries are securely within the old traditions of praise poetry, and no doubt it is one aspect of that ambivalent tradition that allows him to change sides easily. His poem in praise of Lord Glenorchy picks up very competently the style of the seventeenth-century praise-poem in strophic metre:

> Sàr phòitear an fhìon thu,
> 'S tu dh'òladh 's a dhìoladh;
> Fhuair thu fòghlam gach rìoghachd,
> Meòir as grinne nì sgrìobhadh;
> Bu tu sealgair na sìdhne
> Le d'chuilbheir caol dìreach,
>   Nuair a thàrladh tu 'm frìth nam beann àrda

(Excellent drinker of wine, / you could drink and pay for it; / you got the education of every country, / fingers that write most neatly; / you were the hunter of game / with your slim, accurate caliever / when you were in the game-forest in the high mountains).

And 'Cumha Chailein Ghlinn Iubhair' (Lament for Colin of Glenure) takes on just as easily the more vernacular style of the lament.

There can be no doubt that Donnchadh Bàn was influenced strongly by Mac Mhaighstir Alasdair's work. Sometimes this shows up as rather inert imitation, as where Aeolus and Neptune are introduced into four lines in the Song to the King, just as both had appeared in four lines of Mac Mhaighstir Alasdair's 'Oran nam Fineachan' (Song of the Clans), Stanza 3. Whereas the older poet's Aeolus is alive and speaks, and his Neptune acts positively, both have become rather lifeless in Donnchadh Bàn. Again, in his 'Song to Summer' he leans rather awkwardly on Mac Mhaighstir Alasdair, who provided the basic prototype for seasonal poems by four later eighteenth century poets. Probably Donnchadh Bàn was not able to cope with a more abstract subject of this kind, and needed the specificity of Coire Cheathaich or Beinn Dòbhrain to bring his natural talents into play. By contrast, his 'Oran Coire a' Cheathaich', a poem of 144 lines, is packed with detailed description of the flora and vegetation of the corrie, and its wild life, with special emphasis on the deer. Bearing comparison with Mac Mhaighstir Alasdair's poems of natural description, it surpasses these in emotional warmth, though there is little humour in it.

Clearly, however, 'Moladh Beinn Dòbhrain' (The Praise of Ben Dòbhran) is Donnchadh Bàn's outstanding achievement. A poem of some 550 lines, it is a fast-moving, kaleidoscopic celebration of the mountain, the deer and the hunt. There can be no doubt that its core theme is 'the deer', though there are loving descriptions of their terrain, of the guns, of aspects of the chase, and so on. There is no section of the poem without a significant deer presence, but the theme is effectively varied by the digressions e.g. the quality of the water, the place-name litany, the fish that live in the streams, the grasses, and so on. There is a significant degree of planning in the poem, though one has the impression that the deer disrupt the plan from time to time. But putting aside the question of structure, of architectonics, the linguistic texture of the poem is remarkable, and its tone is admirably controlled; there are no forced passages, where the creative tension flags seriously.

Professor William Gillies has argued, ingeniously, that there are strong elements which he labels 'bardic' in The Praise of Ben Dòbhrain: that the praise of the mountain, and of the deer, has various ingredients that are more familiar to us in the bardic verse which praises chiefs and patrons. This thesis can, it seems to me, be accepted without difficulty, but the interpretation of these features is a different matter. Professor Gillies goes on to suggest that the deer's 'right' to Ben Dòbhrain is an image of the Gaels' right to their own country, and that the poem has an allegorical intent. This suggestion is much more controversial. If Donnchadh Bàn had been capable of this kind of sophistication, we might expect it to appear more frequently in his work. It seems more credible that these bardic elements would have seeped into his work from the tradition. Yet it must be admitted that the suggested interpretation adds spice to the modern flavour of the poem.

There can be little doubt that Donnchadh Bàn was at the height of his powers when he composed his most ambitious poem. The probable sequence of composition is as follows: he would have composed his Song to Summer and his 'Oran Coire a' Cheathaich' (Song of the Misty Corrie) after becoming familiar with Alasdair Mac Mhaighstir's work, most probably after 1751, for the Summer Song is modelled on the older poet's seasonal poems, and Mac Mhaighstir Alasdair's 'Allt an t-Siùcair' ends with five stanzas describing a corrie; the Praise of Ben Dòbhrain almost certainly came a little later, and was modelled metrically on Mac Mhaighstir Alasdair's 'Moladh Mòraig'. We can probably envisage this sequence of composition as occuring in the later 1750s and early 1760s, or perhaps mainly in the latter. He had moved to Edinburgh by 1767, and composed nothing comparable thereafter.

Rob Donn (Robert Mackay) of Sutherland was a very different kind of poet to either Mac Mhaighstir Alasdair or Donnchadh Bàn. There are indeed some connecting links, especially with Mac Mhaighstir Alasdair, for Rob Donn (born 1714) seems to have modelled his song 'Iseabail Nic Aoidh' (Isabel Mackay), metrically at least, on 'Moladh Mòraig', the prototype of the 'pibroch' poems, and he also followed his older contemporary closely in his 'Oran a' Gheamhraidh' (Song of Winter), which he constructed by painstakingly substituting winter references for summer ones as these occur in Mac Mhaighstir Alasdair's Song of Summer. But these points of contact are on the periphery of Rob Donn's essential achievement. He was an avid observer of people as Donnchadh Bàn was of landscape and deer, and had a tongue perhaps as fearless as Mac Mhaighstir Alasdair's, but a kinder humour than his. And so he produced a detailed portrait of the society of his time in Sutherland, both high and low (for he was close to some of the native leaders of that society, though he himself moved mainly on a more humble level). Dr Ian Grimble, in *The World of Rob Donn*, has described brilliantly how his poetry illuminates that society. It is largely concerned with people's characters and attitudes, their virtues, weaknesses and idiosyncrasies, and these complexities are woven into a witty and humorous pictorial narrative with malice where it is called for, and a strong moral undertone. Both the nobility and the commonalty would be in little doubt that they were being judged. His plain talking to members of the Mackay and Sutherland aristocracy is in refreshing contrast to Donnchadh Bàn's sychophancy—and that of many earlier bardic poets. In one of his occasional literary forays into the larger world he runs counter to the prevailing Hanoverian mood of his locality, expressing his support for Prince Charles, and his concern for Scotland under the English scourge:

> I see your misery
> As something unprecedented—
> The best part of your hawks
> Chained to a kite.
> But if you are lions
> Retaliate in good time,
> And have your teeth ready
> Before your mouths are muzzled.[11]

Aspects of Rob Donn's originality can also be observed in his 'Lament for John Mackay' (see translation by Iain C Smith in my *Introduction to Gaelic Poetry*, 196 ff), in his poem addressed to Death, in his wry elegy for the Rispond Misers (*Ibid.*, 200 ff), and in his poems about deer hunting (e.g. 'Cead Fhir Bhìoguis don Fhrìth').

Much of the attraction of Rob Donn's poetry is in the neat, witty and detached quality of his comment, as in this metaphor for a man who aims too high and falls by failing to see the slippery flagstone in his path:

> Ach ma thuiteas fear aithghearr
> Le bhith sealltainn ro bhras os a cheann,
> Chan eil fhios agam idir
> Cò 's ciontaich' an leac no na buinn.

(But if a man falls suddenly / by looking too eagerly above him / I do not know at all / which is more to blame the flagstone or the footsoles.)

His quality is difficult to convey in brief, and perhaps more difficult in translation, and I commend to readers Dr Grimble's extended analysis.[12]

Uilleam Ros comes late in the succession of eighteenth century poets. For him the Forty-Five is old history, and Prince Charlie a figure of romance and nostalgia. The writings of James Macpherson have also left a slight romantic tinge on his thought and vocabulary, though this is more than balanced by some of his more realist poems. His Song of Summer, while in the tradition begun some forty to fifty years earlier, is less clinical, his summer landscape more peopled, his touch lighter and more romantic. He is popularly remembered as a poet crossed in love, and dying early because of this, and his love-affair with Mòr Ros has become legendary. It produced some of his finest poetry, in 'Feasgar Luain' (Monday Evening), which is in fact a classically controlled account of his early meeting with Mòr, in 'Oran Eile (Another Song—the inept title, given by an early editor, has acquired its own distinction) in which he faces up to his loss with some realism, though also with a hint of self-pity, and in other poems, probably including a re-working of an older song with the chorus beginning *Fil òro, fil òro*, where we get perhaps the finest passionate expression of his love. His 'Cuachag nan Craobh' (Cuckoo among the Trees) is also a re-working of an older song. But he is capable of looking at himself satirically and realistically, as in the debate between the Poet and the Hag-who-destroys-songs. One or two quotations must suffice here to suggest the flavour of this most personal of love-poets who was also attracted to ideas of literary decorum and order, except in his satires and rumbustious country verse.

> Gur binne leam do chòmhradh
> Na smeòrach nan geugan,
> Na cuach sa' mhadainn Mhàighe,
> 'S na clàrsach nan teudan,
> Na 'n t-Easpuig air Là Dòmhnaich
> 'S am mòr-shluagh ga èisdeachd – – –

(Sweeter your converse / than the thrush on the twigs / than the cuckoo on a May morning / and than the harp of strings, / than the Bishop on the Lord's Day / with the congregation listening to him – – –)

Or from another song, also presumably about Mòr:

I think it was no wisdom / for me to fall in love / with the girl who forsook me / and slighted me so vainly; / if I were to think of it cool-ly / that flame would grow gentle; / I would quench it completely / and she would never diminish me again.

Or from *Fil òro*:

> O 's truagh nach robh mis'
> Agus tusa far an iarrainn,
> Fad sia là seachdain,
> Fad seachd, ochd bliadhna,
> An seòmraichean glaiste
> Le clàimheanan iarainn,
> Na h-iuchraichean air chall
> Agus dall bhith gan iarraidh.

(Alas that we are not, you and I / where I would wish us to be, / for six days of the week, / for seven or eight years, / in locked chambers / with iron bolts, / the keys lost / and a blind man searching for them.)

That is poetry that can and does speak across centuries.

Ros died young in 1792, and in one sense is the last of the eighteenth-century poets, though Ewen MacLachlan is often grouped with them, and other poets such as John Maclean of Tiree carried some of the models of that century into the next one, and to the new Gaelic world of Nova Scotia. But the older mould of the classical Gaelic tradition had been effectively broken and re-formed in a variety of ways by mid-century, and no return to it was possible, except in a spirit of eccentric survival or deliberate archaism.

NOTES

1   D A MacDonald 'Ath-sgrùdadh', in *Gairm* 129, (Glasgow, 1985), pp 84–5.
2   C Ò Baoill, *Bàrdachd Shìlis na Ceapaich* (Edinburgh, 1972), p 76 ff.
3   *See* W J Watson, *Bàrdachd Ghàidhlig* (Stirling, 1959), pp 155–7.
4   R. MacThòmais, 'Bho Làmh-sgrìobhainnean MhicLathagain', in *Gairm* 113 (Glasgow 1981), pp 79–81.
5   Lachlan Macpherson 'A' Bhanais Bhàn,' in T Sinton, *The Poetry of Badenoch*, (Inverness, 1906) pp 142–3.
6   A Sinclair, *An t-Oranaiche* (Glasgow, c. 1879), pp 124–7.
7   *See* D S Thomson, 'Bogus Gaelic Literature, *c.* 1750–*c.*1820', in Trans Gael Soc of Glasgow (Glasgow, 1958), pp 172–88.
8   e.g. D S Thomson, 'Alasdair Mac Mhaighstir Alasdair', in *An Gaidheal* (1961), 56, and *An Introduction to Gaelic Poetry* (London, 1974), pp 160–2.
9   W J Mays, 'Note . . . Oran a' Gheamhraidh', in *Scottish Gaelic Studies*, VIII (Oxford, 1955), pp 53–5.
10 John MacQueen, *Progress and Poetry* (Edinburgh, 1982), p 79. *See also* D S Thomson, 'Gaelic literary interactions with Scots and English work: a survey', in *Proceedings of Aberdeen Conference on Scots and Gaelic* in *Scottish Language*, Winter 1986, No 5, 1–14.
11 Translation as in I Grimble, *The World of Rob Donn* (Edinburgh, 1979), p 73.
12 *See also* D S Thomson, *An Introduction to Gaelic Poetry*, pp. 194–204.

FURTHER READING

Calder, George, *Songs of William Ross* (Edinburgh, 1937)
Grimble, Ian, *The World of Rob Donn* (Edinburgh, 1979)
MacDonald, A and A, *The Poems of Alexander MacDonald* (Inverness, 1924)
Maclean, Donald, *The Spiritual Songs of Dugald Buchanan* (Edinburgh, 1913)
MacLeod, Angus, *The Songs of Duncan Bàn Macintyre* (Edinburgh, 1952)
Morrison, Hugh, *Songs and Poems—by Rob Donn* (Edinburgh, 1899)
Ò Baoill, Colm, *Bàrdachd Shìlis na Ceapaich* (Edinburgh, 1972)
Thomson, D S, *An Introduction to Gaelic Poetry* (London, 1974)
—— *The Companion to Gaelic Scotland* (Oxford, 1983)
Watson, W J, *Scottish Verse from the Book of the Dean of Lismore* (Edinburgh, 1938)
—— *Bàrdachd Ghàidhlig* (Stirling, 1959)

Chapter 11

Theatre in Scotland 1660–1800

ALASDAIR CAMERON

In 1662, theatre in Scotland was limited to short seasons at the Tennis Court Theatre in Edinburgh; it was patronised only by the aristocracy, dominated by English plays and players, and under frequent attack from the Church. By 1800, there were nine permanent theatres spread throughout Scotland, the theatre was becoming the most popular form of organised entertainment in the country and there were the beginnings of an indigenous tradition of playwriting, acting and management, which paved the way for the 'National Theatre' at the Theatre Royal Edinburgh in the early nineteenth century. But the most obvious change was the degree of social and political acceptance which the theatre had secured. By playing a significant role in the victory of the Moderates in the Church of Scotland, the theatre was enabled to flourish in a way which seems almost unbelievable in view of the organised attacks launched upon it by powerful elements within the Church between 1660 and 1760.

One learns little of these changes from the successful Scottish plays of this time. Apart from John Home's *Douglas* and Allan Ramsay's *The Gentle Shepherd*, which still enjoy occasional revivals, there were few Scottish plays which captured the imagination of the Scottish public and which survived their initial performances. Fortunately, however, diverse information about other aspects of the Scottish stage exists for almost every year from 1660 to 1800. Only around 1700, when Scotland was reeling from the effects of the Darien disaster and famine, and social life was under renewed pressure from the Church, are details sketchy. At the same time, the London theatres, on which the Edinburgh theatre depended for its 'dramatic supplies', were under religious pressure from preachers like Jeremy Collier, who published his *Short View of the Immorality and Profaneness of the English Stage*, in 1698.

Although the London stage suffered no lasting harm from such attacks, hostility between the Church and the theatre in Scotland continued until almost the end of the eighteenth century. During that time, theatres were attacked both verbally and physically, actors were forbidden to play in many towns, and were often arrested as vagrants. At least twice, in 1727 and 1756, in the wake of the *Douglas* controversy, concerted attempts were made to anathematize the stage. It is therefore, hardly surprising, that Scottish playwrights often alluded to the hostility of the Church. In his Preface to *Marciano* (1663), William Clerke, an Edinburgh lawyer, while refusing to apologise for plays in general, admits that in Edinburgh they seemed like a 'City-swaggerer in a Country Church' and commented that:

> the peevish prejudice of some persons, who know nothing beyond the principles of base, greazy, arrogant, illiterate Pedants, who, like the grasshoppers of Egypt, swarm in every corner of this Nation, and plague all the youth accordingly, is such, that they cannot have patience to hear of a Comedy, because they never see one acted . . .[1]

Clerke attributed the hostility of preachers to plays to the fact that in them 'such pilfring stinkards as themselves are often discovered in their own colours', and his secondary plot contains interesting echoes of the theatrical situation in Scotland at the time of the play's premiere:

Enter Boy.

Madam, the two Gentlemen you call, Casio and Leonardo, desire to see you.
MANDUCO. Go tell them we are not within.
CHRYSOLINA. Tell them we are not at leasure, Sirrah.

Exit Boy.

MAN. What are they?
PANTALONI. Ranting, young blades, like the times I warrand you, two fellows, that have frequented all your Stage-playes in Italy, and I heard our Chaplain say; and my Sister too (which is more) that Playes are very unlawful and impious.
MAN. Playes are indeed profane, scelerate, abominable, yea abominably abominable—which I will maintain multis argumentis.
PANT. Besides they are great mockers of such Gentlemen as us, who are better than themselves.[2]

Marciano was, 'acted with great applause in front of His Majesty's High Commissioner and others of the nobility' and, like an earlier Scottish Court play *Philotus* (1598), is set in Italy. In *Marciano*, Clerke attempts to fuse a serious plot about the capture of Marciano and the trials of his love, Ariadne, to free him, with a separate comic plot concerning the loves of fops and coquettes. *Marciano* was titled a tragi-comedy, but is in fact an uneasy mixture of tragedy and farce with an almost inappropriate happy ending. This mixture of styles ultimately works against the success of the play.

Marciano was premiered at the Tennis Court Theatre in the grounds of Holyrood House. This was the only permanent theatre in post-Restoration Edinburgh, and it was managed from 1667 by Thomas Sydserf, whose play *Tarugo's Wiles* was premiered in London in 1666, and may also have been performed at the Tennis Court Theatre. Sydserf is also credited with starting the first newspaper in Scotland. This was written in

Scots, and the London Prologue to his play speaks of the writer being 'a stranger to our language'; however, the play itself betrays no sense of a Scot ill at ease with English. It is set in Spain and the main plot concerns an attempt to liberate Livinia who has been locked up by her brother Patricio, who wishes to keep his sister free from the temptations of the world and from 'dangerous curiosities'. Tarugo, lately returned from England, assumes a series of disguises and eventually re-unites Livinia with her lover Horatio. The plot was conventional enough, but the play contains an unusual and very atmospheric scene set in a Spanish coffee house which, though entertaining, seems almost divorced from the plot. The coffee house is, in fact, very English and the conversation concerning blood transfusion and their rejuvenating powers, the effects of coffee, and the qualifications needed to become one of the 'Vertuosi', that of London in the 1660s. There is also a pretentious, and timeless, discussion of Art which consists of trading the names of famous painters. Added to this rich brew is a dance between a baboon or 'Pugge' and a 'Negro Serving-Wench', and some slapstick involving throwing hot coffee around.

The coffee house setting would have been an interesting conceit in Edinbugh, where plays were performed by touring actors in the chocolate and coffee houses, until a proper theatre for them was built in 1715. Few details of such performances survive, but, in a lecture he gave in 1792, William Tytler of Woodhouselee recalled seeing a playbill for Dryden's *The Indian Emperor* at the Queen's Chocolate House. Dryden, as it happens, in a moment of satirical partiality, described an early acting company in Edinburgh:

> Our Brethren are, from Thames to Tweed departed,
> And of our Sisters, all the kinder hearted,
> To Edenborough gone, or Coacht, or Carted.
> With bonny Blewcap, there they act all night,
> For Scotch half Crown, in English Three-pence hight.
> One Nymph to whom fat Sir John Falstaff's lean,
> There with her single Person fills the Scene.
> Another with long use, and Age decay'd
> Div'd here old Woman, and rose there a Maid.[3]

These actors had seceded from the Duke's Company in London and gone North with the Duke of York, later to be James II, when he was appointed Commissioner. During his tenure at Holyrood House there was again, as there had been under James VI, royal sanction for all forms of theatrical activity. But even the Duke of York was forced to suspend 'Masquerades', so scandalised were some influential Scots by this new form of 'loupin agin the Lord'. The Duke's tenure as Commissioner not only saw the introduction of tea as a fashionable drink in Scotland, but also a regular season of plays at the Tennis Court attended by the aristocracy. There was also a performance of *Mithridates, King of Pontus* at Holyrood House in 1680, with the future Queen Anne in the cast, but this was presented for the delight of her family alone.

One of the main sources of information on the Restoration Theatre in Scotland is the Account Book of a member of the Scottish aristocracy, John Foulis of Ravelstane. Foulis attended the theatre regularly between 1669 and 1672 and usually described what he saw as a 'Comedie', only on special occasions specifying what he saw, as in the case of 'Macbeth' in 1770. Play-going was expensive and Foulis paid one pound and nine shillings (Scots) for admission. When his wife accompanied him he purchased cherries, oranges or 'some sweetmeats'. From other entries in his accounts, we also learn that the repertoire of the Tennis Court Theatre in Edinburgh mirrored that of London, that after *Marciano* no specially written Scottish plays were included, and, like the London Theatre, that it was frequented by 'orange sellers'.

Foulis was an eclectic seeker after entertainment and went on several occasions between 1680 and 1705 to see such sights as the 'elephant', 'the puppie [puppet] show', the 'soupple man' [contortionist] and the rope dancers and acrobats. Such shows along with the frequent performances of quack doctors, like John Pontus, were the only theatrical fare available to most Scots. The Scots were so used to acrobats and street entertainers that, until the mid nineteenth century, the country word for actor was 'tumbler'. In the countryside there was also a widespread tradition of folk plays like the Lammas play in Midlothian in which rival villages tried to storm towers built of turf and decorated and ribbons. These folk plays seem to have been primarily an excuse for licensed brawls, rather like the Robin Hood plays in sixteenth century Edinburgh. Of all popular entertainers, however, the rope dancers seem to have been the most popular and Sir Archibald Pitcairne refers to this in his Prologue to *The Assembly*.

> 'Tis a long while since any play has been (Except Rope dancing) in our nation seen.[4]

Pitcairne devoted most of his play, *The Assembly* (1695), to decrying religious pedantry and bigotry in general, and Calvinism in particular. So intemperate was his attack that the *Biographica Dramatica* (1812) describes it as:

> no more than a gross abuse on the Whig party in Scotland, with the most bare-faced profession of Jacobitism, and invectives against all who maintained the cause of King William in Scotland.[5]

This is certainly true, but it overlooks the fact that Pitcairne successfully highlights the hypocritical abuse of religion. This success, however, was the play's undoing, for it was considered too scurrilous to be performed in Pitcairne's lifetime and, although handwritten copies were in circulation from 1695, it was not even published until 1722.

The Assembly contains some very effective comic scenes, but the love scenes are extremely unconvincing. Violetta and Laura accept Frank and Will after little more than a glance and without the audience ever being in any doubt as to the outcome of the wooing. More successful is the scene in which Will and Violetta arrange an assignation in Church using only biblical quotations, and the attempted arrest of Lord Huffy, while besieged by tradesmen whose goods he has broken with his whip. Although much of the humour in *The Assembly* is at the expense of the General Assembly, and of ministers of the Church of Scotland, the outstanding comic creation is the elderly, secular, but devout, Lady Bigot. Her trading of epithets with Will and Frank, disguised as divines for romantic reasons, is one of the comic highlights of the play:

> OLD L. Bring a bowl of Sack . . . O 'tis a sad World Mr Sam
> WILL. An abominable, accursed, unjust, malicious, ill-natured World.
> OLD L. A prying, Censorious, a Soul seducing, Gospel renouncing World.
> WILL. A malignant, backsliding, Covenant breaking, Minister mocking World.
> OLD L. A filthy Idolatrous, Sabbath-breaking Parent dishonouring World; murdering, whoring, lying, coveting World—in a Word, it is an uncharitable worldly World.
> [*Enter* Maid.] There's a poor Man lost his Means by the West Country Rabble.
> OLD L. Come you to tell me that, you baggage? beat him down Stairs—. O Mr Sam, 'tis a troublesome beggarly World, a vain, gaudy, Prayer slighting and Reformation overturning World.
> WILL. [Aside.] Now I can say no more; she has run me out of Breath, she is longer practised in the Trade than I.
> OLD L. But how comes your Friend says nothing?
> FRA. Then, Madam, 'tis an abominable, whoring, drinking, Reformation overturning World.
> OLD L. That's said already.[6]

In spite of its seemingly conventional form, the dialogue has a distinctively Scottish quality which recalls the 'flyting' of earlier Scottish poets like Dunbar. There is so much vigour in the invective, so much life in the satire, that *The Assembly* could perhaps be revived successfully today.

Pitcairne's satire however, no doubt because it gained only private circulation and was never performed, had no influence and for thirty years the Church continued to persecute and to prosecute actors. Apart from sporadic visits of London companies, the years between *The Assembly* and *The Gentle Shepherd*, though witnessing an upsurge of interest in music, saw no similar strengthening in the position of Scottish theatre or dramatic writing. The few plays written by Scots included Alexander Fyffe's opera in doggerel *The Royal Martyr*, according to John Genest one of the worst plays ever written, and David Craufurd's play *Courtship a la Mode* which included a comic servant, Wullie, who spoke in Scots and was to be the prototype for hundreds of similar creations. It is possible that one reason the theatre took so long to become accepted in Edinburgh was that plays were written in English and performed by companies from London. As the fashion for things English took some time to evolve, the theatre might have been regarded with some suspicion in an Edinburgh culturally uneasy about the Union of 1707.

In 1715 a rope dancer, Signora Violante from Dublin, the mentor of Peg Woffington, opened a theatre in the Taylor's Hall in Edinburgh and brought to an end another twenty years without any regular drama in Scotland. She later became a successful teacher of dancing and was followed by many other touring companies. One of these, led by Tony Aston, settled in the city in 1725, grew in favour, and even had some prologues written for it by Allan Ramsay. However, in 1727, after Tony Aston successfully challenged the right of the Church to interfere in the theatre, the Presbytery of Edinburgh caused an Admonition against plays to be read from every pulpit. At first the magistrates of Edinburgh backed Aston but eventually, having been lobbied by the Church, they banned him and all actors from the city. It was in the wake of this defeat for the theatre, that Allan Ramsay began work on *The Gentle Shepherd*—the first major play to be written in Scots since Lyndsay's *Ane Satire of the Thrie Estatis*, published in 1602.

Unlike Aston, Ramsay was used to the wrath of the Church. In 1725 his lending library, which included many plays, had been raided by the magistrates, because, as Woodrow explained in his 'history of remarkable providences', the *Analecta*:

> . . . all the villainous profane and obscene books and playes printed at London by Curle and others, are gote doune from London by Allan Ramsay, and lent out for an easy price, to young boyes, servant weemen of the better sort, and gentlemen, and vice and obscenity dreadfully propagated.[7]

Fortunately, Ramsay had been warned of the raid in time to remove anything which might be considered 'villainous'.

The Gentle Shepherd was very important in the progress of the theatre in Scotland. It appealed to a wide public, and those who read and saw the play realised that it was not the Devil's work. The play thus helped to overcome many prejudices and in 1746 it enjoyed a vastly popular series of benefit performances by the employees of a printer, Robert Drummond, who had been imprisoned for publishing verses critical of, amongst others, the Duke of Cumberland. According to John Jackson, the first but admittedly unreliable historian of Scotland's theatre, it was these performances which broke down prejudice against the theatre among Edinburgh's middle classes, for, having been once to the theatre to show their political support for Drummond, they found the experience enjoyable and returned regularly.

The Gentle Shepherd was commissioned by 'Gentlemen of Haddington' in 1728, in the year and in the town in which Gay's *The Beggars Opera*, to which it owes something of its construction, was first performed in Scotland. Ramsay finished his play by 1731. He set it, not in some timeless Arcadia, but in the Pentland Hills outside Edinburgh immediately after the Restoration of 1660. The play's main strength is its vigorous and idiomatic use of Scots but, as the language becomes more anglicised, so the invention and interest of the play flags. The ending in which the hidden noble birth of

Peggy is almost too conveniently revealed and the newly-returned laird, Sir William Worthy, makes his plea for everyone to behave as he should like them to, is very weak. But the early scenes, especially the dialogues between Roger and Patie and Jenny and Peggy, and the comic scenes in which Bauldy tries to win Jenny by means of witchcraft, work very well. There is an added feminist interest in the scenes with Mause, the supposed witch, who explains the dilemma of the independent educated woman of the time:

> This fool imagines, as do mony sic,
> That I'm a Wretch in Compact with Auld Nick,
> Because by education I was taught
> To speak and act aboon their common Thought.[8]

This may argue the virtues of enlightenment, but, as with so much Scottish literature, the play comes to life when the supernatural is invoked. In his attempt to win the love of Jenny, Bauldy is given a vivid speech in which he describes what he imagines are Mause's magic practices:

> She can o'ercast the Night, and cloud the Moon,
> And mak the Deils obedient to her Crune   [murmurs]
> At Midnight Hours, o'er the Kirk-yards she raves,
> And howks unchristen'd We'ans out of their Graves;   [digs][children]
> Boils up their Livers in a Warlock's Pow;   [head]
> Rins withershins about the Hemlock Low;   [in a contrary direction]
> And seven Times does her Prayers backwards pray,   [flame]
> Till Plotcock comes with Lumps of Lapland clay,
> Mixt with the venom of black taids and snakes.
> Of this, unsonsy pictures aft she makes   [unlucky]
> Of any ane she hates—and gars expire   [causes]
> With slow and racking pains afore a fire,
> Stuck ful of Pins; the devilish Pictures melt;
> The Pain by Fowk they represent, is felt.[9]   [folk]

The play is in essence a kind of 'historical-pastoral', set in time of peace in the aftermath of a great struggle and written when Scotland was again recovering from war and political upheaval. The villagers live a life of democratic paganism, in which neither the Laird nor the Church plays any significant part. In ivew of Ramsay's treatment at the hands of the Church and the state, it is tempting to see this as his political ideal.

Perhaps it was the success of *The Gentle Shepherd* that persuaded Ramsay, in the face of religious opposition, to open his own theatre in Carrubers Close in Edinburgh's Canongate in 1736. Unfortunately for Ramsay, in 1737, in the wake of Fielding's political satire *Tom Thumb* directed against Walpole's government, the Licensing Act was passed by those who had been satirised. This act required a theatre presenting the spoken drama to be granted a Royal Patent, which in turn required an Act of Parliament. The Scottish poet, James Thomson, who wrote for the London stage, was another victim of this Act and had his play *Edward and*

Eleanora banned. This play, like all Thomson's classical tragedies, dealt, in a coded way, with contemporary politics in a prolix and often risable fashion.

In Edinburgh, Ramsay soon rallied support to lobby for a licence to be granted to his theatre. But a counter-lobby was arranged consisting of representatives of the Magistrates, the Church, and the University, and the combined strength of this group ensured that the idea was dropped and the theatre closed. Ramsay lost a great deal of money by this speculation and he also seems to have lost heart in the struggle to establish a Scottish drama, as he never wrote for the stage again. However, from 1740 onwards, a way of circumventing the licensing requirement was found, in which plays were advertised as being offered free between the pieces in a concert of music. By exploiting this device, a permanent theatre at the Canongate Concert Hall was founded in 1746 and ten years later, the most famous Scottish play of the century, John Home's *Douglas*, was premiered there 'gratis', between pieces of music.

Because Home was a minister, his writing of a play for performance and his association with the theatre provoked an outcry amongst the unenlightened sections of the Church. His friend and fellow minister, Alexander Carlyle, was even threatened with punishment for having attended a performance of the play. Carlyle subsequently apologised to the Church for his play-going, but he also wrote an anonymous jeu d'esprit entitled *An Argument to prove that the Tragedy of Douglas ought to be Publicly Burnt by the hands of the Hangman* (1757). This was an attack on his persecutors who seized on the pamphlet as ammunition for their cause, wholly failing to detect the author's irony. The pamphlet began:

> The wiles of Satan are as endless as his malignity is great; and most successful of all he attacks religion in the shape of human virtue . . . by endowing all these fine modern ministers with candour, openness, humanity and an affectionate concern for the welfare of their parishioners, he blinds the casual minds of the people, so that they cannot perceive how deficient they are in true grace: whereas by infusing cunning, envy, covetousness and spiritual pride into the hearts of many godly and orthodox brethren he weakens their hands and destroys the effects of all their zeal and labour.[10]

The Presbytery of Edinburgh followed this with an 'Admonition and Exhortation' to be read from each pulpit in the city. This Admonition was a further attempt by some preachers to make their hatred of the theatre respectable, but this time its effect was to render them ludicrous and to fuel the campaign for a legal patent theatre in the capital. The admonition began:

> The opinion which the Christian Church has always held of the Stage and Players, as prejudicial to the Interests of Religion and Morality is well known; and the fatal Influence which they have on the far greater part of mankind, particularly the younger Sort, is too obvious to be called into Question . . .

To enumerate how many servants, Apprentices and students in different branches of Literature, in the City and in the Suburbs, have been seduced from their proper business, by attending the stage would be a painful and disagreeable Task.[11]

These arguments were constantly challenged as the Enlightenment spread. Those who supported the theatre defended its use as an instrument to ridicule vice and display virtue, to encourage the development of the abilities of young men—and ministers—in rhetoric and deportment, and to assist the understanding and controlling of 'proper passions'. Such improvements were aimed initially at the upper and professional classes and, like many aspects of the Enlightenment, only slowly percolated down to the lower orders.

John Home's *Douglas* was the only play to rival the popularity of *The Gentle Shepherd* in Scotland and its first production highlights many of the strengths and weaknesses of the stage in eighteenth-century Scotland. The controversy provoked by the play was an effective weapon in the hands of the liberal clergy and allowed them to ridicule the fundamentalists who attacked the stage; it provided an opportunity for the greatest minds of the day to rally round and support a cause which the majority of Edinburgh's leading citizens took up; it provided an opportunity for a display of national pride, and it secured the fame of a play destined to become a standard repertoire piece of every theatre in the English-speaking world.

The plot of *Douglas* is simple. Lady Randolph has married Lord Douglas in secret against her father's wishes and their child is born after Douglas has died a hero's death. Both the baby and the nurse who is taking him to a place of safety are supposed drowned. The play opens on the eve of a Danish invasion, when the Scottish ranks are suddenly swelled by the arrival of a new hero, who having been raised in obscurity, turns out to be Lady Randolph's son. The young Norval dies protecting his mother, and the distraught Lady Randolph throws herself from the topmost tower of the castle. The Church was quick to condemn the play as an encouragement to suicide, but the enlightened countered that the play's moral teaching was directed at young women who disobeyed their fathers.

Douglas is an early example of sentimental literature, and Mrs Siddons always played Lady Randolph carrying a huge handkerchief. But tears are shed less in helpless pity for Lady Randolph, as in recognition of her maternal predicament and the loss of the young hero. Audiences responded to the heroic young Norval, said by Henry Mackenzie to have been created in Home's romanticised self-image because, as Pope said of Addison's Cato, 'who sees him act, but envies every deed/who hears him groan, and does not wish to bleed?'.

Douglas works well in the theatre and its initial impact came before the text was available for dissection. The philosopher David Hume, Home's cousin, had a high and often-quoted opinion of the play: 'You [Home] possess the true theatric genius of Shakespeare and Otway, refined from the unhappy barbarism of the one, and licentiousness of the other'. But

Hume was also aware of the play's faults, as he wrote to the author:

> . . . The more considerable objections seem to be these: Glenalvon's character is too abandoned. Such a man is scarce in nature . . . Lord Barnet's character is not enough decided; he hovers betwixt vice and virtue, which though it be not unnatural, is not sufficiently theatrical nor tragic. After Anna had lived 18 years with Lady Barnet, and yet kept out of the secret, there seems to be no sufficient reason why, at the time, she should have been let into it . . . There seem to be too many casual rencounters.[12]

The play succeeded, in spite of these and other commonly voiced objections. 'Crito' ascribed its success to:

> Mrs Ward's amazing powers in Tragedy [and] Mr Digges in the character of young Douglas . . . in copying Nature with judgement . . . in preserving Attention to Recital and in that charming simplicity of Action so long banished the stage . . .[13]

The Scots have always liked a strong sentimental streak in their drama, and perhaps this explains some of the attraction of *Douglas*. It is also an undeniably gripping play, with the strong narrative drive it inherited from its source in the ballad, *Gil Morrice*, and although, as David Hume pointed out, there are loose ends, one should not notice them in a strong production. As Henry Mackenzie characteristically remembers:

> I was present at the representation; the applause was enthusiastic; but a better criterion of its merits was the tears of the audience which the tender part of the drama drew forth unsoaringly.[14]

The fame of *Douglas* also showed how fragile were hopes for a native Scottish drama, as Home's dearest wish was for a success on the London stage. Home had taken the play first to Garrick at Drury Lane. Garrick rejected it. However, it was eventually produced with great success in London at Covent Garden, and this meant more to Home than its success in Edinburgh. He even changed the name of the heroine from Lady Barnet to Lady Randolph when he was told that Barnet was a village near London and the name might occasion laughter in the capital. Home wrote several plays for the London stage but none of these enjoyed the success of *Douglas*. *Agis* and *Alonzo* did not have Scottish settings but *The Fatal Discovery*, 1790, was set in a world of Celtic twilight. However, it proved as unsuccessful as his other plays.

The outcry over *Douglas* both helped to establish the victory of the Moderate party in the Church and underlined the need for Edinburgh to have a licensed Theatre Royal. Nine years later, the Canongate playhouse, in which *Douglas* had first been performed, became Edinburgh's first Theatre Royal. Then, in 1769, in keeping with the dignity of the 'New Town', a new Theatre Royal was opened at the foot of the North Bridge opposite Register House. The interior of the theatre though simple, found favour and was said to resemble that of the Bristol Theatre Royal which still exists today. Unfortunately, according to both the critic William Campbell and the historian of Edinburgh Hugo Arnot, the exterior was without merit and merely served to obscure the view of Register House, one of the finest buildings in the city. Sadly, *Douglas* was the only play of any lasting fame to be premiered at either the Canongate Theatre or the new Theatre Royal for some sixty years. Instead, the new theatre became famous for its managers, most notably Stephen Kemble and John Jackson. Jackson has left a fascinating *History of the Scottish Stage* (1793), more of an 'apologia pro sua vita' filled with anecdote and reminiscence than a serious work of history. Jackson, however, perhaps to obscure the fact that he premiered no outstanding play at his theatre, made great claims for a Christmas spectacle called *Liberty Triumphant*, which he produced in 1790. The play was a reconstruction of the storming of the Bastille but, Jackson's praise notwithstanding, it was ridiculed by another actor, Lee Lewis, who remarked that 'a mass of more timesome absurdity was never before exhibited to a Rational audience'.

Robert Fergusson, though not entirely seriously, regretted the passing of the old theatre in the Canongate which lay for many years in ruins:

> No more the gaudy Beau
> With handkerchief in lavender well-drenched,
> or bergamot, or rose water pure,
> With flavoriferous sweets shall chase away
> The pestilential fumes of vulgar Citz . . .
> Alas how sadly altered is the scene
> For lo! those sacred walls, that late were brush'd
> By rustling silks and waving capucines
> Those walls that late have echoed to the voice
> Of stern King Richard, to the seat transformed
> Of Crawling spiders and detested moths . . .[15]

These lines, partly from their parody of the pomposity of declamatory tragedy, remind us, as, for example, do Kay's caricatures of the audience that watched Clinch and Mrs Yates perform as the Duke and Duchess of Braganza in 1785, that until the end of the century, theatre-going in Edinburgh was very much a fashionable 'English' pastime. According to 'Crito' in the *Dramatic Review* it was Stephen Kemble, who took over the Theatre Royal in 1780, who 'found it fashionable and left it a place which all ranks of society could enjoy'. Hugo Arnot in his *History of Edinburgh* (1788) offers some explanation for the length of time it took to build up a regular audience in the city:

> The fact is that Edinburgh does not give encouragement to the stage proportionable to the populousness of the city. This does not proceed so much from the remaining leaven of fanaticism, as from the poorness of Scots' fortunes, the inconsiderableness of the trade and manufactures, or the smallness of the profits arising from them. These do not admit of ordinary gentlewomen, or the

wives and daughters of shop-keepers and mechanics going often to the playhouse; therefore they keep their penny till some occasion, (no matter what), makes it reported that the house is to be throng, then everyone crowds the theatre, while, without such report the walls would be desolate. As for the gentlemen, the stage has not such attractions for them, as the social pleasures of the bottle, or the pungent emotions of the hazard table.[16]

The truth of Arnot's claim was shown when, during the first visit of Mrs Siddons in 1784, some 2000 applications were made for the 600 seats available at one performance. It was on this visit, so Alexander Carlyle tells us, that the most famous Lady Randolph of all won the battle between Church and theatre:

> ... when the great Mrs Siddons first appeared in Edinburgh during the sitting of the General Assembly, ... the court was obliged to fix all its important business for the alternate days when she did not act, as all the younger members, clergy as well as laity, took their stations in the theatre on those days by three in the afternoon.[17]

With the waning of Church hostility, the theatre between 1770 and 1800 was free to develop and nine theatres opened in Scotland. There were two in Edinburgh, and one in each of Aberdeen, Glasgow, Dundee, Dumfries, Paisley, Ayr and Greenock. There was also a network of fit-up stages and performances by strolling players such as the ones described fictionally but accurately by Rev. Balwhidder in John Galt's *Annals of the Parish* (1821):

> In the month of August [1795] at the time of the Fair, a gang of play-actors came and hired Thomas Thacklin's barn for their enactments ... Their first performance was Douglas Tragedy and the Gentle Shepherd ... the whole pack was in a state of perfect beggary ... I thought I would have liked to have gotten a peek at them myself. At the same time I must own this was a sinful curiosity, and I stifled it to the best of my ability. Among the other plays that they did was one called Macbeth and the Witches ...[18]

After 1730 there were frequent performances of *The Gentle Shepherd* all over Scotland and, because the acting companies were often English, their struggles with the language became an added attraction, providing much unintentional amusement. Richard Sharpe remembers his mother's delighted reminiscence of audiences being convulsed with laughter at the actors' pronunciation. The players' sensitivity to ridicule is apparent in an advertisement for the play in the *Edinburgh Courier* for 1740, which boasts that, 'the utmost care and application has been taken to learn the Scots dialect in this piece as perfectly as possible'. Even *Douglas* was first produced and acted by an English company, though one long resident in Edinburgh and destined to remain so, until profligacy and passion drove the principal actors Digges West and Sarah Ward to Dublin and London respectively. After the Union, however, Edinburgh proved very attractive to English actors and provided them with a very profitable side-line, namely, teaching the genteel how to speak proper English.

While the language of *The Gentle Shepherd* caused the professionals so many problems, it was this which probably appealed to the Pentland villagers who performed the play annually until well into the nineteenth century. Amateur acting in schools, in villages and amongst the upper and professional classes was very widespread in the Lowlands in the eighteenth century. This ranged from the country-house performances of Charles Frank of Dughtrig who excelled, so Maidement in his *Nugae Scotiae* tells us, as Plautus's miser, to benefits for deserving causes in the cities, and village entertainments. The actress Charlotte Deans, who eloped with a poor touring actor, remembered that small companies such as hers could call on local actors in most towns to perform parts in a play when, as often happened, there were not enough actors to fill all the roles. Most professional actors in Scotland were English, but sometimes a talented Scottish amateur actor, like H E Johnston, took to the stage, though this was rare. Perhaps this is hardly surprising, as Scots had little opportunity to train as actors and the repertoire of most companies was overwhelmingly English. It consisted of either declamatory tragedy or verbal comedy, both of which put the Scot, with distinctive speech patterns, at a considerable disadvantage.

In the eighteenth century, new plays could be produced easily, as scenery and costumes were not designed for each production, but came from the theatre's 'stock'. If a play's premiere was successful it could be absorbed into the theatre's repertoire; if not, it had only entailed the actors' learning new parts. Many new plays were tried out on 'national' subjects, like Mary Queen of Scots and William Wallace but they disappeared quietly, to re-appear early in the next century in a form, usually melodramatic, that was to ensure their continuous performance while there were independent Scottish theatres to produce them.

By the late eighteenth century, we find Scottish playwrights still using English models but trying to make them more Scottish. Archibald MacLaren for example in *The Highland Drover*, uses a flimsy plot about the liberation of Lydia from her vile guardian, Mr Hog of Carlisle, who wishes to marry her to Mr Scarecrow. The instrument of her liberation is a Highland Drover who will only speak Gaelic and who finds he is related to Lydia's servant, Betty Campbell, who comes from Inverary and speaks Gaelic too. This play was premiered in Inverness, and MacLaren claims he toured it round the Highlands, 'with universal approbation!'

Possibly the most significant works for the theatre produced in Scotland in the 1790s were Scott's first dramatic translations. From the early nineteenth century his novels in the tactful rearrangements of men like William Terry were to hold the stage for a century or more and to turn the Theatre Royal Edinburgh, under the management of Mrs Henry Siddons and her brother W H Murray, into what was essentially a National Theatre, with Scott as a national dramatist. But, in 1800, the Romantic obsession with Scott and Scotland was only beginning, Ossian had yet to be dramatised, and even Burns, though he wrote in a Prologue for the Dumfries Theatre, 'There's themes enow in Caledonia's story/Wad show the Tragic Muse in a' her Glory', did not feel tempted to test his hypothesis.

Generalisations about the theatre in Scotland between 1660 and 1800, its plays, actors and audience are difficult to make. The period begins with a play like *Marciano*, 'acted with great applause in front of His Majesties' High Commissioner and others of the nobility at the Tennis Court of Holyrood House', and with the Court revels of the Duke of York, and ends with Robert Hamilton's company performing *A Child of Nature* and *The Highland Chieftans*, 'By desire of the Gentlemen of the Montrose Golf Club'. But perhaps we can say that as Scotland changed from a predominantly agricultural to being a mainly industrial nation, as Edinburgh's political importance declined, and the aristocracy emigrated South, as the need to appeal to an elite faded and those who ran the theatres came to realise that it had to appeal to all classes, especially the burgeoning merchant classes in cities like Glasgow and Dundee: as Scotland regained her self-confidence and a sense of national identity; as the Enlightenment spread and the power of the preachers waned, so the theatre followed all these changes and evolved into an acceptable intellectual, social and moral pastime rivalling even the 'hazard table'.

NOTES

1   *Marciano or the Discovery. A Tragi-comedy*. (Edinburgh, 1663), p 3.
2   Ibid., pp 18–19.
3   *The Poems of John Dryden*, James Kinsley (ed) (Oxford, 1958), vol 1, p 374.
4   *The Assembly*. By a Scots Gentleman (London, 1722), p 18.
5   *Biographia Dramatica*, compiled by David Erskine Baker, *et al.* (London, 1812), vol 2, p 40.
6   *The Assembly*, pp 89–90.
7   *Analecta, or Materials for a History of Remarkable Providences, mostly relating to Scotch Ministers and Christians*, by the Rev Robert Woodrow. Maitland Club, (Glasgow, 1843), vol 3, p 515.
8   *The Works of Allan Ramsay*, Burns Martin (ed) (Edinburgh, 1953), vol 2, p 232.
9   Ibid., p 229.
10 *An Argument*, n/a, [Alexander Carlyle] (Edinburgh, 1757), p 16.
11 Quoted in Alice Edna Gipson, *John Home, his Life and Works*. (Yale, 1916) p 72.
12 Quoted in Henry Mackenzie, *An Account of the Life and Writings of John Home, Esq*. (Edinburgh, 1822), pp 100–101.
13 Quoted in James Dibdin, *Annals of the Edinburgh Stage*. (Edinburgh, 1888), p 90.
14 Mackenzie, op. cit., p 38.
15 *The Poems of Robert Ferguson*, Matthew P MacDiarmid (ed) (Edinburgh, 1954), vol 2, p 60.
16 Hugo Arnot, *The History of Edinburgh*, (Edinburgh, 1788), pp 372–3.
17 *The Autobiography of Dr Alexander Carlyle of Inveresk*, 1722–1805 (Edinburgh, 1910), pp 338–9.
18 John Galt, *Annals of the Parish*, (Edinburgh, 1910), p 207.

FURTHER READING

In addition to those texts mentioned in the Notes the following are recommended:

Tobin Terence *Plays by Scots 1660–1800*, (University of Iowa Press, 1974)
Home John, *Douglas*, Parker, Gerald D (ed) (Edinburgh, 1972)

Chapter 12

Historical Writing in the Later Eighteenth Century

GEOFFREY CARNALL

When, in the thirty-fifth of his *Lectures on Rhetoric and Belles Lettres*, Hugh Blair turns from rhetorical topics to a consideration of the various kinds of literature, the first genre that offers itself is 'historical writing'. Being 'an object of dignity' he deals with it at some length, devoting one and a half lectures to it, while he huddles philosophy, dialogue, 'epistolary writing', and prose fiction into a single class hour. Only the varieties of epic and of tragedy demand a greater space in Blair's survey, and it is clear that he has as high a regard for the achievement of Thucydides, or Livy, or Clarendon as he does for Homer, or Virgil, or Milton. Just as epic is 'the recital of some illustrious enterprise' from which moral instruction naturally arises, so history records momentous and important events 'represented in connexion with their causes, traced to their effects; and unfolded in clear and distinct order.' The great difficulty in writing history is to impose narrative order on a wide range of materials, achieving a proper management of transitions and avoiding a prolix detail. The difficulty was increased by the extended scope of historical writing in the eighteenth century, noted by Blair himself in the final paragraph of his discussion of the genre. Laws, customs, commerce, religion, and literature were now seen as part of the regular subject-matter of history. When Voltaire wrote his *Age of Louis XIV* (1751), he not only considered the state and military affairs which were assumed to be the main business of history, but also surveyed the sciences, literature and the arts, and—at some length—the varieties of religion in late seventeenth-century France. This wide-ranging approach was even more apparent in the *Essay on the Manners and Spirit of the Nations* (1756), where he dealt with many aspects of medieval and early modern European society. Historians after Voltaire felt it incumbent on them to realize as fully as possible the social context within which the events narrated occurred; but to do this without loss of narrative impetus was perceived as a condition of success. Blair reserves his highest praise for historians like Tacitus who can evoke past events with the kind of power one expects in epic or tragedy. He is particularly impressed by Tacitus's account of Rome when threatened by Otho: 'no tumult, no quiet; only the silence of terror and anger.' This, says Blair, 'is a conception of the sublime kind, and discovers high genius.' Whatever other concerns the historians of the second half of the eighteenth century may have had in mind, the ambition of displaying as much genius as Tacitus, of showing us what Adam Smith called 'the feelings and agitation of Mind in the Actors',[1] was never altogether absent.

David Hume was not only the most highly esteemed of the Scottish historians in this period, but also one of the earliest. In January 1753, a year before the first instalment of his *History of Great Britain* appeared, he told a friend that there was 'no post of honour in the English Parnassus more vacant than that of History. Style, judgement, impartiality, care—every thing is wanting to our historians'.[2] It is therefore natural to begin this assessment of historical writing with him, the more so as he illustrates so clearly the 'instructive' purpose which is an important feature of Enlightened Scottish historiography.

The doctrine which Hume's *History* is intended to enforce and illustrate is conveniently set out in the political essays he published between 1748 and 1758. The two essays 'Of the Original Contract' and 'Of Passive Obedience' look at the justifications for virtually unlimited submission to authority on the one hand, and for a broad right of resistance to authority on the other. Both speculative systems, he suggests, are unsatisfactory as they are usually expounded. He is particularly anxious to discredit the idea of a social contract, the belief that our submission to authority is conditional on authority's fulfilling its obligations to us. Obedience and subjection, he argues, are in fact accepted as unquestioningly as the principle of gravity or any other law of nature. Nothing could be more terrible for us than a total dissolution of government. But he agrees that obedience should not be unlimited. The British constitution includes an implicit legitimizing of resistance, when a monarch fails to observe the limits placed on his authority, as Charles I and James II did. On the whole Hume clearly inclines to the side of authority, feeling a distaste for the rhetoric of 'patriotic opposition'. Innovations, to be sure, are constantly needed, the more so 'where the enlightened genius of the age' can direct them 'to the side of reason, liberty, and justice'; but, he insists, 'violent innovations no individual is entitled to make.'[3]

Hume began his *History* a few years after the final defeat of the Jacobite cause at Culloden. The Scottish Highlands were being subjected to a comprehensive programme of 'improvement', and the Lowlands were sharing in a quickening tempo of development which was to transform Britain into a mainly manufacturing economy. It was an appropriate moment to reassess the significance of those political upheavals in the previous century which had led to the ejection of the old reigning family, and the establishment of a new system in which the power of the House of Commons was pre-eminent, with an increasingly stable equilibrium between the landed and the moneyed interest.

In rejecting the misleading simplifications of a history inspired by parties and factions, Hume set himself to narrate events with the fullest possible sense of the impulses and motives at work at the time. He takes an evident pleasure in suggesting the precise composition of particular political transactions. There is a characteristic example of this in his account of James I's abortive negotiations with Spain over the proposed marriage between his son Charles and the Infanta. To facilitate it, James had freed Catholic recusants from prison and announced his intention of not executing the penal laws against them—a step so unpalatable to 'the rigid spirit' of the protestants that he felt bound to ascribe it to his own zeal for protecting protestants abroad. His pleas for indulgence, he said, were always 'answered by objections derived from the severity of English laws against Catholics'. Hume then suggests that the king's policy may not have been purely opportunistic: 'if the extremity of religious zeal were ever to abate among Christian sects, one of them must begin.' So far, so good. But Hume goes on to point out that James's abrogation of the penal laws was a striking exertion of the royal prerogative, of a kind which was to cause increasing conflict between king and parliament. It was justified by the immediate result, because it genuinely disposed Philip IV of Spain to promote the marriage, and this would in turn have furthered an important aim of English policy, to restore the Palatinate (in Germany) to James's son-in-law Frederick, who had lost it after imprudently seeking, in 1619, to establish himself as king of Bohemia. Hume suggests that Philip may have been prompted by friendship and generosity rather than reason of state, although he then proceeds to indicate two such politic motives: the desire to conciliate an important maritime nation, and the need to secure an ally against the rising power of France.

Having established in the reader's mind this clear sense of an enlightened policy, Hume goes on to topple the precarious structure with an account of the arrogant impetuosity of the Duke of Buckingham, first inducing Prince Charles to make his romantic visit to Spain, in order to expedite the marriage negotiations, and then turning against the whole project, stirring up hostility to Spain by his partial and misleading account of the whole affair. Buckingham not only charmed Parliament by offering an opportunity for war with papists, but also undermined his royal master's authority by encouraging schemes for abolishing episcopacy and selling church lands to pay for the war. James, for his part, still hoped to temporize, but

> was so borne down by the torrent of popular prejudices, conducted and increased by Buckingham, that he was at last obliged, in a speech to parliament, to declare in favour of hostile measures, if they would engage to support him. Doubts of their sincerity in this respect—doubts which the event showed not to be ill grounded—had probably been one cause of his pacific and dilatory measures. (Chapter 49)

Thus, at the end, Hume suggests yet another aspect of James's enlightened policy towards Spain.

The interaction of motives in this passage helps to account for the satisfying solidity of Hume's narrative. Time after time one is presented with shifts of perspective, often slight, occasionally abrupt, which create an effect analogous to that of landscape painting. His account of the great conflict between Charles I and his parliaments is the outstanding example of his genius for presenting a situation, to use a favourite word of his, *entire*. He emphasises to what an extent the Tudor monarchy was a despotism, and how natural it was therefore for James I and Charles I to take the government as they found it, and to reject the pretensions of the Commons in such matters as the impeachment of Buckingham as an unbounded usurpation which must be opposed by 'a proper firmness of resolution'. On the other hand, his account of John Hampden's resistance to the payment of ship money is an eloquent and detailed exposition of a case which leads irresistibly to the conclusion that 'liberty was totally subverted, and an unusual and arbitrary authority exercised over the kingdom'. (Chapter 52)

Hume is particularly skilful at depicting the interplay of religious and political motives. He is keenly aware of the importance of the spirit of 'enthusiasm', bold, daring, and uncontrolled, without which the civil liberties of the modern British constitution would have been impracticable. He is also alert to the way in which this enthusiasm may coexist with a realistic appraisal of what is actually possible. This is why his portrait of Cromwell is so convincing. He allows him to have been a wholehearted 'saint', transported with the most frantic whimsies, but also endowed with sagacity to regulate enthusiasm in others. He granted an unbounded liberty of conscience to all the protestant sects, and by that means, he both attached the wild sectaries to his person, and employed them in curbing the domineering spirit of the presbyterians'. But the presbyterians, too, enjoyed protection in their establishments and tithes, so they were not ill-disposed to Cromwell's government either. Hume is fascinated by the confusion, embarrassment, and unintelligibility of Cromwell's speeches, and while on the face of it this might appear to be a paradoxical deficiency in Cromwell's genius for government, it is evident that Hume sees Cromwell's obscurities as enabling him to evade some awkward political conflicts. (Chapter 61) A similar tact and empathy appears in Hume's account of Becket's quarrel with Henry II, and in his assessment of Joan of Arc. Joan he regards as an intrepid enthusiast with a genius for encouraging troops in combat. He discounts her abilities as a general, suggesting that the French court fostered this idea with a view to enhancing the divine authority of their cause, but that in fact she was prompted by Dunois and other commanders.

> It is sufficient praise that she could distinguish the persons on whose judgment she might rely; that she could seize their hints and suggestions, and, on a sudden, deliver their opinions as her own; and that she could curb on occasion that visionary and enthusiastic spirit with which she was actuated, and could temper it with prudence and discretion. (Chapter 20)

She eventually fell victim to the envy of French officers who disliked having the merit of every victory ascribed to her, and deliberately exposed her to impossible odds at the siege of Compiègne. Hume tells the story of her trial and condemnation for heresy with a splendid distaste. 'This admirable woman,' he concludes, 'to whom the more generous superstition of the ancients would have erected altars, was, on pretence of heresy and magic, delivered over alive to the flames.'

Hume's *History* is everywhere informed with a generous if ironical appreciation of innocence, good-nature, and benevolence, wherever these qualities are to be found. It is one of the great, and now unduly neglected, monuments of the Age of Sensibility.

The other Scottish historian of the period who was esteemed as comparable to the major figures of antiquity was William Robertson. It must be said at once that he is not so much of an artist as Hume. His tone is unremittingly magisterial, as befits the Principal of Edinburgh University and a man who was for many years Moderator of the General Assembly of the Church of Scotland. He conducts his readers through a mass of firmly-controlled documentation, showing how the characteristic polity of sixteenth-century Scotland was formed, describing the struggle between partisans of different systems of faith and order in the Europe of Charles V, and illustrating the encounter of societies at different stages of development in the *History of America*. He is no less aware than Hume of the range of conflicting policies and ideologies, but where Hume conjures up a sense of these conflicts in precarious and constantly shifting interrelationship, Robertson narrates a series of emphatic and decisive collisions. His account of the Reformation in the *History of Scotland* (1759) focuses on turbulent masses of eager reformers contending with the forces commanded by the bold, aspiring, yet wily and temperate spirit of Mary of Guise, the Queen-Regent. Her reiterated and wanton perfidy confirmed the protestants in their conviction that their safety lay only in armed struggle. Robertson creates an image of people inspired by enlarged notions of religion, and by 'liberal and generous sentiments concerning civil government'. A newly-revived study of Greek and Roman authors intensified the effect, acquainting the reformers with 'exquisite models of free government, far superior to the inaccurate and oppressive system established by the feudal law'. It was from the ancients that Knox derived the arguments for his celebrated blasts against the 'monstrous regiment of women', and Buchanan's dialogue *De Jure Regni apud Scotos* is founded on the maxims of ancient republican government. If this enlarged and generous spirit found its most immediate expression in the excesses of violence committed on churches and monasteries, Robertson does not flinch.

> We are apt, at this distance of time, to condemn the furious zeal of the reformers, and to regret the overthrow of so many stately fabrics, the monuments of our ancestor's magnificence, and among the noblest ornaments of the kingdom. But amidst the violence of a reformation, carried on in opposition to legal authority, some irregularities were unavoidable; and perhaps no one irregularity could have been permitted more proper to allure and interest the multitude, or more fatal to the grandeur of the established church. (Book 2)

The central interest of the *History of Scotland* is in the career of the unfortunate Mary Queen of Scots. Robertson's feelings about her are not easy to determine. He insists on her beauty, her charm, her ability, her reckless imprudence, her guilt. Her warmth of heart was not restrained by discretion, and this led her into conduct which Robertson finds abhorrent. Yet her sufferings were so excessive that

> we are apt altogether to forget her frailties, we think of her faults with less indignation, and approve of our tears, as if they were shed for a person who had attained much nearer to pure virtue. (Book 7)

But although Robertson may have been 'apt' to forget Mary's frailties, he never actually does so, and his impartial portrait left Mary's more romantic partisans acutely dissatisfied.

The main body of the *History of Charles V* (1769) is the least attractive of Robertson's works, an arid succession of political and military transactions in which even Luther's defiance of the established religion is presented in a somewhat perfunctory way. Yet the book has a genuine vitality: the detail of the campaigns is often told with an unclerical zest, as in his account of the siege of Metz in 1552. Robertson is obviously impressed by the Duke of Guise's ruthless preparations for defence, levelling historic churches to the ground (though with pious ceremony), demolishing houses, and destroying corn and forage that could have been of use to the enemy. He did all this with the devoted support of the citizens:

> every other passion being swallowed up in the zeal to repulse the enemy with which he inspired them, they beheld the ruin of their estates, together with the havoc which he made among their public and private buildings, without any emotion of resentment. (Book 11)

Robertson's narrative always takes on a special animation when he sees normally divergent interests concentrating into a single force.

But the *History of Charles V* is mainly remembered for the 'View of the State of Europe' which precedes the main narrative. Robertson displays to us the barbarian hordes overturning an effete and incompetent Roman Empire, producing a state of society unrelieved in its misery. In the whole history of the human race, this was a time 'most calamitous and afflicted'. Contemporaries compared the ruin brought by the barbarous leaders of the time 'to the havoc occasioned by earthquakes, conflagrations, or deluges, the most formidable and fatal calamites which the imagination of man can conceive' (Section 1). But in the midst of this universal dissonance, a few intimations of harmony begin to be audible. Some consequences of the crusades were beneficial to civilization; the growth of commerce led to the establishment of cities which were able to 'shake off the yoke of their insolent lords'; a more regular administration of justice became normal; the spirit of chivalry introduced more gentle and polished manners. By the fifteenth century conditions were ready for the emergence of the modern system of states related by a balance of power; and it was this system that became fully established during the reign of the Emperor Charles V.

Cause and effect interlock here with an impossible precision, but there is a genuine art in the way Robertson relates the firm outline to the vivid and picturesque detail set out in the 'proofs and illustrations' appended to the 'View'. We see here, as we do in parts of the *History of America*, an historian who can set political and military history firmly in a wider history of civilization.

Certainly the *History of America* (1777) has an amplitude that helps the reader to appreciate how ambitious an Enlightenment historian could be.

The two books (IV and VII) that describe the 'savage Americans' and the civilization of Mexico and Peru, are diligent attempts to give an exact and circumstantial account of human societies at particular stages of development. The peoples of many parts of the continent exemplified a state of 'primaeval simplicity' that was quite unknown to Greek and Roman authorities, and this enabled modern philosophers to 'complete the history of the human mind'. Mexico and Peru had left monuments which illustrated the earliest phases of civilization. Robertson follows Warburton in showing how the picture-writing of the Mexicans is one stage in the evolution of hieroglyphics, and sees the first steps towards a system of commerce in their use of cocoa-beans as a sort of currency. Peru provides him with evidence of a remarkably sophisticated system of food-provision, and he notes that it was a far milder and more humane regime than that of the Mexicans. But they had also lost their warlike spirit, and so were unable to put up any resistance to the Spanish invaders. 'The Indians of Peru are now more tame and depressed than any people of America.' (Book 7) One detects here the anxieties of an enlightened philosopher who shared with Adam Smith and Adam Ferguson the conviction that Scotland needed its own militia to sustain its civic virtue.

The narrative part of the *History of America* enters vigorously into the colonizing enterprise of the Spaniards. It supplied the poet Keats with one of his best-known images, that of 'stout Cortez' gazing at the Pacific: of course it was Balboa, but with Robertson one can hardly tell one hero from another. He creates a bleak landscape in which predatory generals engage in astonishing feats of intrepidity and endurance. His account of the native American culture makes one appreciate the sheer destructiveness of the Spanish invasion, and he savours the irony of Las Casas's championship of the oppressed Americans, which only led to the establishment of the new and more terrible oppression of negro slavery in the Americas.

Robertson's *History of America* was published when Britain was in the process of losing her North American colonies; at the same time British officials were busy extending their control over large parts of India. The role of the East India Company moved into the centre of British politics in the 1780s, and a climax of concern was reached when in 1788 Warren Hastings was impeached for gross misrule as Governor-General. In introducing the case against Hastings, Edmund Burke invoked the great systems of law established in the Indian subcontinent, systems which were an integral part of an ancient and splendid civilization. Robertson's last work, his *Historical Disquisition concerning Ancient India* (1791), was written to counteract the prejudice that the peoples of India were 'an inferior race'. If, he wrote at the end of the book, his account of India could help to 'render their character more respectable, and their condition more happy, I shall close my literary labours with the satisfaction of thinking that I have not lived or written in vain.'

The *Disquisition* is in two parts, the first an account of contacts between Europe and India from the remotest antiquity up to the time of the Portuguese settlements; the second a survey of Indian institutions and 'manners'. This second part is an admirable summary of the findings of

European scholars in the latter part of the eighteenth century, and Robertson contrives to set in the strongest light the extraordinary achievement of, for example, the Indian astronomers whose tables are still reliable after 5,000 years. And if the Moderate clergyman and Enlightenment man of letters deplored the policy of the Brahmins in keeping their knowledge to themselves, allowing the populace to remain in superstitious ignorance, they were in this no different from the sages of Greece and Rome.

In the sheer breadth of scope that he exhibits as an historian, Robertson is an exemplary figure of the Scottish Enlightenment. His Indian *Disquisition*, indeed, is something of a high point, as one feels when one turns to the captious insularity of James Mill's *History of British India* published a quarter-century later. A number of works published in the previous quarter-century served to focus attention on the way human societies are constantly changing, but doing so at a variable rate, so that nations coexist in very different phases of social development. Such studies, together with Robertson's own very popular books, helped to modify radically the expectation of what was meant by the writing of history.

A major influence on these Scottish historians was Montesquieu, whose *Spirit of the Laws* first appeared in 1748. the world-wide scope of this treatise, its concern with universal physical and moral causes, proved to be immensely stimulating to speculation about the nature of society. The book was particularly well received in Britain because of Montesquieu's high regard for its political institutions, which illustrated the good effects of the division of powers, and nurtured the energies of its people. He took an evident pleasure in contemplating the English genius, more favourable to 'the bold strength of a Michael Angelo than to the softer graces of a Raphael' (xix 27). One Scottish writer who explicitly acknowledges an extensive debt to Montesquieu is Adam Ferguson, whose *Essay on the History of Civil Society* appeared in 1767. Ferguson examines the various phases of social organisation, from that of 'rude nations' as described by modern travellers in North America, Siberia, and elsewhere, to the corruption of those that are 'polished'. He is constantly concerned with the sources of national virtue, essential to the well-being of any society, and urges the cultivation

> in the higher ranks of those talents for the council and the field which cannot, without great disadvantage, be separated; and in the body of a people, that zeal for their country, and that military character, which enable them to take a share in defending its rights. (V, 4)

The *Essay* was part of a long-sustained political campaign to promote the formation of a Scottish militia, and the merits of the book can only be fully appreciated if one is alert to its polemical purposes.[4] Ferguson is concerned to enhance our respect for the bustle of active participation in affairs, and detects the essentials of liberty as clearly in the savage Tchutzi of Kamtschatska as in the Greeks defending their independence against the Persians. Just as Hume attempts to educate his readers into an appreciation of the balance of influences that make up our felicity, so Ferguson wants to convince us of the possibility of effective action in any circumstances, no matter how discouraging. It is a conviction that informs his energetic *History of the Progress and Termination of the Roman Republic* (1783). People of real fortitude, integrity, and ability can always make an impression on their society. Ferguson's brusque, urgent manner suggests the qualities of 'public affection' that he particularly values, and he draws upon the resources of every age and every quarter of the globe to reinforce his argument.

Ferguson's *Essay* is an example of a genre that became well-established in the latter part of the eighteenth century. Some of the most characteristic monuments of the Scottish Enlightenment are dissertations on aspects of society viewed in a wide geographical and historical context. J F Lafitau's celebrated account of the North American Indians had made familiar the view that primitive societies still existing in modern times belonged to a stage of social development even earlier than that illustrated by the oldest literary texts of Europe. The writings of Lord Kames, Adam Smith, and John Millar take for granted that history is world history. The centre of interest, of course, is in the causes of the wealth of nations or the development of class-distinctions, but the historical evidence is indispensable, endowing the analysis, as it does, with the authority of experience. As John Millar put it in the first preface to his *Observations concerning the Distinction of Ranks in Society* (1771), by looking at social systems in every part of the world, one gleans the results of 'real experiments'. Dependence on 'abstracted metaphysical theories' is avoided, and thus 'human nature is unfolded; the general laws of our constitution are laid open: and history is rendered subservient to moral philosophy and jurisprudence'. Millar's own inquiries into the distinction of ranks are distinguished by the vividness and even the dramatic power of his illustrations. He cites his evidence from the Old Testament, or from Homer, or from modern travellers' narratives, in a way which impresses the reader with a sense of the life he is conjuring up. The forwardness of Ruth in her rustic wooing of Boaz, or the patronizing air which Telemachos adopts, uncensured, towards the virtuous Penelope, are illustrated in a way which enables one to savour the full flavour of the occasion, as well as to see its bearing upon the role of women in primitive societies. The power of life and death which fathers have over their children in some societies is illustrated, pathetically, from Commodore Byron's account of how a South American Indian killed a much-loved three-year-old son for dropping a basket of eggs (Chapter 2). Millar belongs to a generation which expected to learn much from anecdotes illustrating traits of character and the manners of a particular age or society. His *Distinction of Ranks* helped to form the taste which appreciated the notes and illustrations to Scott's *Waverley Novels*.

No less than Hume, Millar saw his inquiries as helping to restrain 'that wanton spirit of innovation which men are too apt to indulge in their political reasoning'.[5] Unlike Hume, however, he adhered to the view that the ancient English constitution was essentially democratic, and in his *Historical View of the English Government* (1787) provided a history that was much more congenial to parliamentary reformers than Hume's had been. In discussing the Saxon witenagemot, while making clear that it was not like a modern parliament, he insisted that it could and did look into abuses, and could call the sovereign to account. A similar emphasis occurs in the writings of Gilbert Stuart, but the temper is much more strident, and more evidently intended to reinforce radical political attitudes. Millar feels at home in a complex, highly developed commercial society: that is where liberty is most firmly secured. Stuart finds liberty fully established in the earliest institutions of the ancient Germans. His *Historical Dissertation concerning the Antiquity of the English Constitution* (1768) takes its epigraph from Montesquieu: the English political system is recognizable in the *Germania* of Tacitus; it originated in the forests. In this book and in his *View of Society in Europe* (1778) he creates an idealized picture of this primitive polity, with its simplicity of manners, respect for women, and stringent constraints on the power of its kings. Any king who grew slack in his martial activity, or imagined himself superior to the laws, was soon humbled and degraded. 'A fierce people set aside his authority.' Stuart is clearly providing ammunition here for the view so fiercely reprobated by Burke, that a free people must have the right to choose their own governors and cashier them for misconduct. It is significant that the *Historical Dissertation* appeared in the same year that John Wilkes entered into the main phase of his challenge to George III and his ministers. The electors of Middlesex would have found it good reading.

Gilbert Stuart's world is inhabited by sternly virtuous heroes and repulsive agents of corruption. David Hume's historical writings exemplify the achievement of the age of sensibility at its most intelligent and discriminating; Stuart is a product of the age of sensibility too, but it is its passion and lack of inhibition that chiefly appears in his writings. His *History of Scotland* (1782) is of some importance as an early presentation of Mary Queen of Scots as romantic heroine. When in 1752 Walter Goodall published his *Vindication of Mary*, showing that the evidence implicating her in the murder of Darnley was forged, his undertaking was regarded as somewhat quixotic. Eight years later, William Tytler made a much stronger impression with his *Inquiry* into the evidence. Stuart takes the case that they make for granted, and presents Mary as an archetypal victim, no match for a skilful Lovelace like Bothwell. This is history where the state of society fades into the background, where we are so caught up in the sufferings of the heroine and the nature of her persecutors that it is difficult to focus upon anything else. No reader of Richardson's *Clarissa* or Frances Sheridan's *Sidney Bidulph* could have resisted Stuart's account of Mary's plight after her abduction by Bothwell and isolation in his castle at Dunbar. His importunity induced her to make the fatal promise of marriage, and then he had no difficulty in manipulating her into what Stuart tactfully calls a 'delirium of pleasure'. Bothwell

> could read in her look the emotions of her heart, and the secret workings of forbidden desires, allure her mind to give itself up to the power of imagination and the senses; take a pastime even in her pangs of remorse, and make them act as a zest to enjoyment; mark the conflicts and progress of expiring virtue; and exult in the triumphs of sensibility over shame. (Book 3)

Robertson had wished to 'draw a veil over this part of her character', but even he agreed that her later sufferings exceeded 'those tragical distresses which fancy has feigned to excite sorrow and commiseration', making her irresistibly sympathetic. It was left to Schiller to give the most complete presentation, in *Maria Stuart* (1800), of the symbolic figure of the beautiful and persecuted queen, whose passionate denial of guilt—'Wo sind die Proben?' [Where is the proof?]—echoes unavailingly through the theatre. But it was Scottish scholars and historians who provided the materials for a myth so congenial to the prepossessions of an age which admired the dark heroes of Byron, and responded positively even to atrocious energies. She was, understandably, too much for Walter Scott, whose line in heroes is notoriously insipid. His somewhat saccharine treatment of her in *The Abbot* reflects his conviction that the charges made against her continued 'to shade, if not to blacken, her memory', and that is something in which he wants no part. Where Scott does show himself to be a genuine disciple of the historians examined here is in his concern with the motives informing his characters' political actions. He doubts whether the story of *Waverley* will be intelligible without some account of 'the feelings, prejudices, and parties, of the times' (Chapter 5). The words might have come straight from Hume, and the panoramic vision that Scott provides owes something to the sense of social process emerging from the writings of Ferguson and Millar.[6] Scott, too, can respond to the passionate sense of resistance to wrong which inspires the myth of the tragic Scottish queen, but does so in a figure like Redgauntlet, uselessly faithful to the Stuart cause, denied even the posthumous gratification of sainthood because of his dedication to old feelings and prejudices. It is in conjuring up such sentiments that Scott gives his readers a glimpse of a history that is, as Hume would have put it, 'entire'.

NOTES

1   Adam Smith, *Lectures on Rhetoric and Belles Lettres*, Lecture 17.
2   J Y T Greig (ed), *The Letters of David Hume*, 2 vols (Oxford, 1932), I, p 270.
3   Hume, *Essays*, 'Of the Original Contract'.
4   The background of Ferguson's *Essay* is fully explained by John Robertson in his admirable study *The Scottish Enlightenment and the Militia Issue* (Edinburgh, 1985). During the eighteenth century, in both Scotland and England, the role of a militia, or citizen army, was an important and controversial question. In England an effective militia was eventually established under the pressure of an invasion threat in the Seven Years' War, providing Edward Gibbon with some unwelcome but not altogether useless experience of military affairs. It was not until 1797, during a later war, that a Scottish Militia Act was passed. Supporters of a militia tended to emphasise its value as a school of civic virtue; opponents remarked on its cost to the economy and poor military performance. *See* J R Western, *The English Militia in the Eighteenth Century* (1965).
5   John Millar, *Observation concerning the Distinction of Ranks* (1771), preface.
6   *See* Duncan Forbes, 'The Rationalism of Sir Walter Scott., *Cambridge Journal* 7 (October 1953), pp 20–35.

FURTHER READING

Black, J B *The Art of History* (1926)

Braudy, L, *Narrative Form in History and Fiction* (Princeton, 1970)

Butt, J, and Carnall, G, *The Mid-Eighteenth Century* (Oxford, 1979)

Forbes, D, *Hume's Philosophical Politics* (Cambridge, 1975)

Meinecke, F, *Die Entstehung des Historismus*, 2 vols (Munich, 1936), trans J E Anderson as *Historism: the Rise of a New Historical Outlook* (1972)

Norton, D F and Popkin, R H *David Hume: Philosophical Historian* (New York, 1965)

Peardon, T P, *The Transition in English Historical Writing 1760–1830* (New York, 1933)

Wexler, V G, *David Hume and the 'History of England'* (Philadelphia, 1979)

Chapter 13

Scottish Hero, Scottish Victim: Myths of Robert Burns

CAROL McGUIRK

> The form [of myth] does not suppress the meaning, it only impoverishes it, it
> puts it at a distance, it holds it at one's disposal.
>
> Roland Barthes

Roland Barthes' notion that myth, while not suppressing meaning, nonetheless 'impoverishes' it, is quite applicable to the myths surrounding Robert Burns. Posterity has always held Burns quite at its disposal; from the earliest days of his career, his very name has summoned a constellation of fixed responses about Scotland, about the peasantry, about native genius. These conditioned responses today flourish almost independently of the poems themselves—and with the very effect Barthes ascribed to myth. Burns the person has been 'immobilized' by Burns the myth, metamorphosed into a 'motionless prototype' (we might name that prototype 'Rab the Ranter') who lives on in place of the complex and notably elusive man behind that assumed mask.

The myth itself is two-sided. On the one hand, it portrays Burns as larger-than-life, a working-class hero and also a national hero—a super-Scot.[1] The opposite side of the myth, however, paints Burns as a victim. Dead at thirty-seven after a life of economic struggle, Burns never received the recognition and support that he deserved. This was the mythic Burns whom Dorothy Wordsworth mourned: 'There is no thought surviving in connexion with Burns's daily life that is not heart-depressing.'[2] And William Hazlitt agrees:

> When a man is dead, they put money in his coffin, erect monuments to his
> memory, and celebrate the memory of his birthday in set speeches. Would they
> take any notice of him if he were living? No!—I was complaining of this to a
> Scotchman who had been attending a dinner and a subscription to raise a
> monument to Burns. He replied, he would sooner subscribe twenty pounds to
> his monument than have given it him while living; so that if the poet were to
> come to life again, he would treat him just as he was treated in fact. This was an
> honest Scotchman. What *he* said, the rest would do.[3]

Hazlitt's remarks also demonstrate the way the myth of Burns-as-victim easily matamorphoses into anti-Scots sentiment, so intimately does the myth identify Burns with his country. In this mythic association of ideas—a larger-than-life Robert Burns and a generic Scotland (whether idealized or, in the case of Hazlitt, vilified)—the poet is again both hero and victim. He dominates (Hugh MacDairmid would have said vitiates) the entire vernacular tradition; but in non-vernacular contexts, Burns is today treated as a marginal figure, outside the mainstream of eighteenth-century British poetry. Raymond Bentman noted in 1972 a trend that has since accelerated: Burns, with Blake one of the two major poets of the late eighteenth century, is nonetheless vanishing from anthologies of eighteenth-century British poetry and even from literary histories of the period.[4]

The most destructive part of the Burns myth, however, is neither the sentimentality of the 'poor Burns' cultists nor the cultural foreshortening by which most literary critics and historians, notwithstanding his worldwide popularity, have seen Burns as speaking only from (and to) 'Scottish' contexts. Those two falsehoods can be corrected by the application of biographical and literary historical information, as in Franklyn Bliss Snyder's and De Lancey Ferguson's myth-shattering biographies of Burns, or in recent collections of critical essays (such as those edited by Jack and Noble and Donald Low) that have begun to define a larger cultural context for Burns's writings. The worst obstacle to a just appreciation of Burns's poems may well be the romanticized view of him as a hero of 'feeling', because this assumption not only ignores critical method but seems to preclude it. In this destructive myth of the 'heaven-taught ploughman', initiated by Henry Mackenzie in 1786 and apparently acquiesced in by Burns himself as a publicity measure, Burns is assumed to have written artlessly, his naive peasant soul expressing itself directly in his poems and songs. While such an assumption greatly magnifies the glamour of the man, it has detracted from our ability even to see, let alone to study, the craft and the art in his writings; for it forbids application of the usual critical criteria to his poems.

This is the dimension of the myth that has led to the cult of Burns's personality, a cult that now intrudes even into the briefest discussions of his poems. In the fragment *Sanditon* by Jane Austen, for instance—it was written in 1817, so this paradoxical myth of unwitting genius was firmly established within two decades of the poet's death—praise of Burns is put into the mouth of the obnoxious Sir Edward Denham, and is received coolly by the heroine, Charlotte Heywood:

> '. . . what think you Miss H. of Burns Lines to his Mary?—Oh! there is Pathos to madden one!—If ever there was a Man who *felt*, it was Burns. . . . Burns—I confess my sence of his Pre-eminence Miss H. . . . Burns is always on fire.—His Soul was the Altar in which lovely Woman sat enshrined, his Spirit truly breathed the immortal Incence which is her Due.—' 'I have read several of Burns's Poems with great delight, said Charlotte as soon as she had time to speak, but I am not poetic enough to separate a Man's Poetry entirely from his Character;—& poor Burn's known Irregularities, greatly interrupt my enjoyment of his Lines.—I have difficulty in depending on the *Truth* of his Feelings as a Lover. I have not faith in the *sincerity* of the affections of a Man

of his Description. He felt & he wrote & he forgot.' 'Oh! no no—exclaimed Sir Edw: in an extasy. He was all ardour & Truth!—His Genius & his Susceptibilities might lead him into some Aberrations—But who is perfect?—It were Hyper-criticism, it were Pseudo-philosophy to expect from the soul of high toned Genius, the grovellings of a common mind.—The Coruscations of Talent, elicted by impassioned feeling in the breast of Man, are perhaps incompatible with some of the prosaic Decencies of Life; nor can . . . any Woman be a fair Judge of what a Man may be propelled to say, write, or do, by the sovereign impulses of illimitable Ardour.'[5]

Austen here places in one elegant nutshell the entire nineteenth-century debate about Robert Burns, pro and con, a debate notable for its immediate divergence from the poetry itself into defence and attack of the poet's motives and conduct.

The Burns myth by now has taken on a life of its own; but originally, of course, the notion of the artist as Scottish hero/Scottish victim came from the personae of Burns's poems (and, to a lesser extent, from the Preface to the Kilmarnock edition and Burns's letters). Tam o'Shanter—henpecked, habitually drunken—nonetheless encounters the preternatural one stormy night and knows instinctively just how to react. The endearing little speaker in 'Tam Glen'—deaved by her Minnie, superstitutious into the bargain—knows exactly, and heroically, what she wants out of life: to marry the lad she loves dearly. The combination of human failings and impeccable instincts-in-a-crisis characterizes virtually all the speakers of Burns's poems, making them seem both vulnerable and heroic. We can never know to what degree these characters functioned for Burns either as wish-fulfillments or self-portraits. But we can trace how inexorably the masks that Burns assumed in his poems and songs have come to be seen as literal renditions of the personality of the man himself.

If the origin of the Burns myth can be traced back to the poems and letters themselves (and the literal-minded or fantasy-prone early biographers and critics who used that material to lay the foundation of his critical reputation), the path to a reading of Burns that looks beyond the myth seems more elusive. But perhaps the best way to dissipate these myths Burns himself promulgated is to go back to the poems and songs, examining them for the artistic methods by which Burns projects such luminous characters, ideals and abstractions out of folk fragments, dialect words, and local subject matter. Practically every poem Burns wrote reminds us (in its subject matter) of his social class and (in his vivid Scottish dialect) of his nation. Yet, as with Burns's personality, we may become so engrossed in our response to these myth-susceptible areas of country and class that we fail to see (in Burns's genial *breadth* of allusion) his equally striking poetic ambitions.

Burns, the balance of this essay will suggest, displaces and transfigures his emotions, his language(s), his literary traditions, and his local subject-matter. This process of displacement or distancing is both what makes Burns more than just a vivid describer of local scenes and why reading Burns too literally leads only to a partial (what I have been calling 'mythic') sense of his enterprise.

In some poems, Burns displaces by translating subject into object: he figuratively links the beauties of landscape with other 'beauties' that he praises: 'O my luve's like a red, red rose'. In others, Scottish points of reference are shown in harmony or dissonance with his speakers, to set (or to offset) their mood:

> Go fetch to me a pint o' wine,
>   And fill it in a silver tassie;   [silver goblet]
> That I may drink, before I go,
>   A service to my bonie lassie:
> The boat rocks at the Pier o' Leith,
> Fu' loud the wind blaws frae the Ferry,
> The ship rides by the Berwick-law,
>   And I maun leave my bony Mary.
>
> The trumpets sound, the banners fly,
>   The glittering spears are ranked ready,
> The shouts o' war are heard afar,
>   The battle closes deep and bloody.
> It's not the roar o' sea or shore,
>   Wad make me langer wish to tarry;
> Nor shouts o' war that's heard afar—
>   It's leaving thee, my bonie Mary!
>
>   'My bonie Mary'[6]

This song conveys a strong sense of placement through such local details as the setting at the port of Leith, the 'loud' wind blowing hard from Queensferry and the embarking boat rocking at the pier. Even the lovely specificity of 'silver tassie' strongly sets and 'places' the song in a pre-Union Scotland informed and permeated with the courtliness of its speaker. Yet in its unforced poignancy the song also conveys a strong sense of dis–placement and estrangement: this speaker is reluctant to be in this place, a point of departure both literally (from Leith) and emotionally (from Mary).

Scots place names and details work here to substantiate Burns's idealizing vision of his speaker and setting (as they do, less successfully, in an analogous song by Allan Ramsay, 'Lochaber No More'). Based, perhaps, on Ramsay's song and also on sensations Burns felt in 1786 when he was involved with Mary Campbell yet in such financial straits that he was forced to book passage for Jamaica, 'Silver Tassie' nonetheless displaces the literal biographical component. A luckless tenant farmer becomes, in Burns's lyric re–vision, a departing soldier; and the time-frame cannot be that of Burns himself. (In addition to the archaic connotations of 'tassie', soldiers did not carry spears in the eighteenth century.) We should not become so preoccupied with the appealing notion of a vivid, direct, dialect, 'peasant' Burns that we fail to acknowledge his self-conscious artistry in such graceful lyrics as 'Silver Tassie'.

No scholar has yet examined this displacement of sentiment into setting in Burns's poetry. Perhaps this is because the myth of Burns as hero of unpremeditated 'feeling' dictates that we see any self-conscious sentiment chiefly as a 'dreadful poison' in his poems, and Burns himself as a descriptive poet who transmitted images of Scotland just as he received them.' Such a view implicitly relies on the myth of a naive Burns, accepting the paradox that this great poet was nonetheless also somehow an unconscious artist, or at most an excellent mimic:

[Burns's] originality was that of his culture . . . At his best Burns dramatizes living and changing individuals who give voice to their feelings idiomatically, tangentially, casually, incoherently, as real people do.[8]

That recent judgement by David Sampson actually echoes George Gleig's approach in the first book-length critical study of Burns, published in 1812:

[Burns selected] all his subjects from low life as it actually presented itself to his own eyes, and [wrote] in the very language which is spoken by the heroes and heroines of his poems.'[9]

If these are accurate accounts of Burns 'at his best', then he is no poet. But the portrait is inaccurate. Many of Burns's most ambitious poems did fail to achieve their 'high' design; but to deduce from the pompous diction of 'The Cotter's Saturday Night' that Burns was incapable of executing any 'high' design is rather like concluding from a perusal of the opening stanzas of 'Goody Blake and Harry Gill' that Wordsworth could not manage rural character-studies.

As J C Weston rightly notes:

[Burns] often integrated English elements into his best Scots pieces . . . He turned the loose Scots tradition of the comic elegy into a true burlesque in 'Poor Mailie's elegy' because, we suspect, he learned about the kind of poetry from Dryden, Pope and Gay.[10]

Indeed, several critics have suggested the way out of myth by laying the groundwork for discussion of Burns's successful deployment of 'high' English diction to convey his transforming (not literal) 'view' of Scotland and Scottish subject-matter. Raymond Bentman, among the first to analyze the mixture of Scots with English elements in Burns's diction, notes that 'Burns wrote no poems in pure vernacular Scots'; although he also concludes that Burns's English usages are often 'tired' or 'insincere'.[11] Likewise, Thomas Crawford's comprehensive study of Burns's poems and songs begins, as it should, with Burns's eclecticism:

the Ayrshire peasantry were hardly strangers to abstract English diction . . . Burns . . . did not start off from an uncontaminated folk culture, shining and incorruptible in its original purity; he began with a mixture of Scots and English.'

Yet, like Bentman, Crawford qualifies his acknowledgement of the 'English' component:

'High English' was apparently reserved for such activities as theological discussion, business correspondence and the writing of certain kinds of love-letter; small wonder then that there clung to it some of that artificiality which always adheres to a polite language which is considerably removed from familiar speech.[12]

While this essay is not, then, unique in assuming that 'high' English diction is no 'alien' language for Burns and that he uses it well in many of his best poems and songs, it may differ from prior criticism in emphasizing that Burns's dynamic mixture of Scots dialect and 'high' English diction is in fact the major vehicle in his best verse that, by its generalizing force, 'transfigures' his images of Scotland, transforming as it transmits them.

Thus, at the center of the myth is a paradox. Far from writing artlessly, Burns consciously manipulates the 'high' strategies of English neoclassical and Anglo-Scottish sentimental diction to convey his idealizing (not descriptive) view of Scotland. As will be seen, Burns's neoclassical diction is often most successful when incorporated into the mock-heroic settings that set off his blend of 'high' and 'low': as in the epic ride of drunken Tam o'Shanter or the portrait of the Bard in *Love and Liberty*, with its high inversion of language ('So sung the BARD') and its invocation to the Muse:

> I never drank the Muses' STANK,   [pond]
>   Castalia's burn an' a' that,   [stream]
> But there it streams an' richly reams,
>   My HELICON I ca' that.
>
>   For a' that &c.

In such short lyrics as 'Silver Tassie', on the other hand, neoclassical diction often serves as an agent of simplicity rather than burlesque; it is a leaven broadening the expressive range of the fragmentary stanzas that often were Burns's sources.

Burns's selection of local detail is often so strongly linked to the emotional peripheries of his speakers' vision that landscape 'views' become transfigured—permeated with speaker-'viewpoints'. Sometimes, as in such middling songs as 'Bonie Bell', the speaker feels in joyful conjunction with the natural setting: the awakening landscape and the certainty of spring's return are linked to the equally certain constancy of his speaker: 'All Creatures joy in the sun's returning,/And I rejoice in my Bonie Bell'. More often, however—and in most of his great songs—speaker and setting are shown, as in 'Silver Tassie', to be in disjunction. This famous song by Burns is another good example:

> Ye banks and braes o' bonie Doon,
>   How can ye bloom sae fresh and fair;
> How can ye chant, ye little birds,
>   And I sae weary, fu' o' care!
> Thou'll break my heart, thou warbling bird,
>   That wantons thro' the flowering thorn:
> Thou minds me o' departed joys,
>   Departed, never to return.—

> Oft hae I rov'd by bonie Doon,
>   To see the rose and woodbine twine;
> And ilka bird sang o' its Luve,   [every]
>   And fondly sae did I o' mine.—
> Wi' lightsome heart I pu'd a rose,
>   Fu' sweet upon its thorny tree;
> And my fause Luver staw my rose,
>   But, ah! he left the thorn wi' me.—

'The Banks o' Doon' (B)

Burns's images of festive nature here contrast poignantly with the melancholy solitude of his eloquent speaker (female, like so many of Burns's most memorable). Heard with the tune, the version above, with its heightened language, is actually more effective as a song than the starker version written around the same time, which is eloquent on the page but less well-matched to its tune:

> Ye flowery banks o' bonie Doon,
>   How can ye blume sae fair;
> How can ye chant ye little birds,
>   And I sae fu' o' care!
>
> —
>
> Thou'll break my heart, thou bonie bird
>   That sings beside thy mate;
> For sae I sat, and sae I sang,
>   And wist na o' my fate.

'The Banks o' Doon' (A)

Both versions transfigure (i.e., describe but *displace*) a Scottish setting; the scene is joyous in every detail, but the song focuses on the speaker's inability to share the pleasures of the natural setting. She is thus displaced (set apart emotionally) from the blooming landscape Burns depicts. That disjunction between the lyric estrangement conveyed by abandoned girl and the lyric 'chanting' of the happily mated birds mirrors and accentuates the discord in her heart, the central focus of the song.

Burns transfigures not only setting but tradition, and in this revisionary use of images traditional in Scottish song (the thorn; the rose), he is much like other poets of the mid- and late-eighteenth century. Speaking of a similar transfiguration of 'borrowed' material in Gray's 'Eton College Ode' and 'Elegy', Leopold Damrosch has noted that '[the best poems of Gray] are built up with borrowed phrases and *topoi* because they reflect the gulf between the poet and his subject, between his feelings and the world to which his feelings are irrelevant.'[13] A similar use of conventional material to convey the poet's intimations of 'otherness' can be seen in songs like 'Silver Tassie' and 'Bonie Doon', where the conventions are—as in Gray—re-crafted in such a way that the tropes simultaneously suggest both integration (of the tradition) and displacement (of the speaker).

So Burns is not unique among mid and late eighteenth-century poets in his revisionary relationship to tradition or his effort to transfigure—to translate images from speaker into setting, setting into speaker. Several other recent studies have seen this complex interplay of private sentiment and traditional expression not only in Burns but in other post-Augustan authors. R D S Jack and Andrew Noble have compared Burns's quick-silver transformations of personae to the problematic protagonist in Diderot's *Rameau's Nephew*:

> To deal with Burns is not to deal with a provincial rustic. He demands of us as close attention as the fictional Rameau's nephew with his disconcerting remark that 'I am myself, and I remain myself, but I act and speak as occasion requires.' With Burns, however, we are not always certain even of this. Nor is it specious to compare him to a fictive, foreign character, for the whole difficulty about the late eighteenth century is that the lachrymose mists that shroud it stem from an inherent confusion of life and art throughout literary Europe.'

In an essay about Burns's letters in the same collection, K G Simpson brings that insight even closer to Burns's poetic dilemma (which is, I would say, that of poets in any century):

> Time and again ... one encounters [Burns's] keen sense of the disparity between man's version of experience and experience itself.[14]

Burns's attempts to achieve a creative synthesis of that 'disparity'—to transfigure setting and personae (particularly in his use of 'place' to exemplify mood)—are not always successful, of course. Yet his later songs have perhaps been too harshly criticized for their pursuit of this integration (or orchestrated disjunction) of place and mood. 'She says she lo'es me best of a'', written in 1794 by the infatuated Burns for flaxen-haired Jean Lorimer, is characteristic of Burns's later work in the speaker's effort not only to express his feelings but to align them with an idealized Scottish landscape. The dim and lovely nocturnal setting of this song, revealed in the concluding stanza, incorporates and serves as a retrospective frame for the speaker's earlier euphoric images of 'Chloris', whose beauty is likewise only partially revealed:

> Sae flaxen were her ringlets,
>   Her eyebrows of a darker hue,
> Bewitchingly o'erarching
>   Twa laughing een o' bonie blue,—
> Her smiling, sae wyling,
>   Wad make a wretch forget his woe;
> What pleasure, what treasure,
>   Unto those rosy lips to grow:
> Such was my Chloris' bonie face,
>   When first her bonie face I saw;
> And ay my Chloris' dearest charm,
>   She says, she lo'es me best of a'.—

> Like harmony her motion;
>   Her pretty ancle is a spy,
> Betraying fair proportion,
>   Wad make a saint forget the sky.—
> Sae warming, sae charming,
>   Her fauteless form and gracefu' air;
> Ilk feature—auld Nature
>   Declar'd that she could do nae mair:
> Hers are the willing chains o' love,
>   By conquering Beauty's sovereign law;
> And ay my Chloris' dearest charm,
>   She says, she lo'es me best of a'.—
>
> Let others love the city,
>   And gaudy shew at sunny noon;
> Gie me the lonely valley,
>   The dewy eve, and rising moon
> Fair beaming, and streaming
>   Her silver light the boughs amang;
> While falling, recalling,
>   The amorous thrush concludes his sang;
> There, dearest Chloris, wilt thou rove
>   By wimpling burn and leafy shaw,   [winding] [wood]
> And hear my vows o' truth and love,
>   And say, thou lo'es me best of a'.—

The song shows Burn's characteristic technique in his late (post-1788) lyrics. Its artistic risk lies in its emphasis on brief, conventional, intensified expression, conveyed through his generalizing and mostly 'English' diction. The song dares, yet I would say avoids, overstatement. There are less sympathetic critics, however. Here is one of Burns's liveliest commentators, writing in general on the diction of Burns's later songs:

> Sad it is again to think that the author of this purest gold [such songs as 'Ae Fond Kiss' and 'The Lea-Rig'] could content himself with such tinsel . . . the endless wearisome catalogues of his later poems—lambs and laverocks, primrose and hawthorn, violet and woodbine, Cynthias and zephyrs, all wimpling and warbling and languishing and anguishing to despair.[15]

Hilton Brown is entertaining, but he isn't quite fair. Burns's later songs—'She says she lo'es me' is, I think, a representative example—do not commit any sin of taste in attempting to puff up folk settings by introducing an 'alien' classicizing diction (the usual criticism). Rather, Burns uses his classicizing diction to displace or transfigure his feelings, to render them as a poet does—indirectly. (Even Wordsworth, with his emphasis on immediacy of diction, knew that such immediacy was a *poetic* device.)

In 'She says she lo'es me,' classical 'Chloris' displaces Scottish 'Jean', and elevated diction alternates with Scots dialect (mostly such cognates as 'amang'). The tryst setting of the last stanza is, of course, as hallowed in folksong as in neoclassical lyric. But the real question posed by this song is not whether its language works. It is whether, despite Burns's use of generalizing language to put the emotion in perspective, the song really manages sufficiently to displace (evoke, not merely tell) Burns's strong feelings for Jean, which the song reveals (perhaps too forthrightly) to be more lustful than lyrical. It is only when the song is heard set to its perfectly-matched melody that an answer can be given. When heard performed to its music, as all Burns's songs (particularly late songs) should be, every one of Burns's diction choices emerges as judicious—even (and I am aware of the extent of my heresy here) 'wimpling burn'. The dramatic, almost breathless urgency of this splendid air simply requires the hightened ardor of Burns's diction: the melody not only accommodates but projects and amplifies the urgency of Burns's lyrics. Indeed, the air also heightens a dimension of ambiguity in the lyrics. The melody, like the metre, stresses 'says' in the refrain, sustaining Burns's half-echo of ambivalence in his stanzas. Does 'Chloris' mean what she says?

Burns was, incidentally, most receptive to the evocative possibilities of the folk-music he adapted. His late letters are full of references to songs' emotional dimensions; their 'querulousness', liveliness, or poignancy. Also incidentally, despite its rather high-flown tone, this is a song in which Burns reveals his farmer-knowledge: unlike city-dweller Keats, whose nightingale is a 'dryad', Burns knew that birdsong was male, territorial, and 'amorous'.

It is not only in Burns's songs that 'Scots' points of reference (setting, melody, language) are transfigured—are made the basis for that broad exemplification of his subjects' or his speakers' moods that makes them so portable as myths. In the poems, as in the songs, 'Scotland' and setting are evoked less as places than as joyous or disquieted states of mind. 'The Holy Fair' is usually seen as straightforward and descriptive (Hilton Brown calls it 'excellent as a descriptive piece, [but] surely too crude for successful satire').[16] Yet actually it is a poem in Burns's mock-heroic mode of transfiguration, opening with stanzas that are clearly burlesques of the neoclassical in their use of personification and provision of a genial ironic 'frame' for the poem. The Mauchline communion gathering is indeed described with what Thomas Crawford calls 'a realistic treatment', but by a detached speaker who accompanies 'Fun' to church just for the lark:

I

Upon a simmer *Sunday morn*,
    When Nature's face is fair,
I walked forth to view the corn,
    An' snuff the caller air: [fresh]
The rising sun, owre GALSTON muirs,   [moors]
    Wi' glorious light was glintan;
The hares were hirplan down the furrs,   [hobbling] [ditches]
    The lav'rocks they were chantan   [larks]
        Fu' sweet that day.

II

As lightsomely I glowr'd abroad,
  To see a scene sae gay,
Three *hizzies*, early at the road,
  Cam skelpan up the way.   [hurrying]
Twa had manteeles o' dolefu' black,
  But ane wi' lyart lining;   [gray]
The *third*, that gaed a wee aback,
  Was in the fashion shining
    Fu' gay that day.

— — — — — — — — — — — — — — — — — — —

IV

Wi' bonnet aff, quoth I, 'Sweet lass,
  'I think ye seem to ken me;
'I'm sure I've seen that bonie face,
  'But yet I canna name ye.—'
Quo' she, an' laughan as she spak,
  An' taks me by the hands,
'Ye, for my sake, hae gien the feck   [majority]
  'Of a' the *ten commands*
    A screed some day.   [tear]

V

'My name is FUN—your cronie dear,
  'The nearest friend ye hae;
'An this is SUPERSTITION here,
  'An' that's HYPOCRISY:
'I'm gaun to ********* *holy fair*,
  'To spend an hour in daffin;   [fooling]
'Gin ye'll go there, yon runkl'd pair, [wrinkled]
  'We will get famous laughin
    At them this day.'

In the first stanza, the festive Scottish high-summer setting is sketched; in later stanzas this setting is shrewdly aligned with the equally exuberant and 'ripe' communicants:

X

Here, some are thinkan on their sins,
  An' some upon their claes;
Ane curses feet that fyl'd his shins,   [fouled]
  Anither sighs an' pray's:
On this hand sits a Chosen swatch,   [sample]
  Wi' screw'd-up, grace-prood faces;
On that, a set o' chaps, at watch,
  Thrang winkan on the lasses   [crowding]
    To *chairs* that day.

XI

> O happy is that man, an' blest!
>   Nae wonder that it pride him!
> Whase ain dear lass, that he likes best,
>   Comes clinkan down beside him!   [sit down smartly]
> Wi' arm repos'd on the *chair back*,
>   He sweetly does compose him;
> Which, by degrees, slips round her *neck*,
>   An's loof upon her *bosom*   [palm]
>   Unkend that day.   [unnoticed]

Like so many of Burns's poems, 'The Holy Fair' evokes a mood of joyous expectancy by juxtaposing the first stanza's ripening grain and rising sun—the near-fruition of August setting and rural landscape—with the mid-poem portrait of the high glee of the young lovers. Burns's speaker thus exploits the first stanza's intonation of natural abundance in his later description of the exuberant 'fairgoers'. Vitality is the dominant mood conveyed by the poem, which may be why it has always been seen primarily as 'descriptive'.

Yet a reading attuned to Augustan strategies of generalization reveals many neoclassical intonations that transfigure the rural setting and characters, displacing them from their own cultural context into Burns's ironic 'classical' frame. Though Burns uses the traditional Scots metre (and festive subject-matter) of *Chrystis Kirk on the Green*, he is nonetheless mock-heroic and Augustan in the distance he asserts from the customs he describes. (He also exploits for ironic purposes the 'distance' between the pretext for the 'fair'—divine worship—and the real purpose it serves in the community—a rare chance for the rural poor to gather, socialize and court.) The speaker's ironic perspective includes (as James Kinsley has noted) outright parody of the communion service itself (the first line of the final stanza above quotes the first line in the metrical version of Psalm cxlvi, but exemplifies 'happiness' in the terms of a downright earthly Paradise).[17]

Mock-heroic design is also evident in Burns's employment of such Augustan satiric tropes as syllepsis ('some are thinkan on their sins,/An' some upo' their claes'). Since Burns's best vernacular predecessor, Robert Fergusson, was also addicted to syllepsis as the instrument of neoclassical 'point', there may or may not be direct influence from Alexander Pope (Burns's other favorite source for mock-heroic strategies). Perhaps there is some echo of Canto V of 'The Rape of the Lock':

> But since, alas! frail Beauty must decay,
> Curl'd or uncurl'd, since Locks will turn to grey,
> Since painted, or not painted, all shall fade,
> And she who scorns a Man, must die a Maid;
> What then remains, but well our Pow'r to use,
> And keep good Humour still whate'er we lose?
>   ('Clarissa' speaking, 11s. 25–30)

For a similar warning against prudery informs stanza XXV:

> O *Wives* be mindfu', ance yoursel,
> How bonie lads ye wanted,
> An' dinna, for a *kebbuck-heel*,   [cheese rind]
> Let lasses be affronted
> On sic a day!

The blithe spring of 'Ye banks and braes' and the festive high summer of 'The Holy Fair' are not the only face of Scotland Burns portrays, of course. Many of Burns's poems are set in the long Scottish winter (and not always his grim poems: 'Boreas' is raging outside while the beggars carouse at Poosie Nansie's in 'Love and Liberty'). Whatever the setting, Burns's Scottish landscapes, like Burns's Scottish characters, express vitality, endurance, survival against bleak odds; fleeting 'springs' of renewal versus long winters of 'innerness' (whether drinking in the refuge of taverns or meditating in response to the season):

> Cauld is the e'enin blast
> O' Boreas o'er the pool.
> And dawin it is dreary,   [dawn]
> When birks are bare at Yule   [birches]
>
> O cauld blaws the e'enin blast
> When bitter bites the frost,
> And in the mirk and dreary drift   [darkness]
> The hills and glens are lost.
>
> 'Cauld is the e'enin blast'

In 'Notes toward a Supreme Fiction,' Wallace Stevens wrote: 'From this the poem springs: That we live in a place/That is not our own and, much more, not ourselves.'[18] This suggests a central issue about Burns and Scotland—about this poet and his 'place'. Stevens's modern assumption that poems spring from the poet's estranged effort to remake coherent meaning through deployment of different levels of language is quite applicable to Burns; though to accept that assumption is to give Burns credit for a level of coherence that posterity has preferred to deny him. But once it be acknowledged that Burns's method is not descriptive (in any simple sense) and that his methods are those of other conscious artists, the cult of personality dissipates and it becomes possible to perceive and value Burns's brilliant transfiguration (not transcription) of folk tradition. It becomes possible to grant Robert Burns what we grant other poets: the assumption that his poems spring out of a relationship not with one particular place but with the world—insofar as a world can be evoked in language. The simple truth is that Burns, no less than his countrymen Henryson or Dunbar, is a Makar, a creator. His goal is to discover (recover) meaning, not to describe simple scenes. His mode is *poesis*, not *mimesis*. Beyond the hero and the victim, in short, was the creative power that summoned and shaped those images.

We have been long in granting this premise because the myth of the 'heaven-taught' ploughman dies hard. Even those who have perceived Burns's sophisticated synthesis of particular and general, 'high' and 'low', English and Scots, in his work have tended to see his eclecticism as a contamination; those fictions Burns creates, they say, are falsehoods. (Andrew Noble links this hostility to 'English' influence on Burns to general Scottish anger at the 'debilitating effects of things English on Scotland.')[19] Yet it is time we acknowledged the protean quality in Burns, for it is his most remarkable poetic trait. No other eighteenth-century vernacular poet managed Burns's seamless synthesis of a variety of traditions (English and Scots, folk and bardic, Augustan and sentimental). Nor did such English contemporaries as Gray, Collins, and Cowper manage the taxing contemporary balancing act of traditions and influences with a better *frequency* of success: in the context of this 'anxious' (in Harold Bloom's sense) literary era, during which most poets experienced slim returns for a lifetime of work, Robert Burns's ratio of successful poetry is remarkable. Like most eighteenth-century poets and also like Shakespeare (that last comparison is often, and justly, made), Burns seldom originated his themes, sentiments or verse-forms. He worked instead, as poets do, to incorporate all he knew of the literary past. But he transfigures inherited conventions by choosing to transmit them in his heterodoxical, radically 'mixed', language.

Using his poet's ability to see through to the heart of a sentiment—or to 'read' intuitively the expressive potential of an old Scots air and then embody it in the best possible language—Burns was just the man to make silk purses out of other poets' sow's ears. These are the famous concluding stanzas for Burns's 'Auld lang syne':

> We twa hae run about the braes,
>   And pou'd the gowans fine;   [daisies]
> But we've wander'd mony a weary fitt,
>   Sin auld lang syne.
>   For auld, &c.
>
> We twa hae paidl'd in the burn,
>   Frae morning sun till dine;
> But seas between us braid hae roar'd,   [broad]
>   Sin auld lang syne.
>   For auld, &c.
>
> And there's a hand, my trusty fiere!   [comrade]
>   And gie's a hand o' thine!
> And we'll tak a right gude-willie-waught,   [cordial drink]
>   For auld lang syne.
>   For auld &c.

Here, by contrast, is the opening stanza of the best-known early eighteenth-century version:

> Should auld Acquaintance be forgot,
> Tho they return with scars?
> These are the noble Heroe's Lot,
> Obtain'd in glorious Wars:
> Welcome my *Varo* to my Breast,
> Thy Arms about me twine,
> And make me once again as blest,
> As I was lang syne.
>
> Allan Ramsay 'The Kind Reception'

The fervent emotions that Allan Ramsay labours to express, Burns conveys with ease. Ramsay's pompous fine lady welcomes back her *Varo* with polite but frigid tranquillity. Burns (apparently) took his first line from Ramsay's version, but then added the world's favourite stanzas of reminiscence and farewell. Burns's dialect, while strongly Scots in flavour, does not present emotional boundaries, even if every word's meaning is not caught by the non-Scot. As David Copperfield describes one of his leave-takings of the Micawbers:

> ... we sang 'Auld Lang Syne'. When we came to 'Here's a hand, my trusty fiere', we all joined hands round the table; and when we declared we would 'take a right gude willie-waught', and hadn't the least idea what it meant, we were really affected. (Chapter 17)

Such songs as 'Auld lang syne' show that it is not only 'high' English diction that serves the purposes of displacement or transfiguration in Burns's works. For many in Burns's audience (including the Micawbers) the 'strangeness' of the dialect diction serves the same distancing purpose as the neoclassical elevation in other works. As Leopold Damrosch notes:

> [Burns uses] a language to which we respond in a special way because of its very strangeness ... By merging himself with folk tradition, Burns is able to be personal and impersonal at once. (645)

David Daiches has noted in several landmark studies that the passing of national autonomy inspired a diverse range of eighteenth-century reactions, from efforts by Scots writers to extirpate all 'Scotticisms' (the path of David Hume and of those legions of anonymous eighteenth-century Scots who took 'English' elocution lessons) to rebellion against English cultural hegemony (seen in the cult of 'Ossian', the rise of the sentimental literati in Edinburgh, and in the brilliant vernacular Scots poems [and burlesque English satires] of Robert Fergusson).

Burns's reaction, which is patterned after Allan Ramsay's and which has been widely misunderstood from his own day to ours, was to incorporate English with Scots. 'Elevated' English ensures breadth of allusion; the Scots, as Damrosch notes above, ensures a vivid diction that (for the English among Burns's readers) works to make the familiar strange. Yet (and this is also true of Ramsay) Burns's permeability to English is best seen not as assimilation but as a form of rebellion. For while, like Ramsay, Fergusson and the other eighteenth-century vernacular poets, Burns felt proud enough of Scotland's continuing cultural difference to embody that difference even in his choice of words and subject matter, his enterprise was never, in intent or in effect, primarily descriptive, local, or parodic. Burns, unlike Fergusson, does not describe Scotland in order to present it in direct competition with England. More like Ramsay in method (though Ramsay lacked the creative power to execute his designs), Burns actually disintegrates English as he uses it by re-embodying it in his Scottish mold. The selective Scottish details actually distract attention from the armature of English that (invisibly, in virtually all Burns's best work) upholds the genial and expansive tone and mood. Being of Scotland but often in English, Burns's best work (quite unlike that of Fergusson, who really was the brilliant, pure 'describer' that Burns is often said to be) transcends specific placement at the same time that it seems quite 'real'. Thus, Burns uses but transforms his many 'influences'; thus, as Damrosch says, Burns manages the poet's trick of seeming 'personal and impersonal at once' (646).

What we find when we put the myths to one side and explore the writings is Burns's self-conscious transfiguration of all his cultural and literary influences (English and Scots) in an effort to evoke 'Scottish' subject matter as truly universal, not local. This is the reverse of assimilation: a re-casting of English elements to wear a Scottish face. By blending English with Scots, Burns often re-animates sentimental and neoclassical English traditions, for his addition of vivid dialect language often enlivens a tradition of petrified wood (as in Ramsay's overly Anglicized version of 'Auld Kyndnes Forʒett'); and by adding English 'elevated' diction to poems of local subject matter, Burns assures, even for his most 'Scottish' efforts, a buoyant allusiveness that excludes no reader:

> But mark the Rustic, *haggis-fed*,
> The trembling earth resounds his tread,
> Clap in his walie nieve a blade,   [ample fist]
>   He mak it whissle;
> An' legs, an' arms, an' heads will sned,   [prune]
>   Like taps o' thrissle.   [tops of thistle]
>   'To a Haggis'

In a recent study, David Daiches follows a tradition established by eighteenth century critics when he—one of Burns's most sympathetic modern critics—nonetheless ascribes Burns's occasional adoption of an 'elevated' neoclassical pose simply to shrewd public relations:

> Fergusson would never have talked of his 'rustic lyre' as Burns did. Burns's pose as an unlettered rustic taught only Nature, the 'Heaven-taught plough-man' hailed by Henry Mackenzie, was deliberately assumed to enable him to be accepted by the arbiters of taste in Edinburgh . . . as a species of natural man who could confront the genteel tradition as a privileged outsider.[20]

While Daiches is clearly correct about Burns's co-operation with the myth in his management of his public persona (what Burns himself called in typically mock-heroic terms the 'machinery . . . of his poetic character' [Kinsley, III, 1537]) such formulas tend to prevent criticism from acknowledging the serious function served by the combination in his work of 'high' with 'low', neoclassical with folk diction. Burns did write, presumably to please the literati, a genteel and empty address to '*Edina! Scotia's* darling seat'; but he also used neoclassical diction in dialect poems where such high-flown tropes as apostrophe and periphrasis successfully broaden his tone: as in 'To a Haggis', quoted above, where the steaming sheeps' stomach is hailed with mock-heroic fervor as 'Great Chieftan o' the Puddin race'; or in 'The Author's Earnest Cry and Prayer, to . . . the Scotch Representatives in the House of Commons', whose title is disrespectfully lifted from its Old Testament point of origin and which offers, in its objection to English laws repressing the Scottish liquor industry, yet another of Burns's mock-heroic portraits of his 'Muse':

> Alas! my roupet *Muse* is haerse!   [husky] [hoarse]
> Your Honors' hearts wi' grief 'twad pierce,
> To see her sittan on her arse,
>   Low i' the dust,
> An' scriechan out prosaic verse,
>   An' like to brust!

Burns's use of 'high' language is almost always successful when deployed mock-heroically, when he casts his homely Scots details into a grandiose 'frame' and invites the reader to share his ironic (in this case, sardonic) pleasure in the disjunction.

In his songs, on the other hand—even those of a jocular nature—Burns generally uses a simpler diction, which is also, however, a varying and carefully controlled mixture of English and Scots:

> Duncan fleech'd, and Duncan pray'd;   [flattered]
>   Ha, ha, the wooing o't.
> Meg was deaf as Ailsa craig,
>   Ha, ha, the wooing o't.
> Duncan sigh'd baith out and in,
> Grat his een baith bleer't an' blin',   [cried]
> Spak o' lowpin o'er a linn;   [cataract]
>   Ha, ha, the wooing o't.
>
> Time and Chance are but a tide,
>   Ha, ha, the wooing o't.
> Slighted love is sair to bide,
>   Ha, ha, the wooing o't.
> Shall I, like a fool, quoth he,
> For a haughty hizzie die?
> She may gae to——France for me!
>   Ha, ha, the wooing o't.

Burns's Duncan Gray (this is his second version, written in 1792—the better-known version was written in 1788) is shorn in both versions of the bawdy specificity traditional for him in folksong, but he keeps (despite generalizing allusions to Time and Chance) all his traditional comic ardor. Burns's jollity is a response to the music here; as he wrote to his editor George Thomson, 'Duncan Gray is that kind of light-horse gallop of an air, which precludes sentiment' (Kinsley, III, 1415).

Ralph Waldo Emerson seemed to take note of Burns's eclectic achievement—and to point the way out of myth—in 1859, when he stressed the power, specifically, of his *language*: '[Burns's is] the only example in history of a language made classic by the genius of a single man' (Low, p 435). This genius who brought 'Scotland' to the world at large is no merely local hero: his vision began at home, but carried 'home' into universal territory. Burns's 'Scotland' seems classic, coherent, and mythic to us precisely because he fashioned it out of diverse and classic literary elements, both traditionally Scottish and English. Like other eighteenth-century vernacular writers, Burns aligned himself with Scotland's continuing cultural difference by emphasizing it even in his vocabulary. But Robert Burns, unlike Robert Fergusson, his only real peer among eighteenth-century vernacular writers, chose dialect not only to assert the substantiality and validity of his Scottish world but also to disseminate it abroad: not so much to reflect Scotland as to evoke it. It was no naive farmer or helpless victim of ungovernable energies who managed this splendid and notably coherent achievement.

When Burns chose to blend English with Scottish dialect in his poems and songs, he was not employing a traditional language. Except for the continuing traditions of bawdry and comic elegy, Scots had died out as a literary language by the Union of 1707—a casualty of the desertion of Edinburgh by James VI's and I's court and the repression of poetry and secular song by the Scottish church throughout the seventeenth century. All vernacular poetry in Burns's century was self-consciously crafted, and in deciding the appropriate ratio of Scots to English in every poem he wrote, Burns was making a self-conscious choice. If the marvelous blend in his language of real and ideal, scene-setting and scene-transfiguration, cooperated in the almost immediate foundation of myths, let us at least acknowledge that the myths did not exist before the *words* did. Burns's enterprise is not unparalleled (Ramsay, Fergusson, and many lesser eighteenth-century vernacular poets preceded him), but Burns is unparalleled in the broad success of his Scots/English mixture, which conveys vivid images of Scotland even to those who will never 'see' any Scotland but the poetic re–vision Burns renders in his burlesque or idealized landscapes.

Nonetheless, the notion persists that this distinctive synthesis in Burns's best work of dialect Scots, anglo-Scottish sentiment, and neoclassical English somehow makes him a *poseur*, rather than an ironist or an artist. Perhaps it is a tribute to the vigour of Burns's projected and self-consciously synthesized 'views' of Scotland and the Scots that the closer scrutiny which dissipates the myth and reveals Burns's art disappoints us. We want him to be a camera, not a poet; we want his 'Scotland' to be real.

NOTES

1   *See* Alan Bold, 'Robert Burns, Superscot', in *The Art of Robert Burns*, R D S Jack and Andrew Noble (eds) (London, 1982), pp 215–38.

2   Dorothy Wordsworth, *Tour in Scotland: AD 1805*, J S Shairp (ed) (Edinburgh, 1894), p 7.

3   Quoted in Donald A Low (ed), *Robert Burns: The Critical Heritage* (London, 1974), p 327.

4   Raymond Bentman, 'Robert Burns's Declining Fame', in *Studies in Romanticism*, 2, no 3 (Summer 1972), pp 207–24.

5   Jane Austen, *Sanditon* in *The Minor Works of Jane Austen*, R W Chapman (ed) (London, 1963), p 397–8. Also excerpted in Low, *The Critical Heritage*.

6   Robert Burns, *The Poems and Songs of Robert Burns*, James Kinsley (ed) 3 vols (Oxford, 1968), I, 445–6. All subsequent quotations are from this edition.

7   The reference to 'dreadful poison' occurs in J C Weston, 'Robert Burns's Satire', in *The Art of Robert Burns*, op. cit., p 55.

8   David Sampson, 'Robert Burns: The Revival of Scottish Literature?' in *The Modern Language Review*, 80, Part 1, (January, 1985), p 33.

9   [G Gleig], from *A Critique on the Poems of Robert Burns* (Edinburgh, 1812). Excerpted in *Robert Burns: The Critical Heritage*, op. cit, p 252.

10 J C Weston, in Introduction to *Robert Burns: Selections*, J C Weston (ed) (Indianapolis, 1967), xxv.

11 Raymond Bentman, 'Robert Burns's Use of Scottish Diction', in *From Sensibility to Romanticism: Essays Presented to Frederick A Pottle*, Frederick W Hilles and Harold Bloom (eds) (London, 1965), p 239. For the reference to 'tired' or 'insincere' English usages *see* his Introduction to Robert Burns, *The Poetical Works of Burns* (Boston, Mass., 1974), p xxvi.

12 Thomas Crawford, *Burns: A Study of the Poems and Songs* (Stanford, 1960), p 3.

13 Leopold Damrosch, 'Burns, Blake, and the Recovery of Lyric', *Studies in Romanticism*, 21 (Winter 1982), p 641.

14 The first quotation is from the Introduction by R D S Jack and Andrew Noble in *The Art of Robert Burns*, op. cit., p 10. The second, from the same volume, is by K G Simpson, 'The Sin of Wit: Sterne and Burns's Letters', p 159.

15 Hilton Brown, *There was a Lad: An Essay on Robert Burns* (London, 1949), p 197.

16 Ibid. p 203.

17 Kinsley, III, 1099.

18 Wallace Stevens, *The Collected Poems of Wallace Stevens* (New York, 1971), p 383.

19 Andrew Noble, 'Burns, Blake and Romantic Revolt', in *The Art of Robert Burns*, op. cit., p 191.

20 David Daiches, *Literature and Gentility in Scotland: The Alexander Lectures at the University of Toronto, 1980* (Edinburgh, 1982), p 59. On p 55, however, Daiches rightly notices the complex mixture in Burns's language: 'The problem of expressing the personality as a whole in Scottish poetry was endemic in the eighteenth century. Those who solved it—Robert Fergusson up to a point, and Robert Burns—did so by balancing Scots and English in a way that combined spontaneity and formality.'

All glosses are based on the glossary in Kinsley's edition of the poems and songs.

FURTHER READING

TEXTS

Burns, Robert, *The Letters of Robert Burns*, J De Lancey Ferguson and G Ross Roy (eds), 2nd edn, 2 vols (Oxford, 1985)
—— *The Poems and Songs of Robert Burns*, James Kinsley (ed), 3 vols (Oxford, 1968)

RECORDINGS

—— *Songs of Robert Burns.* Sung by Ewan McColl. (New York: Folkways [FW8758], 1959)
—— *The Songs of Robert Burns*. Sung by Jean Redpath; arrangements by Serge Hovey. (Vermont: Philo, 1976—). This ongoing series does full justice to the breadth of Burns's lyric output, including his later songs.
There are dozens of good recordings of Burns's songs. McColl and Redpath are suggested because their differing approaches suggest the range of interpretative possibilities afforded by Burns's songs.

CRITICISM

Bentman, Raymond, 'Robert Burns's Declining Fame', *Studies in Romanticism*, 2, no 3 (Summer 1972), pp 207–24
—— 'Robert Burns's Use of Scottish Diction'. *From Sensibility to Romanticism: Essays Presented to Frederick A Pottle*. Frederick W Hilles and Harold Bloom (eds). (London, Oxford, 1965)
Brown, Mary Ellen, *Burns and Tradition* (Illinois, 1984)
Crawford, Thomas, *Burns: A Study of the Poems and Songs* (Stanford, 1960)
—— *Society and the Lyric: A Study of the Song Culture of Eighteenth Century Scotland* (Edinburgh, 1979)
Daiches, David, *Literature and Gentility: The Alexander Lectures at the University of Toronto, 1980* (Edinburgh, 1982)
—— *Robert Burns* (New York, 1950)
Damrosch, Leopold, 'Burns, Blake, and the Recovery of Lyric'. *Studies in Romanticism*, 21 (Winter 1982)
Ferguson, J DeLancey, *Pride and Passion: Robert Burns* (New York, 1939)
Jack, R D S and Andrew Noble, *The Art of Robert Burns* (London, 1982)
Low, Donald A (ed) *Robert Burns: The Critical Heritage* (London, 1974)
—— *Robert Burns: Critical Essays* (London, 1975)
McGuirk, Carol, *Robert Burns and the Sentimental Era* (Georgia, 1985)
Sampson, David, 'Robert Burns: The Revival of Scottish Literature?' *The Modern Language Review*, 80, Part 1 (January, 1985), pp 17–39

Chapter 14

Aesthetic Philosophy: Hutcheson and Hume to Alison

IAN ROSS

Beauty as a subject for philosophic discourse is not usually associated with the work of the men of letters of eighteenth-century Scotland, the *literati* as they liked to call themselves. Thus, Voltaire pretended to be surprised at the appearance of Lord Kames's *Elements of Criticism* (1762):

> It is a wonderful result of the progress of human culture, that at this day there come to us from Scotland rules of taste in all the arts, from epic poetry to gardening. Every day the mind of man expands, and we ought not to despair of receiving ere long treatises on poetry and rhetoric from the Orkney isles. True it is, that in this country we still prefer to see great artists than great discourses upon the arts.[1]

A little investigation brings out, however, that during the century of the poets Thomson, Ramsay, Fergusson, 'Ossian' Macpherson, and Burns; the dramatist Home; the novelists Smollett and Mackenzie; the painters Allan Ramsay, Runciman, and Raeburn; the composer Lord Kelly; and the architects of the Adam family; there was much energetic discussion in Scotland of the nature of beuaty, absolute and relative, and how to delinate and evaluate philosphically its manifestation in human behaviour, artistic productions, and nature. To be sure, a starting point must be found outside Scotland for the discourse conducted there on aesthetics, a term introduced by Alexander Gottlieb Baumgarten in 1748 to describe the branch of empirical psychology dealing with the 'faculty of sensible knowledge', and later restricted to the beautiful and sublime. The inspiration for the Scottish contribution in this field was the thought of Francis Hutcheson, a Presbyterian minister from Ulster who was educated at Glasgow University, 1711–17, and brought to Dublin about 1720 to teach in an academy for the sons of dissenters. Hutcheson was drawn into a circle of intellectuals round Robert Molesworth, a wealthy merchant whose successful government service had been rewarded by an Irish peerage, and who led the 'Old Whigs' in the Irish Parliament. He had been the friend of John Locke and the third Earl of Shaftesbury, enjoying particular intimacy with the latter. Lord Molesworth actively promoted among his circle Shaftesbury's philosophy of benevolence. One result was the appearance in London in 1725 of a book by Hutcheson, said to be the first ever published in the British Isles which dealt with aesthetics: *An Inquiry into the Original of our Ideas of Beauty and Virtue; In Two Treatises. In Which the Principles of the*

239

late Earl of Shaftesbury are explain'd and defended, against the Author of the Fable of the Bees: And the Ideas of Moral Good and Evil are establish'd according to the Sentiments of the antient Moralists, With an Attempt to introduce a Mathematical Calculation in Subjects of Morality. This book attracted a good deal of attention and replies to Hutcheson, who sought to counter the arguments of Thomas Hobbes (*Leviathan*, 1650) and Bernard Mandeville (*The Fable of the Bees*, 1714), to the effect that human nature was basically selfish. The resulting philosophical reputation, together with Hutcheson's distinction as a classical scholar and earlier connection with Glasgow, secured his election to the Chair of Moral Philosophy in his alma mater, a post he held from 1730 until his death in Dublin in 1746. His highly successful teaching in Glasgow, and his further publications, made him the father of the Scottish Enlightenment.[2] It must be acknowledged that he exerted considerable influence with respect to aesthetics and moral science on Hume, who corresponded with him; on Adam Smith who was his pupil; and on Thomas Reid, whose early theorizing about perception was stimulated by reading the *Inquiry* of 1725. Lord Kames also responded to Hutcheson's theories concerning beauty, and Archibald Alison, the last major Scottish aesthetician of the eighteenth century, specifically linked his work to that of Shaftesbury, Hutcheson, and Reid. Hutcheson's teaching may have found all the readier an acceptance in Scotland because the philosophy of Shaftesbury was being discussed there sympathetically, for example, at Aberdeen and Edinburgh in the 1720s.[3]

In their earlier form, the aesthetic doctrines of the 'never to be forgotten' Hutcheson, as Smith called him, seem to be derived in part from a favourite classical source, the *De Officiis* of Cicero, which asserts that morality is beautiful; from the psychology of Locke (*An Essay concerning Human Understanding*, 1690); and from the benevolism and pleasure-principle philosophy, or hedonism of Shaftesbury; also the *Spectator* papers by Addison on the 'Pleasures of the Imagination' (Nos. 411–21). As distinct from reason, Hutcheson posits an internal sense of beauty and an analogous moral sense, which he represents as '*Determinations to be pleas'd with any Forms or Ideas which occur to our Observation*'. Unwilled pleasure, in this connection, is occasioned by a 'regular Form, *a piece of* Architecture, *or* Painting, *a Composition of* Notes, *a* Theorem, *an Action, an* Affection, *a* Character'. The internal sense of beauty responds to the 'Regularity, Order, Harmony' in objects contemplated, whereas the moral sense is activated by the 'Affections, Actions, *or* Characters *of* rational Agents *which we call virtuous*.' Hutcheson adds, further, a theistic component to link aesthetics to morals, bringing in an 'Author of Nature' who '*has made* Virtue *a lovely Form, to excite our pursuit of it; and has given us* strong Affections *to be the Springs of each virtuous Action*' (Preface to the *Inquiry*).

Hutcheson opens the first treatise of the *Inquiry*, itself 'An Inquiry concerning Beauty, Order, Harmony, Design', with a move offered by Locke. When our bodies are acted upon by external objects, this analysis suggests, our passive minds have raised in them simple ideas which are called *sensations*. The mind is active, however, in producing complex ideas by compounding the simple ideas. In addition, our sensitive perceptions are very often accompanied by pleasure or pain, immediately felt, but of varing intensities, without any knowledge of the cause of this pleasure or pain (I.i.5). On his way to formulating a theory of beauty using this Lockian model of the mind, Hutcheson has to face the problem of variation of aesthetic response to combinations of the primary qualities which Locke said inhered in objects, size and figure, for example, and the secondary qualities to which powers in objects give rise in the mind, such as colour and smell and warmth. In this regard, Hutcheson mentions 'Diversity of Fancy' about 'Gardening, Architecture, and Dress' (4th edn 1738: I.i.7). His answer is that colours and fashions in dress in themselves are not disagreeable, but may become so through association with levity of behaviour or low rank or unpleasant occupation. In gardening and architecture, local tradition and fashion can overwhelm or distort whatever generally gives abiding pleasure. In this way, Hutcheson seeks to assert it would be a contradiction to claim that the same simple idea could occasion pain in one person and pleasure in aother. Further, Hutcheson claims that there are 'vastly greater Pleasures in those complex Ideas of Objects, which obtain the Names of Beautiful, Regular, Harmonious'. As one instance, Hutcheson mentions that 'in Musick, the Pleasure of fine Composition is incomparably greater than that of any one Note, how sweet, full, or swelling soever' (I.i.8).

Having cleared these preliminary points, Hutcheson can now state that, in his analysis, the 'word, Beauty is taken for the Idea raised in us, and a Sense of Beauty for our Power of receiving this Idea.' His intention is 'to discover what is the immediate Occasion of these pleasant Ideas, or what real Quality in the Objects ordinarily excites them' (I.i.9). Such discovery is sought by dealing first with 'absolute or original Beauty', and then with 'comparative or relative Beauty'. Both kinds of beauty are mind-dependent, but the first is perceived in objects 'without comparison to anything external, of which the object is suppos'd an Imitation, or Picture, such as that Beauty perceiv'd from the Works of Nature, artificial Forms, Figures, Theorems,' whereas the second kind of beauty is 'that which we perceive in Objects commonly considered as Imitations or Resemblances of something else' (I.i.17). In a brief consideration of original beauty, Hutcheson finds a 'general Foundation' revealed by examining regular figures: those which 'exite in us the Ideas of Beauty seem to be those in which there is *Uniformity amidst Variety*' (I.ii.3). As for relative or comparative beauty, Hutcheson recognises here more complex aesthetic problems. He takes his stand on a theory of imitation: 'All *Beauty* is *relative* to the Sense of some Mind perceiving it; but what we call *relative* is that which is apprehended in any *Object*, commonly consider'd as an *Imitation* of some Original: And this *Beauty is founded on a Conformity*, or a kind of *Unity* between the Original and the Copy (I.iv.1). As Hutcheson sees matters, the imitation may be of some object in nature, or of an established idea. Hutcheson also points out that the imitation of an object may be beautiful, though the original is devoid of beauty. Thus the deformities of age and the rudest rocks in a landscape if depicted well are acknowledged as beautiful. Similarly, in epic and dramatic poetry the imperfect characters who exhibit the inner struggles we experience, according to Hutcheson, touch and affect us, and as represented by a Homer are esteemed the 'Perfection of *Beauty*' (I.iv.2). These hints open up important questions about the problematic relationship of art to reality, however defined, and the aesthetic pleasure afforded by literature in treating painful subjects. This issue is addressed by Hume in the essay, 'Of Tragedy'.

Hutcheson struggles, also, with the shifting taste of his contemporaries who, despite the sway of classical canons of art, were coming to prefer the natural garden to the more traditional ordered one: 'strict *Regularity* in laying out of Gardens in *Parterres, Vista's, parallel Walks* is often neglected to obtain an Imitation of *Nature* even in some of its *Wildnesses*' (I.iv.5). Faced with such phenomena in aesthetics, Hutcheson seeks to argue that though experience of beauty is subjective, there is nevertheless a standard of taste, another topic discussed by Hume and the Scottish aestheticians. Hutcheson argues this standard arises from the uniformity of human nature and the fitness of ends to means in the cosmos, including the provision of the internal senses. These operate, he claims, despite variations introduced by custom, education, and example, to join pleasure to the contemplation of actions which are 'most efficacious, and fruitful in useful Effects' (I.viii.5). Further, they enlarge the mind to receive and retain the most seminal theorems, as the highest level of formal beauty, so that the 'Great Architect' of nature can be discovered as wise and good as well as powerful. Here Hutcheson indulges in the benevolent and hedonistic strain of Shaftesbury, and endeavours to refute the selfish philosophy of Hobbes and Mandeville.

Readers of the foregoing abstruse discussion of beauty, conceived as the pleasurable perception of unformity amidst variety, may have longed for some attention to the more basic but also uniform enjoyment of the pretty face and the well-turned ankle. Hutcheson has something to say about this in the second treatise of his *Inquiry* of 1725. It is presented in the context of his development of the moral sense theory of ethics. This has an aesthetic component in that virtue discernible by the moral sense is beautiful. With respect to the 'External Beauty of Persons', Hutcheson on considering the marks of beauty most commonly admired in faces finds them to be '*Sweetness, Mildness, Dignity, Vivacity, Humility, Tenderness, Good-nature*; that is, that certain *Airs, Proportions, je ne scai quoy's*, are natural Indications of such Virtues, or Abilitys of Dispositions towards them'. He notes, too, that '*Love* itself gives a Beauty to the *Lover*, in the eyes of the Person *belov'd*, which no other Mortal is much affected with' (II.vi.3). Hutcheson wrote these words while courting his wife-to-be, and perhaps the ardour of a lover flighted the pen of the philosopher.

Be that as it may, Hutcheson also deals with literature in the second treatise and again offers some highly interesting thoughts about its aesthetic pleasures, arguing that we find the same *moral Sense* to be the Foundation of the chief Pleasures of Poetry. We hinted, in the former Treatise, at the Foundation of Delight in the *Numbers, Measures, Metaphors, Similitudes* [*cf*. I.ii.13, I.iv.3]. But as the Contemplation of *moral Objects*, either of *Vice* or *Virtue*, affects us more strongly, and moves the Passions in quite a different and more powerful manner than *natural Beauty* . . . so the most moving Beautys bear a Relation to our moral Sense, and affect us more vehemently than the Representation of natural Objects in the liveliest Descriptions.

Hutcheson therefore reckons that dramatic and epic poetry are addressed to the moral sense and raise our passions by the fortunes of the good and evil characters. He goes on to assert that it is because of the 'lively Image' of the objects presented in epics and tragedies that they give a 'vastly great Pleasure than the Writings of Philosophers' (II.vi.7). Here are the seeds of the aesthetic criticism of Hume and Kames and others of the literati.

At the time of the publication of Hutcheson's *Inquiry into the Original of our Ideas of Beauty and Virtue* (1725), David Hume was completing his formal education at Edinburgh University, where he had encountered the 'New Philosophy' of Newton and Locke. At fourteen or fifteen, he turned to private studies with the ambition of making a fundamental discovery in moral philosophy and aesthetics, or as he called this subject 'criticism'. One view of his method is that he sought to apply the observation and experiment approach of Newtonian science to moral philosophy, but another plausible account is that the intellectual revolution Hume projected lay in taking Hutcheson's theory of the role of sentiment in ethics and aesthetics and applying this as a paradigm to the entire subjective world of our beliefs determining the relations we perceive linking matters of fact.[4] The Advertisement to the first two Books of the *Treatise of Human Nature*, which he published in 1739, indicates the nature of his enterprise, also his touching need for some response from the reading public to encourage him to complete his grand intellectual scheme, which by combining scepticism and naturalism aspired to deal with the vexed problems of logic, morals, politics (or the social sciences as we would call them), and aesthetics.

In the event, Hume was bitterly disappointed by the hostility and indifference encountered by the *Treatise*, and he enlisted the help of his good friend Henry Home, then an advocate, and later raised to the Bench as Lord Kames (1752), in getting his publication into the hands of someone who would give it a careful reading. Henry Home had already extended to legal questions the insights of Shaftesbury and Hutcheson about the emotive basis of ethics, as we find in his *Essays upon Several Subjects in Law* (1732), and he prevailed on Hutcheson to write a letter giving a first reaction to the *Treatise*, which was certainly encouraging since he praised the acuteness of Hume's reasoning. However, he drew back from endorsing the young philospher's sceptical tenets.

Scepticism was the issue that came to divide Hutcheson and Hume, and its systematic application of philosophical doubt to vexed questions of aesthetics was Hume's instrument for advancing that subject. In an exchange of letters in 1739, Hutcheson alleged Hume's writing lacked a 'certain Warmth in the Cause of Virtue', and Hume replied by pointing out that Hutcheson's resort to arguments about 'final Causes' was 'pretty uncertain and unphilosophical.' He drew attention to his analysis of morals in this life, with its stress on the role of sympathy. This is the key concept, also, in his aesthetics, as we shall see. Believing that his *Treatise* was unsuccessful because he had published too soon, and because there were 'some negligences' in his reasoning and 'more in the expression', Hume recast his thought in the form of an *Enquiry concerning Human Understanding* (1748), followed by an *Enquiry concerning the Principles of Morals* (1751), also in the *Essays, Moral, Political and Literary*, published from 1741 on, in all of which there is discussion of aspects of aesthetics. He never did write the projected treatise on 'criticism', but he dealt with this subject piecemeal in the *History of England* (1754–62) and in *Four Dissertations* (1757). From these works and the *Treatise*, however, we can discern the grand outlines of a system of aesthetics apparent to his contemporaries and built upon by them, which has also received attention in modern times from careful students of his thought.

Ever the analyst, Hume focused on beauty in itself, what is perceived as beauty, and judgements about beauty. He clears up the confusion that exists in Hutcheson's formulation in hesitating between the identification of beauty as a primary and secondary quality, and declares roundly: 'it is not, properly speaking, a quality in any object, but merely a passion or impression in the soul' (T. 301; II.i.8). As such, to the sceptical Hume, it cannot be defined, but we can describe it by enumerating the circumstances which attend it. In terms of perception, then, 'beauty is such an order and construction of parts, as either by the primary constitution of our nature, by custom, or by caprice, is fitted to give a pleasure and satisfaction to the soul.' Experience, indeed, suggests to Hume that a 'great part of the beauty, which we admire in animals and other objects, is deriv'd from the idea of convenience and utility' (T. 299). However, in a later passage, Hume notes that the 'beauty of all visible objects causes a pleasure pretty much the same, tho' it be derived from the idea of convenience and utility' (T. 617; III.iii.5). This meant to Hume that judgement could be involved in the arousal of the sentiment of beauty, which might occur not only from mere appearance, but also from reflection on the tendency of objects 'to [advance] the happiness of mankind, and of particular persons' (T. 589–90; III.iii.1).

Hume thus offered a distinction between intrinsic and what Hutcheson had called relative or comparative beauty. The former kind he illustrates by referring to the beauty of 'form' of

> some senseless inanimate piece of matter' (T. 363–4; II.ii.5), [also to] some species of beauty, especially the natural kinds, [which] on their first appearance command our affection and approbation; and where they fail of this effect, it is impossible for any reasoning to redress their influence or adapt them to our taste and sentiment (M.173.; I.137).

As to relative beauty, Hume considers that it is seldom we attend only to the 'form' of an object; we enter into judgement about beauty by comparing one object to another and, more importantly, by sympathizing with the owners of objects where our own interests arc not directly involved: 'Most of the works of art are esteem'd beautiful, in proportion to their fitness for the use of man, and even many of the productions of nature derive their beauty from that source' (T. 577; III.iii.1). Such considerations give rise to Hume's utility theory of beauty, but in this connection he stresses the force of human imagination able to enter into the desires and satisfactions of others, as a part of the working of sympathy. It has also to be recognized that beauty judged on the basis of utility has regard to the species, and is culturally relative. One analytic concept of Hume's that proved of seminal value in aesthetics was the association of ideas. As we have seen, Hutcheson made some use of this concept to explain relativity of taste (*Inquiry*, I.vi.3). Previously, Hobbes had offered some interesting hints about guided and unguided trains of thoughts, extending to those present in dreams, and Locke had discussed associations of ideas as a form of unruly mental behaviour, but Hume formulated principles of the association of ideas in terms of '*Resemblance, Contiguity* in time or Place, and *Cause* or *Effect*' as part of his theory of knowledge. For some reason, he dropped from the last authorized edition of the *Enquiry concerning Human Understanding*, published posthumously in 1777, a long passage in Section III which considered some of the effects of the association of ideas 'upon the Passions and Imagination'. Hume focuses chiefly on the issue of unity of action. Offering a form of reader-response theory, Hume argues that the poet with the capacity to enliven imagination and enflame passion must control the unity of the fable or plot strictly, if a reader is not to 'sink into Lassitude and Disgust, from the repeated Violence of the Movements' of the sympathetic imagination. In these 'loose Hints', as Hume calls them, he introduces significant issues to be pursued in that division of aesthetics concerned with the psychology of response to art.

To conclude this segment on Hume's contribution to aesthetics or theoretical 'criticism', it is necessary to make a passing reference to the *History of England*, and then review two late essays, 'Of Tragedy' and 'Of the Standard of Taste', which offer resolution of problems of aesthetics raised in the earlier writings.

In the 1750s, Hume wrote extensively on 'Politics', above all in the *History of England*. This remarkable work in attending to cultural history, however, takes up certain aesthetic issues, particularly when focused on the major English poets. Spenser is said to have created 'great beauties' in versification, elocution, and imagination, but Hume notes that continued allegory drawn from chivalry becomes tedious; in fact, the *Faerie Queene* suffers from defect in poetic unity. Milton is associated with another aesthetic category, that of the sublime: 'when in a happy mood, and employed on a noble subject, [he] is the most wonderfully sublime of any poet in any language; Homer and Lucretius and Tasso not excepted.'

Hume had given some expression to ideas about the sublime, so important to the eighteenth century, in the *Treatise* (T. 112, 373–4; I.iii.9, II.ii.8).

Before embarking on full-scale work on the *History*, however, Hume was drafting another book, finally published in 1757, as *Four Dissertations*, containing 'The Natural History of Religion'; 'Of the Passions'—a reworking of Book II of the *Treatise*; then 'Of Tragedy'; and lastly, 'Of the Standard of Taste'. The sequence of the last three 'Dissertations' makes clear that Hume regards theory of the passions as crucial for understanding his system of aesthetics. From the reworked 'Of the Passions', however, he omitted the treatment of sympathy, because he had further refinements to offer arising from his attempt to account for the pleasure we taken in tragedy. In the *Treatise*, he had offered two analyses. The first suggested that we are imaginately aware that we are watching a performance, and this softens the passion of pity and fear to the pleasurable degree of 'enlivening the mind, and fixing the attention' (T. 115 also 630–1; I.i.9, Appendix. insertion in I. p 123, 1.26). The second dwelt not on the effect of suspension of disbelief but on the pleasure arising from the heightening of our emotions caused by identifying in a sympathetic manner with tragic figures (T. 352–4, 369; II. ii.4, 7). 'Of Tragedy' begins, however, with the concession that the pleasure derived from the representation of 'sorrow, terror, anxiety, and other passions that are in themselves disagreeable and uneasy', seems 'unaccountable'. Existing theories by other authors are only partly helpful for understanding the paradox of tragedy. Hume mentions, first, the argument developed by the Abbé J-B Dubos, in *Réflexions critiques sur la poésie et sur la peinture* (1719), to the effect that the mind abhors vacuity and 'seeks every amusement and pursuit; business, gaming shows, executions; whatever will rouse the passions and take its attentions from itself' (E. 222). A difficulty with this theory, however, is that if distressing objects are really present to us, we might be jolted from mental languor, but at the same time we would be filled with 'unfeigned uneasiness.' A second theory expressed in *Réflexions sur la Poétique* (S.36, 1742) by Bernard le Bovier de Fontenelle, building on the fact that pleasure intensified too much becomes painful, whereas pain when moderated can become pleasure, holds that in the theatre we have some consciousness of the falsehood of what we see and hear (*cf*. T. 115; I.iii.9). Thereby, our sorrow at witnessing distress is weakened and we experience an 'agreeable sorrow, and tears that delight us' (E. 223).

Hume finds this theory convincing up to a point, but supplements this account by referring to Cicero's success in rousing passions to the highest degree by his eloquence in dealing with real subjects. Eloquent representation of the 'melancholy passions' converts their arrousal into delight: 'The impulse or vehemence arising from sorrow, compassion, indignation, receives a new direction from the sentiments of beauty' (E. 225). According to Hume, this is the principle at work in tragedy and, indeed, in all the finer arts:

> The force of imagination, the energy of expression, the power of numbers, the charms of imitation; all these are naturally, of themselves, delightful to the

mind; and when the object presented lays also hold of some affection, the pleasure still rises upon us, by the conversion of the subordinate movement into that which is predominant (E. 227–8).

The 'Dissertation' entitled, 'Of the Standard of Taste', is the most extended and, as it happens, the final statement of Hume about aesthetics. The opening move is recognition of the astonishing variety of taste, 'still greater in reality than in appearance'. Critics will be found to use the same language of approval and disapproval with regard to artistic objects, but inquiry reveals that they affix very different meanings to their expressions. Yet, if there is a 'steady rule of right' which permits us to assess morality, it would appear natural to search for a 'standard of taste' in the area of aesthetics to uphold one 'sentiment' and set aside another.

Though Hume does not mention Shaftesbury in this connection, he had explored the view, albeit in dialogue form, that beauty is a matter of opinion. Hutcheson, of course, had offered a way out of this radical subjectivity by affirming that, 'Men may have different Fancys of *Beauty* and yet *Uniformity* be the *universal Foundation* of our Approbation of any Form whatsoever as Beautiful' (*Inquiry*, I.vi.7). Hume's strategy for developing a theory of a standard of taste in which sentiment has a role is to bring up a 'species of philosophy' which would end the discussion by claiming that all sentiments aroused by the same object are right, in the sense that each is subjectively experienced by the perceiver of the object: 'Beauty is no quality in things themselves: it exists in the mind which contemplates them; and each mind perceives a different beauty.' Answering this, Hume points to the common sense position that there are inequalities in the 'genius and elegance' of authors, and the sentiments of 'pretended critics' who would overlook or confound these would be pronounced 'absurd and ridiculous'. So much for the 'principle of the natural equality of tastes' in practice (E. 234–5).

Reason (or reasoning) and sentiment are both involved in the exercise of taste with respect to artistic productions. Focusing on these, represented by 'compositions', Hume notes that their rules are not fixed from first principles, but have a basis like that of all practical sciences, in experience. Poetry, for example, is confined by rules of art that are revealed to writers by their genius or by observation. Though these rules are based only on experience and observation of human nature, however, it is not to be supposed that human feelings will always conform to them. Very special circumstances are required for the finer discriminations of taste: 'A perfect serenity of mind, a recollection of thought, a due attention to the object; if any of these circumstances be wanting, . . . we shall be unable to judge of the catholic and universal beauty' (E. 237). Still, if the requisite attention flags at any one time, and the 'operation' of a particular beauty cannot be discerned on this or that occasion, over time there is 'durable admiration' of classical works, and the 'beauties which are natually fitted to excite agreeable sentiments, immediately display their energy', as in the case of Homer who, two thousand years ago, pleased at Athens and Rome, and at Paris and London is admired still. Hume concludes that there are structural properties of art giving rise to 'forms and qualities' which are designed to please and some that displease. If these properties fail in their effect, there is something wrong with the organ of taste. This brings Hume to conclude that failure to feel the proper sentiment of beauty arises from 'want of that *delicacy* of imagination which is requisite to convey a sensibility of those finer emotions' (E. 239).

To develop his topic of delicacy of taste, Hume introduces from *Don Quixote* a slightly garbled version of the story of Sancho Panza's kinsmen, one of whom judged a hogshead to contain good wine except for a slight leathery taste, while the other detected a slight taste of iron (II.iii.xiii). They were laughed at, then vindicated when a key with a leather thong was discovered in the drained hogshead. Hume reckons there is sufficient similarlity between bodily and mental taste to permit application of the story. Delicacy of taste exists when the organs are so fine that nothing escapes them. The identification of general rules of composition is like the actual discovery of the key with the leather thong. The kinsmen, who detected the untoward flavours, had delicate taste, though the hogshead had never been emptied: something in the wine itself gave rise to their discriminations. If it were not possible to educe the rules of art, the 'bad critic' might persist in asserting that his sentiment was the appropriate one (E. 241). When he sums up the qualities of the 'true judge in the finer arts', Hume offers this formulation:

> strong sense, united to delicate sentiments, improved by practice, perfected by comparison, and cleared of all prejudice, can alone entitle critics to this valuable character; and the joint verdict of such, wherever they are to be found, is the true standard of taste and beauty (E. 247).

There is debate as to whether Hutcheson or Hume had the more formative influence on Adam Smith. He certainly studied under Hutcheson at Glasgow in the late 1730s and never forgot him, but it is also reported that when he was at Oxford, not long after the publication of Hume's *Treatise of Human Nature*, he was caught reading it by the authorities of Balliol College who punished him for this act of intellectual defiance. Further independent reading undertaken by Smith at Oxford laid a foundation for his extensive knowledge of ancient and modern literature, and through his life he is said never to have neglected cultivating a

> taste for the fine arts:—less, it is probable with a view to the peculiar enjoyments they convey, (though he was by no means without sensibility to their beauties,) than on account of their connection with the general principles of human mind; to an examination of which they afford the most pleasing of all avenues.[5]

For Smith, as for Hume, aesthetics was part of the science of man. When he became a teacher himself, first as a freelance lecturer to young lawyers and ministers in private courses given at Edinburgh (1748–51), then as a

Glasgow Professor (1751–64), he focused on theories of composition and taste as fundamental subjects. The essence of Smith's teaching about composition seems to have been that beauty of language resides not in ornamental features such as figures of speech, but in perspicuous transmission of an author's thought, and effective portrayal of the 'Sentiment' or 'affection' which he wishes to communicate 'by sympathy' to the audience (LRBL 26, 40). It is to be noted, further, that Smith hoped to give a systematic account of beauty in writing, either directly inspired as Hume was by the success of Newton in mathematics and physics or by the teaching of these subjects at Glasgow. In any event, when Smith deals with exposition, he expresses preferences for the 'manner of Sir Isaac Newton', whose aesthetic appeal he characterizes thus: 'it gives us a pleasure to see the phaenomena which reckoned the most unaccountable all deduced from some principle (commonly a wellknown one) and all united in one chain, far superior to what we feel from the unconnected one' of formulating a new principle for each separate phenomenon (LRBL 146).

We shall return to the question of Smith's formulation about the aesthetic pleasure to be found in well-contrived systems when two posthumously-published pieces are discussed: 'The History of Astronomy', and 'Of the Imitative Arts', both appearing in *Essays on Philosophical Subjects* (1795). Meantime, we shall examine *The Theory of Moral Sentiments* (1759), the book based on his Glasgow moral philosophy lectures which brought Adam Smith fame. Here we find his system of aesthetics and the relationship he perceived between this subject and ethics or, more broadly, social philosophy. On the whole, he did not accept Hutcheson's notion that there was a separate, internal, moral sense, but he did posit a 'general taste for beauty and order which is excited by inanimated as well as by animated objects' (TMS VII.iii.3.16). Further, Smith followed Hume in thinking that this 'general taste' was connected with the pleasure arising from sympathy, which a spectators feels in perceiving objects (TMS. IV.1.2; cf. T. 364; II.ii.5).

The original contributions to Hume's theory on which Smith prided himself is the perception that we value the 'exact adjustment of the means for attaining any convenience or pleasure' more than 'that very conveniency or pleasure' (TMS IV.1.3). This provides a link between ethics or aesthetics and political economy, for Smith goes on to claim that the aesthetic perception of successful adaptation of means to ends is a major force in economic enterprise and political organization. To be sure, he pointed out that we are deceived by 'nature' into believing that 'wealth and greatness' are worth the 'toil and anxiety' we bestow on their attainment, because their 'pleasures . . . when considered in this complex view [sympathetic perception of utility], strike the imagination as something grand and beautiful'. Nevertheless, this 'deception' is justified since it 'rouses and keeps in continual motion the industry of mankind' (TMS IV.1.9–10, 11). Smith cautions, however, that in the realm of politics, reformers can become so 'intoxicated with the imaginary beauty of [an] ideal system' of government that they give in to the 'violence of party' and fail to achieve the ends they seek (VI.ii.2.15).

Tempting though it would be to trace further Smith's concept of the seductive power of 'imaginary beauty' residing in ideal political systems, a formulation which must have been of great interest to his friend, Edmund Burke, who discussed its effects in *Reflections on the French Revolution* (1790), it will suffice to end discussion of Smith's aesthetics in *The Theory of Moral Sentiments* by noting that in France his general theory of beauty resting on sympathy was well received, particularly by the ladies, who must be supposed to have appreciated the attention given by him to matters of taste and beauty in a work on morals. In Germany, the first truly distinguished writers on aesthetics reflected an understanding of his teaching: for example, Lessing in *Laokoon* (1766), Herder in *Kritische Wälder* (1769), and Kant in correspondence of 1771 which linked Smith to Kames as author of the *Elements of Criticism*, all suggesting an awareness of the noteworthy progress of the philosophy of beauty in contemporary Scotland.

Before publishing *The Theory of Moral Sentiments*, Smith may well have completed in the previous year all that was preserved of his 'History of Astronomy'. He described it to Hume as a 'fragment of an intended juvenile work', and said that he suspected there was 'more refinement than solidity in some parts of it' (letter of 16 April 1773), but it must be attended to as a landmark statement of the role of aesthetic pleasure in the contriving of ingenious systems which, once contrived, enhance our perception of the beauty of phenomena. Examining the principles which 'lead and direct philosophical inquiries', Smith finds in the history of astronomy an illustration of the improvement of our knowledge through the operation of our 'sentiments' of 'Wonder, Surprise, and Admiration', the last of which he considers to be excited by 'what is great and beautiful' (EPS. 33). Thus, a theory of astronomy arouses, for example, *admiration*, and may be evaluated along with others with respect to its fitness for soothing the imagination and rendering the 'theatre of nature a more coherent, and therefore a more magnificent spectacle, than otherwise it would have appeared to be' (EPS. 46). It is under this aspect, that Smith writes of the 'beauty and simplicity' of the heliocentric theory of Copernicus (EPS. 75), and of the 'superior genius and sagacity' of Newton in making the

> most happy, and, we may now say, the greatest and most admirable improvement that was ever made in philosophy, when he discovered that he could join together the movements of the Planets by so familiar a principle of connection [gravity], which completely removed all the difficulties the imagination had hitherto felt in attending to them (EPS. 98).

When he deals with the 'Imitative Arts', Smith's starting point is one taken up by Hutcheson, namely, there is a relative beauty in the conformity between an original and a copy (*Inquiry*, I.iv.1). Smith notes that subjects other than the 'great, or beautiful, or interesting' such as a 'butcher's stall, or a kitchen dresser', will give pleasure when depicted 'by some Dutch masters', though he believes sculptures of disagreeable subjects would be viewed as absurd (EPS 179). Always the realist, Smith appreciates that goods regarded as scarce and expensive will be valued by the 'rich and the great . . . the proud and the vain' over those having 'exquisite beauty' (EPS 183). He also offers a corrective viewpoint to the one of his own day which would scorn as unnatural the clipping of yew and holly trees into geometrical and other shapes. Smith argues that by this practice a gardener gives to a yew-tree, for example, first, the

> same beauty of regular figure, which pleases so much in porphyry and marble; and, secondly, [intends] to imitate in a growing tree the ornaments of those precious materials: he means to make an object of one kind resemble another object of a very different kind; and to the original beauty of figure to join the relative beauty of imitation: but the disparity between the imitating and imitated object is the foundation of the beauty of imitation (EPS 183).

Smith goes on to deal with the philosophy of the creative arts when he turns to music and dancing. He concerns himself with the superiority of the latter to the former in point of expressive power, and of poetry to the other two imitative arts, because of its capacity to represent the 'reasonings and judgements of the understanding; the ideas, fancies, and suspicions of the imagination; the sentiments, emotions, and passions of the heart' (EPS 189). Yet the power of music to imitate 'endless repetitions of passion' makes Smith echo Plato's claim for wisdom, for he states that the 'proper and natural objects of musical imitation' are 'of all beauties the brightest' (EPS 193).

Smith was succeeded as Professor of Moral Philosophy at Glasgow by Thomas Reid, who taught previously at Aberdeen and made his philosophical reputation with his *Inquiry into the Human Mind* (1764), which offered a common sense answer to Hume's scepticism. Early in life, he sought to refute Hutcheson's 'attempt to introduce a mathematical calculation' into morality, but he remained indebted to Hutcheson for the outlines of his philosophy of beauty. He presented this in an extended essay, 'Of Taste', which formed part of a late work, *Essays on the Intellectual Powers of Man* (1785). Recently there came to light, however, a manuscript version of his 'Lectures on the Fine Arts'. Dated 1774, and thus from his Glasgow professorial period, the 'Lectures' comprehend his most elaborate formulation of aesthetics, and suggest that he was moving towards the position of Kant, in asserting that there is an intermediary branch of intellectual activity between the major ones of the theoretical and practical arts and sciences, namely, that of the 'Fine Arts' or the domain of the beautiful.

Whereas the theoretical arts and sciences address the mind and seek to produce an effect on it, deriving their first principles from the 'philosophy of mind', the practical counterparts are similarly concerned with the body. The fine arts, however, mediate between mind and body: painting presents material objects to the mind it seeks to modify, as does theatre, but poetry and eloquence have the least connection with matter and 'seem to aim more at the mind' than any of the other fine arts (p 21). From this starting point, Reid goes on to consider the mind—body relationship; taste as the power we have to perceive the beauties and deformities of objects of taste; and how to improve taste. He then offers observations on the fine arts, including music, painting, sculpture, gardening, architecture, poetry, and, finally, eloquence, 'undoubtedly the noblest of all the fine arts, for it unites the beauties of them all' (pp 51–2). In his discussion, Reid enumerates the artistic forms of mind-body relationships and thus enlarges on the epistemological significance of the aesthetic domain. In so doing, Reid invokes the roles of judgement with respect to our responses to beauty. Kant followed somewhat the same line of reasoning in his essay, 'Critique of Aesthetic Judgement', in the *Critique of Judgement* (1790) which uses the term aesthetics in its modern sense, and offers the argument that aesthetic judgements differ in kind from moral and scientific judgements. Thus Kant refutes, or seeks to refute, the Hutcheson-Hume school, and asserts that aesthetic contemplation is disinterested, involving the free play of the imagination and the understanding.

The upholder of the Hutcheson-Hume position on aesthetics best known to Kant may have been Lord Kames, because a German translation of his *Elements of Criticism* (1762) by J N Meinhard began to appear within a year of the book's first publication and was completed in 1766. Kames did more than anyone, in fact, to ensure that the philosophy of beauty flourished in Scotland and was attended to abroad, not because of the originality of his ideas, perhaps, but because of the force of personality behind his writings, and the longevity of his career as a man of letters.[6] Voltaire was nettled by Kames's views, as we have seen, and Hume owed to him the first response of Hutcheson to the *Treatise of Human Nature*. In addition, Kames was one of the patrons responsible for launching Smith's career as a freelance lecturer in Edinburgh on composition and matters of taste, and he befriended Reid through sharing with him an allegiance to the Common Sense philosophy as an alternative to Hume's scepticism. Despite this latter strand in his intellectual make-up, the *Elements of Criticism* has many aspects reflecting a grasp of the empirical, sensational side of Hume's thought; for example, Kames's statement of aim is that he intends

> not to compose a regular treatise upon each of the fine arts; but only, in general, to exhibit their fundamental principles, drawn from human nature, the true source of criticism (i. 13)

In part modelled on Newtonian science, and in part on institutional books of Scots law, Kames's own discipline, his work on aesthetics sets out

> To ascend gradually to principles of [criticism], from facts and experiments; instead of beginning with the former, handled abstractedly, and descending to the latter (i. 13–14).

Accordingly, Kames delineates, first, the fundamental rules of human nature and, second, shows how these give rise to aesthetic principles (chs.

i-xv). Third, he demonstrates how aesthetic principles are used in practice, principally by constructing a rhetoric and an art of fiction, but also by giving attention to gardening and architecture (chs. xvi-xxiv). Finally, again in the Hutcheson-Hume tradition, he takes up the question of the standard of taste, which he considers is invoked in formulating and applying critical judgements (ch. xxv).

Kames asserts that the principles of the association of ideas, expanded from those established by Hume in the first *Enquiry*, together with the observable relations between feelings and objects, offer standards for deciding on the naturalness of any work of art regarded as a representation. Like Hume, Kames argues that works of art to be pleasing should be conformable to the natural course of our ideas, with their parts 'like an organic system . . . orderly arranged and mutually connected' (i. 27). This passage gave rise, it seems, to discussion among German critics of the concept of 'organic unity,' which was taken up by Coleridge and reformulated in terms of Romantic aesthetics as the living soul of a work of art. Another concept with a somewhat similar history is the Keatsian one of poetry as 'waking dream'. Kames follows Hume in distinguishing between the original sensation of an object impinging on the mind and the resulting idea in the memory or imagination which has less vivacity. His conclusion is that writers should use vivid and affecting imagery to come as near as possible to natural stimuli. This leads him to posit the creation in art of 'ideal presence' supplying the want of real presence, and he draws attention to the power of language to raise emotions, so that an engaged reader is 'thrown into a kind of reverie; in which state, forgetting that he is reading, he conceives every incident as passing in his presence, precisely as if he were an eye-witness' (i. 93). This takes us to a central motif of the 'Ode to a Nightingale' of Keats, and again to Coleridge with his notion of the 'willing suspension of disbelief' engendered by art.

In the chapter on gardening and architecture, Kames deals, as Hutcheson had before him, with the changing taste of the time and the emerging Romantic sensibility. Experienced himself in gardening in Berwickshire and after 1766 at Blair Drummond near Stirling, Kames was in sympathy with the movement in Scotland seeking to replace the formal garden, associated with the tradition of Versailles, for the natural garden in the style of William Kent, who 'leaped the fence and saw that all Nature was a garden', as Horace Walpole claimed. Kames reckoned that the natural garden could 'raise emotions of grandeur, of sweetness, of gaiety, of melancholy, of wildness, and even of surprise' (ii. 432). With respect to architecture, Kames revealed that his taste had been formed on the revival of classical forms of building associated with the work of Andrea Palladio in sixteenth-century Italy. But Kames also acknowledged the appeal of Gothic architecture in certain settings, amid the 'horrid graces of the wilderness' as Shaftesbury called them. Thus, Kames praises the third Duke of Argyll for constructing his castle in keeping with the 'profuse variety of wild and grand objects about Inverary' (ii.469). In this fashion the Kames's book proved a comprehensive guide to practical aesthetics, and became a staple of the Humanities curriculum in the new colleges and universities of North America, such as Princeton. There is a record, too, of an American medical student in Edinburgh writing home to his father in New York in 1764, recommending that he read the *Elements of Criticism*, 'especially that part of it relating to gardening and architecture, before you go on to improving your place on the north river.'[7]

With his book, Kames may be said to have consolidated the work of the Scottish school of philosophical criticism. There was a flowering of this school associated with the membership of the Aberdeen Wise Club, made up of Professors in the Northern city. One of them, Alexander Gerard, was awarded a prize by the Select Society of Edinburgh, in which Kames was prominent, for an *Essay on Taste* (1759), which he followed up with an *Essay on Genius* (1774) that asserts the primacy of a vigorous imagination for the artist worthy of the name of genius. Another member of the Wise Club, George Campbell, wrote *The Philosophy of Rhetoric* (1776), which explicitly sought to supplement Kames's treatment of eloquence as one of the fine arts by analysing it as a 'useful art . . . closely connected with the understanding and the will' (Preface). Another proponent of Kames's principles of taste and aesthetics, but ready to apply them in practical ways, was his protégé, Hugh Blair, occupant from 1762 of the Edinburgh Chair of Rhetoric and Belles Lettres, the first university post of its kind in Britain which included the teaching of English literature. Blair published his rhetoric lectures in 1783, but previously in the 1760s had made a contribution as a philosophical critic by his promotion of James Macpherson's spurious 'Ossian' as an epic poet of primitive genius. Kames shared Blair's enthusiasm for 'Ossian' which became something of a European cult. Kames's influence is also present in the articles on beauty and taste in the *Encyclopedia Britannica* (1st edn 1771), written by another protégé, William Smellie, who was a printer and the editor of this enterprise of the Scottish Enlightenment sustained to the present day.

Involved in the continuance of the *Encyclopedia* was the philosopher, Dugald Stewart, who became editor of the six-volume supplement of 1816–24. He had lectured on criticism and what would now be called aesthetic principles as Professor of Moral Philosophy at Edinburgh from 1785 to 1810, and he published his views on those subjects in *Philosophical Essays* (1810). It was principally Stewart's former students and associates who produced the second *Edinburgh Review* (from 1802 on). With Francis Jeffrey in the lead, they turned philosophical criticism to good account for periodical reviewing, keeping alive the tradition emphasized by Kames of extolling the social purpose of the arts affirmed by the motto of the *Review: Iudex damnatur cum nocens absolvitur*—the judge is condemned when the guilty person is acquitted.

Stewart in *Philosophical Essays* and Jeffrey in a contribution to the *Edinburgh Review* (May 1811), later expanded into an article on beauty written for the 1816 supplement of the *Encyclopedia Britannica*, paid fitting tribute to the last major work on aesthetics written by a member of the Scottish school. This was Archibald Alison, minister of the Episcopalian chapel in the Cowgate of Edinburgh, whose *Essays on the Nature and Principles of Taste* first appeared in 1790, to be greeted with a favourable reception by Thomas Reid and Robert Burns. It was the second and enlarged edition of 1811, however, warmly welcomed by Jeffrey, which received widespread attention and was reprinted many times. Alison's interest in the beautiful, the picturesque, and the sublime, the three aesthetic categories he investigated, was theoretical rather than practical. He acknowledged wide reading about beauty, including St Augustine and Hogarth, but saw his 'opinions' as coinciding with the 'Platonic school' which he believed to have been maintained in Britain chiefly by Shaftesbury and Hutcheson. Alison also found the tenets of this school affirmed in Reid's book, *Essays on the Intellectual Powers of Man*. The teaching alluded to here is that 'matter is not beautiful in itself, but derives its Beauty from the expression of Mind' (p 114). Alison argues that the emotion of beauty or sublimity is increased by whatever stretches the imagination, and the most original part of his treatise is the resulting analysis of associations as the cause of this intensification of our aesthetic feelings. He differentiates beauty from sublimity in terms of the associations of objects or forms: those connected with delicacy and grace are in common language called beautiful, whereas sublime forms are associated with danger and power (pp 48–51). As for picturesque objects, they commonly strike the mind with surprise and then produce afterwards an additional train of imagery. Alison's examples of this include an 'old tower in the middle of a deep wood', and a 'bridge flung across a chasm between rocks' (p 7). Attention is called here to the expressive power of landscapes specially designed to recreate the effects of the canvases of Claude Lorrain, a feature of contemporary Scottish architectural planning as at Hopetoun House, near Edinburgh. But Alison reserves his most passionate admiration for the beauty and sublimity of wild nature, whose most telling effect he considers to be a moral one. He attests to this in a concluding passage which in one way harkens buck to the effusions of Shaftesbury and Hutcheson as they connect love of beauty with love of virtue, and in another with the contemporary poetry of Wordsworth and Byron who find moral and spiritual significance in the encounter between human beings and the solitude of mountains:

> They hasten into those solitary and those uncultivated scenes, where they seem to breathe a purer air, and to experience some more profound delight . . . They love to feel themselves awakened to those deep and majestic emotions which give a new and nobler expansion to their hearts, and, amide the tumult and astonishment of their imagination,
>
> > To behold omniscient providence
> > In rocks impassable, wild hills and broken cliffs;
> > In raging waves and in the forest night.
>
> (p 118)

To be sure, the artist whose work best exemplified Alison's theories concerning associations of ideas as sources of the beautiful and sublime and picturesque was Walter Scott, whose poetry and fiction drenched the landscape of his native country, particularly the Highlands, with tales of its heroic past, making it forever attractive to the Romantic imagination, but that, of course, is entirely another story.

NOTES

The following abbreviations and short references are used in the text:

Hume, David
 T = *A Treatise of Human Nature*, L A Selby-Bigge (ed) 2nd edn, revsd P H Nidditch (Oxford, 1978)
 M = *Enquiries concerning Human Understanding and concerning the Principles of Morals*, L A Selby-Bigge (ed) 3rd edn, revsd P H Nidditch (Oxford, 1975)
 E = *Essays, Moral, Political and Literary*, (Oxford, 1963)
Reid, Thomas, *Lectures on the Fine Arts, 1774*, P Kivy (ed) (The Hague, 1973)
Smith, Adam, Glasgow edn of the Works and Correspondence (Oxford, 1976–83)
 TMS = *The Theory of Moral Sentiments*, D D Raphael and A L Macfie (eds) (1976)
 EPS = *Essays on Philosophical Subjects*, W P D Wightman, J C Bryce, and I S Ross (eds) (1980)
 LRBL = *Lectures on Rhetoric and Belles Lettres*, J C Bryce (ed) (1983)

1   T R Lounsbury, *Shakespeare and Voltaire* (New York, 1902), p 248.
2   W R Scott, *Francis Hutcheson: His Life, Teaching and Position in the History of Philosophy* (Cambridge, 1900, pp 261–9.
3   M A Stewart, 'Berkeley and the Rankenian Club', *Hermathena*, CXXXIX (1985), 39: ——, 'George Turnbull and Educational Reform', in the forthcoming *Aberdeen and the Enlightenment*, J Carter and J Pittock (Aberdeen, 1987), t/s version pp 1, 9.
4   E C Mossner, *The Life of David Hume*, 2nd edn (Oxford, 1980), p 77.
5   Dugald Stewart, 'Account of the Life and Writings of Adam Smith, LL D', in EPS, p 305.
6   I S Ross, *Lord Kames and the Scotland of his Day* (Oxford, 1972).
7   J B Langstaff, *Doctor Bard of Hyde Park* (New York, 1942), p 61.

FURTHER READING

Edwards, Paul (ed), *The Encyclopedia of Philosophy*, (New York and London, 1967), articles on 'History of Aesthetics' (Monroe C Beardsley), 'Problems of Aesthetics' (John Hospers), 'A G Baumgarten' (Giorgio Tonelli), and 'Beauty' (Jerome Stolnitz)

Hipple, W J, *The Beautiful, The Sublime, and The Picturesque in Eighteenth-Century British Aesthetic Theory* (Southern Illinois 1957)

Jones, Peter, *Hume's Sentiments: Their Circeronian and French Context* (Edinburgh, 1982)

Macmillan, Duncan, *Painting in Scotland: The Golden Age* (Oxford, 1986)

Tait, A A, *The Landscape Garden in Scotland, 1735–1835* (Edinburgh, 1980)

Chapter 15

Literature and the Church of Scotland

RICHARD B SHER

Of the many changes occurring in Scottish cultural life during the age of the Enlightenment, none was more remarkable than the emergence of the Presbyterian clergy as a leading force in polite literature and learning. This development astounded contemporaries, though it would be an exaggeration to say that it happened overnight. For one thing, Scottish Presbyterian clergymen had often shared in an early modern intellectual tradition that was Latin in language, rigorously Calvinist in theology, international in scope, and learned within the confines of its narrowly religious subject matter. For another thing, at the beginning of the eighteenth century some Scottish ministers, such as Principal William Carstares of Edinburgh University, were gradually becoming more tolerant of intellectual endeavours in a wider sphere and more desirous of raising the intellectual standards and stature of Scotland's universities.

In arts and divinity, as in medicine and law, the Dutch influence was crucial. The Netherlands provided the model of a small, Protestant nation in which the boundaries separating sacred and profane learning had become almost imperceptible: the study of nature—from natural philosophy to natural law to natural theology—represented a legitimate means of obtaining knowledge about God and the divine order. By means of their prominence as academics, early eighteenth-century Scottish Presbyterian clergymen such as Carstares worked to reform the institutional structure of the Scottish universities and to establish a broad-based, Dutch-influenced curriculum.

By the 1720s a number of young Scottish clergymen were attracting attention for their progressive views on various aspects of polite culture, including literature. They were born around 1700 and were heavily indebted to the liberalizing influence of the Professor of Divinity (and later Principal) at Edinburgh University, William Hamilton. Sometimes, though perhaps misleadingly, called 'Old Moderates' by nineteenth- and twentieth-century ecclesiastical historians seeking to emphasize their similarities with the culturally liberal 'Moderate' party that rose to prominence in church affairs just after 1750, they included the brothers William and George Wishart, Patrick Cuming, William Leechman, and Robert Wallace. Wallace was a particularly learned and liberal man whose publications included an essay against David Hume's claims on behalf of the superior populousness of the modern world. But secular publications of this sort remained a rarity for Wallace and other clergymen of his generation, at least until the change of climate that occurred in the 1750s. The occasional sermon was their chief medium of publication, and they employed it so effectively in the cause of 'polite'—which is to say rational, moderate, and moral—preaching that the pious Calvinist Robert Wodrow derisively dubbed several of them 'Neu-Lights and Preachers Legal', while admiring Moderate party ministers such as Alexander Carlyle began referring to George Wishart as 'the Tillotson of the Church of Scotland'.[1]

Besides sermons, Scottish Presbyterian clergymen of the early eighteenth century produced their fair share of polemical books and pamphlets against Episcopalians, Jacobites, and fellow Presbyterians affiliated with rival interest groups or ideologies. There were noisy controversies about theology and church government, but there were few signs of the profound clerical literary explosion that lay ahead. An exception that proves the rule in regard to poetry is the literary career of Robert Blair, a member of the Wisharts' generation of clergymen. In 1743 Blair, who lived a quiet life as minister of the rural East Lothian parish of Athelstaneford, published one of the finest poems by an eighteenth-century Scottish divine. Entitled 'The Grave', it is a long, sombre, melancholy, sometimes morbid exploration of death's relentless and seemingly indiscriminate pursuit of human flesh and man's unwillingness to accept the reality of his plight. The poem is tolerably well-crafted and contains several memorable passages exposing human vanity, such as this one which features lines vaguely suggestive of Burns's on the 'best laid schemes o' *Mice* an' *Men*':

> Absurd to think to over-reach the Grave,
> And from the wreck of names to rescue ours.
> The best concerted schemes men lay for fame
> Die fast away; only themselves die faster.
> The far-fam'd sculptor, and the laurell'd bard,
> Those bold insurancers of deathless fame,
> Supply their little feeble aids in vain.

There is a pious and perhaps Calvinist finale in which 'foul monster, Sin' and 'Death' are first presented as the objects of respectful dread and then shown to be 'foil'd' by 'Th' illustrious deliverer of mankind, The Son of God'. Nevertheless, Blair worried about the propriety of his writing such a poem, and a year or two before publication he told Dr Doddridge that he hoped it was 'not unbecoming my profession as a minister of the gospel, though the greatest part of it was composed several years before I was clothed with so sacred a character.'[2] Once a minister Blair does not seem to have been very active as a poet or man of letters, and 'The Grave' stands alone as his only significant literary work, an interesting but isolated episode in the history of Scottish poetry.

History was a second literary field to which Scottish Presbyterian clergymen contributed during the first half of the eighteenth century, but here, too, their accomplishments were relatively slight. In this case Rev Robert Wodrow's *History of the Sufferings of the Church of Scotland from the Restoration to the Revolution* (1721–2), which sympathetically depicted the persecution of the Covenanters during Scotland's last era of Episcopal supremacy, constitutes the rule-proving exception. The product of a decade and a half of scholarship, Wodrow's book has been praised by modern commentators for its extensive use of primary documents and records. Yet some of the same commentators have observed that the work was essentially Presbyterian propaganda and its author no great stylist. If Wodrow's history was learned Presbyterian propaganda, Rev George Logan's efforts to challenge the Episcopalian classicist Thomas Ruddiman on points of Scottish political history during the 1740s represented a cruder sort of polemics. Born a decade before the 'Glorious' Revolution, Wodrow and Logan shared a deep dread of an Episcopal-Jacobite restoration, and for this reason both men wrote Whig-Presbyterian 'controversial' history that subordinated literary merit to polemical purpose.

Only in the field of moral philosophy did a Presbyterian clergyman of this period make a truly lasting mark in polite literature, and he was an Irishman rather than a Scot. Francis Hutcheson combined elements of natural law, civic humanism, and Whig ideology with Christian Stoicism and with Shaftesbury's emphasis on the senses generally and the 'moral sense'—a natural faculty for distinguishing right from wrong—in particular. Significantly, he broke with tradition by lecturing and writing on moral philosophy in English as well as Latin. Closely connected with several of the progressive 'Neu-Lights', to whose generation he belonged, Hutcheson was at the same time able to satisfy most strict Calvinists such as Wodrow. It was therefore possible for his *System of Moral Philosophy* (posthumously published in 1755 with a long list of prominent subscribers and a laudatory introduction by Leechman) to become the foundation of an enduring consensus among Scottish churchmen and men of letters, even though its prose style was considered 'careless and neglected' by a younger generation of literary critics.[3] All subsequent Scottish professors of moral philosophy in the eighteenth century—including the clergymen Adam Ferguson, Thomas Reid, and (in America) John Witherspoon, and the laymen Adam Smith, James Beattie, and Dugald Stewart—would draw directly or indirectly upon his disparate 'system' even if they deviated from it in particular respects. On these grounds there is no denying Hutcheson's role as the 'father' of Scottish moral philosophy.

Thus, by 1746—the year that witnessed both the suppression of the last Jacobite uprising and the premature deaths of Francis Hutcheson and Robert Blair—Scottish ministers had begun to make some headway in the republic of letters. Yet their contributions were still quite modest. Not only were there relatively few Presbyterian clergymen of letters before mid century, but those few demonstrated little more than a workmanlike command of English style and rarely ventured beyond the religious and philosophical concerns that were almost universally considered a proper sphere for the intellectual energies of the clergy. Despite the strong intellectual component in scholastic Calvinism, Blair's memorable but minor poem about death, Wodrow's and Logan's controversial histories, Hutcheson's impressive synthesis of academic moral philosophy, and the liberalizing efforts of a handful of 'Neu-Lights', the fact remains that native-born clergymen in the Church of Scotland produced no major literary works in prose or poetry from the reestablishment of Presbyterianism in 1690 to the middle of the eighteenth century. And this is to say nothing of the stubborn legacy of Presbyterian anti-intellectualism that caused many a Scottish churchman to condemn all secular literature out of hand.

It is against this background that the dramatic developments of the third quarter of the eighteenth century must be seen. In the space of two decades the Scottish Presbyterian clergy not only gained a reputation as a more tolerant, learned, and enlightened body than they had been before but became far and away the most distinguished set of churchman anywhere in the republic of letters and arguably the driving force behind the Scottish Enlightenment. No matter how much attention one pays to precursors and continuity, it is impossible to categorize this development as a merely evolutionary change. By the early 1770s the surprising emergence of the Scottish clergy as a major voice in polite literature was being touted in works as diverse as Thomas Pennant's *Tour in Scotland* and Tobias Smollett's *Humphry Clinker*, where the famous phrase 'hot-bed of genius' was applied chiefly to the Presbyterian clergy in and around Edinburgh.

At the centre of the clerical revolution in Scottish polite literature stood a coterie of Edinburgh-based Moderate party clergymen who were affiliated with other Moderate ministers at Aberdeen, St Andrews, and elsewhere.[4] Born for the most part around 1720, these 'Moderate literati' were evidently sincere Presbyterians who were also deeply committed to the principles of the Enlightenment, including the spread of virtue and polite learning. They happened to come of age at a propitious time for achieving the latter objective. After the unsuccessful Jacobite uprising of 1745–6 the Whig-Presbyterian establishment in Scotland was stable enough to accommodate politeness, and the most powerful Scottish political patrons of their era, such as the third Duke of Argyll and his nephew the third Earl of Bute, were unusually learned and enlightened men. The economic climate of steady though unspectacular improvement also helped, as did an increasing familiarity with the English tongue that made it possible for them to attain an unprecedented mastery of English prose.

The Moderate literati contributed to the development of eighteenth-century Scottish literature and learning in three major respects: as institutional leaders, as literary patrons, and as authors in their own right. In the first of these capacities they were able, thanks largely to enlightened patrons like Argyll and Bute, to gain control of most of Scotland's universities. At Edinburgh University, for example, William Robertson reigned as principal from 1762 until his death in 1793 and was ably assisted by other Moderate ministers such as Robert Blair's cousin Hugh (rhetoric and belles lettres) and Adam Ferguson (natural, and later moral, philosophy). At Marischal and King's Colleges at Aberdeen, similarly, George Campbell and Alexander Gerard held important academic positions, as did William Wight at Glasgow University and Joseph McCormick, George

Hill, and others at St Andrews University. In the Church of Scotland itself the Moderate literati were equally ascendant, and party leader William Robertson dominated proceedings in the General Assembly (the church's highest court) throughout the 1760s and 1770s.

Another area of Moderate institutional prominence was in literary and philosophical societies such as the Select Society, Aberdeen Wise Club, and the Royal Society of Edinburgh. In organizations like these Presbyterian clergymen of letters came together on equal terms with lay intellectuals to exchange ideas and debate important issues. The leading role played by Moderate ministers in universities, church affairs, and clubs and societies had many significant ramifications for the development of Scottish intellectual life, but perhaps the single most important one was the creation of a general climate conducive to the development of polite literature and learning. Owing chiefly to the efforts of the Moderate clergy, censorship and its characteristic byproducts—persecution of men of letters, clandestine publishing of illegal writings, proliferation of devious literary genres such as the cryptic tale, and alienation of men of letters from religious and educational establishments—were as rare in Scotland during the second half of the eighteenth century as they were common in France.

Moderate clergymen who attained institutional preeminence often found themselves in a position to serve as literary patrons for other authors, both clerical and lay. Perhaps the two best known instances of such patronage concern the Scots poetry of Robert Burns and the Gaelic poetry of Ossian that James Macpherson claimed to have discovered in the Highlands and translated into English. The Moderate literati were so deeply involved in the production and defence of Macpherson's Ossianic poetry during the late 1750s and early 1760s that they must be considered indispensable collaborators in that project. John Home and Hugh Blair in particular pressed Macpherson into 'translating' and publishing first some Ossianic fragments and later two full-fledged Ossianic epics, and a large amount of money was raised by them for that purpose. Blair first made his literary reputation with a brief *Critical Dissertation* that praised Macpherson's Ossianic poetry for its admirable mixture of primitive vitality and noble sentiment. By the time Burns brought his poems to Edinburgh in 1786 Blair had been the chief arbiter of Scottish poetic taste for more than two decades. Burns was somewhat resentful that a man whom he judged more distinguished for industry than for genius should have so much literary authority, but to his credit Blair appreciated Burns's poetic ability and took great pride in helping to advance the young poet's career. As he put it in a letter to Burns devoted chiefly to boasting about his role as the leading patron of Macpherson's Ossianic poetry, 'I know no way in which literary persons who are advanced in years can do more service to the world than in forwarding the efforts of rising Genius, or bringing forth unknown merit from obscurity.'[5]

Had the Moderate clergy done no more for literature than the services they performed as institutional leaders and literary patrons, their contribution would be noteworthy. Their most important contribution to Scottish literature, however, consisted in their accomplishments as authors. In field after field eighteenth-century Scottish ministers—nearly all of whom were Moderates—published works that brought them national and often international acclaim. William Robertson wrote histories of Scotland, Charles V, and America that placed him among Voltaire, Hume, and Gibbon as one of the premier historians of the age. Adam Ferguson, John Logan, William Somerville, Adam Dickson, George Ridpath, William Lothian, Robert Watson, Robert Henry, and John Home were among the many other Presbyterian divines who also produced histories on British or European subjects during the second half of the century. A second field of polite literature in which the Scottish clergy distinguished themselves was rhetoric and literary and aesthetic criticism. Alexander Gerard's *Essay on Taste* (1759) and *Essay on Genius* (1774), George Campbell's *Philosophy of Rhetoric* (1776), and Hugh Blair's *Lectures on Rhetoric and Belles Lettres* (1783) were all major publications in this area. A third field was moral philosophy, in which Adam Ferguson and Thomas Reid—leading practitioners of Scottish conjectural history and common sense philosophy, respectively—were the best known clerical names. In poetry there were no major clerical figures but numerous minor ones, including Thomas Blacklock, William Wilkie, John Logan, John Ogilvie, and John Home. Home was a major figure of the age in drama, with six tragedies performed on the London stage including the classic *Douglas*. In mathematics and science Matthew Stewart, John Walker, and John Playfair made impressive contributions. In religion the sermons of Hugh Blair and others set a new standard for polite preaching, while George Campbell and James Macknight produced scholarly biblical criticism. Fiction and antiquarianism were perhaps the only important fields of polite literature in which the Scottish clergy had little to say.

This explosion of polite literature by clerical authors did not go unobserved or unopposed by clergymen in the Popular or orthodox party in the church. By the 1750s, however, the momentum clearly lay with proponents of the clerical Enlightenment. While the most conservative elements in the Church might choose secession rather than tolerate a ministry so deeply involved with polite literature, orthodox clergymen who stayed in the established church found it difficult to resist the spread of Moderate values regarding literature and learning. The case of John Witherspoon illustrates the dilemma such men faced. Dismayed by the rise of the Moderate literati, who were of his generation though not of his austere religious outlook, Witherspoon composed in 1753 a lengthy satirical pamphlet against the Moderates called *Ecclesiastical Characteristics*. It was a sharp and witty performance, ironically advising each Moderate minister to esteem heretics, protect libertines, avoid 'all appearances of devotion', and 'endeavour to acquire as great a degree of politeness, in his carriage and behaviour, and to catch as much of the air and manner of a fine gentleman, as possibly he can'.[6] The irony, however, was double-edged, for the very act of writing a clever satire against the Moderates was an inadvertent endorsement of polite literature. Nor was Witherspoon able to remain consistently austere in his principles. *Ecclesiastical Characteristics* mocked the Moderates for supposedly favouring the liberal thought of Francis Hutcheson and his master Shaftesbury (author of the *Characteristicks* ridiculed in the title), but after becoming president of the College of New Jersey (later Princeton University) in 1768, Witherspoon grew to appreciate Hutcheson's system of moral philosophy and borrowed heavily from it when preparing his own lectures on that subject.

The debate between the two Scottish ecclesiastical parties on polite literature and learning turned chiefly on the question of morality. The orthodox position, as stated by Witherspoon and others, was based primarily on the premise of the immorality of polite literature as such and secondarily on the premise of the immorality of particular works of polite literature composed by Moderate ministers or their friends, such as the notorious David Hume. As the example of Witherspoon's own experience shows, the first of these premises was extremely difficult to maintain because it entailed a thoroughgoing anti-intellectualism that placed Christian philosophers like Hutcheson in the same category as sceptics like Hume. At the time of *Ecclesiastical Characteristics* it seemed wiser for orthodox clerics to focus on particularly pernicious authors and works, but their unsuccessful campaign to censure the 'infidel' philosophers Hume and Lord Kames in the mid 1750s demonstrated how difficult it was to implement this strategy. As polite literature ceased to be considered profane literature, Scottish churchmen grew increasingly reluctant to draw distinctions between philosophical works that were acceptable before the Lord and those that were not.

This is why the controversy over John Home's tragedy *Douglas* was so critically important. In the theatre orthodox clergymen believed they had found a form of polite literature that was unambiguously immoral and reprehensible. When the Moderate clergy produced and attended a tragedy by one of their own number, therefore, they exposed themselves to a furious assault that raged through the early months in 1757. Witherspoon and other orthodox ministers who participated in this paper war based their criticism on the fundamental immorality of theatre as such, but where possible they also tried to show that *Douglas* was a particularly immoral play because it appealed to 'ruling fate' and glorified suicide. The play's defenders, such as Adam Ferguson, countered both these lines of attack by arguing first that theatre could be either moral or immoral depending on the particular play in question, and second that *Douglas* happened to be an exceptionally moral play because it taught virtuous lessons such as maternal love and patriotism. When the *Douglas* case came before the General Assembly in the spring of 1757, William Robertson applied his celebrated oratorical skills on behalf of the view that there was 'nothing sinful or inconsistent with the spirit of Christianity in writing a tragedy, which gives no encouragement to baseness or vice'.[7] The Moderates' triumph on that occasion effectively established the respectability of all species of polite literature and cleared the way for the further growth of the Scottish Enlightenment. Home resigned his parish charge to concentrate on his playwriting and to assist his patron, Lord Bute, in London, but he did not do so in disgrace.

The chief reason for the failure of Popular party clerics like Witherspoon to stop the development of the Moderate-led clerical Enlightenment in Scotland was the fact that the Moderate literati of Robertson's generation were fundamentally moralists, and moralists of an unexceptionable kind. Orthodox clergymen might have desired the Moderates to dwell more on points of doctrine, but few of them would have denied that the polite, moral sermons preached by Hugh Blair and other Moderates were as virtuous as they were elegant. In regard to secular literature, similarly, the Moderates were zealous advocates of morality. This was obviously the case in the moral philosophy classroom, where Ferguson, Reid, and other ministers were explicitly engaged in a quest to instill high ethical principles into their teenage pupils. It was equally true in other branches of polite literature, such as poetry.

Douglas may be used to illustrate this point. It is essentially a morality play in which the evil pronouncements and deeds of the thoroughly wretched villain Glenalvon are contrasted with the consistently virtuous speeches and behaviour of Lord and Lady Randolph and the 'noble' young shepherd Norval. In depicting first the euphoria of Lady Randolph upon the discovery of her long-lost son Norval, and then her despair at losing him again to the treachery of the back-stabbing Glenalvon, the playwright 'waits the test of your congenial tears'.[8] But the pathos he seeks to elicit is wholly in the service of virtue, as shown by these lines on the playwright's aims, spoken in the Epilogue:

> Sadly he says, that pity is the best,
> The noblest passion of the human breast:
> For when its sacred streams the heart o'erflow,
> In gushes pleasure with the tide of woe;
> And when its waves retire, like those of Nile.
> They leave behind them such a golden soil,
> That there the virtues without culture grow,
> There the sweet blossoms of affection blow.

In *Douglas*, as in Home's other plays and most Moderate (as well as Ossianic) poetry, there are no gray areas where ethical issues are concerned. The Moderate conception of literature was fundamentally didactic and moralistic. Hugh Blair's rhetoric course taught that virtue was the end of tragedy, and one of the poems in William Wilkie's *Moral Fables in Verse* began:

> Let every bard who seeks applause
> Be true to virtue and her cause.[9]

Wilkie justified writing a book of fables as a way of overcoming some of the problems associated with other means of conveying moral truths:

In moral lectures treat the case,
Say that is honest, that is base;
In conversation none will bear it;
And for the pulpit, few come near it.
And is there then no other way
A moral lesson to convey?
Must all that shall attempt to teach,
Admonish, satyrize, or preach?[10]

As if in answer to Wilkie's challenge, eighteenth-century Scottish clergymen produced plenty of righteous fables, epics, and shorter poems. But little of their work is readable today, and much of it, like Rev John Ogilvie of Midmar's book-length poems *The Day of Judgment* (1753) and *Providence* (1764), is scarcely even known. David Daiches has attributed the 'unrelieved . . . badness' of the 'establishment poetry of the Edinburgh *literati*' to the Scottish literati's emotional estrangement from the English tongue,[11] and there is undoubtedly a great deal of truth in this linguistic argument. But it is also necessary to remember that much, if not most, of this bad English poetry was written by prudish Presbyterian clergymen whose objectives were as much moral as literary and who lacked much experience in the ways of romance, social gaiety, and other popular poetic subjects at which they sometimes tried their hand—an unpromising foundation for first-rate poetry even among poets with no language problems.

Scholarly English prose was another matter. In this genre command of the English language posed less of a problem than it did in poetry; sentiment and personal experience were of less importance; and moral and religious values could more easily be espoused without compromising literary integrity. Here the Scottish clergy found their proper niche. The Moderate literati of the mature Scottish Enlightenment satisfied the eighteenth-century audience for polite literature by achieving a delicate balance between rational and rigidly pious attitudes, a balance that is well described by the term 'polite Presbyterianism'. Their virtue legitimized their literary endeavours among the pious, much as their moderation and enlightenment made their moralizing more palatable to the polite.

Only extremists of one sort or another were unhappy with the Moderate literati's marriage of Presbyterian religious and moral concerns with polite literature and learning. The literary career of William Robertson demonstrates this point. Robertson's histories were remarkably popular, and they made their author the best paid writer in the world. Their judicious mixture of politeness and Protestantism was certainly one reason for this success. Robertson wrote elegant, formal prose that was greatly admired by contemporaries, and he carefully avoided terms or arguments that might appear to violate the principles of moderate Christianity and conventional morality. Nevertheless, Robertson's efforts did not always satisfy religious zealots and sceptics. The *History of Scotland* was privately criticized by Hume (who was usually full of praise for Robertson's histories) for its

'Godly strain',[12] and Hume or another reviewer in the *Critical Review* attacked Robertson's Presbyterian bias in his treatment of John Knox and the Reformation. At the opposite end of the spectrum, John Wesley was appalled at the thoroughly secular character of Robertson's *History of America.* 'I cannot admire', wrote Wesley, '. . . a Christian Divine writing a history, with so little of Christianity in it. Nay, he seems studiously to avoid saying any thing which might imply that he believes the Bible'. Wesley proceeded to criticize Robertson for 'totally excluding the Creator from governing the world' by attributing events to natural causes or fortune rather than to 'the Providence of God'. Yet even Wesley had to admit that Robertson's style was 'always clear and strong, and frequently elegant', and that his book was 'preferable to any History of America which has appeared in the English tongue'.[13]

Why did Scottish Presbyterian ministers produce so much widely-acclaimed polite literature during the second half of the eighteenth century? Many factors conspired to bring about this development. Among them was the fact that scholarly literature suddenly became highly lucrative during the 1760s, especially after William Robertson received the astonishing fee of £4000 for his *History of Scotland.* Literary endeavours could also lead to translations to more desirable churches, appointments to chaplaincies or university chairs, and the acquisition of international fame and glory. Nor was there any longer a stigma attached to literary activity and the material rewards it might bring. During the 1740s Robert Blair had wondered if publishing a harmless and unobjectionable poem about death was a proper thing for a clergyman to do; in subsequent decades William Robertson grew rich and famous from his secular writings, and upon his death in 1793 he was eulogized by John Erskine, the leader of the orthodox opposition party in the Church, in a sermon that bore the significant title 'The Agency of God in Human Greatness.[14] The production of polite literature by Presbyterian clergymen had become not merely acceptable, but downright respectable.

This would not have been possible if the quest for pecuniary gain had been the only, or even the primary, motive behind the efforts of Scottish clergymen to distinguish themselves in the republic of letters. Material rewards notwithstanding, William Robertson and his Moderate brethren were driven by their sincere commitment to Enlightenment principles. They had a deep love of learning, virtue, justice, humanity, patriotism, politeness, rational religion, and religious tolerance. Their values were embodied in their writings, which included not only grand treatises but pamphlets on social and political issues such as the Scots militia campaign, the American War, and Roman Catholic relief. Their values were also embodied in their personal lives, which were generally conducted with dignity and integrity. While he lay on his deathbed Robertson spoke for his circle when he told John Erskine that he felt joy 'in reflecting, that his life on earth had not been altogether in vain; and his hopes that, through the merits of Jesus, the God, who had so signally prospered him in this world, would, in another and better world, be his portion and happiness'.[15]

What became of the remarkable literary efflorescence that flourished among Scottish churchmen in the age of Dr Robertson? The unfortunate tales of John Logan and William Greenfield, two protégés of the Robertson Moderates, tell part of the story. Both were bright young men who attended Edinburgh University during the Robertson era and subsequently embarked on promising ecclasiastical, academic, and literary careers. Logan, who was minister at South Leith near Edinburgh, published sermons, poems, philosophies•of history, and a tragedy. But ill-health, melancholia, heavy drinking, 'violations of professional decorum', and frustration at failing to secure an academic chair led him to ruin, and soon after impregnating his maid servant he was obliged to resign his church and eke out a living as a hack writer in London from 1785 until his death three years later at just forty years of age. Greenfield's fate was similar, though his downfall was more dramatic. As Hugh Blair's colleague at the prestigious St Giles Church and as Blair's assistant and successor in the Edinburgh chair of rhetoric and belles lettres, Greenfield had a glorious career ahead of him. He was considered an outstanding preacher and a promising literary critic, and he was a good enough mathematician to publish a paper on negative quantities in the first volume of the *Transactions of the Royal Society of Edinburgh*. Burns adored him, and in 1796 his brethren in the Church thought fit to elect him Moderator of the General Assembly. He had a wife and family, including a son named Hugh Blair Greenfield. But in 1798 he threw it all away by committing an undisclosed sex crime that was deemed a hangable offense. Cast out of the Church of Scotland, he spent the rest of his life in England teaching and writing essays and books under assumed names.

Although the sad stories of Logan and Greenfield were not typical, they were symptomatic. 'Polite Presbyterianism'—that delicate balance between traditional religion and morality on the one hand, and polite, secular literature, learning, and manners on the other—was a difficult position to maintain. Tip the balance too far in one direction and the result would be affectation, hypocrisy, and immorality of the sort that brought about the downfalls of Logan and Greenfield. Tip the balance the other way and the result would be a strictly religious approach to literature and learning of the kind associated with pious and sometimes prolific evangelical authors such as John Erskine during the age of the Enlightenment and Thomas Chalmers during the age of the Disruption. For a brief period in the second half of the eighteenth century the Moderate literati achieved a polite Presbyterian hegemony in the Church. During that time a disproportionately large number of Scottish clergymen attained fame, and sometimes wealth, from their literary productions while at the same time retaining their character as respectable churchmen. In no other era in the history of modern Scotland does Scottish literature owe a greater debt to the nation's clergy.

NOTES

1   Alexander Carlyle, *The Usefulness and Necessity of a Liberal Education for Clergymen* (Edinburgh, 1793), pp 38–9; Henry R Sefton, ' "Neu-lights and Preachers-Legal": Some Observations on the Beginnings of Moderatism in the Church of Scotland', in *Church, Politics and Society: Scotland 1408–1929*, Norman Macdougall (ed) (Edinburgh, 1983), pp 186–96. 'New-Lights' became a widely-used term to denote liberal clergymen. 'Preachers legal', according to Wodrow, were those who recommended 'duties only on the powers of nature and without grace, and neglecting Christ as our only strength for performing, and the ground of our acceptance'.

2   Blair to Doddridge, 25 February [1742], in Robert Anderson, *Works of the British Poets*, 13 vols (London, 1795), VIII, p 853.

3   Hugh Blair's review in the *Edinburgh Review* I (1755), p 23.

4   *See* Richard B Sher, *Church and University in the Scottish Enlightenment: The Moderate Literati of Edinburgh* (Edinburgh, 1985).

5   Blair to Burns, 4 May 1787, National Library of Scotland, MS 3408, ff 3–4.

6   John Witherspoon, *Ecclesiastical Characteristics* (Edinburgh, 1753), citing maxims I, II, V, and VII.

7   Quoted in 'An Essay on the Life and Writings of William Robertson', *The Works of William Robertson*, 8 vols (Oxford, 1825), I, p x.

8   *Douglas* (1757), Edinburgh Prologue.

9   William Wilkie, *Moral Fables in Verse* (Edinburgh, 1769), fable III, 'The Muse and the Shepherd'.

10 Ibid., fable I, 'The Young Lady and the Looking-Glass'.

11 David Daiches, *The Paradox of Scottish Culture: The Eighteenth-Century Experience* (London, 1964), *esp*. pp 84–5.

12 Hume to Blair, 27 March 1766, in *The Letters of David Hume*, 2 vols, J Y T Greig (ed), (Oxford, 1932), II, p 31.

13 *The Journal of the Reverend John Wesley*, 4 vols, Everyman edn (London, n.d.), IV, pp 214–15.

14 John Erskine, *Discourses Preached on Several Occasions*, 2nd edn, 2 vols (Edinburgh, 1801), I, pp 240–77.

15 Ibid., p 277.

FURTHER READING

Clark, Ian D L 'From Protest to Reaction: The Moderate Regime in the Church of Scotland, 1752–1805', in *Scotland in the Age of Improvement: Essays in Scottish History in the Eighteenth Century*, Phillipson, N T and Rosalind Mitchison (eds) (Edinburgh, 1970), pp 200–24

Drummond, Andrew L, *The Kirk and the Continent*, (Edinburgh, 1956)

—— and James Bulloch, *The Scottish Church, 1688–1843: The Age of the Moderates*, (Edinburgh, 1973)

Dunlop, A Ian, *William Carstares and the Kirk by Law Established*, (Edinburgh, 1967)

Dwyer, John, 'The Heavenly City of the Eighteenth-Century Moderates', in *New Perspectives on the Politics and Culture of Early Modern Scotland*, Dwyer, John et al. (eds) (Edinburgh, 1982), pp 291–318

Macdougall, Norman (ed) *Church, Politics and Society: Scotland 1408–1929* (Edinburgh, 1983)

Sher, Richard B *Church and University in the Scottish Enlightenment: The Moderate Literati of Edinburgh* (Princeton and Edinburgh, 1985)

—— ' "The Favourite of the Favourite": John Home, Bute and the Politics of Patriotic Poetry', in *Lord Bute: Essays in Reinterpretation*, Schweizer, Karl W (ed) (forthcoming)

Chapter 16

The Language of Sentiment: Hume, Smith, and Henry Mackenzie

JOHN MULLAN

In December 1825, Sir Walter Scott noted in his *Journal* that the eighty-year old Henry Mackenzie had read 'an Essay on Dreams' at a meeting the previous evening of Edinburgh's Royal Society. Scott was evidently impressed by the performance of a person he supposed 'on the very brink of human dissolution', and was prompted by the old man's apparent zest for the ritualized expression of sociability to record a paradox:

> No man is less known from his writings. We would suppose a retired modest somewhat affected man with a white handkerchief and a sigh ready for every sentiment. No such thing. H.M. is alert as a contracting tailor's needle in every sort of business—a politician and a sportsman—shoots and fishes in a sort even to this day—and is the life of the company with anecdote and fun.[1]

The title of Mackenzie's first and most successful book, *The Man of Feeling*, had passed to its author, but Scott was not alone in discovering a gap between the social identity that Mackenzie styled for himself and the exemplary susceptibility of Harley, the 'hero' of that novel. Mackenzie's fellow Edinburgh lawyer Henry Cockburn recollected,

> Strangers used to fancy that he must be a pensive sentimental Harley; whereas he was far better—a hard headed practical man, as full of worldly wisdom as most of his fictitious characters are devoid of it; and this without in the least impairing the affectionate softness of his heart.[2]

Mackenzie was not himself, apparently, 'The Man of Feeling'. The vogue of sentimental fiction over, Scott and Cockburn noted with relief or approval a disparity between 'wordly' action and 'fictitious' ideal. Retrospectively, both men were identifying a special capacity for 'feeling' as incompatible with the necessary faculties of social life.

Condensed in these observations of a banal difference between fact and fiction are some clues as to the failed ambitions of sentimentalism. When Mackenzie wrote to his cousin in July 1769 about how narratives could interest 'the Memory & the Affection deeper, than mere Argument, or moral Reasoning', and described his plan for a fiction 'introducing a Man of Sensibility into different scenes where his Feelings might be seen in their Effects, & his Sentiments occasionally delivered without the Stiffness of regular Deduction,[3] he was following a precedent set most influentially by Richardson. The novels which had come to dominate the market for books in the three decades before Mackenzie produced *The Man of Feeling* habitually professed a desire to teach virtue, but it was Richardson who first effectively proposed the novel as a properly (indeed piously) moralistic kind of text, and insisted on the capacity for 'feeling' as a special trait of those prepared to act virtuously. Mackenzie could follow this lead, though the fashion that he exploited also had to be disavowed. Conventionally, in the period, novels were deprecated (often by novelists) as morally unreliable or pernicious; they were supposed to be titillating, low-minded, beguiling fodder for young women. Mackenzie was merely orthodox in conceiving of his own tale of 'Sensibility' as something other than the kind of text too eagerly devoured by the novel-buying public:

> It has, however deficient in other respects, I hope, something of Nature in it, and is uniformly subservient to the cause of Virtue. You may perhaps, from the description, conclude it a novel, nevertheless it is perfectly different than that species of composition.[4]

As he had inherited from Richardson (whose name is invoked in the Introduction of *The Man of Feeling*) the saving allegiance to 'the cause of Virtue', so he had also taken on the anxiety about the propriety of narrative fiction as such. The story that he tells is to be improving as much as engrossing—'no more a history than it is a sermon'; it equates virtue with an exemplary susceptibility to 'feeling'. This susceptibility is supposed to be as exceptional as it is admirable: Harley, dying a death 'replete with the genuine happiness attendant upon virtue', and witnessed by the few tearful friends who can recognize that virtue, says,

> There are some feelings which are perhaps too tender to be suffered by the world. The world is in general selfish, interested, and unthinking, and throws the imputation of romance or melancholy on every temper more susceptible than its own. I cannot think but in those regions which I contemplate, if there is any thing of mortality left about us, that these feelings will subsist;—they are called,—perhaps they are—weaknesses here;—but there may be some better modifications of them in heaven, which may deserve the name of virtues. (pp 128–9)

Both the protagonist and the narrator of Mackenzie's novel lament the rarity of virtue, which is made a matter of visceral, specialized sensation—unappreciated in a world of misanthropy and self-interest. It is the narrator's sensation when he visits Harley's grave:

> I sit in the hollow of the tree. It is worth a thousand homilies! every nobler feeling rises within me! every beat of my heart awakens a virtue!—but it will make you hate the world—No: there is such an air of gentleness around, that I can hate nothing; but as to the world—I pity the men of it. (pp 132–3)

What Scott and Cockburn were implying was that the Man of Feeling was inappropriate, impracticable, as a model of conduct. Obvious enough

—yet, if a novel was not providing such a model, what could its moral status be?

In a sense, this problem for the producer or consumer of novels in the eighteenth century remains a problem for the historian: what values could novels such as Mackenzie's bespeak? To answer the question it is necessary to describe a 'language of sentiment' of which Mackenzie's fiction was but one influential expression. The popularity of (now scarcely readable) novels such as Mackenzie's is historically significant because it is evidence of the uses to which this language could be put, and of the capacity of such fiction to elaborate a culture's fantasy of 'human nature'. Here again, the remarks about Mackenzie's social persona provide a lead. His social life was stylised and self-regarding in the manner of the Edinburgh ruling-class; he mixed with those for whom the expression of polite, educated sociability had become the nearest thing that they had to a civic duty. It was a class which had found a paradigm of that sociability in the learned or literary club—the kind of social formation whose consolations were nicely hinted at in the name of the grouping of which both David Hume and Adam Smith were founder members in 1754, the 'Select Society'. Scott and Cockburn took Mackenzie's social being—displayed in this kind of forum—to displace his fiction. Yet, whatever the apparent complacencies of polite society in the urban Scotland of the Enlightenment, sociability remained a problem, and Mackenzie's novels demonstrated the fact, for it is just this elusive capacity which they attempted to describe. Their men and women of virtue are typically victims, and most of all victims of sympathetic faculties which cannot be practised in the world: Harley weeping with those few unfortunates who can share his tears; Annesley, in *The Man of the World*, finding a brief 'felicity' in 'the smaller circles of private life' before his reclusive family is destroyed by the malevolent aristocrat referred to in the book's title.[6] The social instinct, justified in tearful acts of benevolence, is what is celebrated and worried over in the novel of sentiment; 'feeling' is discovered to be the raw expression of this instinct. The concern to describe natural human impulses to sociability was not unique to a fashion in novel-writing, and can be traced through many of the other kinds of text by which eighteenth-century Edinburgh could be projected as the 'Athens of the North'. What now gets called the 'Scottish Enlightenment' is distinguished by the new kinds of account offered by writers like Hume and Smith of a commercial world in which differences of interest and specializations of activity were necessary facts; the compensatory assurance of a potential for social solidarity was required by a culture which was learning to describe the effects of competition and self-interest. In Scotland, a nation whose propertied class had to find a substitute in politeness and intellectual cohesiveness for the political identity it had lost with the Act of Union, the ideal of sociability was particularly alluring and difficult. As Mackenzie's novels seem committed (however fantastically) to this ideal, so does the contemporary Scottish philosophy of 'moral sentiments'.

It is a reflection on the national self-consciousness of the Scottish literati of the period that we can make the link between the writer of sentimental novels and the philosopher of moral sentiments by attending to Henry Mackenzie's own tendentious fantasy about David Hume, the most penetrating and finally influential such philosopher. In 1779 there appeared through three consecutive issues of the Edinburgh periodical *The Mirror*, whose editor and main contributor was Mackenzie, a tale of tears and tremulous sensibilities which became known and much anthologized as the 'Story of La Roche'. It was written by Mackenzie, and tells the story of an atheistic philosopher living in France who is habitually solitary until he becomes attached to an old clergyman and his daughter. He comes to admire their simple virtue, and, when the daughter dies, has his scepticism softened by the combined sensibility and religiosity (religion 'of sentiment, not theory') by which the old man becomes reconciled to her death.[7] As he listens to La Roche preach, he is almost swayed: 'even the philosopher felt himself moved and forgot, for a moment, to think why he should not'. As he sees 'The effects of religion on minds of sensibility' (Mackenzie's later title for the story) he almost succumbs to the effects which bind the members of the rural community to which La Roche preaches:

> Mr —'s heart was smitten;—and I have heard him, long after, confess that there were moments when the remembrance overcame him even to weakness; when amidst all the pleasures of philosophical discovery, and the pride of literary fame, he recalled to his mind the venerable figure of the good La Roche, and wished that he had never doubted. (1,xliv, 196)

The story, with its domestic tragedy, its revelation of simple virtue in the capacity for feeling, shows the vogue of sentimental fiction passing over into the polite periodical. It was Mackenzie in particular who pioneered the adaptation of this form—whose most important precedent was *The Spectator*—to the cultural condition of the propertied class in Scotland. Like *The Spectator*, *The Mirror* aimed to produce a polished audience attuned to contemporary 'subjects of manners'—it aimed to socialize its readership. Indeed, it was composed by a club consisting largely of young lawyers, and was thus in origin as well as intent a *social* production. A tale of naturally responsive sensibility was provided as a fashionable diet for readers expected to exercise, in the same moment, moral judgement and literary taste. But the story is something odder than this minor relic of sentimentalism, the 'fine tale' over whose 'unexampled delicacy' Scott enthused.[8] For the character described by Scott as 'a philosopher, whose heart remains sensitive, though his studies have misled his mind into the frozen regions of scepticism' was a peculiarly loaded invention. Mackenzie claimed that when he showed the story to Adam Smith, he recognized its protagonist as his friend and fellow philosopher David Hume, who had died three years earlier. 'This story is purely a fiction founded only on the circumstances of Mr David Hume's living some time in France about the period of his first publications', noted Mackenzie in his own copy of *The Mirror*. Many years later, in his biography of the playwright John Home, Mackenzie referred to his own experience of Hume's company, and that philosopher's tactful avoidance in conversation of religious controversy, in order to justify his fabrication of an episode in Hume's life:

> His good nature and benevolence prevented such an injury to his hearers; it was unfortunate that he often forgot what injury some of his writings might do to his readers. The sentiments which such good nature and benevolence might suggest, I ventured to embody, in a sort of dramatic form, in the story of La Roche in the Mirror.

In the Common Sense philosophy of Thomas Reid, James Oswald, and James Beattie, Hume's name had, through the 1760s and 1770s, been declared synonymous with a scepticism corrosive of moral and religious principle; his death occasioned public attacks on his ideas which were also attacks on his character: Hume's scepticism was a public reputation, and when Mackenzie's sentimental tale was published, many Scottish readers would have been as ready as Smith to recognize its protagonist. The tale shows Hume acknowledging that his sceptical, philosophical spirit isolates him from the benefits of feeling, the privileges of sociability. In this version of natural capacities, sensibility, the submission to the power of sentiment, produces sociability; the Man of Feeling is he who can enjoy sympathetic relations with others. Though Hume was famously a man for 'Company' in a city whose ruling class was attentive to the expression of its own sociability, Mackenzie's tale pictures him cut off from feeling by his philosophy. He may have been, in the Edinburgh of his own lifetime, a paragon of enlightened learning and conversational polish, but his philosophical reputation ('The unfortunate nature of his opinions with regard to the theoretical principles of moral and religious truth', as Mackenzie put it) had to be exorcised:

> He had, it might be said ... two minds; one which indulged in the metaphysical scepticism which his genius could invent; another, simple, natural, and playful, which made his conversation delightful to his friends, and even frequently conciliated men whose principles of belief his philosophical doubts, if they had not the power to shake, had grieved and offended.[9]

Mackenzie could not quite make Hume into a Christian—though others, like Boswell and Johnson, tried—but he could try to redeem his social being from his philosophy.

In fact, Mackenzie found it easier to side with the assault mounted on Hume by James Beattie in his *Essay on the Nature and Immutability of Truth (1770)*, than with Hume's astringent analyses of human beliefs.[10] He regretted a few of Beattie's rhetorical excesses—the product of his 'Ardor of Composition'—but did not see anything essentially wrong with the description of Hume as the leading representative of a philosophy designed 'to divest the mind of every principle, and of all conviction; and, consequently, to disqualify man for action' (Beattie, *Essay*, 2nd edn (1771), p 6). But he also admired Hume as a leading citizen of what he wanted to see as a city of politeness. He attempted to separate out this element of

Hume's reputation by identifying philosophical questioning as a habit which alienates the questioner from the powers of sentiment and therefore from the experience of sociability. In one way, even if mawkishly, his attempt fits Hume's own description of philosophical activity in his *Treatise of Human Nature*—the very work that he composed during that stay in France from which Mackenzie makes his story. In the Conclusion of Book I of the *Treatise*, the philosopher represents philosophy as that which severs him from social existence:

> I am first affrighted and confounded with that forelorn solitude, in which I am plac'd in my philosophy, and fancy myself some strange uncouth monster, who not being able to mingle and unite in society, has been expell'd all human commerce, and left utterly abandon'd and disconsolate.[11]

It is a representation which Beattie, the self-declared enemy to 'Sophistry and Scepticism', could only echo in a puzzled reference to the 'uncouth and gloomy aspect' of the *Treatise*—a puzzled reference to this text's tendency to question its own capacities (*Essay*, p 516). Foreseeing Beattie's objections, and facilitating Mackenzie's fantasy, Hume recognizes that while sceptical doubt is an incurable 'malady' the 'common life' of society depends upon the customary passions and beliefs which the philospher sceptically scrutinizes.[12] Sceptical argument, Hume concedes, is unanswerable in its own philosophical terms, and insupportable outside them: the philosopher is isolated by his malady. In another way, however, Mackenzie's parable seems conveniently blind to the concerns of Hume's most problematic (most 'philosophical') moral philosophy. Much of this is dedicated to the theorization of society, and, in the *Treatise* the communication of feeling or sentiment is the fundamental, common mechanism of society. The language of sentiment in *The Man of Feeling*, as in other novels of the period, is applied to the description of the rare affections of those capable of sympathy; in Hume's moral philosophy, this language is used to portray the basic ('natural') processes of sociability—processes upon which reliable moral judgements come to depend.

Sociability is an approximate synonym for the 'society' to whose workings, in the *Treatise*, Hume applies the vocabulary of 'sentiment', 'passion', and 'sympathy'. In his later *Essays*, society is described at its culturally and historically specific stages, and is understood in terms of its commercial and political organization. In his earliest, and most ambitious, work, however, society is more like a faculty or activity than a set of relations. The *Treatise* is committed to a description of 'human nature', and to the specification of social being as an aspect of this nature. Its effort is to generalize particular models of contact and communication—to establish the principles of social relations by describing 'our' need for, and behaviour in, 'company'. 'We can form no wish, which has not a reference to society' (*Treatise*, p 363): by 'society' here Hume means local relationships, the particular proximity of others; 'company' is, indeed, insistently used in the place of 'society'. The principle which is taken to make possible social transactions is 'sympathy' which allows 'communication of sentiments and passions' (p 592)

> No quality of human nature is more remarkable, both in itself and in its consequences, than that propensity we have to sympathize with others, and to receive by communication their inclinations and sentiments, however different from, or even contrary to our own. (p 316)

'Sentiment' is a word made variously synonymous with 'passion', 'feeling', 'opinion', 'judgement'. This is not so surprising: it would seem consistent with a scepticism about the powers of reason for which the *Treatise* is famous. But then the conflation which the usage permits represents more than an acceptance that human desires and decisions are determined by the vagaries of passion. With sympathy a natural principle, sentiment is socialized. The proximity of feeling and judgement is sanctioned by social existence. 'The sentiments of others can never affect us, but by becoming, in some measure, our own' (p 593)—what sympathy promises is that others' sentiments do become 'our own'.

> The minds of all men are similar in their feelings and operations, nor can any one be actuated by an affection, of which all others are not, in some degree, susceptible. As in strings equally wound up, the motion of one communicates itself to the rest; so all the affections readily pass from one person to another, and beget correspondent movements in every human creature. (p 576)

Every novel of sentiment, and certainly *The Man of Feeling*, sets out to describe such 'correspondent movements'—felt in the fibres of the body, seen in the gestures and tears that need no words:

> When Edwards had ended his relation Harley stood a while looking at him in silence; at last he pressed him in his arms, and when he had given vent to the fulness of his heart by a shower of tears, 'Edwards,' said he, 'let me hold thee to my bosom; let me imprint the virtue of thy sufferings on my soul . . .' Edwards, from whom the recollection of his own sufferings had scarce forced a tear, now blubbered like a boy. (pp 94–5)

But only the especially sensitive can experience the thrill of such sympathy, and they are assailed by misfortunes and persecuted by villains. They exist in an unfeeling world. And the reader is invited to admire a faculty for feeling by a text which presumes that few can manage to recognize that ideal, and which has to distance itself from the usual reputation of novels in order to address its reader as one of those few. So the narrator of *The Man of Feeling* is supposed to ponder the fragmentary nature of the text that he is delivering in order to exclude the insensitive reader: though the fragments contain 'Some instruction, and some example',

> it is likely that many of those, whom chance has led to a perusal of what I have already presented, may have read it with little pleasure, and will feel no disappointment from the want of those parts which I have been unable to

procure: to such as may have expected the intricacies of a novel, a few incidents in a life undistinguished, except by some features of the heart, cannot have afforded much entertainment. (p 125)

If Mackenzie's novels attempt to imagine a virtue experienced in sociability, they perversely demonstrate such sociability at odds with 'the world'—an unusual, defeated solidarity. Misfortune is typically the lot of those who are sentimental and sympathetic in these novels, and is provided in measures which can now appear ludicrous. Indeed, in *The Man of the World*, the virtuous Annesly, seeking social 'felicity' in 'the sphere of sequestered life', is literally struck dead by the intensity of his feelings at the misfortunes that his family experiences. He has sought 'that cordial friendship, that warm attachment which is only to be found in the smaller circles of private life, which is lost in the bustle and extended connection of larger societies', (p 198) but the domesticity which is his ideal exists only to be destroyed by bad luck and the villainy of 'The Man of the World'. Mackenzie's novels actually find it difficult to imagine how social virtues can prevail in an anti-social world.

The elision in 'sentiment' of moral judgement and affecting feeling, bequeathed by Richardson to the novelists of the later eighteenth century, can look like a fatalistic manoeuvre. The idea of sociability may be what the paragon of feeling aspires to in the fiction of the period, but usually this capacity of the individual is shown to be incompatible with the larger society to which this character belongs. This larger society, whose standards the protagonist of a Mackenzie novel habitually laments, knows no sympathies. Novels like Mackenzie's sustain such a representation by addressing as if privately a singular reader who can be trusted to approve of social instinct known in the unusual power of feeling. 'By those who have feeling hearts, and a true relish for simplicity in writing, many pages in this miscellaneous volume will be read with satisfaction', declared the *Critical Review* of *The Man of Feeling*. It is a distinguishing irony of the development of the novel in the eighteenth century that, while this was the most popular, the most widely accessible, kind of text, the effort of novelists, and (when they wished to be approving) critics too was to posit an exclusive, select readership for novels: all except, inevitably, those who were taken normally to read novels. But Mackenzie attempted to be not a novelist but a Scottish Man of Letters. It was as 'Our Scottish Addison' that Sir Walter Scott commemorated him in the Dedication to *Waverley*, in a phrase whose pretensions signal a patriotism always close to a sense of inferiority. Mackenzie's was a writing career symptomatic of the aspirations of the educated ruling class of Enlightenment Scotland (not least in that he continued in a successful and remunerative legal career all the time that he was a writer). He looked for other ways of prescribing sociability, other ways of constructing a socialized readership, in the polite journalism of *The Mirror* and *The Lounger*.

These periodicals elucidate an ethics of 'manners' for their polite Scottish readership, even if worrying whether they can find a sizable, sophisticated audience such as that supposed to exist in England. They deal, as Mackenzie declared in a retrospective manifesto to *The Mirror*, with 'subjects of manners, of taste, and of literature', (2, cx, 279) striving for an 'intercourse of sentiment', an 'invisible sort of friendship' with 'the virtuous and the good' who are imagined to constitute their readership. Yet the metaphor of this intimate, conversational relationship (a dominant one—both periodicals take conversation as the ideal of their styles) should not obscure the difference between the model of sociability envisaged in these texts and that produced in the tear-soaked pages of Mackenzie's novels. The Addisonian essay was one of the culturally desirable forms to the manipulation of which the literary arbiters of the Scottish Enlightenment aspired. Hume's *Essays*, as he acknowledged in the Advertisement to the first edition, were originally devised for serial publication in this mode. But then Hume's recourse to this form was also a retreat from the uncommon sense of his earlier philosophy—a retreat without that saving lightness of irony which had distinguished the professions of *The Spectator* to improve its readers:

> It was said of *Socrates*, that he brought Philosphy down from Heaven, to inhabit among Men; and I shall be ambitious to have it said of me, that I have brought Philosophy out of Closets and Libraries, Schools and Colleges, to dwell in Clubs and Assemblies, at Tea-Tables and in Coffee-Houses (*The Spectator*, No. 10).

This declaration by Mr Spectator calculatedly courts bathos for the benefit of a readership finally untroubled by the pretensions of 'philosophy'; Hume's essays, for all their elegance, have none of this confidence, and are the more gripping for their tendency to veer from tact into difficulty or iconoclasm. Though avoiding the unconsoling lures of scepticism, the polite essays devised by Mackenzie and his collaborators to socialize a provincial readership were also less culturally complacent than they sometimes proclaimed themselves. The 'science of *Manners*' fitted to 'a state of society so advanced as ours',[13] was what they were designed to promote, but in doing so they had to qualify, or even repudiate, the model of a limited but elemental sociability based on sentimental susceptibility.

It is not enough for refined journalism to rely on 'those delicate strokes of sentimental morality, which refer our actions to the determinations of feeling'. (2, ci, 231) Readers of *The Mirror* are advized that 'there are bounds beyond which virtuous feelings cease to be virtue; that the decisions of sentiment are subject to the control of prudence'. (p 236) Mackenzie's collaborator and fellow lawyer William Craig takes literally the possibility of sensibility being the distinguishing quality of social being and emphasizes the instability of that ideal of sociability:

> Refinement, and delicacy of taste, are the productions of advanced society. They open to the mind of persons possessed of them a field of elegant enjoyment; but they may be pushed to a dangerous extreme. By that excess of

sensibility to which they lead . . . they may unfit their possessor for the common and ordinary enjoyments of life. (1, x, 40)

Mackenzie discloses the ambiguity of the code of social virtue which gets described in *The Mirror* and *The Lounger* with the parables that he devises for *The Mirror* concerning Mr Umphraville, a spectatorial critic of the luxurious excesses of a 'commercial' society. He is a man of 'spirit and sensibility', who retires from a world in which 'the sentiments of public virtue are extinguished'. (vi, 26) Yet while his 'sensibility' permits insights into fashionable corruption (and politeness must always be distinguishable from mere fashion, which is the surrender of sociability to fantasy), he cannot be a model: the narrator of his exploits has to step in to tell us that 'in his apprehension of facts he is often mistaken, and the conclusions he draws from those facts are often erroneous'. (xxviii, 126) The 'sensible' critic of corrupted manners cannot conduct the world's necessary 'business'; his potential for social understanding isolates him from the practical contacts of a civilized existence. The capacity for feeling which, in Mackenzie's novels, is the equivalent of sociability is shown as impractical, even pathological: 'There is a certain fineness of soul, and delicacy of sentiment, with which few situations accord, to which many seemingly harmless ones give the greatest uneasiness'. (xxxii, 139)

These strictures echo Hume's essay 'Of the Delicacy of Taste and Passion', and bespeak the same concern that it shows with the conception of civic virtue, or at least propriety, achieved in the self's adaptation to a social life. Hume writes to correct 'a certain *delicacy of passion*', an extreme 'sensibility of temper' liable to deprive a person of 'all relish in the common occurences of life; the right enjoyment of which forms the chief part of our happiness': 'men of such lively passions are apt to be transported beyond all bounds of prudence and discretion, and to take false steps in the conduct of life, which are often irretrievable'.[14] The logic of what was the opening essay in Hume's *Essays: Moral and Political* of 1741 is an odd one; it is contradictory in the same way as Mackenzie's description of the relation between sentiment and civilization, feeling and refinement. 'Taste', the faculty shown in *The Mirror* and *The Lounger* to be the desirable achievement of the citizen, is what Hume puts forward as a guarantee of sociability. Hume proposes the displacement by 'delicacy of taste' of the 'delicacy of passion' which it 'very much resembles'. (pp 4–6) Indeed, as 'taste' covers the appreciation not just of 'the productions of the nobler arts' but also of 'conversation', 'company', or 'the characters of men', the two are barely distinguishable; 'taste' looks like a minimal support to the idea of a social identity adapted to 'the accidents of life' rather than abandoned to fickle currents of passion. In fact, Hume concedes that 'taste' is not so far removed from 'passion':

> But perhaps I have gone too far in saying, that a cultivated taste for the polite arts extinguishes the passions, and renders us indifferent to those objects, which are so fondly pursued by the rest of mankind. On farther reflection, I

find, that it rather improves our sensibility for all the tender and agreeable passions. (p 6)

'Taste' should distinguish the responsible citizen in a commercial world, but it does so by specializing society to 'the company of a few select companions': 'a delicacy of taste is favourable to love and friendship, by confining our choice to few people, and making us indifferent to the company and conversation of the greater part of men'. (p 7)

The elitism of this is insecure. The essay is significant to a history of the language of sentiment because, whilst it starts by outlining the requirements for a practical 'conduct of life' in society, it ends by detecting the essential experience of society in the particular, exclusive contacts of 'select companions' - in a limited exercise of 'sensibility'. It attempts to embrace what, in Mackenzie's writings, is the contradiction between the sentimental paragon of the novels and the polite codes of the essays. This contradiction was indicated in one of the letters of Robert Burns, whose poetry received some of its earliest sponsorship from an article by Mackenzie in the *Lounger* (one of the less wishful efforts at the puffing of a new Scottish 'literature'). Burns described *The Man of Feeling* as 'a book I prize next to the Bible', a text whose moralizing, socializing effects were assured:

> From what book, moral or even pious, will the susceptible young mind receive impressions more congenial to humanity and kindness, generosity and benevolence—in short, more of all that ennobles the soul to herself, or endears her to others—than from the simple affecting tale of poor Harley?[15]

So far these are just variations on the conventional justification of narrative given throughout the century by the writers and readers of novels. But immediately Burns remarked, 'with all my admiration of M'kenzie's writings, I do not know if they are the fittest reading for a young man who is about to set out, as the phrase is, to make his way into life':

> among the favored few of Heaven in the structure of their minds (for such there certainly are) there may be a purity, a tenderness, a dignity, an elegance of soul, which are of no use, nay, in some degree, absolutely disqualifying, for the truly important business of making a man's way into life?

This seems a disabling caveat; what kind of virtue might it be that could not be practised? If the literati of the Scottish Enlightenment were self-consciously committed to the explication of a kind of virtue practicable in a commercially progressive, politically dependent province, Burns indicates how the novel of sentiment fails to fit the model. We might say now that the Man of Feeling was never a serious ideal—that the remarks of Scott and Cockburn with which I began pointedly demonstrate that he must always have been a fantastic figment. Yet as fantasy (and a popular and influential one over which readers claimed to weep even if they did not) it is symbolic of at least a wishfulness at the heart of complacent refrains about the social sophistication of modern Scottish citizens. It is the fantasy of a ruling class about what it has lost. Harley and his likenesses stand for a capacity for sympathy unsustained by society at large.

In this sense, and precisely because he is fantastic, inimitable, the situation of the Man of Feeling dramatizes a difficulty encountered in moral philosophy of the period (Hume's in particular), a problem still perceptible in 'Of the Delicacy of Taste and Passion'. Hume's *Enquiry concerning the Principles of Morals* rhetorically poses the question, 'but why, in the greater society or confederacy of mankind, should not the case be the same as in particular clubs and companies?': it is easy to read this as plaintive.[16] For at stake in the enquiries of both Hume and, later, Adam Smith is the relation between the experience of sociability exemplified by 'particular clubs and companies', those limited groups to whose formation the educated of Edinburgh devoted themselves with an anxious seriousness, and the wider world of competing interests and prejudices. 'Every human creature resembles ourselves, and by that means has an advantage above any other object, in operating on the imagination', writes Hume in the *Treatise*, (p 359) but this resemblance is experienced, as 'sympathy', in particular contacts. It is this sympathy, in the *Treatise*, which secures moral judgements: such judgements may not be referable to any absolute (certainly not any God-given) standard, but, if sentiments are completely communicable, they can at lest be shared. The problem is to model the relations and allegiances constituting a political society on such particular fellowship of feeling. In the *Treatise*, Hume attempts to generalize sympathy to an 'extensive concern for society', (p 579) a capacity to appreciate the social utility of institutions and actions by imagining, and sympathizing with, those whom they might benefit: 'the good of society, where our own interest is not concern'd, or that of our friends, pleases only by sympathy'. (p 577) Where there is sympathy, there are no strangers.

The *Treatise*, however, trusts to the socializing of 'the passions' more completely than any other attempt in the period to use moral philosophy to understand the nature of social agency. It relies on a sympathy by which 'the ideas of the affections of others are converted into the very impressions they represent': 'an idea of a sentiment or passion, may by this means be so inliven'd as to become the very sentiment or passion'. (p 319) In his later moral philosophy, Hume abandons the discourse 'Of the Passion', and substitutes for 'sympathy', in the *Enquiry concerning the Principles of Morals*, a 'natural sentiment of benevolence', (p 230) and a willingness and ability to calculate what is 'beneficial to human society'. (p 195) The effort to make sympathy secure social identity and moral consistency was always strained (the strain that shows in another way in the hyperbole of sentimental fiction), and the *Enquiry* abandons the flow of sentiments for the influences of 'utility' and 'public interest', upon which a 'political society' must depend. 'Sympathy', on the rare occasions when it is used, is merely a synonym for 'a general benevolence' (p 298)—that 'universal affection to mankind' with which Hume was philosophically impatient in the *Treatise*. (p 481)

It took a philosopher as penetrating and unsuperstitious as Hume to push the discourse of moral philosophy far enough for it to begin to *fail* to explain how members of a society were actually bound together. The enquiry into the nature of social cohesion, some of whose other products were the incipient sociology of Ferguson and the political economy of Adam Smith, had a particular significance for educated Scots, whose situation was an incentive to new ways of thinking about social being. In the wake of J G A Pocock's *The Machiavellian Moment*, the revivification in England in the eighteenth century of humanist vocabularies of civic identity has been seen to dominate political thought. But because civic humanist theory, as adapted from a writer like Machiavelli, was a theory of the citizen's political identity (that is what a citizen was—a political agent) it was scarcely applicable to the inhabitants of what, since 1707, had been a province rather than a politically independent nation. For Scots in particular it was evident that such theory could not describe modern forms of society. But the alternatives were difficult. The progress from Hume's early writing, through his later writing, to the use made of each by Adam Smith, illustrates the failure of moral philosophy to explain social relations as the language of sentiment falters. Hume's *Treatise* attempts to reconcile reasonable discourse to the limitations of reason, most importantly by placing its faith in a sociability conceived of as 'sympathy'—a principle of 'human nature'. Here, though not in his later works, Hume describes how 'passions', made synonymous with 'sentiments', can bind individuals together. Smith's *Theory of Moral Sentiments*, first published in 1759, capitalizes on Hume's vocabulary to justify a logic of 'propriety' to its educated readers, but in examining every detail of the possible operation of sympathy it announces the limitations of that principle. In order to adapt social identity to the facts of a commercial world, whose operations he analyzed in *The Wealth of Nations*, Smith constructs as his social animal a responsible agent—a 'spectator' of actions and passions. His is not a subject defined by instinctive sympathies, but a self-possessed citizen practising sympathy carefully, reservedly. So, for Smith, sympathy can be corrective as much as responsive:

> Sympathy . . . does not arise so much from the view of the passion, as from that of the situation which excites it. We sometimes feel for another, a passion of which he himself seems to be altogether incapable; because, when we put ourselves in his case, that passion arises in our breast from the imagination, though it does not in his from the reality.[17]

Indeed, it is a kind of duty to moderate passions sufficiently to arouse a sympathy that can always be withheld. The socially adjusted individual cannot just feel a passion,

> He must flatten, if I may be allowed to say so, the sharpness of its natural tone, in order to reduce it to harmony and concord with the emotions of those who

are about him. What they feel, will, indeed, always be, in some respects, different from what he feels, and compassion can never be the same with original sorrow . . . These two sentiments, however, may, it is evident, have such a correspondence with one another, as is sufficient for the harmony of society. (p 22)

Sympathy, in Smith's moral philosophy, is about arriving at 'sentiments' by the regulation and tutoring, as much as the sharing, of 'passions'. It should proceed only from a willed uninvolvement, an achievement of a condition removed from the more dangerous effects of passion. Writ large in the *Theory* is the Stoic virtue of self-command: 'from it all the other virtues seem to derive their principal lustre'. (p 241) Sympathy in the *Treatise* involved a letting loose of the self which the language of Stoicism in the *Theory* is to guard against. Sympathy, indeed, becomes for Smith not the experience of shared feeling but the basis of the regulation of behaviour according to an abstracted standard—'by regard to the sentiments of the supposed impartial spectator': 'Without the restraint which this principle imposes, every passion would, upon most occasions, rush headlong, if I may say so, to its own gratification'. (pp 262–3) Extending sympathy beyond the possibility of any practical contact, any actual transference of feeling, the *Theory* makes 'moral sentiments' the product of discriminating, internalized reasoning—the reference of judgement to the supposed standard of an 'impartial spectator':

> All such sentiments suppose the idea of some other being, who is the natural judge of the person that feels them; and it is only by sympathy with the decisions of this arbiter of his conduct, that he can conceive, either the triumph of self-applause, or the shame or self-condemnation. (p 193)

The effort of self-command, trusting more readily to a 'sympathy' with an imagined 'impartial spectator' than to the actual passions discovered in others, is the only guarantee of an understanding superior to the compulsions of particular feeling. It is symptomatic of the progress through which Scottish moral philosophy has gone that whilst, in Hume's *Treatise*, these compulsions were supposed the very stuff of social relations, in Smith's less ambitious moral theory they are impediments to the proper judgements which the educated and responsible few might be expected to achieve.

Yet Smith has forsaken the ambition to imagine a sociability which could be a common habit, a shared possession. In a sense, the ideally socialized individual has become, in his moral theory, the abstracted spectator. Philosophy cannot now propose, as Hume's *Treatise* did, the experience of society in shared passions. When Smith's philosophy of 'moral sentiments' is set alongside Mackenzie's 'sentimental' novels, there become visible the limitations of a theory which could only warn against the loss of self in excessive feeling. However formulaic it might have been, the fiction could express needs unstated by the philosophy. Illuminatingly, in a moment of condescension Smith concedes that there can be an excessively 'stoical apathy' which is 'never agreeable': 'The poets and romance writers, who best paint the refinements and delicacies of love and friendship, and of all other private and domestic affections', he says (and lists several, including Voltaire, Richardson, and Marivaux), 'are, in such cases, much better instructors' than the Stoic philosophers. (p 143) It is a moment of condescension because it exploits what was the conventional notion of novels as fit to represent 'only' 'private and domestic affections'. Yet we can perhaps be more willing than Smith to believe that novels are liable to tell of the aspirations or anxieties of the culture that produces them. If it was finally a slight relief to Scott and Cockburn that Mackenzie was not his Man of Feeling, the relief was some indication of their recognition that his sentimental fiction had articulated a version of virtuous feeling which could not be acted on in the world. It was perhaps some indication too that a text like *The Man of Feeling* spoke for its polite culture of a dream it could not fulfill—a dream of the true virtue and true sociability which could not be reconciled to a supposedly modern society. The language of manners and taste which that culture was learning to call its own was one which as determinedly respectable a writer as Mackenzie was always able to adopt, but it could not always embrace 'private and domestic affections'. The appeal and the limitation of the sentimental novel was that it was these 'affections', cut off from all public forms, which it celebrated.

NOTES

1 *The Journal of Sir Walter Scott*, J G Tait (ed) (1939; repr Edinburgh, 1950), p 31.
2 Cited in David Craig, *Scottish Literature and the Scottish People 1680–1830* (London, 1961), p 45.
3 Letter of 8 July 1769, in *Henry Mackenzie, Letters to Elizabeth Rose of Kilravock*, H W Drescher (ed) (Münster, WG , 1967), p 13.
4 Letter to Elphinston, July 1770; cited in H W Thompson, *A Scottish Man of Feeling* (London, 1931), p 112.
5 Henry Mackenzie, *The Man of Feeling*, Brian Vickers (ed) (1967; repr. Oxford, 1970), p 4. All subsequent references are to this edition.
6 Henry Mackenzie, *The Man of the World*, in *The Works of Henry Mackenzie*, Vol II (Glasgow: 1818) p 198. All subsequent references are to this edition.
7 Henry Mackenzie (ed), *The Mirror*, first published 1779–80 (London, 1794), 2 vols, Vol 1, No. xlii, p 190. All subsequent references are to this edition.
8 Walter Scott, 'Henry Mackenzie', in *The Lives of the Novelists*, (London 1910), p 297.
9 Henry Mackenzie, *An Account of the Life and Writings of John Home, Esq.* (Edinburgh, 1822), pp 20–21.
10 See *Letters to Elizabeth Rose*, pp 80–81, where Mackenzie rejects the notion that Beattie has misrepresented Hume's ideas and arguments.
11 David Hume, *A Treatise of Human Nature*, L A Selby-Bigge (ed), 2nd edn, revised P H Nidditch (Oxford, 1978), p 264. All subsequent references are to this edition.

12 See *Treatise*, Book I, Part IV, Section I, 'Of scepticism with regard to reason', ibid., pp 180–7.
13 Henry Mackenzie (ed), *The Lounger*, first published 1785–6, 2nd edn, 3 vols, (Edinburgh: 1787), Vol 1, No. 2, pp 8–9.
14 David Hume, *Essays Moral, Political, and Literary*, E F Miller (ed) (Indianapolis, 1985), pp 3–4. All subsequent references are to this edition.
15 *The Letters of Robert Burns*, J De Lancey Ferguson (ed), 2 vols (Oxford, 1931), pp 14, 19–20.
16 David Hume, *Enquiries Concerning Human Understanding and Concerning the Principles of Morals* L A Selby-Bigge (ed), 3rd edn, rev P H Nidditch (Oxford, 1972), p 281. All subsequent references are to this edition.
17 Adam Smith, *The Theory of Moral Sentiments*, D D Raphael and A L Macfie (eds) (Oxford, 1976), p 12. All subsequent references are to this edition.

FURTHER READING

This list does not include those works of Mackenzie, Hume, and Smith to which I have referred in the text.

Craig, David, *Scottish Literature and the Scottish People 1680–1830* (London, 1961)

Daiches, David, *The Paradox of Scottish Culture; The Eighteenth-Century Experience* (London, 1964)

Drescher, H W (ed), *Henry Mackenzie, Letters to Elizabeth Rose of Kilravock* (Münster, WG, 1967)

Hont, Istavan and Michael Ignatieff (eds), *Wealth and Virtue. The Shaping of Political Economy in the Scottish Enlightenment* (Cambridge, 1983)

Ignatieff, Michael, *The Needs of Strangers* (London, 1984)

McElroy, D D, *Scotland's Age of Improvement. A Survey of Eighteenth Century Literary Clubs and Societies* (Washington, 1969)

Mossner, E C, *The Forgotten Hume* (New York, 1943)

Mossner, E C, *The Life of David Hume*, 2nd ed (Oxford, 1980)

Phillipson, Nicholas, 'Culture and Society in the 18th Century Province: The Case of Edinburgh and the Scottish Enlightenment', in *The University in Society*, Lawrence Stone (ed), 2 vols (Princeton, 1975)

Phillipson, Nicholas, 'Hume as Moralist: A Social Historian's Perspective', in *Philosophers of the Enlightenment*, S C Brown (ed) (Brighton, 1979)

Thompson, H W, *A Scottish Man of Feeling* (London, 1931)

Todd, Janet, *Sensibility. An Introduction* (London: 1986)

FURTHER READING

Chapter 17

The Culture of Science in Eighteenth-Century Scotland

JOHN R R CHRISTIE

We have as yet no adequate notion of the place of science within the overall range of Enlightenment culture in the West. There is a growing sense that science, in various forms and guises, bulked large in Enlightenment centres, playing a part in practical reformist programmes, performing as exemplar of intellectual and educational change, and in turn gaining from the ideological impetus which the Enlightenment gave it. This process was, however, subject to considerable local variation. As we move from metropolitan Paris to provincial Edinburgh, from Philadelphia to Naples, science is a constant factor only in its presence. The activities it generated, the support it gained, and the meanings it possessed were produced by and within particular settings, as much as by a self-contained, cosmopolitan 'Enlightened' community of scientists and philosophers.

It might be said that a consistent set of assumptions nonetheless characterized the pursuit of natural science in the context of Enlightenment: that, for example, science was universally held to be rational, progressive and useful. Yet even such apparently unexceptionable characterizations are laid open to doubt within a range of well-known texts of canonical significance for the Scottish Enlightenment. Are the theories of science produced by David Hume and Adam Smith unquestionably rationalist and progressivist? In what senses, and with what associated values, was science designated as useful by the eighteenth-century movements of Improvement? To pose such questions and provide detailed answers to them will be to undo the vacuous certainties with which Enlightenment science has often been globally characterized.

In the course of this chapter, such questioning is undertaken within an overall depiction of the nature and role of science in the development of eighteenth-century Scottish culture. That culture is striking in comparison with some other Enlightenment centres, Paris for example, in its relative lack of a substantial literary dimension. Diderot and Rousseau are as much the territory of the literary historian as of the historian of philosophy and science. It may be that Hume, Smith and certain scientists such as John Robison thought of themselves as 'men of letters', but that did not make them producers of notable imaginative literature. The distinctively literary works associated specifically with the Scottish Enlightenment, John Home's *Douglas*, Henry Mackenzie's *Man of Feeling* and James Macpherson's

Ossian, are thin on the ground, and the latter in particular formed a curious and less than glorious chapter in the literary history of eighteenth-century Scotland, given the tangled story of its origin, composition and critical reception. Such literature is also contrasted with the native power and vigour of the vernacular writings of poets such as Fergusson and Burns, admired to a degree by Enlightened culture but definitively consumed, rather than produced, by that culture.

For whatever reasons then, creative talent and energy tended to be channelled into philosophical and scientific endeavour, rather than literary, and it is true to say that Enlightenment imaginative literature in Scotland produced nothing to stand comparison with the works produced by Hume, Smith, Ferguson, Reid, Cullen, Black, Robison and Hutton. These men and their colleagues produced representations of mind and body, of planet and polity, of nature and society, which arguably had a decisive and shaping effect upon the modes and substance of modern thought. Their energy and ability produced classics of philosophical and scientific investigation whose effects were paramount for providing many of the basic assumptions and practices of the century which followed. This point can be made in exemplary fashion. If we stand in 1850 and view the recent historical landscape through the eyes of Karl Marx, two features stand out: the 'bourgeois science' of classical political economy, and the machine-filled factories driven by steam power. If we then ask for ascertainable origins of these epochal phenomena, for an account of when, where, and how they began to attain their distinctive modern form, we are led to the arts faculty of the University of Glasgow in the middle decades of the eighteenth century. It was there that Adam Smith, in his lectures on jurisprudence, first gave shape to the doctrines eventually published in *The Wealth of Nations*, and it was there that James Watt initiated the improvements in steam technology which became embodied in the Watt engine.

The point gains added force with the realisation that these are only two among many possible examples of epochal change whose source is eighteenth-century Scotland. Comparable cases could be maintained for the sciences of heat and electricity; for geology and the chemistry of gases; for the philosophy of human nature, society and history. The culture of the Scottish Enlightenment was one devoted to the production of theoretical, empirical and practical enquiry, and to pose the historical question of the origins and development of this cultural change should be to recognise in the first instance that, to a quite remarkable degree, the enterprise of knowledge provided the form and substance of lowland Scottish culture.

In the year 1700, the chances of such development occurring must have appeared slim. Scotland was a small nation with a weak economy, on the brink of losing the coherence of identity provided by its central political institution, the Scots parliament. It maintained nonetheless institutions whose survival and eventual expansion would prove to be of capital importance for the enterprise of knowledge.[1] These institutions, the universities and the colleges of physicians and surgeons, were in a state of some disarray in 1700. This was less to do with a lack of able and talented men than with the tensions and fissures present in the culture, between Jacobite and Whig, Episcopalian and Presbyterian, anti-Unionist and Unionist. The troubled history of the universities and medical colleges in the years preceding the Union was largely the result of the polarization and factionalism induced by such stresses and strains. The culture which survived in this environment was humanist in character, typified best perhaps by Archibald Pitcairne, who combined an urbane and poetic Latinity with a commitment to the most recent mechanistic medical theory, a cultural range which the intellectual specialization witnessed in the eighteenth century would render increasingly rare. Cultural initiatives at this time centred on the figure of Sir Robert Sibbald, like Pitcairne a medical man. However, Sibbald's projects, which may at one time have included plans for a Royal Society of Scotland, were unable to thrive in the absence of a permanent patronage base of monarch and court. Thus, although Scotland undoubtedly possessed the resources of learning and talent to support a Virtuosi culture such as could be found in England, a similar culture never emerged in the pre- or immediately post-Union years in an institutionally coherent form. What survived were shifting groups of Virtuosi, their interests focused on natural science, medicine, history and antiquarianism.

Lowland Scottish culture benefited from the Union insofar as it helped to bring about some resolution of pre-Union tensions, and created the conditions in which a settled political and religious establishment could take shape. But the form and content of much pre-Union culture became increasingly marginal in comparison with more novel developments. Ruddiman's classicism, Pitcairne's mechanistic medicine, and Sibbald's natural history, indeed survived into the post-Union world, but did not finally generate the support and enthusiasm necessary to place them at the centre of a flourishing and expanding culture. Of more significance for the next fifty years of cultural development were structural features of institutional change and the introduction of novel intellectual currents, and new cultural styles. In the field of higher education, the University of Edinburgh underwent a process of radical reform which replaced the old regenting system with a more specialised series of professorships, culminating in the establishment, in 1726, of a new medical faculty. The new faculty took over the relatively minor elements of medical education which had persisted in the work of the College of Physicians and the Surgeons Incorporation and in so doing transformed them into a systematic form of medical education whose success provided the basis of the university's massive expansion in the eighteenth century. The appointment of Colin Maclaurin brought a leading Newtonian mathematician and natural philosopher to the university. Outside the university, an enthusiastic prosecution of the idealist philosophy of George Berkeley was undertaken by the young members of the Rankenian society, while the members of Allan Ramsay's Easy Club espoused aspects of polite Augustan culture in their readings of the *Spectator*, and by their adoption of 'characters' such as Bickerstaff and Newton in their meetings. Landed society developed a strong and socialised commitment to agricultural improvement in an institution devoted to that end.

These were all signals indicative of a responsiveness to non-native culture, a desire to remake intellectual and social life in and through forms which would attune cultural life in Scotland with developments in England and abroad. As a process of cultural adaptation it was to prove enduring, for the elements which were in place by the mid 1720s were to gain in significance throughout the rest of the century. Medicine, natural philosophy, idealist empiricism, polite literature, and agricultural improvement, pursued in an institutional and social environment constituted by university and learned society: these were among the major elements whose combination formed the culture of the Scottish Enlightenment.

In institutional terms, medicine and natural science became the recipients of continually increasing material and social resources. The numbers of academic positions devoted to these subjects increased throughout the century, while the stream of new clubs and societies for the pursuit of science and medicine testified to a massive investment of social energies in these fields.[2] The detailed history of these developments is complex and beyond the scope of this chapter; suffice it momentarily to say that it reveals a complex process of adaptation to a number of factors. These include the changing ambitions and preoccupations of elite landed society, who held the instruments of patronage; the growth of an international educational market; and the development of disciplinary specialisations. In intellectual terms, there was an equally complex and dialectical pattern of growth whose determinants would include secularization and quantification, together with debate over the logical nature and status of science.

It is important to realise that scientific knowledge in eighteenth-century Scotland cannot be characterised in specifically cultural terms through its content alone. Scots scientists produced experimental and theoretical work on a vast range of topics, from mathematically technical extensions of the Newtonian calculus to the psychology and significance of dreams. What characterises this culture of science is less its subject-matter, which it shared substantially with colleagues of other nations, than its posture towards the scientific enterprise itself. We have to deal, in other words, not only with a culture hooked on the production of knowledge, but a culture which actively and critically thought about the economic, social, psychological and philosophical implications of the knowledge-producing enterprise on which it had so enthusiastically embarked. Science was both accompanied and stimulated by reflection upon the meanings which the activity and its representatives embodied. To this considerable extent, the culture of science was therefore critically self-aware, alive to the broader significances of its own processes. If, as could be argued, science signified modernity and progress for eighteenth-century Scots, then that modernity and progress were seen to be double-edged and problematic, and it is the analytical self-awareness producing such realisations which marks the cultural distinctiveness of Scottish science.

There are numerous works and moments through which this thematic awareness in its various modes may be demonstrated, but a preliminary sketch of science's major developmental aspects is first required, to anchor the discussion which follows. The generation of scientists installed in the 1720s were typified by their commitment to two general scientific systems. First, the professors of Edinburgh's new medical school were dedicated in their educational endeavour to the exposition of the system of their teacher, Herman Boerhaave of Leyden, whose medicine was based on a predominantly mechanistic conception of the human body and its ailments, which emphasised the body's fluid systems, such as circulation and digestion. Secondly, Colin Maclaurin taught Newtonian mathematics and natural philosophy. But neither Alexander Monro *primus* and his medical colleagues, nor Maclaurin, were solely teachers. Monro was a notable comparative anatomist, while Maclaurin's work on the calculus and the theory of tides confirmed his reputation as a major scientific *savant* of international standing. The element which unified these diverse endeavours was a common commitment to a religious version of the natural world. This appeared in the notion on which Monro's comparative anatomy was based, the principle of gradation. It appeared in Maclaurin's rigorous defence of mathematics from some of the accusations contained in Berkeley's tract on the infidelity of mathematics, and in his popular exposition of Newtonian philosophy.[3] It also appeared in the chemical theory of Andrew Plummer, professor of chemistry in the medical school. For all of these men, nature was itself an artefact, to be understood ultimately in terms of the causes and purposes which the Deity had used and installed in the design of Creation. This natural science was therefore contained within a framework of religious teleology, and possible conflicts with Christian orthodoxy were thereby marginalised.

This framework was progressively disrupted from the mid 1740s onwards, and the main instigator of disruption was David Hume. Read from a cultural perspective, one of the principle drives of Hume's whole philosophical endeavour was secularization. Whether one considers his theory of knowledge, his moral theory, his political theory, or the vision of culture depicted in his essays, Hume's attempt was to envisage human nature and society in secularized terms. With respect to the framework of religious teleology within which natural science had hitherto been pursued, Hume mounted a severe critique against the sort of metaphysical and quasi-theological reasoning which attempted to explain the phenomena of nature by reference to the agencies of divine causation and purpose. This campaign was continued from first to last in his philosophy, as is seen in the precautions he made to ensure the posthumous publication of his *Dialogues Concerning Natural Religion*, a work containing many of his most powerful arguments against the religious interpretation of nature, and quite incompatible with the still broadly religious world-view of Monro *primus* and Maclaurin.[4]

Had Hume's work found no positive echo among his compatriots, its cultural significance would be lessened. As it was, aspects of the clerical reaction against Hume in the 1750s indicated that, so far as the religious were concerned, they had to cope less with an isolated individual than a formidable cultural initiative which possessed a powerful appeal. If the view of Hume they adopted, as mechanistic, materialistic and atheistic, was a caricature unable to do justice to the sceptical, flexible and undogmatic style of Hume's thought, clerical objectors were nonetheless correct to sense Hume's potential appeal. Part of the evidence for this appeal is located in the theoretical innovations introduced by Hume's friends and colleagues in the natural sciences, notably William Cullen and Joseph Black.

Cullen's and Black's rise to intellectual eminence was through the science of chemistry. Hitherto taught as an adjunct to medicine, chemistry in Cullen's hands took on a separate and independent disciplinary existence. Part of this process involved providing chemistry with a new theoretical basis, which served to validate it as a properly conceived science, as distinct from a series of practical techniques whose value was solely to medicine and manufacture. The theory which Cullen adapted for these purposes was derived originally from the speculative queries of Isaac Newton, who had postulated an aether (an extremely attenuated, subtle and elastic fluid) which, pervading all space and matter, and endowed with appropriate dispositions and forces, could account for the phenomena of heat, electricity, magnetism, gravitation, and sensory perception. Hume himself had recommended the aether as an explanatory option for science, in preference to reliance on a realm of divine causation in nature.[5] It is less than coincidental to find Cullen taking this option in his chemical theory, partly because of Cullen's enthusiasm for Hume as a prospective colleague at the University of Glasgow, but more specifically because of the explicit recapitulation of Hume's position which is to be found in Cullen's chemistry. There, as Hume had done earlier, Cullen offers aetherial explanation as an alternative explicitly preferable to explanation by divine causation. Reliance on divine causation to explain the chemical phenomena of matter was, according to Cullen, an unnecessary limitation upon enquiry itself.[6] In broad terms, the outcome of Cullen's theoretical departure was therefore a newly distinct science of chemistry with a definitively secular public image. In this strong sense, Cullen had developed and exploited the cultural potential of Hume's programme of philosophical secularization.

Cullen did not rest there, but developed the theoretical range of the aether to underpin his explanations of the phenomena of life and disease in his theoretical physiology, a practice which aroused some strong opposition amongst medical colleagues such as John Gregory. Here again Cullen was exploiting the potential of his environment. The generation of professors who succeeded the original Edinburgh medical faculty from the mid 1740s onward, a group which included Cullen, had adopted a critical rather than positive attitude towards their master, Boerhaave. Instead of emphasizing the body's fluid systems, this new generation now concentrated on the body's solid systems, pre-eminently upon the nervous system. They prodced notable technical advances in the understanding of the structure, function and action of the nervous system, and of the nature and treatment of diseases of nervous and hysterical origin. In this context, Cullen's use of the aether, envisaged as an active, fluid medium distributed throughout the nerves and responsible for many of the body's life functions, constituted a materialistic and deterministic account of the human, and it was upon this recognition that hostility towards Cullen's theoretical medicine was grounded.

In the physical sciences, the direction of technical development moved strongly towards defining and quantifying the interaction of active agencies such as heat and electricity with ordinary matter. Once again, the theory of the aether, now identified as the subtle fluids of heat and electricity, underpinned much of this work. It issues in such chief discoveries as Joseph Black's, of latent and specific heats, and John Robison's, of the force law governing the action of electrical charge, definitive investigations which stand comparison with anything produced elsewhere in the eighteenth century. In 1748, at the close of his *Enquiry Concerning Human Understanding*, Hume had written, somewhat drastically:

> When we run over libraries, persuaded of these principles, what havoc must we make? If we take in our hand any volume; of divinity or school metaphysics, for instance; let us ask, *Does it contain any abstract reasoning concerning quantity or number*? No. *Does it contain any experimental reasoning concerning matter of fact or existence*? No. Commit it then to the flames: for it can contain nothing but sophistry and illusion.[7]

That intense No, and its implied Yes, may stand emblematically for the direction of Scottish scientific culture in the three decades after which it was written, insomuch as that culture was premised on the rejection of divinity, and the pursuit of knowledge through the productive combination of 'reasoning concerning quantity or number' with 'experimental reasoning concerning matter of fact'.

It would be quite wrong, however, to imply that Scottish science remained locked within an aggressively secular and positivist mould, for men such as Hume and Cullen, despite their pre-eminence in philosophy and science, were nonetheless atypical of the last quarter of the century. Hume's philosophy provoked a vigorous response from Thomas Reid and his Aberdonian colleagues, as did Cullen's medicine from John Gregory, a medical cousin of Reid's who shared the teaching of the theory and practice of medicine with Cullen in Edinburgh. In essence, this response aimed to combat the scepticism and necessitarianism which were seen as the outcome of systems such as Humes' and Cullen's. It did so by attempting to demonstrate an indubitably secure ground for human knowledge in the beliefs common to all men: the reality ofthe external world, the validity of our perception of that world, the rationality of properly conducted intellectual inquiry, the active agency of free will, a presiding and benevolent deity.[8] Thomas Reid's often technically adroit defence of these propositions assumed considerable importance, as this Common Sense philosophy, as it was called, spread from Aberdeen to Glasgow and then Edinburgh. Through Reid himself, through notable pupils such as Dugald Stewart, and through kin such as John Gregory, Common Sense gained a much firmer place in university education than Hume's thought was ever allowed to, and it became the staple philosophical diet for generations of Scots in higher education. For science, its significance was twofold. First, it re-established the framework of religious teleology, encouraging the sort of re-moralization of nature which Hume and Cullen sought to eschew. Secondly, in its strong methodological bias towards the careful establishment of natural laws which avoided speculation as to casual agency, it militated against the deployment of hypothetical causes such as the aether. The aether, indeed, received such rough handling from Common Sense philosophy and its scientific adherents that there is little doubt that a major motive for the origin and continuing use of Reid's methodological canons was the negation of aether-based scientific speculation.

In the latter decades of the century, although physical science remained flourishing, new and reformed types of scientific enquiry also rose to prominence, notably the earth science of James Hutton and the science of natural history.[9] Hutton's earth science was capable of provoking religious unease, in that it postulated a virtual infinity of time for the planet's history, and so refused conformity with any aspect of the biblical narrative of the earth's origin and destiny. Hutton's theory was nonetheless conceived within a deeply teleological framework. The problem it tackled was the progressive denudation and erosion of earth's surface, its degeneration as a habitable space. Hutton was able to show, through a consideration of igneous rocks, that this degeneration was compensated by a productive process within the earth's crust, whereby new rock was consolidated and elevated to form, in its turn, habitable land. He claimed to show, moreover, from the composition of certain strata, that this process had probably occurred many times. Hutton's geology envisioned a perpetual, stable, cyclical system, in which forces of degeneration are always compensated by forces of renewal. This was a conception of the earth remarkable for its confident theoretical systemization from a slim basis of observation, and for its methodological assumption. Hutton assumed constancy and uniformity of causation for the earth's history, by accepting that the forces which now shape the face of the earth are those which have always done so and will continue to do so. Using Huttonian uniformity, there was no need to invoke single and catastrophic upheavals, such as the biblical flood, to explain aspects of earth's history. It might seem then that Hutton's theory, produced relatively late in the century, invoked that secular and speculative form of science pioneered in the 1750s. This is indeed partly the case. Hutton's closest friends, Adam Smith and Joseph Black, were men of that earlier generation. Yet it does not do to ignore the form of Hutton's problem, which focused upon the globe's habitability, an entirely humanized and anthropocentric conception of the earth's purpose and meaning. At a religious level, Hutton's theory vindicated the idea of a creative and benevolent deity who had ensured that the earth remained a fit habitation for mankind. The theory may have appeared unchristian with regard to a literal interpretation of Scripture, but it was nonetheless religious in its framing and solution of the problem. The possibility that it may have been written in part as a response to Hume's subversive attack on the idea of a benevolent deity in the *Dialogues Concerning Natural Religion* should not be ruled out.

Hutton's geology tends to overshadow that other science of the earth and its inhabitants, natural history, though at the time natural history was more popular and of more educational significance. After Sir Robert Sibbald, natural history remained for many decades relatively low on the agenda of Scottish science, confined in the main to the activities of the successive professors of botany in Edinburgh's medical school. In comparison with Hutton's dynamical and historical geology, it appears almost anachronistic, for it assumed a static and hierarchically ordered creation, which it was the natural historian's task to name, classify and describe. These taxonomic activities were however highly technical exercises, and increasingly controversial. Botanists such as John Hope and John Walker used the Linnaen system of classification, which designated the character of a plant through the number, form and arrangement of its reproductive parts. At the same time, the limitations of the 'Sexual System', as it was known, were also recognised, for it operated on the arbitrary abstraction of one aspect of plant appearance through which to assign its character, and thence its classification. John Hope and his pupil and successor John Rutherford both therefore attempted to extend the practice of taxonomy beyond its Linnaen limitations. John Walker also broke with standard natural history practice in his mineralogy. Natural history had long been the science of the external, visible surface of things, and the meticulous recording of the visible surface in descriptive writing which had developed its own restricted and technical vocabulary.[10] Walker's attempts at mineral classification went well beyond this standard and canonical practice, which he found to be of limited use in deciding the relation of one kind of mineral to another. He therefore adopted a system of classification which utilized an aspect of internal constitution, namely chemical composition, for classificatory purposes.[11] Linnaen natural history, useful and practical though it was for certain purposes, did not therefore limit Scottish efforts to extend the boundaries and methods of natural history.

Natural history, moreover, did not remain confined to the limited technical practice of taxonomy. In the hands of William Smellie, a non-academic naturalist, as well as a printer, pamphleteer and poet, natural history became a much broader and more accessible science of nature, and of man within nature.[12] Smellie treated nature in terms of broad categorical topics, such as Love, Generation and Gregariousness, in a style which deliberately avoided the hard-edged technicality of academic naturalists like Walker. This approach, apparently innocuous, nonetheless had subversive implications, for man was treated within these categories along with other species. Additionally, Smellie was inclined to emphasize instinctual aspects of human behaviour, which tended to assimilate his account of the human to the animal. Even natural history, an apparently limited and technical form of scientific discourse, was capable of registering divergence and tension in the accounts of nature and of man which it delivered.

This sketch of the development of eighteenth-century Scottish science has so far dealt with its philosophical context, its developmental course, and its characteristic theories, practices and achievements. A cultural historian might rest content with the account so far, underpinned perhaps by more social and institutional detail, and by an additional appreciation of the ways in which almost all Scottish scientists involved themselves in practical, utilitarian activity for the improvement of agriculture and manufacture. This chapter, however, aims to provide a more thorough sense of the complexity of scientific culture by demonstrating the conflicting and contradictory meanings which science embodied for eighteenth-century Scotland. By 'meaning' is indicated not only the evident ideological significance attached, say, to the secularity and determinism of aether theory, or to Smellie's animalistic account of man, important though these were. The Scots, whether reflecting historically and philosophically upon science, or actively engaged in its prosecution, became profoundly aware of what science itself was, and what its implications were for modern culture. It is these meanings which are now pursued.

In the preceding account, science has appeared as largely validated and supported by Scottish culture, philosophically, socially and materially. What follows suggests that this is less obviously the case than might be supposed, because the enterprise of knowledge contained its own critique within it. This appears very obviously in Hume's theory of knowledge. Hume set out to revolutionize philosophy through the application of the methods of empirical science, and ended his formal epistemological enquiry by advocating the burning of any books which lack scientific content. Yet in between these strikingly scientistic moments, Hume managed to case in doubt almost all the grounds of scientific inquiry. Most notably, he called the logic of science into question by pointing out that no universal proposition can be derived from a number of individual instances, no matter how large that number. If science proceeds from experimental instances to general laws based upon them, it could not, according to Hume, do so logically. And even if we set aside Hume's sceptical account of the senses and of reason, his view of the self as no more than a mobile bundle of perceptions offered little purchase for the autonomous, coherent and controlled observer which scientific enquiry assumed. If science offered the best model of intellectual enquiry, as according to Hume it did, then even the best was performed non-logically by an incoherent self.

The ground of science therefore appears as less than secure in Hume. The fundamental reasons for this are seen in the theory of science written by his closest philosophical follower, Adam Smith. In an essay written most probably in the 1750s, Smith undertook an investigation of scientific enquiry in an essay on the history of astronomy. The essay opened with a strongly psychological account of the roots of enquiry, then proceeded to illustrate this account with the example of the history of astronomy. Smith's view of science saw it as the product of human imagination. Confronted with novel appearances in nature, the mind exhibits two passions, surprise and wonder. These in turn are the product of the mechanism of the association of ideas which govern the workings of the mind. Surprise and wonder are the feelings which arise when the mind is unable to incorporate a novel appearance within its normal associative patterns. According to Smith, prolonged failure of the mind to produce an explanation of the novel appearance will lead to frenzy, lunacy and even death. To attempt to restore the smooth and regular associative process, the imagination must therefore originate a new chain of ideas, on the principle of analogy with existing chains. This new chain is an analogically plausible hypothesis which bridges the perceived gap in association occasioned by the novel appearance, thereby eliminating surprise and wonder. This psychological account of theory invention was remarkable in its de-emphasis of terms like reason, truth and reality. Smith's analytical categories are passion and imagination, and he was quite explicit in disavowing claims that the new chain of ideas which constitute scientific theories have any warrantable correspondence with the real world of external nature. As products of human imagination, they conform to criteria of imagination, and these criteria—unity, simplicity and harmony—are aesthetic in character. Smith was willing to emphasise these claims even with reference to the Newtonian system of the world. It was, like all others, 'a mere invention of the imagination'.[13] Smith had taken Hume's associationist account of the mind and focused it exclusively on the topic of scientific theory. In so doing he had moved science into the world of passion and imagination, and transformed it into, in the Addisonian phrase, a pleasure of the imagination. What then was the image of science which he portrayed? Instead of being a realist account of external nature, the imaginative projection of our ideas onto nature was much more akin to something like fiction, for these ideas, the theories of science, correspond with the inward aesthetic demands of imagination rather than with external constraints of natural appearance. In the work of Hume and Smith we therefore find an account of scientific knowledge which entirely subverted the realist and rationalist accounts which had hitherto been unproblematically accepted. Scientific theories were the provisional fictions through which human imagination is obliged to apprehend and control the world.

It was this deeply disturbing view of science which prompted Thomas Reid's attempt to reground science in the realism of Common Sense. This Common Sense reaction had other significant dimensions, however, which can be seen in the work of John Gregory. Gregory, a practising medical scientist, was nonetheless deeply concerned about certain aspects of his scientific culture. He complained, for example, of the scepticism and materialism prevalent in Edinburgh. His critique of contemporary science

was less philosophical than social, an argument about the social implications of the practice of science in modern commercial society. Although
man was naturally rational, the faculty of reason was weak. In modern
society, 'knowledge, instead of combatting a vitiated taste and inflamed
passions, is employed to justify them'. Modern culture tended to over-
value rationality, which participated in the creation of 'false appetite and a
deluded imagination'.[14] Those who cultivated universal knowledge and
genius became too 'inwardly directed', which resulted in a 'gloomy and
forlorn Scepticism, which poisons the chearfulness of temper'. Social
affections languish, men are rendered 'unfit for business'. Science in
modern culture was a form of existential corruption for Gregory, because
its false consciousness distracted men from active pursuit of virtue, the
public good, and real objects of material improvement. Gregory's critique
of science as the fetish of modern reason was actually launched within, and
perhaps provoked by, his appreciation of the values inherent in the
recently recovered antiquity of the *Ossian* poems. These poems, according
to Gregory, described a world of strong social and kinship bonds, martial
spirit, love of liberty and patriotism, which stood as a positive exemplar
against the corruption, effeminacy and private satisfactions which characterised the modern culture of reason.

A comparable series of attitudes can be found, in much more sophisticated and elaborate form, in Adam Ferguson's *Essay on the History of
Civil Society*. Like Gregory, Ferguson attacked certain tendencies inherent
in modern commercial society, and valued the virtues of primitive cultures.
Also like Gregory, Ferguson did not exclude the modern enterprise of
knowledge from his analysis. Much of this analysis concentrated on the
increasing division and specialization of labour witnessed through history,
and on the social and moral effects of this process. The separation of arts
(practical skills and techniques) from professions, of the role of statesman
from that of warrior, were examples of a process which produced the
material benefits of more efficient occupational specialization. At the same
time, they illustrated the breaking of social cohesion, as men became
fractionized into specialized interest groups which pursued their own
benefit in competition with others. Ferguson did not exempt the figure of
the 'man of science' from complicity in the divisive process of interest and
competition. In modern society, knowledge is commerce. 'The productions
of ingenuity are brought to the market; and men are willing to pay for
whatever has a tendency to inform or amuse'.[15] By implication then,
science itself is increasingly produced by occupational specialization, and
knowledge, as commodity, feeds into the ascending spiral of desire and
gratification which is the psychological principle of market-based society.
For Ferguson, the name of this process of division and privatized consumer
satisfaction was corruption.

The examples of Gregory and Ferguson indicate the strong persistence
of a series of civic and humanist values in Scottish cultural life, and further
indicate the ways in which the modern project of scientific knowledge
could not be easily harmonised with those values. A comparable dilemma
is illustrated in the attitudes of the natural historian and practical agricul-

tural improver, John Walker. Much of Walker's career centred on the Scottish Highlands, on whose exploration and scrutiny much of his natural history was based. He was simultaneously involved in efforts to civilize Highlanders and Islanders, through the spread of Presbyterian religion, and to improve their agriculture and fisheries. In the 1760s, Walker moved through Highlands and Islands with the eyes of the lowland scientist-improver, superior in knowledge, and therefore in the management of human and material resources. He devoted his efforts towards incorporating the Highlands as far as was possible within the modern productive and commercial activities of Great Britain. But Walker lived long enough to witness the effects of improvement upon the Highlands, and by the close of his career had changed his attitudes. Instead of the settled and prosperous Highland community run by local owners organised in 'Economical Societies', which he had earlier imagined, improvement in practice had brought about severe depopulation, through the combined effects of grazing farms, sheep farming, and the greater rewards obtainable in southern labour-markets. Walker therefore now deplored the effects of the improvement he had eagerly sought. His contradictory experience of science and improvement with regard to the Highlands marks yet another movement where modern, science-based Scottish culture was required to confront critically problems which admitted no ready solution.

The aggregate effect of these interpretations of Hume, Smith, Gregory, Ferguson and Walker is to suggest that the culture of science in eighteenth-century Scotland cannot be easily and simply understood by assimilation to the model of a progressive society in pursuit of modernity through the acquisition of positive, scientific knowledge. That 'modernist model' is true. Hume was a scientistic and positivist thinker; great scientific innovations were produced, many intellectual energies and social resources were devoted to science; and many scientists devoted themselves to the material betterment of their society. Yet it is equally true that science could be defined as approximate to fiction rather than positive knowledge, that its nature and role in modern society could be seen as both contributing to and suffering from corruptive forces, and that the effects of its practical application through improvement brought about uncontrollable and undesirable consequences. Whether viewed philosophically, psychologically, socially or materially, the culture of science produced its own reflexive negations. To acknowledge this is to acknowledge that scientific culture was less a seamless devotion to and accretion of knowledge, than a critical and dialectical process which contained the contradictions and dilemmas which are characteristic of all modern knowledge-based societies. The Scots met and realized these problems earlier and more profoundly than other comparable cultures, and it is precisely in this encounter that the modernity of eighteenth-century Scottish scientific culture consisted.

Notes

1 For a more detailed description of this process than is possible here, *see* J R R Christie, 'The Origins and Development of the Scottish Scientific Community, 1680–1760', *History of Science* 12 (1974), pp 122–41.

2   *See* A C Chitnis, *The Scottish Enlightenment: A Social History* (London, 1976), chs. 6, 7, for treatment of these subjects.
3   C Maclaurin, *An Account of Sir Isaac Newton's Philosophical Discoveries* (London, 1748).
4   D Hume, *Dialogues Concerning Natural Religion* (Edinburgh, 1779)
5   D Hume, *Enquiries Concerning the Human Understanding and Concerning the Principles of Morals* L A Selby-Bigge (ed) (Oxford,1902), p 73.
6   W Cullen, Royal College of Physicians of Edinburgh, Lectures on chemistry, MS C10.
7   Hume, *Enquiries*, 165.
8   T Reid, *An Inquiry into the Human Mind* (1765)
9   R M Porter, *The Making of Geology* (Cambridge, 1977), is a good treatment of these topics in an overall British context.
10 M Foucault, *The Order of Things* (Tavistock, 1970), ch. 5, contains an excellent analysis of this aspect of natural history.
11 Walker claimed he adopted this procedure as advocated by Cullen and Lord Bute.
12 W Smellie, *The Philosophy of Natural History*, 2 vols (Edinburgh,1790).
13 A Smith, 'Of the Principles which Lead and Direct Philosophical Enquiries, Illustrated by the History of Astronomy', in W Wightman and J Bryce (eds), *Essays on Philosophical Subjects* (Oxford, 1980), p 105.
14 These quotations are taken from the preface to J Gregory, *A Comparative View of the State and Faculties of Man with those of the Animal World*, 2nd edn. (Edinburgh, 1771).
15 A Ferguson, *An Essay on the History of Civil Society*, D Forbes (ed) (Edinburgh, 1966), p 183.

FURTHER READING

Chitnis, A C, *The Scottish Enlightenment: A Social History* (London, 1976)

Christie, J R R, 'The Rise and Fall of Scottish Science', M P Crosland (ed), *The Emergence of Science in Western Europe* (London, 1975), pp 111–26

Olsen, R, *Scottish Philosophy and British Physics, 1750—1880: A Study in the Foundations of the Victorian Scientific Style* (Princeton, 1975)

Phillipson, N T 'Culture and Society in the Eighteenth-century Province: the Case of Edinburgh and the Scottish Enlightenment', Stone, L (ed) *The University in Society: Studies in the History of Higher Education*, 2 vols (Princeton, 1976), vol 2, pp 407–48.

Simpson, A D C (ed) *The Early Years of the Edinburgh Medical School* (Edinburgh, 1976)

Chapter 18

Scotland and Romanticism: The International Scene

ANDREW HOOK

Scottish literary romanticism, with its roots firmly in the eighteenth century, produced those images which, for better or worse, continue to provide Scotland with a meaning and identity for the outside world. What has to be recognized is that these familiar images—whatever their subsequent fate in terms of nationalistic self-indulgence, commercial exploitation, or the development of the Scottish tourist industry—were, in their origins, imaginative responses to the realities of Scottish life and culture at a particular historical moment. Romantic images of Scotland, and the mythology they helped to create, that is, began life as necessary fictions: imaginative attempts to order and interpret historical realities. What called them into being was a combination of the particular cultural circumstances in which Scotland found herself in the eighteenth century, and the forces at work both inside and outside Scotland which in the same period transformed the imaginative sensibilities of Scotsmen, Englishmen, Europeans, and Americans. The conjunction was potent enough both to refashion Scotland in the eyes of the world, and to wrap the country in a shiny romantic package from which she has never wholly escaped.

Before the eighteenth century, Scotland was a little-known country on the remote, northern periphery of Europe. The Romans had defeated the barbarian people who lived there, but never subjugated them. (Romanticism would subsequently find both this geographical location and ancient history very much to its taste.) In the Middle Ages the Scots may or may not have invented the concept of nationalism, but there is little evidence that the rest of Europe paid much attention. The Florentine historian Villani, writing in the fourteenth century, alludes briefly to Edward I's invasion and subjugation of Scotland; but his reference to the leader of Scottish resistance as a man of humble birth called 'Robert of the Wood'— perhaps a conflation of Robert the Bruce and Robin Hood— hardly suggests a detailed knowledge of the historical realities. Two extant accounts of Scotland in the fifteenth century by foreign observers agree on at least one basic point: the country and society they are describing are unfamiliar and unknown. Of the two accounts, the earlier, by Aeneas Sylvius Piccolomini, later Pope Pius II, who visited the court of James I in 1435, is the more negative. For the Italian humanist and man of letters, Scotland is clearly a backward country on the very edge of civilization. For Pedro de Ayala, Spanish ambassador to the court of James

IV in 1495, Scotland is somewhat less uncivilized. But even for Ayala, who is doing his diplomatic best to recommend Scotland to his Spanish masters, the country of James IV is unfamiliar territory. When in 1505-08 Pinturicchio came to portray episodes from the life of Pius II on the walls of the Piccolomini Chapel in the cathedral of Siena, he included a panel on his subject's Scottish visit. What is striking is the romantic, Gothic quality with which the painter has invested the Scottish landscape which looms behind the figures in the foreground. Scotland emerges as a mysterious, unknown land. Ariosto, in *Orlando Furioso* (1532), describes one of the protagonists of his poem as a son of the King of Scotland, and gives a detailed account of a Scottish army joining forces with the Irish and English on the banks of the Thames; but apart from a suggestion of the natural warlikeness of the Scots, there is little to suggest any real knowledge of Scotland or its people.

In the early modern period Scotland did from time to time impinge upon the European consciousness: the execution of Mary Queen of Scots was clearly one such moment; James VI of Scotland's accession to the throne of England and Scotland as James I, was no doubt another. Nor in the later medieval and early modern periods was Scotland in any sense cut off from European contact. Significant trading links existed between Scotland and Flanders, France, and the Baltic states, and such trading links helped to promote cultural ones. Scottish scholars had always travelled on the continent, and studied at the great French and Italian universities. The Scottish monarchy frequently had diplomatic and political links with European powers, and European artists and musicians were sometimes to be found at the Scottish court. Scots mercenary soldiers were frequently prominent in the service of European princes.

These links between Scotland and Europe, significant as they are, particularly for the cultural history of Scotland, were a long way from bringing Scotland to the centre of the European stage, and by the end of the seventeenth century and the opening of the eighteenth, Scotland's European standing had certainly deteriorated. Her status as an independent country had gone, and her political and religious history in the recent past had probably served to underline the view that she was a particularly uncivilized, poverty-stricken and backward country, with a special taste for cruel and internecine violence.

Such was the situation at the opening of the eighteenth century. By its close a dramatic change had occurred. The Scotland that had been remote, obscure, neglected, had achieved an ever-increasing fame. North Britain had become a distinguished centre of Improvement, Progress, and Enlightenment. The country which the *Edinburgh Review* in 1824 described as 'a little shabby scraggy corner of a remote island, with a climate which cannot ripen an apple' had gained a reputation for intellectual and cultural achievement which, at least in relation to its size and population, could not be rivalled elsewhere in Europe. In history and philosophy, in medicine, in science and technology, in polite and popular literature and literary criticism, in architecture and painting, Scots had made, or were making, contributions of such note that Scotland itself had become identified as a land of learning. The Scottish universities had gained international pre-stige: Thomas Jefferson was not alone in regarding Edinburgh as the finest university in the world, and students arrived there from England and Ireland, from America and the West Indies, from France and Germany and most of the countries of Europe. And by 1800 the city of Edinburgh had become one of the great cultural capitals of the world.

Yet in the long term, it was not the Scottish Enlightenment, whatever the scale of its achievements, which gained for Scotland its new and enduring identity. The eighteenth-century Enlightenment everywhere promoted the values of reason, objectivity, moderation and tolerance; it celebrated the life of the mind. But its very success, and the progressive social and material ideals it advanced, inevitably set in motion a counter-movement. In certain areas of experience at least, the configuration of attitudes, habits of mind and feeling, transcendent dreams and visions, which define roman-ticism, came into being as a reaction to the world of the Enlightenment. In one of its essences at least, romanticism repudiated the rationalism of the Enlightenment.

Paradoxically, the Scottish Enlightenment itself contributed to the emergence of romanticism both inside Scotland and beyond. Like the proponents of Enlightenment everywhere, the Scots philosophers saw themselves as progressives, men of a new and modern world, based on a more rational approach to human nature and human society. But the Scots thinkers' interest in a more rational and analytical study of man and society inevitably led them back to examine such questions as the origins of human society, how civilization developed, the movement from one stage in social progress to the next. Given the speed of social change within Scotland itself it was perhaps inevitable that they should be interested in such questions of social development. In turn, this emphasis on the past structures of human society helped to bring about a situation in which those who found the modern, enlightened world somewhat unexciting and uninteresting could begin to look back to the past, and find there modes of life and experience infinitely more apealing than those of the mundane present. Enlighten-ment ideas about the nature and development of language provide another excellent illustration. The Scots philosophers and rhetoricians did a great deal to promote the idea that the forms of language used in primitive, uncivilized societies, were characterized by a natural spontaneity and figurative power. Such language may well have been less accurate and less controlled than that of modern, sophisticated societies, but it was full of colour and passion. Thomas Blackwell, the Aberdeen classical scholar, for example, argued in his pioneering *Life and Writings of Homer* that the finest epic poetry was the natural product of a society still emerging from barbarism. And Hugh Blair did not hesitate to suggest that the language of the primitive Celtic tribes, whose descendants still inhabited the Scottish Highlands, like that of latter-day Red Indian tribes in America, possessed a natural, poetic power missing from the world of more civilized speech. It is easy to see how such ideas could contribute to the development of romantic theories on the nature of poetry and poetic language. Thus, leading exponents of Enlightenment in Scotland helped to bring about a situation in which their own values, and the new, commercial and progressively-minded North Britain they were helping to create, could begin to be subtly subverted from within.

Exactly such a process of subversion had been underway from early in the eighteenth century. At the end of the day, in the nineteenth and twentieth centuries, what Scotland came to mean to the outside world was not a land of learning and intellectual distinction. And this is true even if learning and intellectual achievement are seen as not unconnected with the patterns of economic development that made central Scotland in the nineteenth century an industrial and technological power-house. It was another, quite different image of Scotland, an alternative mythology, which was to prove decisive. And this counter-image prevailed because it both echoed and helped to create those forms of romanticism which in the later eighteenth and nineteenth centuries invaded and transformed individuals' structures of thought and feeling throughout the western world. Scotland's thinkers had gained for her a distinguished reputation; but it was Scotland's poets and writers who took possession of the feelings and imaginations of the outside world, giving their country an irresistible attraction for romantic sensibilities everywhere. It was her writers who recreated Scotland as a land of poetry and song, and who finally made her into an archetypal land, not of learning, but of romance.

In the creation and dissemination of this alternative and potent romantic image of Scotland certain writers and works played a crucial role. These were: Allan Ramsay's pastoral drama, *The Gentle Shepherd* (1725); John Home's tragedy *Douglas* (1756); what James Macpherson published as translations of the poems of *Ossian* in the 1760s; the poetry of Robert Burns (1786); and the poems and novels of Sir Walter Scott published between 1805 and 1832. Numerous other works and writers played their part in producing the situation through which in the nineteenth century Scotland gained its mythopoetic identity throughout Europe and America—James Beattie's poem *The Minstrel* (1771–4) for example, or Jane Porter's novel *The Scottish Chiefs* (1810) with its sentimental celebration of William Wallace, Robert the Bruce, and the Scottish Wars of Independence—but those listed provided the crucial impulse.

Of course a century stretches between *The Gentle Shepherd* and the Waverley Novels. What happened with Scotland's cultural life was a gradual process, not a sudden transformation. It was only with the passage of time, with the slow waning of the dominance of Augustan or neo-classical critical and aesthetic values, with the gradual shift in taste and sensibility occurring as the eighteenth century went on; it was only, in other words, as the romantic movement began to emerge in Europe as whole, that the Scottish writers began to make their major impact and so began to create a new and enduring vision of Scotland.

Ramsay's *The Gentle Shepherd* was a success when it was first staged in the 1720s and remained successful for well over 100 years. But the work was at the height of its fame and popularity in the period 1780-1820. It was then that the majority of its some 120 editions were produced, and it was then that the majority of its 160 or so separate productions in Scotland, England, and America occurred. This publication and theatrical history makes it clear *The Gentle Shepherd* enjoyed its greatest vogue in the period when romantic attitudes were beginning to dominate literature and the arts generally. Yet the play had also appealed to a world in which Augustan critical values held sway. There is a clue here to the extraordinary popular success achieved by all the major works of Scottish literary romanticism. The Scottish writers succeeded in looking backward and forward simultaneously; their romanticism was attractive and appealing, but it was never unqualified. Above all their romanticism was never revolutionary. As a result, their writings were safe, offering no kind of threat to established society and its conventional forms. Such lack of threat perhaps explains both the success and the limitations of Scottish literary romanticism.

The Gentle Shepherd is a pastoral drama, concerned with the lives and loves of shepherds and shepherdesses; nothing could be more orthodoxly classical. It is written throughout in rhyming couplets, Augustan poetry's most widely-used form. Hence the conventions of the play are highly traditional. So in many ways is its content. The shepherd of the play's title is 'gentle' in the sense that he is of gentle birth; he is a gentleman who happens to be living the life of a shepherd. The shepherdess he marries also turns out to be of gentle birth. Their origin explains their excellent qualities. For Ramsay there is no question of *real* shepherds possessing the superior traits ascribed to them by a genuine Romantic such as Wordsworth. Similarly, the plot of the play hinges on the return from exile of Sir William Worthy, a supporter of Charles II, at the time of the Restoration in 1660. The Scottish peasantry rejoice at the restoration of their old master; good times are returned, old buildings will be restored, the land recultivated. The good life is seen to lie in a recreated past, not a revolutionary future. The politics of the play are clearly Tory, aristocratic, and Jacobite. A similar conservatism pervades the ideas and sentiments of the piece: the values of reason and commonsense take precedence over those of feelings and passion.

Yet if this were all that could be said, how could this play have continued to grow in popularity long after neo-classical critical values were superseded? The answer is that *The Gentle Shepherd* from the beginning included a potentially romantic strain which a changing sensibility could register and bring to the fore. The play revealed the social forms and way of life of a part of rural Scotland which appeared increasingly remote from modern, sophisticated society. It seemed to take seriously the feelings of simple people. The language in which it was written possessed the natural spontaneity of an unpolished vernacular. (For performances in England the language of the play was often anglicized.) And most important of all perhaps: the pastoral play included versions of about twenty traditional Scots songs. This musical dimension of the play undoubtedly contributed largely to its success. And it is equally clear that, in incorporating this folk material, Ramsay was both catering to, and helping to create, a fast-growing taste for the unaffected simplicities of traditional Scottish airs and songs. These then are the characteristics that largely explain *The Gentle Shepherd's* success in the age of romanticism. The play creates an image of the rural peasantry of Lowland Scotland which is attractive and appealing; they are a simple, unsophisticated people, dignified, loyal, and with a strong sense of traditional, communal values. The process through which the common people of rural Scotland will be everywhere identified as naturally intelligent, devout, loyal and the inheritors of a living folk tradition of poetry and song, has begun.

Most modern readers can find much to admire in Ramsay's *Gentle Shepherd*. This is perhaps less true of John Home's tragedy, *Douglas*, which began to do for the Scottish Highlander what Ramsay's play had done for the Lowland peasant. *Douglas* caused an immense sensation when it was first produced in Edinburgh in 1756—and not only because its author was a Church of Scotland clergyman. As one contemporary put it: 'The town was in an uproar of exultation, that a Scotchman should write a tragedy of the first rate . . .'. Home was in fact a familiar figure in North British circles in Edinburgh, a close friend of David Hume, William Robertson, Adam Ferguson, Hugh Blair and the rest. Despite their successes in so many fields, imaginative literature was not an area in which the Scots *literati* had distinguished themselves; hence perhaps their rapturous delight over Home's play.

In fact there is much about *Douglas* that relates it to many other forgotten eighteenth-century sentimental dramas. It exploits the pathos and sentiment of its plot. Young Norval (the Douglas of the title) has been brought up as a simple shepherd in the Grampian Mountains; a chance encounter allows him to show his martial prowess in saving his step-father, Randolph; as a result he is reunited with his mother and is in a position to reassume his rightful dignities. However the machinations of Glenalvon, the villain of the piece, bring about the death of the youthful Douglas, and the suicide of his heartbroken mother. Full of long declamatory and expository speeches, the play is written in a largely conventional language and style. The unities of time, place, and action, are observed in the best neo-classical tradition. Yet this apparently unexceptional mid eighteenth-century drama was immensely successful everywhere. It was published in at least 75 editions. Ten editions appeared in America between 1790 and 1821. Amedée Pichot, that major impresario for Scottish culture in France, published a French translation in 1822; an Italian translation appeared in Genoa in the same year. For almost a hundred years the play held the stage. It was performed in America for the first time (in Philadelphia) as early as 1759; in 1825 the *New York Literary Gazette* could still refer to it as 'one of the best modern tragedies.' All the leading actors and actresses of the day played in it: Mrs Siddons (Lady Randolph), John Philip Kemble,

John Howard Payne, Edwin Forrest, Charles Kean (Douglas). An Italian writer, G B Niccolini, wrote a play, *Matilde*, consciously modelled on it (1825). And it was an Italian critic, commenting on Niccolini's play in the important Italian periodical *Antologia* in 1826, who made the crucial observation that *Douglas* itself occupied a middle ground between the classical and romantic traditions.

As in the case of *The Gentle Shepherd*, *Douglas's* capacity to seem to look both backward and forward in aesthetic terms, helps to explain its continuing success. This mid eighteenth-century play contained elements which could make it a hit in the high romanticism of the 1820s. What these are is easy enough to identify: its setting in some remote period in the Scottish past; its vague and melancholy Highland landscapes; its valorous Highland characters who seem to belong to a distant but heroic society and age; its sense of inevitable defeat and loss. But in the case of *Douglas* these potentially romantic elements were given an enormous boost by a new factor in the Scottish literary situation which emerged in the 1760s. The appearance of the works which James Macpherson asserted were translations from the Gaelic of the ancient Celtic bard Ossian transformed the context within which audiences everywhere responded to *Douglas*.

Compared with Macpherson's *Ossian*, the works so far described played but a minor role in conferring upon Scotland her new, romantic identity. *Ossian*'s role, on the other hand, was crucial: at least until the appearance of the Waverley Novels, no other work even begins to compare with its significance. This is especially true if one looks beyond the confines of Great Britain to Europe and America. The truth of the matter is that Macpherson's work has never been given its rightful place in English literary historiography. From the beginning in the 1760s, because of Macpherson's association with the powerful Scottish Earl of Bute, and the administration of George III, *Ossian* became caught up in the complexities of Anglo-Scottish political relations. What this meant was that almost from the moment of initial publication, Anglo-Scottish interest in *Ossian* centred on one question only: were the works of Macpherson genuine or fraudulent? Were they actually translations from the Gaelic or literary hoaxes passed off by Macpherson as the real thing? As a result of this preoccupation with the authenticity question, *Ossian*'s impact in England, despite the enthusiasm of writers such as Thomas Gray and Horace Walpole, was relatively muted. Such was not the case elsewhere. In Germany, France, Italy, Spain, Russia, in fact in every European country, and in America, *Ossian*'s vogue was astonishing and enduring. Scholars and readers in all of these countries were of course in no way unaware of the authenticity controversy. But it seems everywhere to have been regarded as only a minor problem; compared with the impact of the works themselves, it was nothing.

Fingal, *Temora*, and the rest of the Ossianic material appeared in Edinburgh and London in the 1760s. And Hugh Blair's highly influential *Critical Dissertation on the Poems of Ossian* (subsequently included as a Preface to many editions of the poems themselves) also first appeared as early as 1763. But the impact of *Ossian* was not immediate. The ripples it produced on the contemporary sensibility were at first small; but as the later decades of the eighteenth century passed, the ripples grew larger until at last the vogue for *Ossian* became a great wave sweeping across Europe and America. The pattern of response is then similar to that towards *The Gentle Shepherd* and *Douglas*, though now on an immensely greater scale. The scale in question is the scale of romanticism itself. The Ossianic vogue is at the heart of the emergence of the new romantic sensibility; Macpherson's work both helps to create, and is sustained by, the new romanticism. Thus *Ossian*'s impact in Germany, a cradle of romanticism, begins to occur several decades before its power is felt in France, a country where romanticism had a harder struggle to establish itself. The earliest German translations of fragments of Macpherson appeared in 1762; a complete translation was made by Michael Denis in 1768 and 1769. Not all German readers were satisfied that Denis had caught much of the spirit of the original, but his translation was nonetheless immensely influential. From the 1770s, *Ossian* was a potent force in German culture. Most of the major German writers were admirers: Herder, Klopstock, Lessing, Schiller, Novalis, Burger. And Goethe's decision to make the protagonist of his famous novel, *The Sorrows of Young Werther* (1774), an *Ossian* enthusiast—the text of the novel contains lengthy excerpts from Goethe's translation of the *Songs of Selma*—both reflected, and helped to spread, *Ossian*'s European vogue. Commentaries and criticisms; translations of *Ossian*; imitations in prose and verse; German publication of the English editions—German interest in *Ossian* did not flag until well into the nineteenth century.

In Italy a translation of Macpherson's work appeared amazingly early: that by Melchior Cesarotti published in Venice in 1763. But that original Cesarotti edition had little impact. It was only in the 1780s and 90s, with the republication of Cesarotti's translation in Bassano, that the Italian vogue for *Ossian* really got underway. It was at its height in the early decades of the nineteenth century when editions of Cesarotti appeared in almost every major Italian city: Venice, Pisa, Florence, Milan, Naples. As a result *Ossian* became a key work in the emergence of Italian romanticism. Again, a complete French translation of *Ossian* appeared relatively early: that of Letourneur in 1776-77. But French enthusiasm for the Ossianic world did not really kindle until the early years of the nineteenth century when romantic writers and theorists, such as Madame de Stael, Lamartine, and Chateaubriand, found in *Ossian* an authentic articulation of the kind of sensibility that fascinated them. *Ossian*'s French vogue is best symbolized by the enthusiasm of a single reader: Napoleon himself. Throughout all his military campaigns, the poems of Ossian—in Cesarotti's version—remained Napoleon's favourite reading. In conversation with Lady Malcolm, wife of the naval commander of St Helena, in 1816, he expressed his continuing admiration for *Ossian* and asserted that it was his influence that had brought the poems into such vogue throughout Europe: 'It was I—I made them the fashion. I have been even accused of having my head filled with Ossian's clouds.' Clearly there is an element of megalomania here, but Napoleon's enthusiastic patronage of the poems was inevitably important. Painting's commissioned for the imperial apartments at the Quirinal in Rome in 1812 included Ingres's 'The Dream of Ossian,' while Malmaison, the Empress Josephine's Parisian house, was also decorated with paintings of Ossianic heroes and heroines. Bernadotte, whom Napoleon made King of Sweden, named his son Oscar—he was later King Oscar I of Sweden—as a gesture of respect towards Napoleon's admiration for the Ossianic hero. In fact Oscar and Malvina became popular Christian names in various European countries, and in the end translations of *Ossian* appeared not only in German, French, and Italian, but in Spanish, Dutch, Danish, Russian, Swedish, and Polish.

In America the Ossianic vogue got underway in the 1790s. The first American edition dates from 1790; between that date and 1823 another eight editions appeared. Thomas Jefferson had been an enthusiastic reader as early as 1773: he decided that Ossian was the greatest poet who had ever lived, and, like a true son of the Enlightenment, wrote to Edinburgh for a grammar and a dictionary that he might learn the language of the originals. But it was another twenty years or so before an American versifier of an extract from *Ossian* could assume that 'the source whence I draw, is in every library.' 1796 saw the production in Boston and Charleston of a theatrical work based on Macpherson's writings: *Oscar and Malvina: or, the Hall of Fingal. A Grand Scottish Heroic Spectacle*. Such an American spectacular reminds us that the Ossianic vogue was everywhere expressed in a wide range of artistic forms: Ossianic plays and melodramas in Scotland, France, Germany and Italy; settings of songs from *Ossian* by Schubert, Brahms, Weber, and a variety of other less famous composers; at least two operas; a great range of paintings on Ossianic subjects in France, Germany, Scotland, and other countries. In the early nineteenth century the Ossianic world had become part of the permanent romantic landscape of Europe and America.

The pervasiveness of *Ossian*'s impact throughout the western world is clear. What exactly was it that all these enthusiastic readers responded to in Macpherson's prose poems? They responded to the vision of a strange, remote, exotic ancient world, peopled by grandly heroic characters who move with a kind of stately dignity across wild and barren landscapes of mountains, crags, rivers, seas, clouds and mists. What particular enterprises these characters are actually engaged in is not always very clear: plot lines are not one of Macpherson's stronger points. But every episode involves battles or epic contests of valour and heroism; victory or defeat are equally worthy of celebration. Most of all what contemporary readers responded to was the consistent mood or tone of the poems. *Ossian* is pervaded by sentiments of regret and melancholy; it communicates a sense of elegiac sadness at the loss of home and country, loss of fame and reputation, loss of life—at the fading and failing and passing away of all the brightest things in the days of man. This above all is the note of Ossianic gloom and melancholy which seems to have captivated Europe.

In the debate over the authenticity question most of Macpherson's friends among the Scots *literati* rallied to his defence. But ironically, Macpherson's Scotland was not their Scotland. The new Scotland, the North Britain of enlightened Progress and Improvement, had nothing in common with the 'Grand Scottish Heroic Spectacle' that Macpherson was concerned to evoke and make familiar to so many readers everywhere. In the end *Ossian* represented a challenge to the new, material and commercial civilization of Lowland Scotland and to the intellectual and cultural hegemony it had so brilliantly established; *Ossian* was a kind of Highland counter-attack, an attempt to impose upon Scotland, as her truer and more traditional self, a romantic, Celtic image created out of the wild grandeur of her Highland scenery, and the heroic simplicity of a poetic Highland past. And it was to this mythopoetic vision of Scotland that romantic Europe was responding at the end of the eighteenth century; early in the nineteenth that vision would be reinforced and expanded by still more powerful literary forces.

Meantime, the capacity of a work such as *Douglas* to hold the stage throughout the romantic period, is largely explicable in terms of the success of *Ossian*. *Douglas* could very readily be seen as belonging to the Ossianic world. Young Norval and Randolph seem to prefigure the grand, heroic protagonists of the Ossianic poems; landscapes and settings; melancholy mood and sentiments—all of these elements in Home's play seem essentially consonant with the world created by Macpherson's *Ossian*. *Douglas*, in other words, could be readily assimilated to the developing romantic image of Scotland which *Ossian* did more than any other work in the eighteenth century to create.

By the opening of the nineteenth century, Scotland was beginning to emerge as a kind of romantic archetype, its very existence offering confirmation of what were becoming key aspects of the ideology of romanticism. Scotland's geographical position on the northern periphery of Europe became significant. As a result of the influence of Madame de Stael and others, the notion that romanticism was the natural cultural and artistic means of expression for northern latitudes became increasingly familiar. The classical world had emerged in the Mediterranean countries of the south. Classical values were thus related to the geographical, climatic, and other characteristics of their countries of origin. Germany and northern Europe possessed different characteristics; of these romanticism was a true reflection. Thus northern romanticism offered a viable alternative to the classical tradition which had dominated European culture for so long. Scotland's place in this ideology was crucial: after all the Scottish Highlands, as early as the third century, had possessed an admirable civilization and culture, testified to by the existence of the Northern Homer, Ossian, his epic poems in no way unworthy of comparison with those of his classical rival.

But Scotland was increasingly identified as a supremely romantic country not only because of its geographical location. Its scenery was wild, sublime, awful (as *Douglas* and *Ossian* attested, and as the earliest books of prints and engravings of Scottish scenes confirmed); but it also contained softer, milder, more pastoral scenes (*The Gentle Shepherd*). Its common people, whether Lowland peasant or Highlander, displayed a natural simplicity of manners, and a spontaneity of language and feeling, which made its poetry and song expressive and affecting beyond anything that could be achieved in more 'civilized' societies. Ramsay's successful use of the tradition of Scottish folksong in *The Gentle Shepherd* and elsewhere was followed up in the later eighteenth century; it culminated in the achievement of Robert Burns.

Today we see Burns as a highly intelligent, and in no way ill-educated, poet, whose work is perhaps best understood within the context of the Scottish Enlightenment. But to his contemporaries at home and abroad Burns appeared in a quite different light. He was a natural poet, an untutored bard, an unsophisticated peasant farmer with a spontaneous gift for song. Henry Mackenzie spoke in the authentic voice of romanticism when he called Burns a 'heaven-taught ploughman.' The phrase pinpoints exactly the Burns that Mackenzie and his contemporaries wished to see: the peasant-poet. (James Hogg would soon emerge as another such figure.)

How well-known was Burns and how far did his existence contribute to the romantic mythology of Scotland's poetic identity? His frequent use of the Scottish vernacular did create problems for non-Scottish readers. (In early nineteenth-century anthologies of poetry Burns is usually represented by some of his English language poems.) In America, though, there seems to have been little problem. Burns was widely appreciated from the start, and Americans often seem to have prided themselves on responding with more understanding to the vernacular poems than their English contemporaries were able to do. The problem was greater in Europe. No extended translation of Burns appeared in Italian until 1896. In Germany and France the situation was better. Burns was first heard of in France in the earliest years of the nineteenth century; in the 1820s, when the first translations begin to appear, he became widely known as a Scottish poet of an almost ideal simplicity and naturalness. In Germany Burns was known in literary circles before the end of the eighteenth century, and full-scale translations and editions of his poems became common in the 1830s and 1840s. In all these countries it is the notion of Burns as the 'heaven-taught ploughman' that appears most regularly. Thus even before his actual poems were widely-known, Burns's existence was seen as confirmation of the essentially poetic nature of rural and peasant Scotland.

By the early nineteenth century, then, a great deal of romantic enthusiasm had been kindled by the landscapes and scenery of Scotland, and by the language and way of life of the common people of rural Scotland. By then, however, Scottish history and the Scottish past were also beginning to exhibit a powerful, romantic appeal. The Ossianic poems had shown Scotland to possess an heroic and honourable culture and society in the ancient past; *Douglas* had depicted medieval Scotland in a rather similar light; *The Gentle Shepherd* had delineated seventeenth-century Scotland in an appealing manner. The Scottish past was acquiring a general romantic gloss. In time other particular historical episodes were picked out for romantic attention. Jane Porter's novel, *The Scottish Chiefs* (1810), which had a great American and European vogue, did much to make Wallace and Bruce into romantic heroes. A translation appeared in France immediately after the initial English publication; and this French translation was reprinted in 1814 and 1820. A play based on the book was written by Pixérécourt in 1815 but not produced in Paris until 1819: the play had been suppressed in 1815 because it expressed hatred towards the English! In Italy *The Scottish Chiefs* was translated and published in Milan in 1823. In the same year an opera, *Wallace, or the Scottish Hero*, by Felice Romani, clearly derived from the novel, was presented at Padua.

A figure even more to the romantic taste than either Wallace or Bruce was Mary Queen of Scots. Schiller's *Mary Stuart* (1800) is paralleled by several other French and Italian dramatic versions of Mary's tragic fate. European prejudices were very much on Mary's side with the result that in every account Mary emerges as the innocent martyr, or victim of Elizabeth's unworthy jealousy. Mary Queen of Scots and her fate seemed to sum up the romance of Scottish history, bloody and violent as for the most part it is allowed to be. Soon the ill-fated Jacobite risings of the eighteenth century would be added to the romantic landscape of Scottish history. Scottish scenery, Scottish Highlanders and Lowland peasants, Scottish folk-song and poetry, Scottish history, all of these were coming together at the close of the eighteenth century to make Scotland into perhaps the most romantic country in Europe. This then was the new meaning, and the mythopoetic identity, that Scotland was acquiring. Perhaps it is not entirely surprising that in the heady atmosphere of Paris in 1815, after its occupation by the allied victors of Waterloo, one of the sights that most fascinated Parisians was that of the soldiers of the Scottish regiments in their tartan uniforms. The Allies too were welcomed at the Paris Opera by a new ballet—*L'Heureux Retour*, performed with special additions including a party of Highlanders dancing reels.

For literate Americans and Europeans, then, Scotland in the later eighteenth century, and in the early years of the nineteenth, may well have meant both learning and romance. But as the nineteenth century went on, the pattern clearly begins to change. Scotland's romantic identity acquires a new and still more potent force. This achievement, if that is what it is, was the result of the work of one man, the most famous Scotsman of his time, perhaps of any time: Walter Scott. Scott it was who completed the process begun by Ramsay, Home, Macpherson, Burns, Jane Porter, and the rest. Scott it was who—despite the complexity of his own attitude towards the romantic impulse—extended, completed, and definitively propagated Scotland's romantic image. The triumph of the Waverley Novels everywhere in Europe and America was unprecedented. For Scott himself his success brought unparalleled wealth and fame for a writer; but his success was also critical for Scotland and Scottish culture. By setting so much of his work in Scottish contexts, Scott moved Scotland squarely to the centre of the romantic map of Europe. As a result, all the earlier strands in Scottish literary romanticism were now brought to a brilliant consummation. Through Scott the aura of romance finally settled upon Scotland; Scotland's colourful and passionate history, her lochs and rivers and mountains, her loyal, valorous, and proud people, her tradition of poetry and song—all those aspects of Scotland that had already acquired considerable romantic appeal—now appeared in a new and totally irresistible form.

However, not even the Waverley Novels were an instantaneous success everywhere. In Italy, for example, where the struggle between upholders of the classical tradition and proponents of the new romanticism was, partly for political reasons, particularly bitter and hard-fought, Scott met with considerable resistance. But in time Scott appealed over the heads, as it were, of literary establishments, and the response of the reading public swept aside all opposition. In the end Scott's vogue in Italy was to be as great as in the rest of Europe. Commentators were forced to admit that such was his fascination that the geography of Scotland had become more familiar to Italians than that of their own country: Loch Lomond and the banks of the Tay were better known to Italians than the lakes and Alps of Italy. Italian children were given the names of Scott characters, and for a time the children of rich families were frequently dressed in kilts.

Soon Scott was being translated into all the languages of Europe. In France, particularly in the 1820s, the vogue for Scott, and hence for Scotland, was tremendous. Tartan became high fashion. The Duchess of Berry gave masked balls in Paris in which all the guests appeared as characters from the Waverley Novels. Cravats and bonnets 'à la Walter Scott' were popular everywhere. Much more significant was the way in which the Scott vogue manifested itself in music, painting, and the theatre. In the field of literature, American and European enthusiasm for Scott helped in the development of national literary traditions: writers in different countries were encouraged to try to do for their own nations what Scott had done for Scotland. Schools of historical novelists emerged everywhere, from the United States to Russia. But in music, painting, and the theatre, the vogue for Scott and Scotland produced a different result: Scottish topics and themes invaded all these fields. For a time the arts of Europe began to take on a distinct Scottish coloration.

On the same evening in Paris in 1827 the theatre-goer could have chosen to attend one of four Scott plays, all derived from different Waverley Novels: *Quentin Durward*, *Woodstock*, *Kenilworth*, *The Monastery* and *Guy Mannering*. On other occasions he might have seen plays based on *The Bride of Lammermoor*, *Old Mortality*, *The Abbot*, and *Rob Roy*. Victor Hugo's *Amy Robsart* (from *Kenilworth*), written in 1821 and staged in 1828, was only one of the less successful of these Scott-inspired French plays.

For opera writers and audiences, the appeal of Scott was irresistible. Some Scott operas of course remain part of the modern repertory:

Donizetti's *Lucia di Lammermoor*, Bizet's *The Fair Maid of Perth*, Rossini's *La Donna del Lago*, Bellini's *I Puritani*. But these represent only the tip of an iceberg. In all not far short of 100 Scott-inspired operas were produced in the nineteenth century. Some of these were immensely popular: *La Dame Blanche* (from *The Monastery* and *Guy Mannering*) with music by Boieldieu and a libretto by Scribe was performed over a thousand times after its initial production in 1825. And of course it was not only in opera that the fascination with Scotland manifested itself musically: Berlioz' overtures for *Waverley* and *Rob Roy* are familiar, as are Mendelssohn's 'Fingal's Cave' overture and his Scotch Symphony. (Mendelssohn was one of the many Americans and Europeans who undertook a tour of the Scottish Highlands.) But above all it is the taste displayed by a wide range of classical composers for Scots songs and airs, and for the setting of Scots poems—a taste with origins deep in the eighteenth century—which testifies best to the pervasiveness in musical terms of the Scottish theme. The settings of *Ossian* by Schubert, Brahms, and Weber have already been referred to; Schubert set a series of Scott texts from *The Lady of the Lake*; Schumann and Weber set a variety of poems by Burns. Pleyel, Haydn, Beethoven, and Hummel all set poems by Burns and other Scots poets.

In painting, too, the romantic, Scottish theme is much in evidence. Reference has already been made to *Ossian*'s impact on the visual arts. This was certainly on a large enough scale to allow a major *Ossian* exhibition to be mounted in France and Germany in 1974; works were exhibited from a wide variety of European countries. The Scott vogue inevitably provided painters with a new set of subjects. At the Paris Salon exhibition in 1831 over thirty canvases were directly inspired by the Waverley Novels. Delacroix was a particular admirer of Scott: his 'Murder of the Bishop of Liège' (from *Quentin Durward*) shows Scott's creative stimulus at its dramatic best.

In drama, in opera, in music, in painting, European culture in the first half of the nineteenth century reveals itself as immensely responsive to the Scottish theme. Thus when Bournonville came to create *La Sylphide*, the earliest and most influential work in what was to become the established canon of classical ballet, no accident was involved in his choice of a Scottish story and setting; nor was it surprising that musical and dance elements in the work should derive from ideas of popular Scottish dance and song.

Final evidence of the nature of the appeal of Scotland for both Americans and Europeans is provided by those who, having made their way there, proceeded to publish accounts of what they saw. Few came before the 1780s but after 1800 their number begins rapidly to grow; and in the 1820s, 30s, and 40s the surprising thing is that the reading-public in America, France, and Germany had not had more than enough. But the taste for descriptive accounts of travels in Scotland seems to have been insatiable. Only a few such accounts derive from Italy, many more from France and America, perhaps most of all from Germany. By and large the travellers go to the same places, look at the same things, and very often say similar things about what they see. It is true that some broad discriminations can be made. The small band of foreign visitors who arrived in Scotland in the later eighteenth and very early nineteenth centuries and subsequently published an account of their visit were on the whole not attracted by Scotland's romantic appeal: often scholars or scientists themselves, they were drawn by the land of learning. But for the great majority who arrive after 1815, the land of learning is much less appealing than the land of romance. To turn the pages of these travellers' accounts—be they American, French, German, or Italian—is to turn the pages of Scotland's romantic history and literature. The same scenes are described over and over again—and they are essentially the scenes that today's tourists feel obliged to see: Edinburgh Castle, Holyrood Palace, the Scott country, the Burns country, the Trossachs, including Loch Katrine and Ellen's Island, Glencoe, Loch Lomond. At every point it is Scotland's poets and novelists who guide and direct the traveller's steps. In its origins, the pilgrimage through Scotland was essentially a literary one; the amazing successes of Scottish literary romanticism had made Scotland itself, in foreign eyes, into a new 'classic ground.'

As the nineteenth century passed, however, the foundations upon which Scotland's 'classic' reputation had been built proved unstable. The early exponents of Scottish literary romanticism, up to and including Scott, had responded passionately and creatively to the complex political, social, and cultural problems facing Scotland after the Union of 1707. But the images they created proved to have a life independent of the literature which had sustained them. The consequences of that circumstance remain a problematical part of Scotland's cultural situation today.

FURTHER READING

Bentman, R, 'The Romantic Poets and Critics on Robert Burns', *Texas Studies in Literature and Language*, 6 (1964), pp 104–118

Chapman, M, *The Gaelic Vision in Scottish Cuture* (London and Montreal, 1979)

Donaldson, W, 'Bonny Highland Laddie: the Making of a Myth', *Scottish Literary Journal*, 3 (December, 1976) pp 30–50.

Hook, A D, *Scotland and America, 1750—1835* (Glasgow, 1975)

MacQueen, J, *Progress and Poetry: The Enlightenment and Scottish Literature* (Edinburgh, 1982)

Mitchell, J, *The Walter Scott Operas* (Alabama, 1977)

Muir, E, *Scott and Scotland* (London, 1936)

Simpson, K G, 'Rationalism and Romanticism: the Case of Home's *Douglas*', *Scottish Literary Journal*, 9 (May, 1982), pp 21–47

Smart, J S, *James Macpherson: An Episode in Literature* (London, 1905)

INDEX